LA BO UR

THE NEW ZEALAND

LA

LABOUR PARTY

BO

1916–2016

UR

PETER FRANKS & JIM McALOON

VICTORIA UNIVERSITY PRESS

VICTORIA UNIVERSITY PRESS
Victoria University of Wellington
PO Box 600 Wellington
vup.victoria.ac.nz

First published 2016

National Library of New Zealand Cataloguing-in-Publication Data

Franks, Peter, 1950-
Labour : the New Zealand Labour Party, 1916-2016 /
Peter Franks and Jim McAloon.
Includes bibliographical references.
ISBN 978-1-77656-074-5
1. New Zealand Labour Party—History. I. McAloon, Jim. II. Title.
324.29307—dc 23

Cover design by Todd Atticus
Index by Timothy Vaughan-Sanders

Printed by Printlink in Wellington, New Zealand

To all the men and women of the New Zealand Labour movement; past, present and future

Contents

Foreword

by Andrew Little

Leader of the New Zealand Labour Party

The Labour Party was forged from a spirit of not just seeking justice, but fighting for it. The founders of the party saw the need to create a political force that put the levers of government power in the hands of those representing all citizens, not just the few at the top.

The driving force of the party in its early years was scrappers from the union movement, leaders like Peter Fraser, Bob Semple and Paddy Webb. All would be members of the first Labour cabinet. They pushed hard and challenged the establishment, but they also knew they needed a wider appeal than to just those in unions. Unlike other Labour parties around the world, the New Zealand Labour Party consciously embraced progressive liberal supporters from across the political landscape at the time of its formation.

As Jim McAloon and Peter Franks' history shows, Labour in government has ushered in the major changes that have modernised our social support and economic institutions. And those changes have endured. From social security, quality public health and a modern education system in that first government to KiwiSaver and Working for Families tax credits in the fifth, Labour has shown itself to be the party of practical measures and deep-seated change aimed at giving all New Zealanders a better chance. It is Labour governments that have pushed the pendulum of fairness and equality back in favour of the people.

Harnessing the power of government to promote greater equality of opportunity has defined Labour. But equally, the party has never shied from making morally correct but politically difficult choices. Supporting the Allied effort in the Second World War without surrendering decisions on troop deployment to the British generals; pulling out of the Vietnam

War; standing up to the nuclear madness and becoming nuclear free; advancing the cause of human rights, including gender equality and sexual identity: these were progressive causes and the decisions often attracted much controversy, but they were the right things to do.

Jim and Peter's history has an incredibly difficult task to perform: to account for a hundred years of a major political party in a style that is free from political jargon and that tells a coherent and recognisable story that is readable. They have fulfilled that mission amply. This is not an insider's account full of untold tales of cunning and intrigue, rumour and speculation (for the Labour Party, that would fill volumes). It is two historians' digest of the significant historical features—the directions taken and the changes undergone—of New Zealand's social democratic party.

Issues and challenges may be repeated throughout history. I was recently shown a 1933 Timaru parish newsletter decrying the obscenity of the five big banks at the time reporting record profits amidst widespread poverty and hardship (the parish openly supported one of Labour's longest-serving MPs, former Congregationalist minister Clyde Carr, who served as member for Timaru from 1928 to 1962). It all sounds a bit familiar when we look at the conduct of our major trading banks today. How we face those challenges will depend on the historical context, and this book is careful to describe the circumstances in which difficult calls were made.

It is often comforting to look backwards to historical events. We rejoice in past victories and achievements. They give us confidence and we draw upon the legacy of those past times. But progress lies in the future. Labour has always prided itself, as I think this book demonstrates, on looking well ahead and preparing New Zealand for long-term change.

At the beginning of its first hundred years Labour was the party advocating for those increasingly left out and left behind, and challenging a government increasingly governing for those at the top. A hundred years on, we are doing the same. But the way we prosecute issues and conduct ourselves in opposition is different. The story of our first hundred years gives us good cause to be strong in our hearts and determined in our resolve as we continue the fight for a just society.

Andrew Little MP
April 2016

Foreword

by Nigel Haworth

President of the New Zealand Labour Party

This book is a welcome contribution to the literature on New Zealand politics. It is an important way to mark an important milestone in New Zealand's oldest political party's history, and to reflect on the fundamental role played by the party in the creation of a fair, inclusive and decent society. The authors have produced a serious and readable account of that history, admirably based on a combination of primary and secondary sources. Theirs is a job well done.

This is, of course, a book written about, not for, the Labour Party. It is a work of scholarship, safeguarded against partisan pressures to follow any particular interpretation. I am particularly pleased that the text has been subjected to standard academic review and assessment by the publisher. There are sections in the book which will challenge the party to reflect on both organisational and political matters, and I sincerely hope that it will engender constructive debate, not just about past events but also about the future.

To the extent that the authors were offered any input from the party, it consisted of a simple message: Labour owns its history, both ups and downs or, as was sometimes mentioned, 'warts and all'. A party cannot survive in the rough and tumble of politics over a tumultuous century without enjoying high points, and enduring the low. One lesson of the book is that, despite that tumult, the Labour Party is resilient, and able to renew itself to face the demands of a changing environment. It identifies that resilience in the fundamental values and principles of the party, established at its foundation and still the driver of all we seek to achieve.

Labour parties such as ours were formed to provide a democratic socialist voice for working people otherwise excluded from political power. It was at first a hard row to hoe, but, from the 1930s, the rise of the Keynesian accommodation empowered social democracy. In New Zealand, as elsewhere, the Labour Party became the guardian of economic and social policy orthodoxy. From 1935 to 1984 Labour's story was New Zealand's. Since the 1980s the certainties of that long era have been disrupted, challenging Labour to once more do the hard intellectual and policy work required to build a decent society in the face of contemporary policy settings that dismiss inclusion and contemplate growing inequality with equanimity. This book helps us to understand what drives the Labour Party to remain true to its values and principles and to the interests of all New Zealanders. For me, that is the strength of this book. In looking back at a complex and, at times, rugged history, it illustrates, with erudition and clarity, why the Labour Party moves into its second century undiminished in its adherence to social democratic principles and to the interests and needs of New Zealand.

Nigel Haworth
President, New Zealand Labour Party
April 2016

Preface

The New Zealand Labour Party was established in July 1916—literally in a smoke-filled room—at a conference of representatives of a number of political and industrial organisations. It is New Zealand's oldest existing political party, and its antecedents extend, in a formal sense, to the first years of the twentieth century.

The Labour Party is a social democratic party. It began as the political wing of organised labour: industrial unions were essential actors in the party's foundation and have always had the right to affiliate. Fundamental to the party's thinking and practice, however, have been an unqualified commitment to parliamentary democracy, a belief in equality (however that may be defined), and a belief in the possibility and desirability of political action to reform and shape economic and social institutions. Like other social democratic parties, too, Labour has emphasised economic modernisation in whatever terms have been perceived as necessary at a given time, however much that might at times have complicated the party's relations with its industrial affiliates. Sometimes it has been difficult to balance the imperatives of social justice and economic development. Social democracy emphasises what one American scholar has called the 'primacy of politics': that is, the future can be made.[1] Not, as Marx noted, entirely as we please; certainly within constraints. But it can be made. Political action can shape economic development, can make a fairer and more just society. Social democracy rejects inequality and rejects the uncontrolled market. It rejects self-interest as the fundamental principle in economic and social life. Social democracy advocates solidarity and the common good.

The New Zealand Labour Party, like other social democratic parties, was born out of the industrial labour movement, but its founders included radicals and progressives who were not directly involved with unions. Like other social democratic parties, Labour has always been a broad coalition, its members espousing and drawing on many strands of political thought and organisational models. The range of perspectives that have shaped the party has made it accommodate economic modernisers, liberal progressives, Christian socialists, rationalists, social democrats and democratic socialists. And, like other social democratic parties, as society has changed the party has had to change too. Social democratic parties in former settler colonies like New Zealand have particular issues to work through, about colonisation and decolonisation, about full economic and social citizenship for the indigenous and displaced. Particularly since the 1960s, it has become evident that 'equality', or 'social justice', has many meanings, and Labour has engaged with the third wave of feminism, with ethnic and cultural diversity, with gay and lesbian and transgender communities, and with environmental and green movements. In some ways this last presents the most important challenge of all, given the powerful mobilisation of such movements into Green parties in this country and overseas. At best, all these strands of political thought have existed in a healthy and creative dynamic; at worst, there has been internecine bloodletting. While Labour became a broad-based party, like most political parties in democratic states Labour has experienced in recent decades the decline of politics as a mass activity.

The New Zealand Labour Party was established later than similar parties overseas. The Australian Labor Party was formed in 1901 on federation (the New South Wales Labor Electoral League having been established in 1891). The British Labour Party was formally established in 1906 when the Labour Representation Committee, formed in 1900, was renamed. Elsewhere in Europe, the Social Democratic Party of Germany, for instance, was formed in 1875, the Norwegian Labour Party in 1887 and the Swedish Social Democratic Party in 1889.[2] Despite its later formation, the New Zealand Labour Party, like the Scandinavian parties, was an early mover in successfully inaugurating social democratic welfare policies. Swedish social democrats worked creatively to develop such policies from the mid-1920s, drawing on English liberals such as John Maynard Keynes and J.A. Hobson, as well as advanced thinkers in their own Stockholm School. As we suggest in this book, New Zealand Labour Party parliamentarians worked equally hard, with fewer resources, to similar effect. The Swedish party was well prepared for office when it led a majority government from 1932, and the other Scandinavian parties followed suit before 1940.

The Australian Labor Party was not so fortunate. Although it formed majority federal governments from 1910, its policy approach was little different from that of the New Zealand Liberals. Some scholars have emphasised a continuity in Australian (and indeed New Zealand) policy from the 1890s to the 1980s, but we suggest there was a 'Keynesian break' in the 1930s and 1940s, in Australasia as elsewhere.[3] That this break came later in Australia than in New Zealand was for a number of reasons, but the Scullin government of 1929–31, as well as being unlucky, vacillated in its response to the Depression and had not developed a coherent economic approach. Only from 1941 was an Australian Labor Party government able to enact Keynesian reforms. The fate of the Scullin government—splitting apart over Depression policy, with former members joining a conservative administration—was also that of the second, minority British Labour government, also of 1929–31. The British Labour Party, likewise, had little coherent policy to deal with the Depression (the Liberals, under David Lloyd George and advised by Keynes, advocated reflationary policies but were not in a position to influence events). Labour in Britain was out of office until it joined the wartime coalition in 1940, and formed a majority government, implementing far-reaching reforms, under Clement Attlee between 1945 and 1951. As a result of the Depression, and even more of the Second World War, social and economic policy regimes were reshaped in most democratic states.[4]

As a very broad generalisation, the effects of this reshaping lasted until the late 1970s. This was as true in New Zealand as elsewhere, and in the English-speaking nations moderate conservative administrations during the 1950s adopted the principal elements of 1940s social democracy. For a number of reasons, the German social democrats did not form a post-war administration until 1969, and the French social democratic forces were fragmented until the mid-1970s; a stable social democratic administration was only formed under François Mitterrand in 1981. In the United States, of course, F.D. Roosevelt's New Deal had social democratic elements, but the language of social democracy was unacceptable.[5] Social democratic parties were more successful in retaining office in Scandinavia: the Swedish party had a virtually unbroken period in government from 1932 to 1976. One explanation for Scandinavian success was the prevalence of proportional representation. While the Scandinavian parties, like those in New Zealand, Australia and Britain, could count on an electoral base of around 40 per cent of the vote, centrist and conservative forces in Scandinavia were fragmented and social democrats could usually ally with agrarian or moderate parties. Simple plurality ('first past the post') was a powerful incentive to a two-party system, and once the British Conservatives, the Australian Liberals and the New Zealand National Party had adopted the essentials of the welfare state, they held enough middle-class voters to ensure long terms in office.

A problem common to all social democratic parties after 1950 was developing a policy direction that went beyond simple maintenance. In Sweden, in the 1950s the non-social democratic parties ('bourgeois parties', as they are usually called)

> began intimating that with these reforms the Social Democrats had eliminated the grounds for their own existence: they had abolished the impoverished proletariat by making it secure, affluent and unideological. Consequently, the party ought to step aside and allow efficient bourgeois executives and politicians to administer the new society.[6]

Much the same was true in Britain, Australia and New Zealand, although the answers differed. Tony Crosland, that most attractive English revisionist, suggested that 'the future of socialism' amounted to more equality and better public amenities.[7] Crosland believed that regulated capitalism had made ownership irrelevant and overestimated the long-term strength of Conservative commitment to the post-war settlement. In New Zealand, Arnold Nordmeyer, another moderniser, while no fan of the acquisitive society, thought that there was 'no place . . . for what used to be called the class struggle'. Out of office, the English-speaking labour parties experienced a degree of impotence; the Swedish party endeavoured to further develop social provision and enhanced equality. Scandinavian social democratic governments, generally, relied on a high degree of consultation, in which governments brokered policy agreements with the economic interest groups. As well as full employment, Scandinavian policy emphasised price stability and export competitiveness, with the implication that the demise of outdated industries should be carefully managed and workers retrained in the interests of productivity and efficiency.

The anglophone parties were seldom enthusiastic about Scandinavian-style liberal corporatism, and the industrial federations generally insisted on free collective bargaining. When the anglophone Labour parties returned to office—in Britain from 1964 to 1970, in Australia only in 1972–75, and in New Zealand in 1957–60 and 1972–75—they espoused economic modernisation and egalitarian social reform. Ultimately, in all cases, including the British Labour administration of 1974–79, they were defeated by economic difficulties and problematic relationships within both the political and industrial labour movements. Chastened, all three parties adopted or accepted more deregulated economic policies after 1983. The Australian and New Zealand parties implemented substantial neo-liberal economic measures in the 1980s, while attempting to maintain social services and welfare; there was also a new attention to gender and ethnic equality, at least in the formal sense. The British Labour Party, out of office until 1997, followed a similar path thereafter. By then, in Britain as well as in Germany and in France, social democracy had been rebranded as the 'Third Way', espoused by Britain's Tony Blair and United States president Bill Clinton. This trend was rather less evident in Scandinavia, although Swedish ideas about employee shareholding leading to gradual collective ownership did not survive the changed ideological climate of the 1980s. If the Scandinavian parties remained committed to comprehensive welfare regimes, the anglophone parties in government (Australia, 1983–96 and 2007–13; New Zealand, 1984–90 and 1999–2008; Britain, 1997–2010) attempted to maintain a degree of public social services and income support while developing or accepting deregulated markets in many spheres. The balancing act was tricky to say the least, and a fruitful source of controversy.

The New Zealand Labour Party, then, shared with the Scandinavian parties a degree of success in the 1930s, a success not enjoyed by the Australian and British parties until the 1940s. Having substantially reshaped economic and social policy, the New Zealand Labour Party struggled to win office between 1950 and 1984, when the Scandinavian parties enjoyed considerable success. The Australian party was similarly unsuccessful, as was the British until 1964. A pragmatic, if complacent, moderate conservative party combined with non-proportional voting is part of the explanation; reluctant renewal of personnel and policies were other factors. After 1980, the challenges confronting social democratic parties included a changing global economy and emboldened neo-liberal ideologues, as well as fundamental changes around gender, culture, identity and the nature of work. Economic growth, in the context of new environmental concerns, was now problematic as well.

Political parties, as parties, are rather neglected in New Zealand historical literature. The most recent substantial history of a party, Barry Gustafson's study of the National Party, appeared 30 years ago.[8] Gustafson also wrote the last substantial book to appear on the history of the Labour Party and its predecessors: it covered the period to 1919 and came out in 1980. If there was a 'standard work' before that, it was Bruce Brown's *The Rise of New Zealand Labour*.[9] Brown's book was published in 1962—four years before the party's half-century—and he concluded his account in 1940. The need for a new history is evident.

The writing of New Zealand's political history is dominated by biography. Biography, of its nature, deals with the individual. Political parties, as institutions, have lives of their own. But if histories of political parties are few, histories of governments are even scarcer, with the single exception of the fourth Labour government (1984–90), which, because of its far-reaching reform programme, has been the subject of many discussions. There is an obvious lack, not only of studies of the equally important first Labour government (1935–49), but also of conservative administrations. The gap is only very partially addressed, for both Labour and National administrations, by some studies of particular government departments, such as Malcolm McKinnon's history of the Treasury, and by studies of policy issues, such as Margaret McClure's discussion of social welfare and Malcolm Templeton's works in diplomatic history.[10]

Biography has some advantages: by emphasising the life of a significant individual it may provide an accessible 'way in' to that person's historical context. Yet, of course, biography emphasises the subject's perspective, and political biography, like memoir, usually emphasises those who achieved high office and flamboyant mavericks. Since 1964 there have been substantial biographies of, in order of appearance, Harry Holland, Walter Nash, John A. Lee, Michael Joseph Savage, Peter Fraser, Arnold Nordmeyer, Geoffrey Palmer and Norman Kirk.[11] All except Lee led the party, and Lee, to say the least, wanted to. Other published work includes a biography of the 1950s minister Phil Connolly, and various studies of Kirk, Bill Rowling, David Lange and Helen Clark; some of these foreshadowed election campaigns, and some were interim assessments.[12] A related genre is participants' memoirs; by far the most substantial is Michael Bassett's account of the Lange cabinet.[13] Margaret Hayward's *Diary of the Kirk Years* is an important account of Kirk's actions and thinking.[14]

Few Labour figures, apart from Warren Freer, have written conventional autobiographical memoirs. Lange's rather brief memoir was dictated towards the end of his life; Palmer's memoirs combine autobiography with substantial discussion of policy issues, while some of Mike Moore's writings are informed by his autobiography.[15] Unusually, John A. Lee wrote voluminously about his political engagement, but much of this, while entertaining, is hardly reliable. A telling example is Lee recalling that Fred Cooke, at the funeral of his old comrade Ted Howard, made the socialist gesture of taking off his red tie and dropping it on the coffin.[16] No doubt Cooke would have made such a gesture, had he not died nine years before Howard. A number of publications arising out of conferences involving the Association of Former Parliamentarians and edited by Margaret Clark combine memoir and analysis; Fraser, Nordmeyer, Kirk, Rowling and Lange have been the Labour subjects of these publications.[17]

Bruce Brown's book began as a master's thesis, written in the mid-1950s. When his book was published, Labour had been through the disappointing experience of the one-term Nash government, and a slightly elegiac tone permeates the book. Brown was writing in the middle of the National Party's long post-war ascendancy, an ascendancy secured by National's adoption of much of the 1935–49 Labour government's achievements. Gustafson, likewise, wrote his thesis on the Labour Party in 1960 and when he published his book in 1980 Labour had been scarcely more successful in winning office than 20 years previously. Both historians may have thought that Labour's best days were behind it. Explaining the party's formation, however, was necessary, and both regarded the organised labour movement's increasing distance from the Liberals after 1905 as fundamental to the new party's eventual formation.

Much of the explanation for the New Zealand Labour Party's relatively late formation is that the Liberal government satisfied the political aspirations of many working people for some years after it took office in 1891. The Liberal government's progressive legislation itself reflected a sustained political mobilisation by labour and other progressive organisations and by working people. Where Brown and Gustafson perhaps treated the period before 1905—the first election contested by an independent 'labour' party—as something of a prelude, we suggest that when the Labour Party was established in 1916 it was heir to decades of radical and democratic activism. In going back to 1840, we revisit a period dealt with by J.D. Salmond as long ago as 1924.[18] Salmond's thesis was revised for publication in 1950 by Desmond Crowley; it carefully dealt with early claims for an eight-hour day and with the formation of some skilled workers' unions in the 1860s and 1870s, and with the wave of unionisation in the 1890s. To a modern reader Salmond's careful and detailed work is more narrative than analysis, but it remains valuable. Some of the struggles of the years before universal suffrage in 1893 remained relevant after 1916, and indeed some still do. In showing that New Zealand has a longer history of political radicalism than is sometimes allowed, we hope to, in E.P. Thompson's classic phrase, ameliorate 'the enormous condescension of posterity'.[19] William Tanner, a shoemaker who was a Christchurch member of parliament from 1890 to 1908, looked for co-operation rather than materialism; over 125 years later some share his hope.

The books by Brown and Gustafson were both important, although they have been criticised on one common point: an excessively simplistic division between 'moderate' and 'militant', whereby direct action was always the province of the movement's left wing, and parliamentary organising always right-wing. Gustafson suggested that the dominant ethos in the new party was pragmatic reformism, much influenced by progressive Christianity. If we think that Gustafson slightly overdoes that argument, we agree that Christian socialism has been a significant strand in the party's history. Some of the most consequential parliamentarians may be so described: Nash, Nordmeyer and Lange. Biblical language was often deployed by the formally irreligious, like James Thorn and Peter Fraser; and Tim Armstrong, perhaps the most left-wing of Savage's cabinet, was (like his Christchurch colleague Dan Sullivan) a practising Catholic. It remains the party's good fortune, though, that religious argument never caused a major, long-lasting split, unlike the devastation which right-wing Catholics wrought on the Australian Labor Party in the 1950s and 1960s.

We are by no means the first to suggest that parliamentary socialists could be at least as radical in their ambitions as industrial militants, although we agree with both these older historians that industrial defeat in 1912–13 made parliamentary organisation more acceptable to erstwhile militants. Gustafson, in particular, suggested that public dissatisfaction with the government's prosecution of the war contributed to Labour's good result in the 1919 election. We go a little further and argue that opposition to wartime conscription was the fundamental common ground on which the party began.

Neither Brown nor Gustafson wrote simple narratives of inevitable progress. Gustafson, then active in the party, had too much experience of its organisation to underestimate the hard work that goes into making a successful political party (not to mention the inherent disputatiousness of a reformist organisation). Gustafson highlighted the ongoing fractiousness within the infant organisation, not least over the drink question before 1919, a threat resolved by the decision that the party would not have a position on it. Gustafson, naturally, dealt with this, and conscription, in more detail than Brown, but implied that the 1919 election, in which Labour secured eight seats, was dreams coming true. More sceptically, Brown described the election as only a 'minor triumph'. They differ, too, over whether the new party should have remained in informal alliance with the Liberals or sought to become a truly national party. The latter decision prevailed, and Brown suggests that this cost two or three seats in 1919.[20]

Brown discussed the organisational problems of the 1920s in some detail, suggesting that the revived radicalism among transport workers and their Alliance of Labour reflected ongoing ideological divisions within the wider labour movement and hindered the party's advance (Harry Holland, the leader at the time, shared this view). Brown also discussed the difficulties of policy development in the context of successive general elections. For Holland's biographer, Patrick O'Farrell, however, Holland himself was the problem—a rigid and humourless ideologue, incapable of creatively developing policy and, by his unyielding Marxism, condemning Labour to opposition and impotence. O'Farrell, it seems, never departed from this view, which has become an orthodoxy.[21] We are pleased that some scholars are now rethinking Harry Holland, and we think Holland was more creative than he has been given credit for.[22] We suggest, too, that Labour's failure to advance much during the 1920s had something to do with an electoral system that was unfit for purpose, and to open intimidation by police and political censors. Yet the 1920s were also a decade of laying the foundations, a bedrock of electoral support that would hardly waver for decades. One dimension of this was the cautiously developed relationship with the Rātana movement; these efforts went back to the mid-1920s, and Brown is surprisingly brief on these discussions.

On one fundamental point, though, we agree with previous studies: it is most unlikely that Labour would have formed a government in the mid-1930s without the Depression. Perhaps there is a temptation to regard 1935 as an inevitable fulfilment. The 1935 victory, we suggest, was rather tentative, although we maintain that the party's parliamentarians were more than ready to embark on wide-ranging reform. However qualified its victory, on winning government in 1935 the party was in a position to reshape New Zealand's economic and social policy regime earlier than happened in many democratic states, a distinction shared with Scandinavian comrades. That reshaping involved a historic compromise, in which capitalism was to an extent tamed but not reformed out of existence. Social democrats accepted not only the logic of modernisation, but also that of accumulation. For New Zealand, as a small, trade-dependent nation, this implied significant challenges.

There is a pervasive strand in writing on the Savage and Fraser governments which charges them with missed opportunities, whether that opportunity was to implement a more radical socialist programme or merely to launch New Zealand on an economic path of industrialisation and independence. Keith Sinclair described this strand, with some justice, as 'the Lee–Sutch syndrome'.[23] It is not clear why W.B. Sutch reserved so much vituperation for Fraser and Nash, but his accusation was, in effect, that they preferred to conciliate British investors and their local collaborators rather than strike out boldly.[24] Sutch, in fact, regarded Lee as the lost tribune of such independence, a notion which Lee in his voluminous writings happily encouraged. Leaving aside Lee's egomania, the notion of timid parliamentarians betraying socialist ideals is far from uncommon in social democratic parties. As we suggest, such criticisms often ignore the real constraints, internal and external, under which reformist governments operate. Moreover, as the British historian Jim Tomlinson has often pointed out, social democracy has traditionally entailed programmes of economic modernisation as well as of redistribution.[25]

In contrast to the Lee–Sutch line of criticism, the standard biographies of Savage and Fraser are generally positive about their subjects and offer alternative interpretations. Gustafson's Savage is the ultimate humanitarian, although at the same time a canny political organiser. Perhaps inevitably, Savage is almost portrayed as the government, with little enough said on most of his ministerial colleagues. Writing as he was during the Lange–

Douglas years, in the context of a policy direction and approach to government which he deplored, Gustafson implicitly portrays Savage as the ideal of a Labour prime minister—humanitarian, pragmatic and of warm personality. Yet he concedes that Lee's conflict with Savage does not reflect well on either man. Erik Olssen says as much, observing that the two men destroyed each other; in this account, Lee was an enormously creative, but very flawed and ultimately tragic politician. If, as Michael Bassett suggests, by 1939 Fraser was convinced Lee was irredeemable, more sensitive handling in 1936 might—or might not—have had a different outcome. While we suggest that the impact of Lee's expulsion in 1940 has been exaggerated, we agree that it did the party no good, and reflected an enduring problem whereby loyalty was given undue priority over open debate. Fraser himself, as we agree with Bassett and Michael King, may justly be regarded as New Zealand's greatest prime minister, and that biography emphasises Fraser's domination of, first, social policy and then foreign and defence policy as he led a small nation through world war and to disproportionate influence in 1945. Bassett, who had the major responsibility for the biography, deftly noted the difficulties inherent in Fraser's social democratic vision, particularly that of fostering an ongoing ethic of solidarity rather than individualism. In the end, Sidney Holland and the National Party outmanoeuvered Fraser by promising security with instant gratification.

If it is valid to characterise the period to 1949 as one of rise and success (as it is), the years after 1949 were more difficult. After 1945, as in many democratic states, conservatives accepted much of the social democratic settlement. Labour's triumph was thus Labour's problem: how was the party to maintain its relevance? Robert Chapman summed up the conventional wisdom, that there was little policy difference between Labour and National in the 1950s, with the phrase 'parallelism of opinion'.[26] The party did itself some disservice in the 1950s when renewal was avoided, although the political climate was far from hospitable to extensions of reform. The major published work on the party in the 1950s consists of the biographies of Nash and Nordmeyer. Sinclair gave Nash due credit for mobilising support in 1957, but it is hard to avoid the conclusion that Nash, and the party, would have been better off had he retired before then. A master's thesis on the last years of the Fraser government, and the Bassett–King biography of Fraser, noted that the failure to renew the caucus went back to the 1940s and, in part, reflected a culture that placed a high priority on loyalty.[27] Nordmeyer was, arguably, a principal victim of this culture and Mary Logan's biography confirms the established impression of a capable and principled politician. We can only wonder what might have happened had Fraser realised in 1943, rather than 1950, that he wanted Nordmeyer to succeed him. The Black Budget of 1958 was not the only reason Labour was defeated in 1960; Barry Gustafson has pointed to the general failure to develop relevant and attractive policies in the mid-1950s.[28]

Labour was more successful in articulating independent visions of nationhood in the 1970s and 1980s. Perhaps surprisingly, the Kirk–Rowling government has attracted little attention, and it was only in 2014 that a substantial biography of Kirk appeared. The author, David Grant, wrote a sympathetic account of that complex man, and captured something of the idealism of the time. Kirk's strength was in foreign affairs; Brian Easton has observed that he had too little appreciation of economic management and his relationship with Rowling, as minister of finance, was not always easy.[29] Rowling himself awaits a posthumous biography, but the government had a number of very capable ministers; a detailed examination would need to move beyond the understandable nostalgia with which the Kirk years are sometimes viewed. Some useful theses have discussed party organisation in the 1970s, but the opposition years, 1975–84, provoked introspection and, perhaps, a temporary loss of confidence. As we have already noted, the fourth Labour government has been the subject of extensive analysis. Much of that government's record remains contentious. Foreign policy, and particularly the anti-nuclear dimension, have been litigated by participants and others, and the same is true of economic and social policy. Many accounts are emphatic in approval or denunciation; nuanced discussion is more rare. When necessary economic reform descended into every free-market, back-of-the envelope fantasy, the damage to the party was serious and, again, in the aftermath of heavy defeat in 1990 some professed to wonder whether the party had a future. Not all of those wondering were disinterested. From the mid-1990s Labour successfully developed a social democratic politics for a globalised world and in winning three consecutive elections, 1999, 2002 and 2005, Helen Clark became the most electorally successful leader the party has yet had (as well as the longest-serving). Although political chronology places some emphasis on the long periods in opposition between 1949 and 1984, since 1984 Labour has been in government for 15 of 32 years, which is not a bad record.

In writing this history we have drawn on a wide range of sources. We owe much to the insights of other historians, especially those whose work we have discussed above. Much valuable work lies in university theses, and we have used many. Given the large gaps in coverage, though, this book could not be a synthesis of an existing literature, and we have relied on many original sources. These include, obviously, the records of many party organisations, as well as interviews, either undertaken for this book (by Peter Franks and Rob Carr) or archived from earlier projects. Parliamentary debates and other official sources have been important, and, especially for the period before 1945, we have been able to access a wide range of newspapers through the National Library's Papers Past website. In researching and writing this book, we divided the initial drafting of chapters equally between ourselves, and then read, critiqued and amended each other's drafts. The whole book, therefore, can be regarded as having been jointly written, and, of course, we take full responsibility for what we have written.

This book has been written with the support of the Labour Party's New Zealand Council, although it is not an 'official' history. We have both been members of the Labour Party for many years and obviously therefore have a degree of political commitment. We hope, though, that we have been able to write this book with a degree of detachment proper to historians. Clearly enough, we see much that is positive in the Labour Party's hundred years, and much that was done badly or was plain wrong. We are, however, not seeking to whitewash, still less to tell consoling or uplifting stories: 'where the desire to edify prevails, there can be no history'.[30]

We offer this book as our informed interpretation of the Labour Party's history, an interpretation with which readers and other historians will wish, we hope, to engage and debate.

1

The Democratic Tradition 1840–1904

In February 1840, at Petone, a newly arrived carpenter, Samuel Duncan Parnell, insisted to a prospective employer that an eight-hour working day be observed. The employer tried to impose the longer hours prevailing in London. Parnell's reply was pithy: 'We're not in London.' He got the eight hours, and then persuaded others to adopt the principle.[1] Parnell lived to see universal male suffrage in New Zealand, dying shortly after the 1890 election which resulted in the Liberal–Labour government led by John Ballance. The 1890 election reflected a newly assertive labour movement and the possibilities of a settler democracy, and our argument in this chapter is that the Labour Party came out of a long tradition of radical and democratic politics, the influence of which is still evident. We emphasise that this was a politics of struggle: class conflict did not suddenly emerge about 1889 but was evident from the 1840s. Conservatives then deployed familiar language, blaming the poor for their own plight and arguing that labour organisations undermined the proper balance of society and natural co-operation between employers and workers. Debates were often complex and nuanced, and not infrequently disputatious. Arguments about the balance between collectivism and individual opportunity continued for decades, as did the tension between assertiveness and at least a tactical respectability. The proper balance between workplace issues—wages, hours and conditions—and other progressive movements was another ongoing debate, and if nineteenth-century labour activists frequently sought to exclude non-white immigrants, then again the labour movement continued to struggle with cultural diversity in later decades. At least from the 1870s labour activists were advocating economic diversification and industrial development: social democracy's modernisation agenda has something of a genealogy. More generally, there were always debates over how much reform would be sufficient, and a persistent language of New Zealand as a classless land of opportunity. Sometimes this language was deployed to describe an ideal to be achieved, and sometimes as a description of reality.

A glorious country for the labouring man?

Even before Parnell died his activities in 1840 were becoming reshaped into myth. To describe the Parnell story as a myth is not to deny its truth but to emphasise that the episode took on a retrospective importance in the context of 1890.[2] Parnell's observation, 'We're not in London', suggests a new start, a break from Old World oppression and inequality. Parnell's own career suggests some complexities. His ambition was independence. He became a self-employed builder, and owned a farm in Karori. He apparently took little part in political affairs, but in the intense debates of the later 1880s about the type of society New Zealand should be, Parnell willingly identified with labour's political mobilisation.

Many immigrants sought more independence and respect than they had experienced in Europe. The New Zealand Company's 'gorgeous fantasies' implied that colonisation would be easy and rewarding for capitalists and labourers alike. 'Company ships were fertile fields for those with a vision of a new world and a commitment to an improved place for labour.'[3] This first pulse of migration to New Zealand came from a United Kingdom much influenced by radical agitation, particularly Chartism, which demanded at the very least universal male suffrage, the secret ballot and a reformed parliament. Middle-class progressives shared some of these ambitions and 1850s New Zealand was, for white inhabitants anyway, a markedly more liberal society than Britain.[4] If working men's organisations in the 1840s and 1850s emphasised respectability and self-improvement, they were nonetheless assertive. With labour often scarce, workers' bargaining power was sometimes strong. One disgruntled Nelson gentleman complained that New Zealand was 'a glorious country for a labouring man' and another of the 'insufferable cheek' of female servants.[5] Labour shortages and a democratic ethos combined from the beginning to shape a new society.

Perhaps rashly, the New Zealand Company had promised to provide work for all 'emigrants' whom it had brought out on free passages. Workers had to insist on this several times. In Nelson the 'Working Men' wrote in a long memorial in 1843:

> we did not come here under the dishonourable apelation of Convicts we came here not with characters branded with Infamy but with characters that would bear the strictest scrutiny as honourable and Industrious men wishing only to live by our Industry and to procure a comfortable maintenance for ourselves and families.

Unemployed Nelson labourers were given work building roads. Conditions were so strict that the labourers organised what would now be called a work-to-rule, limiting progress. They occupied the company offices when officials proposed fortnightly, not weekly, wages. They threw one particularly unpopular overseer into a ditch.[6] Direct action aside, the arguments were about what one historian has described as a fundamental contract: the opportunity to work, with public authorities as the employer of last resort. This idea would be profoundly influential in labour politics.[7]

Working men's organisations also emphasised self-education and political representation. At the end of 1840 a Wellington Working Men's Association established a workers' library 'to furnish [them] with knowledge, the real source of power'. The existing public library's £5 subscription obviously excluded workers. Over 200 attended the founding meeting of this Port Nicholson Mechanics' Institute, which had a committee of 20, 'eight of whom shall be working men'.[8] A prominent figure was Rowland Davis, who had organised trade unions and campaigned for parliamentary reform in London. In Wellington (and, later, Lyttelton) he was a hotelkeeper, and no doubt his premises hosted political meetings.[9]

The infant colony's Legislative Council enacted a Municipal Councils Ordinance in 1841, which allowed a settlement with a European population above 2000 to establish a council, for which all adult (white) men who paid a registration fee of £1 (credited against rates) would be entitled to vote. This represented an opportunity for those of modest means. In February 1842 a committee, chaired by George Scott, who had been prominent in the library agitation, organised 'to watch over the interests of the working classes at the . . . Municipal elections'.[10] George Earp, a member of the appointed Legislative Council, complained that this would breed party spirit, 'prevent that good feeling which does exist, and ought always to exist, between the higher and lower classes' and 'sow the seeds of distrust and insubordination'. Letting the rabble vote, Earp thought, was 'a near approach to universal suffrage in its most objectionable form', for if labourers won political power the 'higher classes' would 'be taxed without mercy'.[11] The working men's committee warned that without workers' representatives the council would impose taxes 'infinitely more oppressive in a Colony than in the Mother-country'. Moderately, the committee hoped for a balanced representation of landed, commercial and working classes, 'so that no class should command a preponderance in the Council'.[12] Labour's moderation was not matched by the well-heeled advocates of the rights of property.

There was increasing agitation for self-government. Auckland merchants opposed Governor George Grey's autocratic style, which, they held, blocked economic development.[13] In Wellington and Nelson, settlers' constitutional associations emerged at the end of 1848. At a crowded meeting in Wellington Rowland Davis described the nominated Legislative Council as a 'miserable abortion'. A grand reform banquet drew more than 200 men in March 1849, Davis's hotel catering. By the end of August 1849, 780 men had signed a petition to the Queen, out of a jury list of 839.[14] In Nelson there was at least as much enthusiasm and in December 1850 a public meeting of 300 ran for 13 hours, calling for universal male suffrage, triennial parliaments of two elected chambers, and the secret ballot.[15] The associations reflected the ongoing alliance between middle-class liberals and artisan radicals. The Nelson association's committee was chaired by W.T.L. Travers, a lawyer, and the most prominent working man was John Perry Robinson, who had been a turner in Birmingham and observed that 'when he left England, he left it in the hope that he never should have occasion to take again an active part in politics, but since he had been in this colony he had witnessed such extraordinary doings and undoings on the part of the governing powers'.[16] The *Sydney Herald* thought 'ultra-Chartism' was rampant in New Zealand.[17] Even in Canterbury, one prominent settler complained that a Lyttelton Colonists' Society was 'composed chiefly of the people and working classes, and therefore . . . takes a democratic and republican, or Chartist tendency'.[18]

The 1852 constitution was less democratic than some hoped, with five-year parliamentary terms, an upper house of lifetime appointments, a property qualification and no secret ballot. The property qualification was low enough that the right to vote was widespread among Pākehā men (small numbers of Māori men qualified by individual property).[19] Provincial elections saw regular appeals to 'the working classes' and, by conservatives, to 'the property and intelligence of the province'.[20] Few 'working men's' candidates won election to provincial councils during the 1850s; the most notable was Robinson, in Nelson, whose support among artisans and small farmers made him provincial superintendent from 1856 until his accidental death in 1865. Robinson's ideal society was democratic and decentralised:

> Local self-government makes freemen always to do folk-right among each other . . . [it] brings law and folk-right, and the exercise of all political functions, home to every man's door, speedily, frequently, and costlessly . . . Local self-government unites all classes and interests in one effort for the common weal, making every proposition to be freely and fairly discussed before all, and to be determined only after such discussion.[21]

At the same time, Robinson's ideal society of independent producers would not always be hospitable to labour's notions of collectivism.

The right to work remained a key theme, especially as provincial governments, now in charge of immigration, continued to deploy rosy images of New Zealand in their recruiting campaigns. In 1860 Marcus Collison, a 'delegate from the working men of Carterton and Greytown', told a meeting:

> we have come to this country from the United Kingdom and elsewhere, not as agriculturalists nor capitalists, nor men of independent means, but as working men under the auspices of the Provincial Government's Agents, and under an assurance from them that we should find abundance of employment from public and private sources, and that in the event of the latter failing, we should have the public works of the Province as a resource.[22]

Unemployment was noticeable in the early 1860s, and while local government authorities and philanthropic individuals were willing to organise relief work, Collison and those of like mind expected something more. The press often described them as 'noisy demagogues, too idle to work themselves, too selfish to allow others to work, who conceive that it is their special mission to create an antagonism between the laboring classes, and those who provide the capital to pay for that labour'.[23] Some newspapers blamed the unemployed for their own plight. In 1864, with 200 men unemployed around the small town of Kaiapoi, the Christchurch *Press* maintained that the distress was 'chiefly, but not exclusively, among those of the Lancashire immigrants who have never become sufficiently capable workmen to secure regular employment, we have also no doubt that it has been greatly exaggerated'.[24] In May 1867 a meeting of several hundred Auckland workers called for public works to be stepped up. There, too, newspapers blamed workers: 'if the working men of Auckland had been a saving, thrifty body, there would not be any distress'. The issues were not simply pragmatic but ideological: 'trades-unions and combinations, the short-time movement, and the other specious pretences . . . divert the minds of the majority from their own individual interest, and induce them to look upon themselves as members of a caste or class', which prevents 'the one great motive . . . self-advancement'.[25] If many workers had only a strictly qualified interest in 'self-advancement', the ideal of opportunity was always in an uneasy tension with collective values.

In 1865 a Canterbury Working Men's Political Protection and Mutual Improvement Association organised to campaign for manhood suffrage, secular education and the secret ballot.[26] Samuel Andrews, a plasterer, campaigned as a working man for the provincial council, emphasising land settlement, public works and a free public library as well as the association's democratic agenda. He came sixth in a field of seven for four seats.[27] In 1871 a Working Men's Mutual Protection Society in Christchurch warned prospective immigrants about the shortage of work, communicated with the International Working Men's Association (commonly called the First International) and circulated some pamphlets by a leading figure, Karl Marx.[28] Also in 1871, an Auckland Working Men's Protection Society held a large meeting of the unemployed and discussed electoral mobilisation; 250 men took a petition for work at fair wages to the superintendent. They occupied the provincial government offices when the superintendent, Thomas Gillies, a flinty Scottish-born Free Church lawyer and landowner, questioned their good faith, refused to address them and offered stone-breaking at three shillings a day. The wages were starvation, but there was a deeply entrenched belief that elected office-holders should give petitioners the courtesy of addressing them.[29]

In Wellington, one Cornelius Ryan called a public meeting for 'the working classes of Wellington' to select two parliamentary candidates.[30] One newspaper was 'utterly opposed to this system of dividing the electors of Wellington into classes . . . We cannot see what end is to be gained by introducing class distinctions.'[31] Very moderate, and so crowded that it moved from the advertised hotel to a nearby paddock, the meeting resolved to support the long-serving politician and civil servant J.C. Richmond and the radical Irish lawyer W.T.L. Travers.[32] Neither was successful, and both opposed the colonial treasurer, Julius Vogel's, loan-funded developmentalism, partly from financial rectitude and partly because they foresaw duties on basics like tea and sugar increasing to repay the loans.[33] Travers won election in 1875, supported by the *Evening Post*: 'Every working man . . . who possesses a vote, would do well to remember to-morrow' the implication of supporting Travers's opponents. 'These gentlemen belong to a class bitterly opposed to the imposition of a tax upon property, or to any attempt to compel wealth to contribute its fair share to the revenue.'[34]

As the mid-1870s economic boom slowed, unemployment began to increase. In July 1877 the Amalgamated Iron Workers of Dunedin called a public meeting to discuss the problem. A thousand people, employers as well as workers, attended. A torchlight procession a few days later drew at least 1500, including ironworkers, tailors, labourers, printers, bricklayers, carpenters, plasterers and tanners, accompanied by bands and floats. After the procession a crowd of 3000 heard calls to 'Encourage Local Industry': speakers urged that the government should have railways rolling stock and other infrastructure requirements built in New Zealand rather than imported from Britain.[35] This was an early, and eloquent, statement of an agenda of economic development, not only for employment but also for economic independence.

In 1877 George Grey, now in his mid-sixties and drawn out of retirement by opposition to the abolition of provincial governments, formed a nominally radical government. His parliamentary allies included some among a new political generation who identified as Liberals. Grey adopted the role of radical tribune, 'persuading the public that principles such as manhood suffrage, the breaking up of the great pastoral estates and fairer systems of taxation were his inventions'.[36] Despite the rhetoric, Grey's government achieved very little in its two years, but the language of radical liberalism became firmly established in political discourse and once intermittent labour organisation became more persistent.

In 1879 the Auckland Amalgamated Society of Engineers called a meeting of unions which established a Working Men's Political Association, 'whose object shall be to secure the better representation of the working classes in Parliament'.[37] Grey advised a deputation of Wellington workers that if the 'industrial classes' wanted legislation to reflect their interests 'they must send their own class to represent them in Parliament', and at its first meeting the Auckland Working Men's Political Association resolved to seek direct parliamentary representation, and discussed tariff reform that would encourage industrial development and processing New Zealand resources rather than exporting raw materials.[38]

Grey was replaced later that year by a conservative administration led by John Hall, who had 'cleverly committ[ed] himself to liberal reforms', including triennial parliaments and manhood suffrage (albeit with continuing extra votes for the propertied).[39] The Hall government reduced public spending, including cutting public sector wages by 10 per cent. When new pay scales were promulgated at the Addington railway workshops the workers eventually and reluctantly accepted the reductions. Mostly skilled tradesmen, they understood that wages would be restored once the public finances improved, and when in September 1881 railways administrative staff received the restoration but tradesmen did not, many of the latter gave notice to strike. Eventually 68 men walked out, issuing an 'appeal to the working class of Christchurch.—We, the blacksmiths, fitters, turners, machinists, hammermen and labourers of the Addington workshops, do earnestly solicit the help and sympathy of all engaged in a similar class of trade', asking 'the help of all honest, good men, to refrain from applying for our situations'.[40] They were quickly replaced. Strikers' representatives addressed public meetings and met Hall, who of course refused to consider dismissing the strikebreakers, promising only that those who had walked out might be taken on again if there were fresh vacancies. Some of the strikers went to Victoria.[41]

Historians have argued about whether it is appropriate to speak of a developing liberal–conservative divide before, or even after, 1890. Contemporaries had fewer doubts. The lawyer and parliamentarian John Sheehan told a meeting in Napier in 1879 that there were liberals and conservatives 'though the Conservatives repudiated their title'. Sheehan identified a number of key differences. Tax policy was one: whether it should emphasise customs duties, to the detriment of working people, or rely more on property and particularly land (land taxes would also discourage aggregation). Liberals advocated universal male suffrage and triennial parliaments. Sheehan declared that he 'was not a revolutionary *sans culotte*, for he believed in the rights of capital as well as labor; but he believed also that labor had not had all its rights, and that capital had had more than its share'.[42] In Christchurch, Samuel Andrews stood as a Greyite and added to the basic liberal platform a land policy which would allow purchase on deferred payment. This, he thought, would allow workers to improve their position: 'he was a plasterer, and worked at his trade, but he believed that every mechanic had a hope beyond their trade'. Andrews won, but proved more conservative than his supporters hoped; even his support for manhood suffrage was qualified.[43] In 1881 he was defeated by a contractor and timber merchant, William White, who also campaigned as a Liberal, and supported universal male suffrage and at least some admission for the working classes to secondary education. White's views on these questions and taxation accorded with those of the local Working Men's Political Association.[44]

Another aspiring parliamentarian, Richard Seddon, thought, on education, that the government should provide only 'elementary instruction, not Latin, French and music'. Seddon wished 'to be an exception to the most of the other candidates who termed themselves Liberals, he would call himself a Radical'. His platform included expanded public works, not least to diminish Māori isolation and autonomy, and while he wished to encourage local industry and introduce an income tax, much of his 'Radicalism' was defined by virulent anti-Chinese rhetoric.[45] Similarly, the Auckland Working Men's Political Association president, Thomas Thwaites, a shipwright, complained in late 1879 that a bill to restrict Chinese immigration was 'worse than useless . . . unless something were done, several industrious classes would be starved out'. The Chinese were 'a pest, not only by their unfair competition, but by the evil example of their manners and ways'. He was loudly applauded, and such statements would be a central element in labour rhetoric for decades.[46]

Until 1880, most efforts to organise working men's votes lasted no longer than an election campaign. During that decade, though, labour's political organising became more systematic, and sometimes unlikely alliances with middle-class reformists were regarded with some caution. The Auckland Working Men's Political Association survived the 1879 election, with over 200 members and a committee of over 40. Membership was open to 'all working men of known good character' on payment of a shilling entry fee and sixpence a month; 'employers of labour and other gentlemen' could become honorary members.[47] The organisation advocated industrial development, as well as running lectures on political affairs and history.[48] In September 1880 the committee prepared a report discussing the recent royal commission on colonial industries; the Christchurch *Press* dismissed it as 'a remarkable illustration of the singular want of judgement which too often characterises the efforts of the self-constituted representatives of the working classes to secure political influence'.[49] For the 1881 election the association resolved that 'the candidates whom this association shall support shall be working men'.[50] It is unclear what occupation its candidate for Auckland West, a Mr Laing, followed, but Laing's platform was standard radical liberalism, including land reform, industrial protection, the abolition of property votes in general elections, and the total exclusion from the country of Chinese. Laing also opposed women's suffrage and supported the Contagious Diseases Act, which many feminists strongly condemned.[51] A Working Men's Political Association in Christchurch was established or revived a month before the 1881 election with a similar platform.[52]

In Dunedin, the Otago Trades and Labour Council (consisting of individual members rather than affiliated unions) had some difficulty deciding which candidates to support. Some were 'far below the standard . . . suitable for very ordinary working men's candidates—that is to say, if the working classes could not produce more able men than some of those now seeking their suffrages they don't deserve to be represented'. In the end the council supported Matthew Green, a Primitive Methodist preacher, two lawyers, John Bathgate and W.D. Stewart, and the journalist and poet Thomas Bracken, as well as the master painter Henry Smith Fish.[53] All were elected, probably owing little to the Trades Council. (Fish became notorious for his vituperative opposition to women's suffrage, and, although he liked to pose as a working men's champion, there was little substance in his claims.)[54]

During 1883 a trades council revived in Auckland, initially campaigning against Chinese as well as for the rights of white workers.[55] By 1884 the Auckland and Otago councils claimed a fairly numerous membership, as did the Christchurch Working Men's Political Association. Councils or associations were formed or discussed in Napier, Blenheim, Wellington, Greymouth and Oamaru at least. Most supported Grey 'as the leader of the Liberal party' (although some branches of the Christchurch association did not).[56] Grey was a symbol of the aspirations felt by many working men and liberals; the lack of specificity did not matter so much as people feeling that they had a champion.[57] The labour organisations generally sought to influence elections rather than stand their own candidates, although at least two members of the Christchurch Working Men's Political Association stood, unsuccessfully.[58] They usually emphasised their moderation, disavowing strikes and emphasising industrial arbitration (Otago was horrified at the suggestion that its 'object was to raise class warfare').[59] At the same time these organisations insisted on their own definitions of liberalism. One Christchurch parliamentarian supported land and property taxes, settlement by deferred payment, the state as employer of last resort and secular education; but he also supported plural voting and an unreformed Legislative Council, and George Dorney, the Working Men's Political Association president, called him 'a stumbling block to New Zealand, and especially to the working classes'.[60]

Dunedin's labour movement, based in New Zealand's most industrial city, was the most visible in the mid-1880s. It was dominated by the skilled men of the artisan trades, whose moral order was challenged by mechanisation and monopoly. They responded with a mobilisation that was defensive, but more than defensive. Their political mobilisations stressed not only the rights of man and the dignity of labour, but also the duty of self-improvement. Temperance, and the moral precepts of dissenting Protestantism generally, informed this movement. 'Literacy and knowledge, useful in many skilled trades and essential in some, were indispensable to full legal, political and social equality, or, in a word, citizenship.'[61] Thus, radicalism and respectability were in creative tension. In January 1885 the Otago Trades Council called the first New Zealand Trades and Labour Congress, attended by 36 delegates. Charles Thorn, the Otago president, told delegates, 'Labour has not been represented and organised as it ought to have been. That has been our own fault', and he called on those present to 'Agitate and organise'. The platform was familiar enough: extended voting hours, abolition of the property vote, to advocate for labour interests in parliament, technical education, and reduced hours for shop-workers. He conceded that 'we have up to the present time entirely lost sight of our female co-workers', and organising women workers would also assist local industry, as would organising mining and farming workers.[62] Moderate and respectable, the congress affirmed its faith in arbitration 'as it considers a strike only becomes legitimate when every other means has failed'. Six hundred workers paraded with trade banners and bands in front of a Saturday evening crowd of thousands.[63]

A second congress met in Auckland in January 1886. 'Hard times were at the bottom of the fact that many societies were unrepresented.' The chairman, H.W. Farnall, observed:

> the enormous wealth of the Colony was to be kept by men who monopolised it, and . . . the majority, who had helped to produce it, were to starve or clear out or do anything they liked as long as they did not interfere with the money interest . . . the question of all questions was, Were the people to be divided into two classes—the landlords and the landless, the governing and the governed, the wealthy and the poverty stricken, the slaveowners and the slaves; or whether they were, by wise and judicious legislation, to secure to everyone a home and a competency.[64]

The congress joined the annual Eight Hours' Demonstration, again with many trades banners, which was followed by an afternoon of sports. At the public meeting which followed, one speaker 'insisted that every working man in the community should belong to a trades union. The necessity for this was shown by the fear and dread which the propertied classes had of trades unions.'[65] The congress established a parliamentary committee and resolved that it was desirable to elect to parliament 'good and true men from the working classes'. A general principle was endorsed of 'co-operation in the case of long strikes'.[66]

Labour agendas were less visible in the 1887 election, perhaps because of continuing depression. The working men's political associations and the trades councils seem to have gone into recess and the national congress did not meet. Only in Canterbury was there a concerted effort, through the Canterbury Electors' Association, to organise progressive forces. The association urged voters against

> men who study only the selfish interests of the small clique they represent . . . legislation for a Class, and that Class a small minority of Wealthy Speculators, Wealthy Commission Agents, and Wealthy Importers . . . men who would destroy that grand heritage which the People have acquired, our

> System of Free and Ample Education . . . men who would strangle our Local Industries, and who would have the Working Men clear out or starve . . . who would Tax the Necessaries of Life, and who would free the Wealthy from all inconvenience.

Twelve of the 14 endorsed candidates were elected, including W.P. Reeves.[67] The overall result, however, was a cobbled-together Scarecrow Ministry in which the relatively moderate Harry Atkinson depended on the support of a number of hard-line right-wingers.

Transformation, 1887–90

The 1887 election was like those of 1928 and 1978: an oddly subdued affair in which many voters voted to not decide anything very much. The quietness was artificial, for, just as in 1928 and 1978, paralysis gave way to a burst of reforming energy in a decade of ideological ferment. Campaigning for universal suffrage intensified. In 1889 the parliamentary opposition reshaped itself under the leadership of the Whanganui newspaperman John Ballance, and a liberal–labour coalition developed. Universal male suffrage was won in 1889 and women's suffrage followed in 1893. Most importantly, trade unionism grew rapidly and unionists began to stake out radical positions on work, employment and the distribution of wealth. The high tide of 1890 receded, but the labour movement was fundamentally transformed in these years.

Coal miners' unionism had been increasing in strength since the late 1870s. Fifty South Yorkshire miners, imbued with the ideals of solidarity and Methodism, were recruited for the Westport Coal Company in 1879, but when they arrived in Nelson the company's managing director, A.J. Burns, 'allowed his prejudice against unionism and Methodism free reign' and refused to engage them.[68] The miners dispersed, but within a few years the company was 'forced to take what miners it could get—unionism and Methodism notwithstanding' to develop its Denniston mine.[69] In September 1884 the Denniston miners formed a union. Despite their moderation—they sought only 'customary miners' holidays, recognition of the negotiating role of union officials, and an agreement that in future only experienced colliers would be employed'—the employers cut their wages.

The miners struck for six months and won because the company could not find suitable strikebreakers. John Lomas, the union president, sought to federate all New Zealand and Australian coal miners, and included labourers and railway workers up and down the West Coast.[70] Given the close links between coal and shipping, it was unsurprising that larger companies like the Union Steam Ship Company had a dominant position in both industries. This in turn prompted miners, seafarers and watersiders to federate in the Maritime Council, formed in Dunedin in October 1889 with Lomas as treasurer and the Seamen's Union secretary, John A. Millar, as president.

In October 1888 a Dunedin Presbyterian minister, Rutherford Waddell, preached a sermon, 'The Sin of Cheapness', exposing the conditions in which many women were forced to work, with very low wages for take-home work.[71] Remarkably, the city's establishment shared Waddell's concern and the *Otago Daily Times* launched an investigation, which vindicated him. The newspaper emphasised the respectability of many of the women affected, noting that one front room was 'scrupulously clean and tidy, and by no means ill-supplied with books of a religious character'. One woman was pessimistic: 'It's of no use speaking of trade organisation amongst women. They never will combine', for it would cost even that meagre livelihood, when unemployment had recently become much worse.[72] Waddell advocated uniform rates set by workers' and employers' representatives. He argued that women needed to unionise as men had done. 'Strikes are morally justifiable. The worker who has nothing to sell but his labour has an incontestable right to withhold his commodity from the market if he thinks he is not getting a fair remuneration for it. And that is the simple meaning of a strike.'[73]

Clothing trades workers, men and women, organised in Dunedin, Christchurch and Wellington, supported by middle-class liberals, including some parliamentarians and clergy. The Dunedin Tailoresses' Union included, as vice-president, Harriet Morison, a working tailoress, while Waddell was the president and Millar the secretary. The union drew up a log of rates in July 1889, and when employers refused to accept it, 500 workers voted to strike. Within a few days agreement was reached.[74] In Christchurch, the Tailors, Tailoresses and Pressers' Union president, F.S. Parker, noted that there had previously been a union but it had gone into recess and 'the result was that they were now in a frightful condition. Had they come out to a new land to suffer the same hardships which they had in the Old Country?' The committee comprised equal numbers of men and women, and also prepared a log. Most employers accepted it, with the notable exception of the big Kaiapoi mill, which employed 500 workers and where management refused to accept a closed shop. Four hundred workers struck, maintaining that the closed shop was the very basis of unionism and essential to deter freeloaders. The strike lasted three weeks, with every step being debated by meetings of up to 500 union members and pickets persuading the recalcitrant to join. In the end, management accepted that all workers had joined the union and, saving face, accepted the closed shop, and eventually agreed on the log. This resounding victory was also notable for the moral and financial support contributed by other unions throughout New Zealand.[75]

Workers at the Wellington Woollen Mill, in Petone, objected to long hours, with 13 a day common, especially on the night shift. Citing a downturn in trade, the company closed the nightshift and sacked 58 workers—all but one of them men—who had formed the union. The Wellington Trades Council spent several weeks trying to negotiate reinstatement, and at the end of February 1890 about 60 young women walked out in support of their dismissed comrades. Unions across the country contributed strike pay. There were frequent mass meetings, including one in late March when 200 Wellington supporters took a steamer up the harbour and joined 300 workers in Petone for a rally, speeches and evening dancing. Eventually, in late May, the Maritime Council's John Millar negotiated reinstatement and recognition of the union. With slack trade, not all the unionists were reinstated.[76] While some newspapers, including the *Evening Post*, supported the workers, others maintained that the union was overreaching itself and in accepting arbitration had learned 'a valuable lesson, which . . . seems to have been needed', for while combination of labour is necessary, 'when labour begins in its turn to be tyrannous as well as strong . . . it is time to give labour a lesson'.[77] Bourgeois liberalism had its limits.

The wave of organisation extended far beyond mining and the clothing trades. Within a few weeks of its foundation in November 1889, the Canterbury Trades and Labour Council represented 1500 workers, including bootmakers, carpenters, printers, clothing workers, boilermakers, shipwrights, painters, butchers, and farm and general labourers.[78] The Otago council, in recess for some years, revived in January 1890.[79] In March 1890 railway construction labourers in the Grey Valley sought improved conditions, threatened to strike, and got most of what they wanted. A manure factory in Belfast, Christchurch sacked eight union men and the Canterbury council eventually won reinstatement.[80] Bakery employees in Christchurch, working 60 hour weeks, organised to seek a reduction and gave notice to strike. The council negotiated a settlement, which the workers reluctantly accepted. A Catholic priest, Fr le Menant des Chenais, addressed a public meeting in support of the bakery workers and essentially laid out a liberal platform, including land reform and co-operation. 'Labour produced capital, and when capital was not properly divided it caused misery.'[81]

By March 1890 newspapers estimated that there were over 20,000 union members across New Zealand, in a total population of fewer than 700,000. Unionism was concentrated among transport workers (13,000) and the textile and footwear trades (3000). Another estimate is that 35,000 workers, or 27 per cent of wage and salary earners, were union members in 1890. A liberal newspaper thought that 'so large a body, most of whose members must be entitled to the franchise, could exercise no small power in the election of the next Parliament' and advocated a colony-wide labour federation.[82] Some thought this could be based on the Knights of Labor, an American organisation which had recently become influential in New Zealand. Founded in Philadelphia in 1869, the Knights of Labor became a mass organisation in the United States in the 1880s, and the first New Zealand organisation to adopt the Knights platform was the Canterbury Labour Union, shortly after forming in November 1887. The Knights combined the language of radical liberalism with much ritual and secrecy, and attracted support from political luminaries such as Grey, Reeves, and a number of other current and future Liberal parliamentarians. Although generally seeing the strike as a last resort, Knights supported textile and clothing workers in 1889 and 1890 and spoke at strike meetings. Aileen Garmson, a Christchurch clothing worker, was a master workman, as the Knights called branch chairs. Dunedin Knights were the high command of the Otago labour movement. The Knights faded after 1890, but for a brief time they were a powerful, colony-wide political force, certainly more of an organisation than the Liberal Party itself until after 1893.[83]

The Knights of Labour's fondness for ritual and secrecy perhaps limited their appeal. Workers had no shortage in 1890 of enthusiasm for open mass meetings. Rutherford Waddell and John Lomas toured the country in the autumn of that year. Waddell described unions as 'only a half-way house to a much larger boon that would be secured . . . in the form of co-operation'.[84] Lomas urged the benefits of combination, particularly encouraging unmarried women to involve themselves: 'the ladies were the best Union men', although he 'had no sympathy with women being made to work against men. The working men should be in such a position that they should be able to keep their wives and daughters in their homes, and not be the slaves of anybody.' Lomas's advocacy of organising across occupational particularism so that, for instance, gold and coal miners would be in the same union, and his belief that only mass organisations could meet the employers from a position of strength differed only in the rhetorical flourishes from the Red Fed agenda of 1908–13.[85]

The working class mobilisation of 1887–90 was a major challenge to the capitalist order, and a confrontation was inevitable. The trans-Tasman maritime strike of September and October 1890 directly involved miners, watersiders and seamen in New Zealand, but affected workers and unions across the country.[86] The strike began when the Australian shipowners refused to allow ships' officers to join the Australian Maritime Council. The dominant New Zealand shipping company, the Union Steam Ship Company, secure and prosperous, might have conceded something, but smaller shipowners were 'absolutely implacable' in opposing such ideas.[87] Most of the larger Australian shipowners were likewise opposed, and the strike began there in early August. The Union company decided after a week to support the Steamship Owners of Australia, of which they were members. Thus emboldened, the Steamship Owners resolved to ban ships' officers from joining any union, and to use non-union labour as it saw fit. 'The fight was now over basic principles' of unionism.[88] Two hundred railway workers at Lyttelton, ordered to work the wharves in place of striking watersiders, refused and were dismissed.

West Coast coal miners had only just recovered from a year of conflict over union membership, wages and conditions: the unions had deployed restrictive practices to good effect, but when unemployment rose again early in the winter of 1890 the employers locked them out for a month.[89] When the maritime strike spread to New Zealand, Denniston miners demanded that their employer not supply Union ships and struck. The Grey Valley miners went out a little later. With summer approaching, there was less pressure on coal supplies, and high unemployment meant little difficulty in finding strikebreakers. The miners' defeat allowed employers to 'destroy mining unionism in the colony'. Most miners applied for their old jobs by the end of October and union leaders were blacklisted.[90] In Christchurch, the booksellers and printers Whitcombe and Tombs had refused to recognise the Typographical Association, and in August the Maritime Council called a boycott of the firm. Railwaymen, watersiders and seamen refused to handle the firm's goods and were sacked. A public meeting, called by the Trades Council, drew 3000 men and women. Despite this massive show of support, the printers were beaten when their dispute merged with the maritime strike at the end of August.[91]

The aftermath of the maritime strike: labour politics remade

The maritime strike ended in comprehensive defeat. 'Rapid though union growth had been in the late 1880s, unions were neither organisationally nor ideologically ready for a large-scale dispute.'[92] But it would be mistaken to suggest that labour organisation disappeared. The general election in December 1890 demonstrated that workers could still mobilise (and their strength was reinforced because multiple voting for property owners had been abolished). Even before the election, workers staged a major show of defiance in the Labour Day processions on 28 October. Thousands marched with their union banners and bands across the country, 'a chance to salvage dignity from rout'.[93] In many parts of the country 'a new socialist discourse lay to hand and had been absorbed into popular attitudes . . . Paine's view of the Rights of Man, Ricardo's labour theory of value, the assaults on industrialisation by Thomas Carlyle and John Ruskin, not to mention the indictments of land monopoly spelt out by George and Mill'.[94] Henry George and John Stuart Mill attacked land monopoly as the foundation of economic injustice, and these ideas resonated powerfully in New Zealand as in other 'new world' societies. The opposite of land monopoly was an ideal society of independent producers and artisans, or at least one in which work was respected and rewarded with modest comfort. Thomas Paine's 1791 *Rights of Man* attacked hereditary status and defended the French Revolution's liberty, equality and fraternity. Chartism renewed these claims in the 1830s and 1840s. In later decades, a Whiggish belief in the British genius for peaceful reform endowed the democratic agenda with a certain respectability. Ruskin's critique of the dehumanising aspects of industrialisation was accompanied by a belief in co-operation and service which reflected the famous co-operative efforts of Robert Owen in the 1830s, and would go on to influence Walter Nash and others in the 1920s and 1930s. Edward Bellamy's utopian novel, *Looking Backward*, sold out in New Zealand and was serialised in the *Canterbury Times*. Bellamy foresaw a world in which there was free education, equal distribution of work and income, radically shorter working hours, state control of industry, and marriage out of love rather than women's economic dependence. As the great American socialist Eugene Debs wrote, Bellamy 'not only aroused the people but started many on the road to the revolutionary movement'.[95] In the middle of 1890 the liberal Christchurch newspapers printed a series of articles on socialism by William Pember Reeves, which further legitimated the use of the word. The strike's defeat did not end the ideological ferment, a ferment which shaped and reshaped labour politics for some time to come.

The 1890 election, with one man one vote, returned a liberal and radical majority to the House of Representatives. How many of them were identified with labour depends on definitions, and is complicated by the considerable common ground which existed between left-wing liberals and labour activists.[96] The president of the Canterbury Trades and Labour Council, F.S. Parker, stood unsuccessfully in Halswell; his election addresses were no more or less 'labour' in orientation than those of William Hall-Jones, a master builder who won Timaru.[97] David Pinkerton, from Dunedin, would later identify 'the men in the House who have come straight from the ranks of labor', who included himself and William Earnshaw, William Tanner from Christchurch, James Kelly from Invercargill, T.L. Buick from Wairau and Charles Mills for Waimea–Picton. Yet Mills, a commission agent, was no more 'from the ranks of labor' than Masterton's radical newspaperman Alexander Hogg, whom Pinkerton explicitly excluded. Pinkerton also recognised 'men who have been returned in the labor interest, but who are not workers', like Dunedin's bad-tempered maverick Henry Fish, and three members from Christchurch, R.M. Taylor, Westby Perceval and Reeves.[98]

Labour's electoral strength was concentrated in Dunedin and Christchurch and was mobilised by the trades councils, reinforced in Christchurch by the People's Political Association.[99] Certainly a key factor, as Pinkerton suggested and Tanner had made very clear, was 'that working men . . . would not be satisfied with "working men's friends" but would insist on the genuine article'. Tanner, a shoemaker whose father and grandfather had been involved in radical movements in England in the 1840s and 50s, thought 'this new democracy looked ultimately to a rearrangement of society on the basis of a true commonwealth, eliminating the individualism of the present materialistic age'.[100] The success of Dunedin and Christchurch labour politicians reflected not only the importance of industry in those cities but also, and perhaps more, the greater discipline of labour organisations. In Auckland in 1890 some unions formed a United Labour Election Committee, but the Knights of Labour backed their own candidates. Similarly divided efforts were evident in Wellington.[101]

In parliament the 'labour' members joined the Liberal caucus.[102] They could hardly have done otherwise, although that did not mean they quietly accepted a cautious middle-class liberalism. When Ballance and his colleagues sought to establish a National Liberal Federation in the middle of 1891, Earnshaw noted the existence of distinct Tory and Liberal parties 'and he was glad to say that in the Liberal party there was a good sprinkling of the socialistic element'.[103] The federation promoted a broad progressive platform, including universal suffrage, guaranteed employment, public ownership of land, mines, railways and coastal shipping, rent and interest controls, and basic public education. These would be advanced by progressive land and income taxes, a minister of labour, a state bank of issue, and an elected governor and revising committee to replace the Legislative Council. All the 'labour' parliamentarians, except the printer John Rigg, who had been appointed to the upper house in 1892, openly supported women's franchise.[104]

Nor did trade unionism disappear. The movement was defeated and diminished in the maritime strike, not annihilated. In June 1891 delegates from the trades councils in the four large cities met for several days to discuss labour legislation before the House, and organised a very large public meeting of support for the Liberal government, including a presentation to the now aged Grey.[105]

Remarkably, Auckland bootmakers—and the wider movement—sustained a six-month strike in 1891. In February, footwear manufacturing employers across the country agreed to a national standard of wages and conditions. Many Auckland employers refused to comply, and in March the Auckland Operative Bootmakers' Union gave notice to strike unless the national standard was adopted. Two hundred and five men and 55 women walked out of 11 factories, with strong support from the Auckland Trades Council and the Knights of Labour. Unions all over the country and in

Australia raised about £6000 in strike pay. The union assisted several dozen strikers to find work in other parts of New Zealand, but even at the end of July over 100 were still out and a meeting voted by 176 to 32 to stand firm. Public meetings in support drew as many as a thousand. The strike suffered a blow in May when the union president resigned and went to work in a non-union shop, but his erstwhile comrades retaliated with an elaborate mock funeral procession in which his effigy was subjected to various indignities. Eventually the union accepted the employers' terms when the strike pay ran out, but clearly unionism was far from being a spent force.[106]

In Dunedin the Trades Council's Workers' Political Committee 'established control over the selection of candidates' for the 1893 election. Given the dwindling membership of the unions, this success 'was little more than astonishing'.[107] The 1893 election was dominated not by the struggle of 1890 but by a feeling of consolidation, added to the interest aroused by universal suffrage. Labour's success in 1893 was a high tide, and the greater victory in that election was of the Liberal party's rural wing. Even before the 1893 election, Seddon, who became premier when Ballance died in April, had scolded the Auckland Liberals for issuing a manifesto sufficiently radical to 'alienate . . . every country district in the Colony'.[108] The manifesto had been no more than the advanced liberalism of 1890.[109] The Dunedin Workers' Political Committee manifesto was very similar, but that committee was independent of, although aligned to, the Liberal organisation. It included, moreover, the Women's Franchise League, which sought to mobilise working women in the suffrage campaign.[110] In 1896 the Workers' Political Committee issued another manifesto along the same lines. Although Dunedin and Christchurch labour members still supported the government, their identification with it was qualified.[111]

David Hamer dismisses the labour members as 'few in number and not of high calibre'. Many Liberals, he suggests, thought that 'more was being done for labour than seemed justified by its strength and importance as a sectional interest'.[112] Even before Reeves left for London in 1895, labour was being marginalised in the Liberal coalition. Having got the Industrial Conciliation and Arbitration Act 1894, which gave unions legal recognition and machinery for the compulsory resolution of industrial disputes, through parliament on the basis that it would not apply to rural workers, Reeves could achieve little more; Seddon publicly warned that labour should not push its luck.[113] He took over the labour portfolio, and, although he defended the legislation that had been passed until then, he was prepared to accept only modest and incremental further reform.[114] Certainly, Seddon accepted the 'social contract', implying ultimate state responsibility for a basic level of economic security, frugal comfort and a degree of opportunity.[115] Thus 'the achievement of 1891–4 was sacrosanct, and that was a major political gain for labour'.[116] Labour activists agreed, but their agenda in 1890 had been bigger than that, and the larger agenda would be revived after 1900.

By 1900 labour's political organisations were becoming fractured, especially over the drink question. In Auckland and Wellington, labour organisations were, in 1896, 1899 and 1902, unable to agree over candidates or even whether candidates should be supported. In 1896 the Dunedin Workers' Political Committee split over prohibition, and the impact was also felt in Christchurch. As Seddon moved to the imperialist right, labour became increasingly marginalised within the Liberal caucus, even as a number of left-Liberals continued to win election, including George Laurenson, Harry Ell, T.H. Davey and Tommy Taylor in Christchurch. Ell and Davey had been printing tradesmen; Laurenson, who always enjoyed strong support from working-class voters, was a ship's chandler; and Taylor was a land agent. Taylor, in particular, was a fanatical prohibitionist, and some of the south Dunedin labour prohibitionists shared his anti-Catholic bigotry. In 1899 the liberal lawyer T.K. Sidey won Caversham as the labour vote split over drink.[117]

Some labour activists thought that the Liberal alliance was diminishing in usefulness and were involved in forming the New Zealand Socialist Party in 1901. In order to ensure that it wasn't immediately swamped by Liberals, the Wellington inaugural meeting was advertised by word of mouth, and 100 turned up. The new party owed much to the arrival, in 1900, of a group of settlers inspired by the English socialist paper the *Clarion*. The Clarionettes' legacy was the influence of the British Independent Labour Party on the New Zealand labour movement. Two of the Clarionettes, Fred and Ida Cooke, settled in Christchurch, joined the Socialist Party, and were prominent in left-wing politics for 30 years. Fred was a tailor, and when he went into business on his own account Ida kept the books. They joined the Labour Party after 1916, Fred serving as president in the 1920s. The great-granddaughter of another Clarionette, Thomas Clark, would achieve even greater eminence after 1999.[118] The new party intended to educate people towards 'the organisation of New Zealand as a Co-operative

Commonwealth in which the land and all the instruments of production, distribution, and exchange shall be owned and managed by the people collectively'.[119] Branches followed in Auckland and Petone (in August) and in Christchurch (launched by the Trades Council in January 1902). George Laurenson supported the new party, for 'reforms were as merely beating the air until the people owned the land', and Harry Ell thought the new party's aims 'were really what true Liberals had been fighting for for years past'.[120] The Christchurch branch owed something, too, to the Socialist Church, established in 1896 by Harry Atkinson, a nephew of the former premier. Atkinson had been inspired by a similar organisation in Manchester, where he had lived for some time. Like the Independent Labour Party, the Socialist Church emphasised an ethical, co-operative socialism and the importance of educating citizens in such principles. Although the Socialist Church faded around 1905, some of the people associated with it remained very influential in the labour movement.[121]

During 1902 the English socialist Tom Mann, who had recently arrived in New Zealand, was appointed organiser, but after some months, with the party unable to pay him, Mann left for Australia (he would return to England in 1910). Then another recent arrival, Robert Hogg from Scotland, established *Commonweal* as the Wellington branch newspaper. Hogg espoused revolutionary politics, as did Mann's American replacement, Robert LaMonte, and, in Bert Roth's severe judgement, the pair 'succeeded in undoing all Mann's good work . . . Theoretical discussion now prevailed, electoral work was ignored, and the trade union struggle for better wages and conditions was dismissed as unworthy of revolutionary socialists.' As a result 'the party quickly lost all influence in the Trades Councils', and indeed all branches except Wellington went into recess.[122] A revival in the party's fortunes would only come with the revolt against arbitration after 1907.

The trades councils were likewise moving towards an independent labour party. By 1904 the union movement was more self-confident. Legal recognition was a necessary but not sufficient condition for this strength, which relied on the commitment of thousands of working men and women. The labour movement had often struggled, and before the 1880s its organisation was fragmented. As it had developed by 1900, there were evident continuities with the decades since 1840. However sporadically, labour activists had advocated decent wages and hours, democratic reform, a measure of economic equality, secure work, and economic development (less meritoriously, often in the language of a White New Zealand). From the late 1880s this had become a more coherent political agenda, and after 1900 there was an increasing argument that the agenda could be realised only by an independent labour party.

2
Labour Parties
1904–19

At Easter 1904 the trades and labour councils' annual conference, held in Christchurch, resolved to form a Political Labour League. There was increasing dissatisfaction with the Liberal government, or at least a feeling that organised labour needed to be represented by its own party. Establishing the Political Labour League was a first step, leading to the formation of the New Zealand Labour Party in 1916. Labour politics over the decade and a half from 1904 would be tortuous to say the least. Many have written about this period in the party's history and we draw on this work. Sometimes, perhaps, discussions of the party's origins have been written from the hindsight of 1935. Foundation stories are sometimes constructed to emphasise the founders' heroic virtues, which later generations fail to achieve. For this reason, and because of its dramatic qualities, the role of the direct-action militants is sometimes unduly stressed. We do not minimise their importance, but, with other historians, emphasise the movement's gradualist wing. There was no simple division into 'moderates' and 'radicals'; philosophies and perspectives varied widely. Regional differences also mattered. If we emphasise the political mobilisations and creativity of many hundreds of men and women in these years, we also argue, as others have, that the Labour Party's shape owed much to circumstances, especially the politics of the First World War.

Infant might: the Political Labour League, 1904–08

In 1904 Chris Watson formed a minority Australian Labor government, 'an object-lesson to New Zealand Unionists to "go and do likewise"'.[1] Moving the league's formation at the conference on behalf of the Otago Trades Council, the Victoria-born John Thomas (Tom) Paul argued that it was 'no use . . . to pass resolutions year after year' on labour matters 'unless there were members in the House to see that requests of the Conference were attended to'. The league would advocate for labour, but did not aspire to winning office. Nor was there unanimity over the platform, or even the league's existence. Ironically, in view of later mythology, one Westland delegate thought 'an Independent Labour Party would frighten a great number of moderates'. Suggestions that coastal shipping, coal and oil should be nationalised he thought 'ridiculous . . . The Conference was a Conference of Unionists and not . . . of Socialists. If motions of this kind were carried the labour Unions would lose the support of . . . moderates.'[2]

The league's platform included a state bank with sole right of note issue, an end to sale of Crown land, an emphasis on leasehold tenures, universal suffrage for local government, preference to unionists, an end to borrowing, state factories and nationalisation of mineral wealth. Parliamentary candidates would, as in Australia, pledge themselves to vote in accordance with caucus decisions. This pledge defined labour parties against progressive Liberals.[3] Tom Paul was himself for years ambivalent about radical liberalism: a Congregationalist and typographer, he epitomised the respectability and constitutionalism of self-improving Dunedin labour, and accepted a Liberal appointment to the Legislative Council in 1907. Press response to the league was tepid, the Liberal-aligned *Star* warning that a labour party 'might have to wait many years' for power.[4] One provincial newspaper, however, welcomed the league as an antidote to Seddon's increasing autocracy.[5]

Speakers at the league's Wellington inauguration accused Seddon of departing from the progressive ideals of Ballance's administration (ironically, 30 years later Labour propaganda would claim Seddon's mantle). John Rigg, another printer, whom Ballance had appointed to the Legislative Council, was the league's first president.[6] Branches were established in Dunedin and Christchurch in January and February 1905.[7] There was very little enthusiasm in Auckland, where the Trades Council was strongly Liberal. Eventually a branch was formed without Trades Council support, but by April 1905 there were also branches in Taihape, New Plymouth, Southland and Midhirst, as well as three in Wellington. The Westland Trades Council remained aloof.[8]

The league's first conference, in April, claimed a thousand members. The debt to radical Liberalism continued: the conference confirmed the nationalisation of land but not other means of production and distribution, and voted unanimously for a White New Zealand.[9] In Christchurch the league first sought unsuccessfully to enlist sitting left-Liberal members of parliament as candidates, and then debated whether to challenge them.[10] These parliamentarians had been associated with a good deal of reform, but their electorates were precisely those which a labour party would need to win. Some in the Political Labour League, particularly the railways tinsmith Jack McCullough, were in any case now openly espousing socialist politics and for them the Liberals were the past. McCullough was one of the most influential figures in the Canterbury labour movement. Belfast-born, he had emigrated with his parents and siblings as a young man. Tom Paul's equal in seriousness of mind, McCullough had been introduced to socialism by Harry Atkinson and the Socialist Church, and he remained a radical socialist for the rest of his life. The Liberal government dismissed McCullough from the railways in 1907 for his political activities; soon afterwards, the unions elected him workers' representative on the Arbitration Court. He filled this role with a painstaking sense of duty, taking advantage of official travel to encourage labour's political mobilisation across the country.

McCullough's young protégé, James Thorn, another railways metal tradesman, stood in Christchurch South and declared that 'the land question was the paramount question of the hour', and accused the Liberals of 'propitiating conservatives and wool kings'.[11] In Wellington the waterside unionist David McLaren also emphasised the land issue, but argued that the Political Labour League should formally ally with the Liberals.[12] Of nine candidates in the 1905 elections, seven lost their deposits and only Thorn received more than 1000 votes, which was a substantial portion of the league's 3850 nationwide.[13]

The league admitted that the contest 'was somewhat in the nature of a forlorn hope', but while maybe 'premature . . . it must not be overlooked that there must be a beginning to all reforms'.[14] The league faced powerful opposition within the unions, many of which emphasised Liberal reforms from which workers had benefited.[15] The debate would become intense in the next few years and the centre of gravity in labour politics would shift to the left.

The leftward shift is often discussed in terms of the industrial mobilisation of the 'unskilled' in the Red Federation—miners, watersiders, labourers, shearers and the like. That had a major impact on labour politics in New Zealand, but is far from the whole explanation. The Red Feds had the good stories and the good lines, and some particularly able propagandists, but there were other important factors. One was the pace of unionisation after 1900: New Zealand in 1913 was 'the third most unionized society in the world'.[16] Enthusiasm for unionism increased markedly among miners after 1905, in Auckland and Christchurch among unskilled workers and in Wellington among the skilled. Growth in Dunedin, by contrast, was steady rather than spectacular and in absolute numbers Dunedin lagged well behind by 1910.[17] Unionisation was essential but did not inevitably mean a labour party, even if 'most unionized workers were acquiring a stronger sense of collective identity and purpose' and came to regard the Liberals and the arbitration system as unsatisfactory.[18]

The miners' strike at Blackball in February 1908 has been mythologised as the beginning of the 'revolt against arbitration', but it was not the first time workers had struck for direct bargaining. Slaughtermen struck in many parts of the country early in 1907, demanding direct negotiation with employers, arguing that this was more relevant to the industry than a court whose members had no experience of it. They won a significant wage increase, and largely ignored the fines imposed for an illegal strike. Blackball was immediately about the inadequacy of a 15-minute meal break, and more generally about the determination of a radical group to challenge the arbitration system. It made a great story and the best telling was by one of those involved, the young, Nelson-born Pat Hickey. Seven miners simply took 30 minutes to eat; when they were dismissed the rest of the miners struck. The union was prosecuted for an illegal strike, and the judge opined that 15 minutes was perfectly adequate, immediately before calling a luncheon adjournment of 90 minutes. When the miners' goods were seized and auctioned to pay the fine, a number of miners made very sure that the bidding was derisory, and the 'purchasers' then returned the goods to their owners.

Disillusionment was reinforced when the Arbitration Court refused, also in 1908, to make an award for Canterbury farm labourers. Unionists, and their dissenting court representative, Jack McCullough, saw this refusal of legal protection as a naked expression of class power. The revolt of militant unions has been well discussed by historians, but the increasing demand for radical reform by so-called 'moderate' skilled workers has received less attention. Their dissatisfactions focused on wages, job control, the intensification of work and skill dilution. The government's response was to increase the coercive aspects of arbitration law, and many unionists resented the fact that the architect of coercion was none other than the 1890 Maritime Council chief and then-minister of labour, J.A. Millar.

In August 1908 the miners' unions formed a federation and in 1909 invited other unions to join what was renamed the New Zealand Federation of Labor, popularly known as the Red Federation. In 1911 the federation took over the shearers' newspaper, the *Maoriland Worker*, and made it an eloquent advocate of militant unionism and socialism. Two of the Blackball strikers, Hickey and Paddy Webb, were leading figures, and they were joined by another miner, Robert Semple, Australian-born like Webb. The Socialist Party became the federation's political ally. Strongly influenced by Britain's Independent Labour Party, as we have seen, the party advocated 'making socialists' through education and agitation rather than prioritising electoral contests. The trades councils did not share the federation's enthusiasm for militant action, but many unions were expressing more radical intentions even as they supported parliamentary campaigning. The Political Labour League claimed a 'paying membership' of 2000 at the beginning of 1908, and in Wellington, at least, along with many local unions called for the nationalisation of the means of production, distribution and exchange.[19]

The 1908 and 1911 elections required a second ballot if no candidate won an absolute majority. This encouraged more Labour candidates to stand, however loosely affiliated to the Political Labour League.[20] Supporters could now hedge their bets by voting Labour the first time and Liberal the second. Labour's first-round vote increased. In three seats Labour candidates won more than 2000 votes, and the 12 Political Labour League candidates got 20 per cent of the vote across the electorates they contested, while seven socialists took 7 per cent.[21] David McLaren won Wellington East on the second ballot; despite having won only a quarter of the first ballot, McLaren secured most of the Liberal votes to defeat a Reform candidate.[22] McLaren's politics were left-Liberal. He continued to insist that land policy was 'the most vital problem that this country has to face', and he was unenthusiastic about the cabinet's decision to donate a Dreadnought to the Royal Navy.[23] He had some foresight anticipating the Labour Party's attempt in the 1920s to make common cause 'between the trade-unionist of the city and the legitimate working-farmer', and suggesting that the British Empire should develop 'as a confederation of free States'.[24] Understandably, as a lone member McLaren struggled to make an impact in parliament; he narrowly lost his seat to Reform in 1911, but was elected mayor of Wellington the next year.[25] During the First World War McLaren would abandon the labour movement and support conscription.

Division and dissension, 1909–12

After 1908 the labour movement became increasingly divided. In opposition to the Red Federation, the trades and labour councils formed a Federation of Labour (confusingly enough) in 1909. The Red Federation's model implied that mass organisation at the point of production would deliver more to the workers than would parliamentary organisation. The Red Federation strategy, as it developed, was for affiliated unions to cancel their registration under the 1894 arbitration law and register instead under the Trade Union Act 1878. Awards under the 1894 act invariably proscribed strikes during the term of an award, and the 1878 act had no such provision. The debate was about more than tactics; it was about visions of means and, sometimes, of ends.

This is not to revive excessively simplistic distinctions between moderates and militants. Some skilled unionists were very radical and by no means all unskilled unions were militant. Radical parliamentary socialists like Jack McCullough argued that a reformed arbitration system was essential for workers who did not enjoy the miners' and watersiders' strategic location, that universal suffrage presented opportunities for radical politics, and that major strikes could not be won. 'Organized Capital . . . can beat us 99 times out of every 100 times we challenge them to a trial of strength.'[26] Sometimes these radicals seemed to be on the defensive, not least because their parliamentary road emphasised patient, unglamorous and incremental organisation. The Red Federation and the Socialist Party emphasised a direct and vigorous mass participation rather than (as they would have said) 'merely' marking a voting paper at regular intervals. The Red Federation's rhetoric and imagery also frequently emphasised a muscular and rather traditional masculinity.

So far as parliament was concerned, the Trades Councils' Federation of Labour's first step, rather than building on the 1908 result, was to ask a number of left-Liberal MPs if they would 'form an Independent Labour party within the House, but the replies received were far from encouraging'. Perhaps one reason for this initiative was an attempt to conciliate Liberal unionists; in Christchurch at least, the division between Liberals and advocates of an independent labour party dominated trades council affairs.[27] Eventually, McLaren used the parliamentary recess to promote labour's political unity around the country.[28]

The trades and labour councils' conference in 1910 debated 'the establishment of an Independent Political Labour Party'; the Political Labour League had evidently faded. Dunedin unions instead favoured local labour representation councils, including 'representatives of all organised labour or progressive bodies' and, subject to general principles, having 'a free hand' in their platform.[29] This was a recipe for incoherence and was not adopted. The platform committee drew up a manifesto which moved beyond radical liberalism. Land settlement was again prioritised, including 'resumption of native and other lands, for closer settlement'. Other policies included nationalising monopolies, unemployment insurance, arbitration reform, a minimum wage and a 48-hour week reducing to 40.[30] The names 'Progressive Labour Party' and 'Independent Political Labour Party' were rejected in favour of 'New Zealand Labour Party'.

Considerable debate produced an objective of maintaining 'all the progressive legislation that has already been enacted', as well as reform leading to 'equality of opportunity, also the moral, material and educational advancement and the general comfort and well-being of the whole people, based upon the gradual public ownership of all the means of production, distribution and exchange'. This objective was proposed by Edwin (Ted) Howard from the Canterbury General Labourers' Union, who would soon become much more militant. Some Auckland delegates preferred 'Socialisation of the means of production, distribution and exchange', and the difference between 'public ownership' and 'socialisation' occupied delegates for some time. Paul thought the former could be applied to monopolies but equated socialisation with confiscation and thought it counter-productive.[31]

One of the Auckland delegates was a 38-year-old Victoria-born labourer, Michael Joseph Savage. Savage had come to New Zealand in 1907 at the invitation of his old friend, the miner Paddy Webb. Rapidly immersing himself in labour politics, by 1911 Savage was a prominent Socialist Party radical. Howard, Bristol-born and four years older than Savage, was his Christchurch counterpart. Formerly a seafarer, Howard also joined the Socialist Party, and turned the Canterbury General Labourers' Union into a large and powerful organisation. His mission in life was to persuade the 'unskilled' that they had as much right to respect and the good things of life as anyone else: for years he wrote in the *Maoriland Worker* as 'The Vag', his columns by turns whimsical, pungent and enraged.

Joseph Ward took the Liberal party further to the imperialist right with the Dreadnought in 1909 and compulsory military training in 1910. Consequently, more came to feel that the balance of argument lay with the Labour Party.[32] The party, however, continued its unsuccessful attempts to recruit sitting Liberal MPs. Most of the left-Liberals were mavericks, unamenable to party discipline. Tommy Taylor was the most glaring example, and kept Jack McCullough and the New Zealand Labour Party on a string for more than two years.[33] The left-Liberals were also stuck in the politics of 1890, when too much had changed, even as they hoped that a Labour party might be a vehicle for their own ambitions.[34] It was a small world, though: Taylor's sister Lillian married Jack McCullough's brother Jim.

By 1911 'the potential strength of the urban Labour vote' was evident.[35] With all residents now eligible to vote for local councils, five Labour candidates won seats on the Christchurch City Council in April. Taylor was elected mayor with labour support but died soon afterwards. In the general election, the New Zealand Labour Party won 25 per cent of the total vote across the 17 electorates it contested, and the Socialist Party over 15 per cent across seven electorates. Barry Gustafson notes that in three seats where Socialist and New Zealand Labour Party candidates both stood, the latter did far better.[36] However, as Erik Olssen observes, the New Zealand Labour Party's platform was 'well to the left of any other labour party in the English-speaking world'; the 'moderation' of working-class voters can be overstated.[37] David McLaren narrowly lost Wellington East, but four other labour candidates won. John Robertson in Ōtaki was nominated by the Manawatu Flaxmill Workers' Union and scraped in by 21 votes.[38] John Payne won Grey Lynn by 28 votes, calling himself the 'People's Popular Labour Candidate'. He was 'flamboyant, mercurial, voluble and controversial and was remembered as the most fastidiously dressed man in Parliament'.[39] Alfred Hindmarsh won Wellington South for the New

Zealand Labour Party: a lawyer with origins in the Hawke's Bay pastoral elite, he had been involved in labour and union affairs for many years.[40] William Veitch won Whanganui as an independent labour candidate. An engine-driver, Veitch had the most orthodox union background, but as a parliamentary novice began angling for a position in the shortlived 1912 Liberal ministry. Jack McCullough privately reproached himself: 'to think that I was mainly responsible for his securing the nomination of the Labour Party'.[41]

While 1911 indicated that a significant labour vote now existed, controversies within the labour movement became much more intense.[42] In 1912 one Auckland Red Fed accused the New Zealand Labour Party of heading down a path that would 'get unions to organise themselves into voting cattle to put into power the Prohibition, wowseristic, Single Tax, Lib.-Lab. Labor Party, who will continue upon the lines of the rapidly-decaying party of Ward and Co'. Paul accused the Red Federation leadership of acting like dictators, imposing their own views on the majority.[43] The first New Zealand Labour Party was shortlived, being replaced from Easter 1912 by the United Labour Party, which proved even more shortlived.

The United Labour Party story is entwined with that of one of the more extraordinary political organisers to cross the New Zealand stage: 'Professor' Walter Thomas Mills. Mills's experiences in the American Midwest had convinced him that the working class lacked the numerical and organisational strength to bring a socialist society into being; broader alliances were necessary. Although his personal and financial probity were questionable, Mills was a capable political writer and a compelling orator (his stagecraft enhanced by his height, all four foot six of it).[44] Having been impressed by some of Mills's books, Jack McCullough took the lead in organising a lengthy speaking tour for him in New Zealand during the winter of 1911.[45]

In August 1911 Mills assisted the trades councils and the New Zealand Labour Party in drawing up a plan for labour unity. Mills's plan was addressed 'to the useful people of New Zealand' and envisaged one organisation which would combine industrial and political matters. With 12 large industrial departments, including farmers, professional workers and women's organisations, the intention was clearly inclusive. So far this reflected the view, shared by many in the New Zealand Labour Party, that a broad progressive coalition was necessary. One United Labour Party member in Palmerston North was a shopkeeper who had emigrated from the English Midlands with his young family in 1909. Walter Nash found that the party's ethical base fitted his own Christian socialism, and the platform's appeal to all those performing 'necessary service' anticipated his political language in the 1930s. The third objective, promoting workers' 'good citizenship' and increasing their 'efficiency', would not have allayed Red Federation suspicions that Mills was a stalking-horse for the bourgeoisie.[46]

In December a visiting Australian socialist, Harry Scott Bennett, debated the issues with Mills on behalf of the Red Federation and the Auckland Socialist Party. While Mills espoused prohibition, Scott Bennett 'integrated his Marxist diagnosis of capitalism with a cultural critique of bourgeois society which made hostility to "wowsers" a central element in the revolutionary faith. When he drank to excess, as he sometimes did, it made a political statement'.[47] There was no meeting of minds between these two brilliant platform orators. Scott Bennett declared that 'we are all very anxious for working-class unity, but . . . upon sound and scientific lines' based on 'clearly understanding the class nature of modern society'. It followed that including middle-class reformers diluted revolutionary purpose.[48]

The United Labour Party was formally established at Easter 1912. Its constitution was essentially Mills's unity scheme. Paul was elected president and a Dunedin gunsmith, Arthur McCarthy, secretary, while Mills was retained as organiser. Mills received the high salary of £12 weekly plus expenses, but that may have been intended to compensate his wife, Hilda, who ran the party office, as well. Veitch, Robertson and Hindmarsh all joined, but Payne did not.[49] The debate between Mills and Scott Bennett highlighted the problem with each organisation. The Red Federation was elitist; the ULP's inclusiveness could become mushy attempts to be all things to all people. McCullough certainly recognised that risk: he thought that a strong union element in the new party was essential 'as only in this way could we prevent it being captured by Liberals & respectables'.[50]

Ideological and regional divisions overlapped. In Dunedin, where Paul was the dominant figure, the right wing of the party set the tone, a political line which reflected the respectable artisan world of the southern suburbs. Christchurch was more evenly divided: the Red Federation and the Socialist Party enjoyed some support, and many of the ULP unions espoused radical socialism to be achieved through constitutional means.

McCullough reflected this radicalisation of the skilled, and Howard the militant Red Federation line. Wellington was likewise divided, with a more moderate ULP group and an increasingly radical waterfront. The new party also enjoyed some support from unions in provincial towns. Auckland was the only one of the main centres where the United Labour Party had little traction among unions, for the dominant figure there was the draper, single-taxer and erstwhile Liberal, George Fowlds. Auckland's rapid growth, especially of its port, led to a strong Red Federation and Socialist Party, which were also dominant in mining towns both on the South Island West Coast and in the North Island.[51]

It was at Waihī, in the Coromandel goldfields, that a defining crisis for the New Zealand labour movement developed in 1912.[52] Waihī's goldmining was industrial in scale and manner. The miners' union—the Waihī Workers' Union—had affiliated with the Red Federation, and withdrew from the arbitration system in February 1911. Initially the union secured a substantial wage increase, but some workers had always had reservations about the new direction. Early in 1912 some of the mine's engine-drivers registered their own union under the Industrial Conciliation and Arbitration Act. Arguing that there should be one union for each workplace, Workers' Union militants demanded that the company refuse to recognise such unions under threat of strike action, and the president, Bill Parry, 'to save his union and his own authority' brought the Workers' Union behind the demand.[53] And so on 14 May 1912 the Waihī strike began. Sustained by financial support from both sides of the Tasman, the strikers remained out for many weeks. The company's counter-demands included that the Workers' Union register under the Arbitration Act. This was unacceptable. In July 1912 the climate in Wellington changed when the Liberals lost a confidence vote and the Reform party's William Massey began his long tenure as prime minister. Massey was determined to use state power against the Waihī miners, and the Red Federation in general, and he sanctioned much more aggressive policing by the new commissioner of police, John Cullen. Strikers and union leaders were arrested and imprisoned. Strikebreakers appeared from early October, backed up by armed and mounted police. On 12 November, Black Tuesday, a crowd of strikebreakers and police charged the union hall, and in the fracas which followed, police and strikebreakers beat a striking miner, Frederick Evans, to death.

Significant as 'the tragic story of the Waihī strike' was in itself, the consequences were far-reaching. The Red Federation had been internally divided over the strike, and some leading figures in the ULP and the trades councils had openly condemned it. Bitterness extended beyond Waihī: in Christchurch, Dan Sullivan of the ULP, a furniture craftsman, frequently criticised the strike as evidence of the Red Federation's violent and barbaric disposition, and Ted Howard responded by describing Sullivan as a 'paid servant of the master class'.[54] Paul, Mills, Fowlds, McLaren and other ULP leaders wanted to condemn the strike as early as June, but McCullough and the four sitting Labour MPs refused to consider this 'betrayal of labour principle . . . to do anything which might be used to the detriment of workers who, right or wrong, are fighting common enemy'.[55] The divisions, it seemed, were as deep as ever, but Waihī was a catalyst for organisational progress.

Tentative unity, 1913–14

Black Tuesday traumatised and enraged the labour movement. Among the United Labour Party leadership, 'all but the most fanatical enemies of the Red Federation' were reduced to silence, and the Red Federation executive took a major initiative in convening a unity conference for January 1913.[56] The federation emphasised problems with arbitration, where small minorities could undermine 'the work and will of big majorities', and even many unions that remained within the system felt it was not advancing workers' interests. Otherwise, the federation left the agenda open.[57] Some ULP leaders were publicly unenthusiastic. Paul held to his grudges about the vituperation dished out by Red Feds to ULP unions. The Wellington Trades Council advised affiliates not to attend, maintaining that the normal Easter conference round should have been kept to. Mills, strangely, wanted the decisions to be spelt out in advance.[58]

A large number of ULP unions simply ignored Paul and his friends and sent delegates. Perhaps these unions were aware that the party was struggling financially. In any case, 112 delegates attended, representing 88 organisations. Motions from the floor, carried after long debate, invited both the ULP and the Socialist Party to join the conference. Thus political parties, as well as unions, were represented. The conference prepared a draft plan for unity, with one industrial and one political organisation.

The United Federation of Labour constitution owed much to the Red Federation: its objective was 'to organise systematically upon an industrial union basis, in order to assist the overthrow of the capitalist system, and thus bring about a Co-operative Commonwealth, based upon industrial democracy'. A Social Democratic Party would merge the ULP and the Socialists for 'the socialisation of the collectively-used means of production, distribution and exchange'. The new party's name was suggested by a recent arrival from Scotland, Peter Fraser. Fraser had arrived in Auckland at the beginning of 1911 and quickly associated himself with the labourers' union and the Socialist Party. He moved to Wellington at the end of 1912 to pursue his duties as a member of the Red Federation executive. Fraser, like other Red Federation leaders, was now thinking about the importance of parliamentary engagement alongside industrial organisation.[59] The success of the conference was 'unexpected . . . all along the line'. As well as the willingness of most participants to find a way forward, John Rigg's masterly chairing was crucial.[60]

A further conference was convened in July, before which the unity committee barnstormed the country, wisely appointing the two debating antagonists of 1911, Scott Bennett and Mills ('a most adaptable little person', in Pat Hickey's sardonic estimation) as organisers.[61] The campaign's reception varied across the country. Most of the Red Federation strongholds supported the campaign, as did the Canterbury Trades Council. Some ULP affiliates in provincial towns were less enthusiastic, and the same was true of Wellington and (particularly) Dunedin. David McLaren, who lost the Wellington mayoralty in April 1912, was the most vocal critic; a frustrated McCullough wrote to Arthur McCarthy that McLaren's 'tripe . . . is the stuff that has convinced so many honest workers that the most effective way to destroy the usefulness of a Labour man is to put him into Parliament'.[62] However, the July conference convened with 391 delegates representing 247 organisations and 61,000 workers. 'There had never been such a large conference of trade unionists in Australasia.'[63] It sat for ten days and confirmed the new organisations by very large majorities, albeit with some minor dilution of militant rhetoric.

As one old printer, John Petterd, put it, unity was

> a movement of the rank and file, as workers, as men, we have too long been separated—our aims are identical, our hopes, our dangers, the same—we have

> wasted valuable years fighting amongst ourselves—and our would-be leaders are to a great extent to blame—the rank-and-file want to see these differences swept away—want to feel that the working-class movement is a forward movement.[64]

Unity remained imperfect; the ULP rump kept up a flow of objection, and Paul, Veitch and Hindmarsh all walked out over defence policy (the new party opposed the military training law).[65] Some saw the unity platform as a Red Fed jack-up, but the Red Feds were in a minority on the drafting committee. Waihī had catalysed a significant leftward shift in the centre of gravity, a process that would be intensified by the great strike at the end of 1913.[66]

The great strike was triggered by two separate disputes. At Huntly, in early October, the Taupiri Coal Company sacked 16 union activists, and 500 miners voted to strike until they were reinstated. In Wellington, shipwrights had affiliated with the waterside workers in May 1913 and had been negotiating a new agreement since then. In mid-October the employers rejected the shipwrights' claims. The shipwrights struck, and a few days later the watersiders held a stopwork meeting to discuss the shipwrights' case. While they were meeting the employers put other workers on; the watersiders refused to return to work until the other workers were taken off and they were reinstated. The employers maintained that the stopwork meeting amounted to terminating the industrial agreement and that the watersiders had gone on strike. The watersiders regarded it as a lockout.

By the end of October, after Cullen, the police commissioner, had organised special constables, all major ports were on strike. Armed naval troops patrolled in Wellington and there were machine guns on the wharves. Farmers and employers organised strikebreakers, special constables and supplies. The mounted specials, carrying long batons, quickly came to be known as Massey's Cossacks. There were frequent confrontations, with stoning and gunfire, particularly in Wellington and Auckland. Miners came out in most districts, and when specials occupied the Auckland waterfront there was a general strike in the city. Slowly, state power won the upper hand. Employers and government refused to negotiate, and Massey politicised the police force to an extreme degree.[67] The strike was over by mid-December.

The strike was 'not a fight over wages and conditions: it was a power struggle'.[68] Employers, farmers and the Massey government sought to destroy the new labour organisations at birth. In February 1913 the New Zealand Employers' Federation established a defence fund to 'combat Socialism, Syndicalism and Anarchy'.[69] The Canterbury Employers' Association had a secret meeting in August to plan the recruitment of strikebreakers.[70] One of the first things Massey did as prime minister was introduce legislation that prevented unions from cancelling registration under the Arbitration Act, imposed severe penalties for striking and included in the definition of striking a union refusing to sign a new contract. Almost as soon as the strike began in Wellington the employers demanded that the watersiders' union register under arbitration.[71]

The strikers' defeat was due to a number of factors. The new United Federation of Labour's strength was much the same as the Red Federation's; most other unions had not joined by October 1913. To that extent, the employers succeeded in pre-emptive action. While miners, watersiders, drivers and some seamen struck, most other unions did not. Crucially, railway workers and shearers stayed at work. Shearers, vulnerable to strikebreaking, sought to preserve their own organisation, while the railway unions' priority was their longstanding agreement with the government over terms and conditions. They had walked out of the unity congress. More generally, 'the conditions for a successful general strike were the conditions for a successful revolution', and they did not pertain in 1913.[72] Unity remained partial, but, as Erik Olssen emphasised, the strike shifted things very much to the left: 'all had changed utterly', and even so-called moderates like Sullivan and the seamen's Tom Young supported the strike once battle was joined. While three-quarters of the country's unionists did not join the strike, many of that majority were at least sympathetic. Politically, 'the middle ground passed to the advocates of a socialist labour party'.[73]

Two by-elections in 1913 made this clear. In both, the Social Democratic Party positioned itself as the heir of the radical Liberals. In June the Liberal member of parliament for Grey, Arthur Guinness, died. Guinness, a lawyer, enjoyed good relations with the miners (his father had been a Knight of Labour). Paddy Webb, a key figure in radical mining unionism since the Blackball strike, literally rushed away from the unity congress to contest the by-election. Webb campaigned on collective ownership of land, mines and industry and the repeal of conscription. The first ballot was evenly divided, the Reform candidate taking 2160 votes, Webb 2074 and the Liberal 1982.

Webb naturally led in the mining booths, but the Liberal and Reform candidates achieved big tallies in the larger towns, Greymouth, Cobden and Reefton. Reform Party campaigners accused Webb of irreligion, fostering mob rule and threatening economic ruin. Webb easily won the second ballot by 3433 to 2763. The Liberals had split two to one for the Social Democrats. Their own candidate, Michael Hannan, a Catholic, publicly supported Webb, partly because the Reform campaign indulged in sectarian attacks.[74]

In the middle of the great strike, on 19 November, George Laurenson, Liberal member for Lyttelton since 1899, died. No labour candidate had ever stood against Laurenson and a thousand striking watersiders marched behind their band in his funeral procession in Wellington. Inevitably this by-election was a referendum on the government's conduct in the strike. The Social Democrat candidate was James McCombs. McCombs was neither a Red Fed nor a manual worker. Irish-born, he had come to New Zealand as a child, and had at one point undertaken Anglican theological training, although he was not ordained. He had been a radical Liberal and a member of a draper's assistants' union. McCombs headed the poll on the first ballot, with 2075 votes to 1560 for the Reform candidate, 922 for the official Liberal candidate and 360 votes divided between two other Liberals. McCombs led in all but the farming districts of Banks Peninsula and the electorate's prosperous suburban enclaves. In the second ballot McCombs won more narrowly than Webb, by 2628 to 2402. Arguably McCombs had picked up more Liberals on the first ballot than Webb, but the two by-elections were a great boost to Social Democratic Party morale.

Yet the strike was a defeat for militant industrial organisation. Reprisals followed, as a number of prominent figures were imprisoned. The most severe sentence, a year, went to an Australian-born radical journalist, Harry Holland, whom the Red Federation had invited over to lecture in support of the Waihī strikers, and who by 1913 was editing the *Maoriland Worker*. The United Federation of Labour conference in July 1914 revised the organisation's constitution with less militant language. Hiram Hunter, the new president, observed that the 1913 version had been 'perfect, but . . . not adhered to' and 'somewhat in advance of the times in this country'—a delicate way of recalling that most unions had not struck. The new version emphasised the concentration of economic power and the need for labour unity so that 'the workers may . . . by the power of concerted and well-considered action, wage successfully the battle of humanity against the power of wealth'.[75] The SDP conference, held immediately afterwards, noted that the strike had done much damage, although, with 8000 members and 49 branches represented, there was room for optimism. Strike funds from the Australian Workers' Union were gifted to the party, paying for three full-time organisers (the Millses, however, had suddenly returned to America). There was intense debate about whether socialists should support Liberals in the event of a labour alternative, and distinctly unenthusiastic agreement that this was acceptable.[76]

The 1914 election was a difficult one. The First World War muted political controversy, and the Social Democratic Party was running out of money. More serious was the continuing influence of trades council-based labour representation committees, particularly in Dunedin and Wellington. Where the SDP maintained its socialisation objective alongside a platform of radical social and political reform, the labour representation committees (LRCs) continued to espouse policies that a left-Liberal could comfortably have supported (the Wellington committee went so far as to include upholding imperial unity). The liquor question was another divisive issue, with vociferous arguments for both prohibition and continuance. The SDP resolved that the matter should be decided by a simple majority at a referendum, but controversy continued. Not least because the second ballot had been abolished in favour of a return to simple plurality, the SDP and the labour representation committees had to work together, however unenthusiastically. This labour coalition and Liberal candidates made mutually beneficial arrangements in Wellington and Dunedin.[77]

In the end there were nine SDP candidates (in Christchurch, Auckland, Grey, Palmerston North and Ōtaki), five LRC (all in Wellington and Dunedin) and three other labour candidates: the incumbents Veitch and Payne, and Gains R. (Bob) Whiting, who had been prominent in the ULP, in Christchurch South. The result was ambiguous. Of the incumbents, the SDP's Webb and McCombs won easily, as did Hindmarsh (Wellington LRC), Veitch and Payne. John Robertson (SDP), however, lost Ōtaki. McLaren (LRC) very narrowly failed to win back Wellington East, and the other Wellington LRC candidate fared poorly enough. The Otago LRC claimed two seats on the night: Andrew Walker was confirmed but James Munro lost Dunedin Central on a recount. The other Christchurch labour candidates all made creditable showings, not least as their Liberal opponents were generally on the party's radical wing.[78] 'Labour went into the 1914 election with six Members of Parliament . . . [and] emerged . . . still with only six.' Significantly, five of the six had not had to face a Liberal opponent. The SDP share of the vote across its nine contested electorates was one third, while the LRC candidates, who picked up Liberal votes, secured nearly half the popular vote across five electorates. The *Maoriland Worker* cheered that 'Labour Unity Brings Victory', but fragmentation remained.[79]

War and unity, 1914–19

The war was of fundamental importance in the formation of the Labour Party in 1916. But there was nothing inevitable about this, or the way things played out across the country. Certainly, whether SDP or LRC, there was from 1911 'in Wellington, Christchurch, and Dunedin . . . a secure electoral base' for labour.[80] This base was bridging divisions (such as they were) between 'skilled' and 'unskilled' working-class communities and beginning to attract middle-class progressives. Of as much significance was the shift in Auckland. Most of the growth among Auckland unions before 1914 had been among the unskilled, whose radicalisation had been reflected in the city-wide general strike in 1913. In the strike's defeat these workers 'had learned the limits to their power' and a parliamentary road to socialism came to seem more promising.[81]

The Social Democratic Party was struggling, and knew it. The labour representation committees' continuing appeal had been evident in the 1914 election. The SDP's 1915 conference claimed a membership of 6230, but only 1672 were individual branch members; the rest were members of affiliated unions, not all of whom would have been active.[82] The party's travelling secretary, Peter Fraser, had been busy but most of his efforts had been directed to Christchurch and the West Coast, where the party was strong anyway. High-mindedness could only go so far. Even in wartime, Fraser noted, despondently, even on the West Coast, 'the all-victorious picture shows have made the work of propaganda rather difficult'; but '[w]hile Demosthenes or Cicero could not compete against Charlie Chaplain [sic], it is still possible to get a crowd to listen to Socialism before King Charles, or Fatty Arbuckle or the incomparable Mabel, are let loose, or "released," as the technical phrase now goes.'[83]

Many in the LRCs and the SDP quietly sought a better understanding. The one issue that more than any other shaped this rapprochement was conscription for overseas service. While there was a wide range of opinion within the labour movement about the war, the greatest agreement was that conscription was unacceptable, at least without conditions that the government refused to contemplate.

In August 1915 Reform and Liberal formed a coalition and the 'Parliamentary Labour Party'—Hindmarsh, Veitch, McCombs, Webb and Walker—refused to join. Adopting this label was itself significant. The labour group had been offered one seat in the coalition cabinet. Payne, who had withdrawn from the labour caucus, publicly debated with Holland that this should be taken up in order to demonstrate—particularly to white-collar workers—Labour's fitness to govern.[84] The *Maoriland Worker* argued that refusal was justified by the resolution of successive congresses that labour had to remain independent of other parties, as well as the now minute policy differences between the Liberals and Reform.[85]

The *Worker*'s position was predictable enough. More significant was the position of the Otago Labour Council (as the Otago Trades Council had become in 1914) and Paul, who, from the Legislative Council, supported the caucus line, although maintaining that the 'Labour Party . . . bowed to no other party in its patriotism and in its desire to see the war brought to a successful conclusion'. He noted that a single Labour seat in the coalition cabinet would have meant powerlessness, while collective cabinet responsibility would have silenced any criticism whatever.[86] When the United Federation of Labour called a conference on conscription at the beginning of 1916, the Otago Labour Council forwarded its views. While Otago 'affirm[ed] its unqualified faith in the righteousness of Britain's attitude and entry in the present war' it thought 'voluntary . . . enlistment is more in harmony with British history and British instincts than any form of conscription'. Conscription would be unnecessary if soldiers and their dependants were better paid, and any conscription 'must be in practice and essence national service', including the conscription of wealth. Nor did Otago support joining the coalition: 'until the National Government gives some indication that it intends dealing with the exploiters in an effective manner the workers would be well advised to keep clear of the representatives of capitalism'.[87]

The conference included representatives of 87 organisations, and declared that conscription was an unacceptable denial of liberty and that soldiers and dependants should be properly provided for, with the highest artisan wages and pensions as of right not by proven need. 'Charity and doles from patriotic funds are not what is wanted'; drastic taxation was. All this was common ground: those who did not share Otago's faith in the British cause had the manifesto quote Pope Benedict XV's appeal for peace on reasonable conditions, and called on the allies to state their terms.[88] Veitch left the caucus over conscription, but the other Labour parliamentarians stressed the common ground on the issue in debate on the Military Service Bill in June 1916. Paul argued that conscription meant adopting precisely the illiberal militarised society that the British Empire professed to oppose, and would be unnecessary if soldiers were properly paid. Bourgeois patriots in the Legislative Council accused him of descending to a 'sordid' level in discussing money.[89] Hindmarsh was not absolutely opposed to conscription, but opposed the bill because the government had no idea how to make a better world after the war, nor any intention of doing so. McCombs also emphasised liberty, and Webb urged the conscription of wealth.[90]

The United Federation of Labour and SDP conferences were scheduled to meet in early July. There was, as the federation president John Dowgray pointed out, increased interest in coherent political organisation, but localism remained a problem, Otago continuing to favour regionally autonomous labour representation committees.[91] The SDP invited both Federation of Labour and LRC delegates to its conference, to discuss 'the advisability of forming a N.Z. Labour Party, with which all present Labour organisations and Unions could affiliate'.[92] Both Paul and Sullivan had urged this step. Paul told the Federation of Labour conference that 'it was dangerous to leave the name Labor Party lying around'.[93] The danger, as Sullivan had made clear, was that Payne and some Liberals might form a conscriptionist Labour Party. Sullivan urged, too, that the name change would itself be a means to greater unity: the SDP should 'drop the fancy name under which it is disguised at present, and revert to the homely title of the New Zealand Labour Party'.[94] Fraser also now thought that the name 'labour' was 'the only asset worth a moment's consideration'.[95]

The joint conference met on 7–8 July at the Wellington SDP's Alexandra Hall in Abel Smith Street and referred the proposal to a sub-committee, which prepared the new constitution. The New Zealand Labour Party would be based on labour representation committees, comprising unions, trades councils, Social Democratic Party branches 'and other properly constituted Progressive organisations which subscribe to the constitution and platform of the Party'.[96] As Jack Vowles has said, in a real sense the new party was prompted by opposition to conscription, the one point on which there was wide agreement (conversely, particularly in Dunedin, pro-conscription union leaders refused to support the new party).[97]

The new party's beginning was low-key to say the least. The party almost immediately had to borrow £10 from the United Federation of Labour.[98] Money was one problem; another was the difficulty of translating formal unity into substantive unity. The constitution allowed SDP branches to continue as constituent organisations, and some influential SDP figures intended to fill the role of ideological conscience. While some activists, like James Thorn, agreed with Paul about the imperative of unity, the Wellington SDP seemed to regard the new party as an unfortunate necessity. In Dunedin, Arthur McCarthy had similar views, as did Ted Howard in Christchurch.[99] Christchurch SDP branches refused to join the Labour Party, which meant they were unrepresented at the new party's first conference in 1917. Even worse, James McCombs, Labour's first president and a diehard prohibitionist, walked out of the 1917 conference when the liquor platform was amended to include a referendum question on state control.[100] In Auckland there was a quite different problem: the Trades Council was in recess. Only in the middle of 1917 did local unions establish an Auckland Trade Union Congress, which in turn formed a labour representation committee and affiliated to the party. Thereafter, though, progress was rapid. There was clearly a good deal of latent support for political unity, including from the Women's Political League and the Women's International League.[101]

Ideological and factional tensions continued. It would be misleading to describe the divisions simply as being between 'moderates' and 'militants', although the language of the protagonists could reinforce such an impression. 'Moderates' like Sullivan and Paul discussed co-operation and worker participation in industry. Sullivan welcomed the federation of unions engaged in the same industry—thereby moving beyond the particularism of craft unions—while warning that 'instilling visionary and unreal ideas into the minds of the masses is worse than useless'. A revolutionary general strike, Sullivan emphasised, would never happen and the patient accumulation of power and responsibility was a surer way of transformation.[102]

Where they differed from former Red Feds like Fraser and Holland was in their attitude to the war. Sullivan was 'sincerely desirous of seeing Great Britain and the allies victorious in the present world conflict'. He also wanted 'to keep this a white man's country; we want to keep its blood pure, and its civilisation, manners, customs, and ideas uncontaminated by admixture with peoples of barbaric or twisted development. In saying this I exempt from inclusion within the statement our own Maori race'.[103] Some of the 'militants', like Fred Cooke, deprecated such ideas, and Cooke was one of many radicals imprisoned during 1917 for opposing conscription. While opposition to conscription was the point of greatest agreement, it was the militants who openly challenged the state. Cooke, H.T. (Tim) Armstrong, Thorn, Semple and Fraser were among the several dozen who were imprisoned for sedition in 1917, when half the party's executive were in jail. In Christchurch, Labour's effort for the 1917 local elections emphasised anti-conscription protest, despite McCullough's and Sullivan's misgivings on tactical grounds. Excessively high hopes were not fulfilled, but the five Labour councillors who were returned increased the representation by one. Among the five was Ada Wells, a feminist and pacifist, and the first woman on the city council.[104]

State coercion extended even into the parliamentary caucus. In May 1917 Paddy Webb was imprisoned for three months after saying that miners, in opposing conscription, were striking a blow for liberty.[105] As a fit single man, Webb was under pressure to enlist, but his mining constituents clearly believed that it was more important that he continue to represent them as the only former miner in parliament. When he was released from prison Webb was conscripted and again appealed to the needs of his constituents, this time by resigning and forcing a by-election. 'Despite bitter press criticism of Webb, no government candidate could be found and Webb was re-elected unopposed' in December 1917. The party then appealed for Webb to be exempt as his occupation was of national importance; the Military Service Board rejected the appeal, thereby declaring that the legislature was of no significance. In March 1918 Webb refused to serve and was jailed for two years. As a consequence he forfeited his parliamentary seat and after the war, like some 2000 other resisters, lost his civil rights for ten years.[106] The Massey government's pursuit of Webb was as vindictive as it was remorseless.

Labour selected Harry Holland for the seat of Grey's second by-election, and, although Holland lacked Webb's easy charm and local appeal, he won the seat. Grey was one of six by-elections in 1918, which together indicated much popular unhappiness with the government and its management of the war effort. An 'independent Labour' candidate won Taranaki and the Labour candidate, Alex Galbraith, came close in Palmerston North. In 'safely conservative' Wellington North, some weeks before he won Grey, Holland doubled the Labour vote over 1914. Then, in October, Peter Fraser took 56 per cent of the vote in Wellington Central, winning two and a half times the votes achieved by his nearest rival, a conscriptionist 'independent Labour' candidate.[107] Finally, Alfred Hindmarsh died of influenza and Robert Semple held Wellington South for Labour with 56 per cent. Semple could not resist pointing out that he, Holland and Fraser had recently been in prison and were now headed for parliament.[108] (In 1922 another former political prisoner, Tim Armstrong, would win Christchurch East. He is reputed to have commenced his maiden speech with: 'Mr Speaker, this is not the first of His Majesty's institutions of which I have been a member. When I was there I saw many who should be here, and now that I am here, methinks I see many who should be there.' It deserves to be true.)[109]

Labour's morale was greatly boosted by these events. Membership almost doubled in the year to July 1919, to 21,500, and 75 electorates counted some party presence.[110] As in 1914, there was debate about whether to contest as many electorates as possible or to concentrate on winnable seats. Paul, the party president, warned that this risked letting some Reform candidates win. The contrary argument was that Labour had to demonstrate its appeal across the country. Savage, the secretary, 'insisted that the paramount objective in 1919 was not the defeat of Reform but the establishment of an independent Labour Party'.[111]

The party fielded 48 candidates and went into the election with five MPs: McCombs in Lyttelton, Holland in Grey, Andrew Walker in Dunedin North, and Fraser and Semple in Wellington. Walker and Semple lost their seats, but Dan Sullivan won Avon, Ted Howard Christchurch South, Savage Auckland West, Bill Parry Auckland Central and Fred Bartram Grey Lynn. John Payne had won the latter seat as independent Labour in 1914, but the other victories generally showed that Labour had made substantial inroads into the Liberal vote in Auckland and Christchurch. Two of the most significant defeats—Walker and Paul, both in Dunedin—reflected very strong support for conscription in the city's unions; Walker lost to a conscriptionist trade unionist. The government was also keen to have Semple out, insisting on a straight fight with army colonel George Mitchell.[112]

After 1919 Labour would be a permanent fixture in the parliament and politics of New Zealand. This was far from inevitable, even with the deeper social processes which were an essential condition for a Labour party to emerge. In some parts of the country, notably Auckland and, for even longer, Dunedin, organised labour and working-class voters continued to support the Liberal party. In Dunedin this allegiance remained significant into the 1920s. The industrial and political wings of the movement alike had experienced years of philosophical controversy; in 1912 unity must have seemed a very distant prospect. Unity in 1913 was incomplete. We have emphasised the significance of conscription as a basis for unity in 1916 but there were many reasons, not all mutually consistent, for opposition to conscription. The 1919 election was no more than a beginning.

3
Building a Party 1919–35

The 1919 election had confirmed that Labour was a serious political force, but it would be another 16 years before the party formed a government. The party increased its parliamentary representation in each election from 1919 with the exception of 1925, but the popular vote increased more slowly. From the other side of 1935 it is easy to see a story of gradual and inevitable advance, but the reality was more ambiguous and messy. The party faced considerable challenges in organisation and in finance. Electoral politics during the 1920s were complex. Most accounts of the long march to government emphasise the limited appeal of militant socialism and the necessary transition from party of protest to party of government. Harry Holland is often portrayed as an obstacle to this transition, but policy development was continuous through the 1920s and Holland was a more creative thinker than is usually admitted. For much of the 1920s, party activists and even parliamentarians were regarded with deep suspicion by the conservative mainstream, and even in 1931, with the Depression near its worst, Labour was unable to overcome this suspicion.

Elections and parliament

The 1919 election gave Labour eight MPs, joined after a 1922 by-election by a ninth. Caucus increased to 17 in the 1922 election, but dropped to 12 in 1925, before increasing again in 1928 and 1931. One factor was the distorting effects of three parties (and independent candidates) in a simple plurality voting system, but more generally the party struggled to overcome the hostility of mainstream newspapers and to appeal to voters, especially outside the cities. Elections during the 1920s saw plenty of wild cards in the electoral pack and not a few jokers.

Party activists sometimes suggested that simple plurality voting denied Labour its proper share of parliamentary representation. Such claims assume that everybody who voted for a Labour candidate would have voted Labour under proportional representation. That cannot be known, but even some of Labour's leading parliamentarians could not count on an absolute majority of the vote in a three-way contest. While the party's platform called for proportional representation, the 1922 conference rejected suggestions that Labour make an electoral deal with the Liberals to introduce proportional representation, with a number of speakers dismissing the Liberals as thoroughly untrustworthy.[1] As one MP put it in 1920, organised workers had spent years 'joined with that once great and glorious party known then as the Liberal and Labour alliance. We got a decree of separation on the ground of want of maintenance.'[2] To secure power, Labour had to displace the Liberals as the dominant progressive force. The state into which the Liberal party had fallen by 1919 should have made that easy, but many Liberal politicians enjoyed significant support in their electorates. Particularly in Dunedin, a centre of the Liberal–Labour politics of the 1890s, old loyalties died hard. Paul resigned from the Legislative Council in 1919 to contest Dunedin South, but failed to beat T.K. Sidey in a straight fight by an agonising 84 votes, and did not contest another election.

Labour's electoral record between 1919 and 1928, while showing a slow increase in support across the country, thus often reflected the circumstances of individual electorates. Labour's share of the popular vote in 1919 was around 24 per cent, but split votes could work both ways. While Labour led the popular vote in the five Wellington electorates, with 40 per cent of the three-party vote against 30 per cent each for the other two parties, Reform won three seats with less than 45 per cent in each case. Almost a quarter of Labour's vote in the region came from Fraser's 4257 votes in Wellington Central, which he won in a straight fight with an old Liberal, Fred Pirani. Harry Holland in Buller and Ted Howard in Christchurch South also won straight fights. Dan Sullivan won Avon with 58 per cent in a three-way contest. In Lyttelton, McCombs held on with only 39 per cent. Labour won three Auckland seats on minority votes: 48

per cent for Parry in Auckland Central, 44 per cent for Savage in Auckland West, and only 39 per cent for Bartram in Grey Lynn.[3]

The 1922 election saw 17 members returned but, as James McCombs warned, no increase in the share of the popular vote.[4] Straight fights with Reform in Auckland saw convincing wins for Savage, Parry and Bartram, and a surprise win by the young John A. Lee in Auckland East. Lee, brought up in some poverty in Dunedin, had been a swagger and petty criminal before 1914. As he reached adulthood he educated himself in socialism. He served with some distinction on the Western Front, where he lost an arm, and on returning to New Zealand established himself as journalist and aspiring politician of considerable ability. An independent bled off just enough Reform votes in Manukau to give Labour the seat. However, in straight fights Labour managed to take only one of the five Dunedin seats, where James Munro held Dunedin North. Robert McKeen took Wellington South in a straight fight and McCombs likewise held Lyttelton. Armstrong won Christchurch East with 47 per cent, and Sullivan held Avon with an embarrassing 42 per cent. Alex Monteith took Wellington East and Frank Langstone won Waimarino, each with 42 per cent. Victories in Napier and Westland came from less than 40 per cent of the vote.

Labour parliamentarians' priority between 1919 and 1925 was establishing credibility and learning the legislative process. In the 1919 caucus, only James McCombs had been in parliament for more than a year. The learning curve was steep, but years of experience in trade union organising and unsuccessful parliamentary campaigns were a valuable training. Ted Howard may not have been the only new Labour MP who was wryly amused to find himself in parliament: 'when I first came to the House I sat in a corner seat, but when the Gentleman with the Black Rod came in I thought he was after me and I shifted'.[5]

The 1922 election produced a hung parliament and some speculation that the Liberals would return to office with Labour's support or abstention. The Liberal leader, Thomas Wilford, dismissed the idea and some in Reform advocated merging with the Liberals, contrasting 'a progressive, enlightened and constitutional democracy and . . . communism or extreme socialism'.[6] That would have suited Labour strategy. When parliament finally met, Massey intended to secure the government's majority by appointing a speaker from the opposition (in 1993 Jim Bolger would play the same trick). Charles Statham, a Dunedin lawyer, was an independent and had recently tried to establish a National Progressive and Moderate Labour Party and, after that failed to go anywhere, a United Progressive Liberal and Labour Party. Labour members, particularly Holland, deployed some skilful tactics to embarrass the other parties, nominating McCombs for speaker as a vote of no confidence in the government. McCombs and Statham exchanged gentlemanly compliments, and, as Labour expected, the Liberals joined with Reform to elect Statham.[7]

The 1925 election suggested Labour's forward march had stalled. Labour went into the election with 17 seats and emerged with 12 (it was small consolation that the popular vote increased from 23 per cent to 27 per cent). The election was a triumph for Reform's able and personable Gordon Coates (and the cheque-books of his business supporters), but 1922 had exaggerated Labour's strength.[8] Four of the five seats Labour lost in 1925 were straight fights and had been won in 1922 on minority votes: Napier, Waimarino, Wellington East and Westland (Westland and Lyttelton, which McCombs lost on the night, both went to appeal).[9] The fifth loss was Munro in Dunedin North. On the other hand, Parry held Auckland Central with 65 per cent against two rivals. Lee held on to Auckland East with 45 per cent. Savage and Bartram held their Auckland seats in straight fights, as did Fraser and McKeen in Wellington, Armstrong, Sullivan and Howard in Christchurch and Holland in Buller.[10]

Coates's victory soon lost its shine. Coates was one of the youngest and most progressive in the Reform Party; the landslide had brought, not a new generation, but older men of 'a decidedly conservative, even reactionary disposition'. Coates himself, while a capable minister, 'lacked the political skills to capitalise on the stunning vote of confidence he had been given' in the election and proved not to have the strategic sense essential to a successful prime minister.[11] In April 1926 Rex Mason won a by-election in Eden (with less than 42 per cent of the vote) and in 1927 Lee Martin won another in Raglan.[12] Martin was Labour's first farmer MP, and Mason, a lawyer, theosophist and vegetarian, would have an unbroken, and distinguished, 40 years in parliament. The immediate consequence of Mason's victory was to make Harry Holland leader of the opposition. Martin's victory, with 36 per cent of the vote, demonstrated the fractiousness of many North Island farming communities. Although the mining townships gave him his victory, an independent Reform candidate and a Liberal meant the government faced an unwelcome four-way race.[13]

Coates's weak hold over the Reform Party combined with continuing economic uncertainty is the explanation for the upset 1928 election, when the old Liberal label was grafted onto the unscrupulous genius of Reform's erstwhile political organiser, A.E. Davy, who worked closely with the Whanganui MP, W.A. Veitch. Veitch, who entered parliament in 1911 as a United Labour Party candidate, ratted over conscription during the war, joined the Liberals, and in 1935 would finish in the extreme right-wing Democrats. The result was the United Party, led by the ailing Joseph Ward. Reform remained the largest party, but was almost halved, from 55 to 28 seats. United had 27 and Labour 19 (the remaining six were held by a motley collection of independents).

Once again there was a good deal of variation in the results. In Auckland, Lee and Bartram were narrowly defeated. Savage held on with 47 per cent and Mason won a new seat with 44 per cent. In Christchurch, Howard held his seat with 45 per cent and McCombs his with 47 per cent. More positively, Langstone retrieved Waimarino with 47 per cent and Munro got Dunedin North back with 40 per cent. On the other hand, straight fights sometimes benefited Labour: William Barnard won Napier back and Clyde Carr began a 34-year tenure of Timaru. Without a United rival, Semple finally returned in Wellington East, and the party similarly retrieved Wellington North.[14]

Labour in 1928 had barely improved its share of the popular vote over 1919, however, increasing it by only 6 per cent in city electorates, 4 per cent in the provincial towns and 2 per cent in rural electorates. The United Party was 'an alternative conservative party of the city with a strong appeal to the middle levels of small business, shopkeepers, tradesmen and skilled workers . . . Labour was still not a party for which the "respectable" could easily vote.'[15] The problem was evident in the 1929 Hutt by-election, which Walter Nash won with fewer votes and a smaller percentage than he had lost with in 1928 (40 per cent compared to 45 per cent, edging the United candidate out by 212 votes: the difference, of course, was that 1928 was a straight fight). Labour's position in 1928 could easily have induced pessimism.

When parliament met, Labour voted with United to unseat the Coates government. Some later scholars have suggested that doing this, rather than abstaining and forcing the two older parties to merge (as Labour had attempted in 1923), reflected a loss of confidence.[16] In 1928 Labour parliamentarians may have been surprised at Ward's victory, and almost certainly felt that, having campaigned on the basis that the party would vote against Coates, there was no alternative but to do so.[17] Despite Holland's dislike of Ward, the Labour caucus placed no explicit conditions on allowing Ward to form a government.[18] The election result may have knocked Holland's confidence: when parliament met he emphasised land settlement and breaking up the big estates in language indistinguishable from that of an 1890s Liberal, even if he also argued for more generous pensions, family allowances and workers' compensation, along with industrial development.[19]

Ward's health collapsed almost as soon as he had taken over as prime minister. At the same time the economy began to slide into depression. The decade had been volatile, but real difficulty emerged as export prices dropped. The government drifted through 1929, with policy largely shaped by the dour George Forbes, who, with his colleagues, was quite unable to respond creatively to the worsening economic situation. In 1931, as the country's trade totally collapsed, Reform joined United in a coalition. Only in the election at the end of that year did Labour exceed 30 per cent of the popular vote, but even then the result was just over 34 per cent, and four more seats for a total of 24. While some of the senior members, like Savage, Parry and Fraser, won well over 55 per cent in their seats, some of the wins were decidedly narrow and relied, again, on split votes. Only as the Depression, and the Coalition's management of it, became even worse did Labour become an alternative government. One straw in the wind was the 1933 by-election in Lyttelton, where, on James McCombs's death, his widow, Elizabeth, succeeded him to become the country's first female member of parliament, the marginal Labour seat becoming extremely safe. More generally, as the Depression worsened Labour parliamentarians found themselves engaged in constant defensive action to preserve what they could for working people. Conviction and astute parliamentary practice sometimes delivered surprising victories. In 1932, for instance, the Coalition proposed to end compulsory arbitration and remove women workers from the arbitration system altogether. Fraser's and Lee's genuine outrage resulted both in their suspension for a day and in the government backing down on women workers.[20]

The 1920s were a decade of struggle for Labour. New parties need time to establish themselves. Labour also faced considerable establishment hostility which, in a variety of subtle and unsubtle ways, presented the party as not legitimate. Labour's meetings, parliamentarians and activists were

Above: Samuel Duncan Parnell (1810–1890) in 1890. An original advocate of the eight-hour day in 1840, Parnell became a farmer and well-regarded builder in Wellington. As workers mobilised in the late 1880s, Parnell willingly identified with the new labour movement. Wright, Henry Charles Clarke 1844–936: Negatives. 1/1-020462-G, Alexander Turnbull Library

Right: Samuel Andrews (1836–1916), a plasterer, was one of a number of 'working men' who sought elected office in Canterbury in the 1870s and 1880s. He served on the provincial council from 1872 to 1876 and was elected to a single term in parliament, 1879–81. Although he campaigned as a 'Liberal' he espoused a number of conservative positions, and as his interest in politics declined he became a successful businessman.1/2-022086-G, Alexander Turnbull Library

Left: Harriet Morison (1862–1925) was born in Ulster, Ireland, came to New Zealand with her family in 1874 and worked as a tailoress. She became involved in the Tailoresses' Union in Dunedin in the late 1880s and soon became secretary. She was also a key figure in Dunedin's women's suffrage movement. During the 1890s she spent much time organising tailoresses in various parts of New Zealand, and was also active in social work and in the Bible Christian and Unitarian churches. From 1906 until 1921 she held various positions in the Department of Labour, not always sitting comfortably with the civil service ethos of the day. Guy photograph, Otago Witness, 13 December 1905, p.44. S13-099c, Hocken Collections Uare Taoka o Hākena, University of Otago

Below: Railway workshops were major industrial undertakings and the workers, especially the skilled, were particularly conscious of the dignity of labour. This photograph shows the blacksmiths' shop staff at Addington in 1886, five years after the blacksmiths and other workers struck in protest at a continuing wage cut. Railways Magazine, 1 April 1931

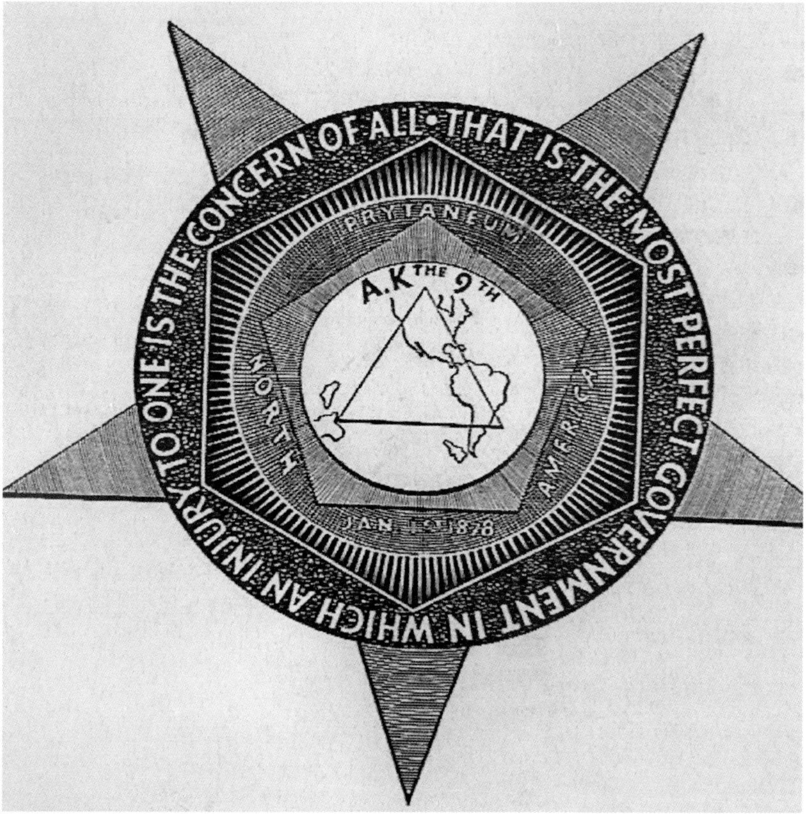

Above: The Knights of Labour began in Philadelphia in 1869 and by the 1880s claimed many thousands of members across North America. Branches were established in New Zealand from 1887. Although the Knights were supplanted by occupationally based trade unions, they were an important influence, especially in Dunedin and Christchurch, and for a few years a significant national organisation. Robert Weir, Knights Down Under: the Knights of Labour in New Zealand, Cambridge Scholars Press, Cambridge, 2009

Left: David Pinkerton (1836–1906) was born near Edinburgh and apprenticed as a bootmaker. Emigrating to Otago in 1860, Pinkerton worked at his trade at a time when mechanisation was increasingly threatening traditional skills and workers' livelihoods. Embodying the respectable and democratic culture of South Dunedin's skilled workers, Pinkerton became increasingly involved in the city's growing trade union movement during the 1880s and sat in the House of Representatives as a labour supporter of the Liberal government from 1890 to 1896. After losing his seat he was appointed to the Legislative Council. General Assembly Library: Parliamentary Portraits. 35MM-00142-a-F, Alexander Turnbull Library

Above: Although later activists caricatured the liberal–labour politics of the 1890s as devoid of any radical fire, contemporaries saw the labour movement as extremely assertive. Conservatives, like this cartoonist, often suggested that labour's demands were excessive. Hunter, Ashley John Barsby, 1854–1932: A large order, New Zealand Graphic and Ladies' Home Journal, 29 April 1893, p.898. A-312-8-007, Alexander Turnbull Library

Opposite, top: John Alexander (Jack) McCullough (1860–1947) and John Thomas (Tom) Paul (1874–1964)—here back row, second and sixth from left among delegates to the 1903 trades and labour councils' conference, Greymouth—were leading figures in the independent labour parties that were organised before 1916. Both were skilled workers, committed to self-improvement and the rational use of democratic institutions to secure progressive reform. McCullough, born in Ulster, was a railways tinsmith before being elected as workers' representative on the Arbitration Court in 1907, the same year in which the Victoria-born Paul, a printer, was appointed to the Legislative Council. But while Paul's politics were essentially those of a radical Liberal, McCullough was committed to achieving radical socialism through parliamentary means. MB14, Canterbury Trades and Labour Council Records, reference code 16, Macmillan Brown Library, University of Canterbury

Opposite, bottom: The New Zealand Socialist Party was established in 1901 and most of its branches merged into the Social Democratic Party in 1913. The Socialist Party's priorities were usually agitation and education in order to change the ideological climate; 'making socialists' was more important than winning elections. The party was, however, effectively the Red Federation's political wing from 1910. While never enjoying much apparent electoral success, the party claimed around 3000 members at its height. Regardless of its organisational weaknesses, the Socialist Party was a significant force in shifting labour politics to the left after 1905 and its members included two future prime ministers, Michael Joseph Savage and Peter Fraser. Pictured here are the attendees at the party's conference in 1908. Vera Wood photographs of New Zealand Labour Party and socialist groups. MSS & Archives Vault 30, Special Collections, University of Auckland Libraries and Learning Services

SOCIALISM

Above, left: Dan Sullivan (1882–1947) was born in Christchurch and served an apprenticeship in the furniture trade. He became involved in the Canterbury Trades Council and, successively, in the Political Labour League, the first New Zealand Labour Party, the United Labour Party and then the Social Democratic Party. Usually described as a 'moderate', Sullivan actively explored ideas about workers' participation in industrial management and was a lifelong advocate of New Zealand's industrial development. Labour MP for Avon, 1919–47 and mayor of Christchurch, 1931–35, he was minister of industries and commerce, 1935–47, and, at times, acting prime minister. R. Holland Collection. PAColl-4415-01-010, Alexander Turnbull Library

Above, right: Sarah Snow (1864–1939) was born in Wellington and made her living as a boarding house keeper. She was involved in labour movement organisations from the first decade of the twentieth century. In the context of party organisations dominated by trade unions, Snow and others of like mind urged that women's organisations such as the Wellington Housewives' Union should also be allowed to affiliate and, thus, to exercise influence. She advocated for statutory inclusion of women in party conferences, and insisted that male parliamentarians consult women's branches and organisations about legislation which affected women and children. R. Holland Collection. PAColl-4415-04, Alexander Turnbull Library

Opposite, top: Ted Howard (1868–1939) and Bob Ross (1873–1931) were *Maoriland Worker* colleagues—Ross as editor and Howard contributing notes from Christchurch and writing a weekly column as 'The Vag'. Both espoused radical socialism and had a distinct hostility to social hierarchy, pretension and conservatism; they were united in their determination to advocate for labourers and the impoverished to receive their due share of the world's wealth. Ross, an Australian, was only in New Zealand from 1911 until 1913, when he returned home, but Howard, born in Bristol, lived in Christchurch from the mid-1890s. As a union organiser he made the Canterbury General Labourers' Union into a powerful body, and he represented Christchurch South in parliament from 1919 until his death. Holland Family Collection. PAColl-4415-06, Alexander Turnbull Library

Opposite, bottom: The remote mining settlement of Denniston, in the Buller district. Living conditions were harsh, and mining work was arduous and dangerous. Denniston was an early centre of mining unionism, and union activists from Dennision played significant roles in successive waves of labour organisation in the 1880s and again after 1905. PAColl-6348-47, Alexander Turnbull Library, Wellington, New Zealand

"IF BLOOD BE THE PRICE
OF YOUR CURSED WEALTH,
GOOD GOD WE HAVE BOUGHT
IT FAIR"

Above: Ada Wells (1863–1933) was the first woman elected to the Christchurch City Council, as a Labour member in 1917. Born in England, she emigrated to New Zealand with her parents as a child. She trained in Christchurch as a teacher, and was a leading figure in the city's radical feminist movement. After universal suffrage was achieved in 1893, Ada Wells was one of those who formed the National Council of Women in 1896 to campaign for complete equality. She worked for welfare reform, prison reform, and the right of women to sit in parliament. Ada Wells was also a pacifist and campaigned vigorously against conscription before and during the First World War. Photograph of Ada Wells from *Woman Today* magazine. Ref: 1/2-C-016534-F. Alexander Turnbull Library, Wellington, New Zealand. http://natlib.govt.nz/records/22728937

Opposite, top: The annual Labour Party picnic was a fixture for decades in many New Zealand towns. As with other organisations like unions and lodges, the picnic provided party members, friends and their families with a chance to socialise and raise a little money at the same time. The Canham family, among those at this picnic in Wellington in the 1920s, were grassroots activists in the labour movement for many years. G.E. Canham (Estate). PAColl-5687-001, Alexander Turnbull Library

Opposite, bottom: Michael Joseph Savage (1872–1940) arrived in Auckland from his native Victoria, Australia in 1907 and within a few years became a leading figure in the Auckland branch of the Socialist Party and the Red Federation, expressing at that time very militant views. The Auckland labour movement was relatively slow to join the New Zealand Labour Party when it was formed in 1916, but did so during 1917. Savage's campaign flyer demonstrates the importance of proposing immediate and achievable social reform alongside more radical aspirations. New Zealand Labour Party, Auckland Regional Council records. MSS & Archives A-161, box 42, folder 1, Special Collections, University of Auckland Libraries and Learning Services

M. J. SAVAGE.

City Councillor, and Member Hospital and Charitable Aid Board, Auckland and Suburban Drainage Board.

Selected Labour Candidate for Auckland West.

GENERAL ELECTIONS, 1919.

To the Electors of Auckland West.

Ladies and Gentlemen,—I beg to announce that I have been selected by the New Zealand Labour Party to solicit your suffrages at the forthcoming elections. My qualification to fulfil the task of representing the mental and manual workers in the Parliament of the Dominion is due to my experiences in office, mine, field, and workshop, covering a period of more than 30 years, and to my association with the Labour movement for a quarter of a century.

During the course of my rather strenuous career in the Labour movement, I have been entrusted by my fellow workers with every position of trust known to the movement outside of Parliament, until to-day, when I hold the position of National Secretary to the Party responsible for my nomination in this constituency.

At an early date I shall take the opportunity of fully explaining the Party's Platform, to which I am pledged, and shall be pleased to meet friends and opponents alike, in a spirit worthy of the great movement which I have the honour to represent.

Yours faithfully,

M. J. Savage

Above: Numerous and regular social events were a key factor in the various labour parties' political success. The Grand Ball—this one at the Auckland Trades Hall on 3 October 1918—is one of the more formal occasions, but branches of the Labour Party and its predecessors organised a wide range of cultural, social and educational events that strengthened the relationship between working-class parties and communities. Classes in economic and political theory developed the mind, classes in public speaking developed the ability to advocate, choirs and orchestras enlivened meetings and welcomed visitors, and picnics provided a relaxed day out. New Zealand Labour Party. MSS & Archives 2015/10, Special Collections, University of Auckland Libraries and Learning Services

Opposite, top: The great strike of 1913 involved thousands of workers, mostly on the waterfront and in the mines, but it became a general strike in Auckland. Seen as the high tide of industrial militancy, it was as much a defensive struggle as unions sought to preserve non-arbitrationist organisations against government and employer determination to enforce arbitration. The strike was defeated by state power—by the use of troops, armed police, strikebreakers and special constables (the latter became known as Massey's Cossacks). But it was also defeated by continuing divisions within the labour movement. Price, William Archer, 1866–1948: Collection of post card negatives. 1/2-000186-G, Alexander Turnbull Library

Opposite, bottom: Bill Parry (1878–1952) and Bob Semple (1874–1955) were two of the many Australian workers who settled in New Zealand and shaped the labour movement after 1905. Both miners, they quickly became leading figures in the Red Federation, although their commitment to industrial unionism was as much based on pragmatic calculation as on ideological considerations. Both served long terms in parliament—Parry from 1919 until 1951 and Semple from 1918 to 1919 and 1928 until 1954—and both were ministers from 1935 to 1949. Parry's tenure at Internal Affairs saw the department actively promote the arts, culture, and physical welfare and recreation; Semple was a flamboyant and energetic minister of public works. Holland Family Collection. PAColl-4415-07-01, Alexander Turnbull Library

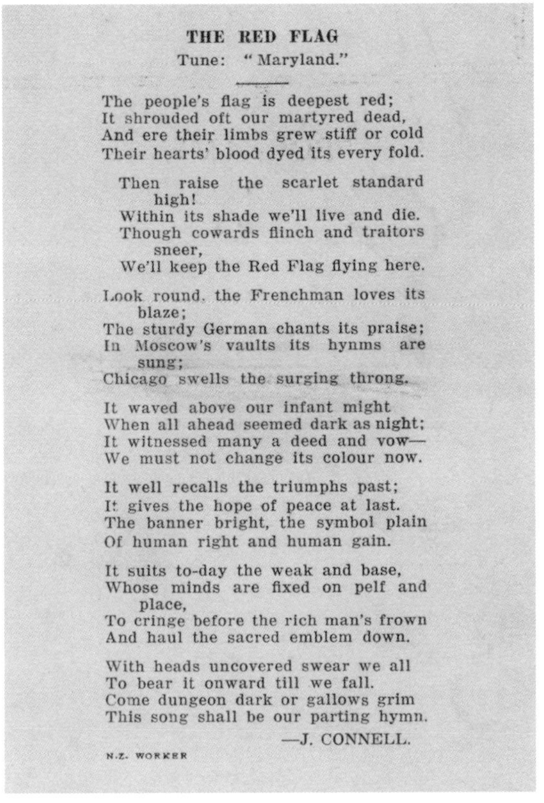

THE RED FLAG

Tune: "Maryland."

The people's flag is deepest red;
It shrouded oft our martyred dead,
And ere their limbs grew stiff or cold
Their hearts' blood dyed its every fold.

Then raise the scarlet standard high!
Within its shade we'll live and die.
Though cowards flinch and traitors sneer,
We'll keep the Red Flag flying here.

Look round, the Frenchman loves its blaze;
The sturdy German chants its praise;
In Moscow's vaults its hynms are sung;
Chicago swells the surging throng.

It waved above our infant might
When all ahead seemed dark as night;
It witnessed many a deed and vow—
We must not change its colour now.

It well recalls the triumphs past;
It gives the hope of peace at last.
The banner bright, the symbol plain
Of human right and human gain.

It suits to-day the weak and base,
Whose minds are fixed on pelf and place,
To cringe before the rich man's frown
And haul the sacred emblem down.

With heads uncovered swear we all
To bear it onward till we fall.
Come dungeon dark or gallows grim
This song shall be our parting hymn.

—J. CONNELL.

N.Z. WORKER

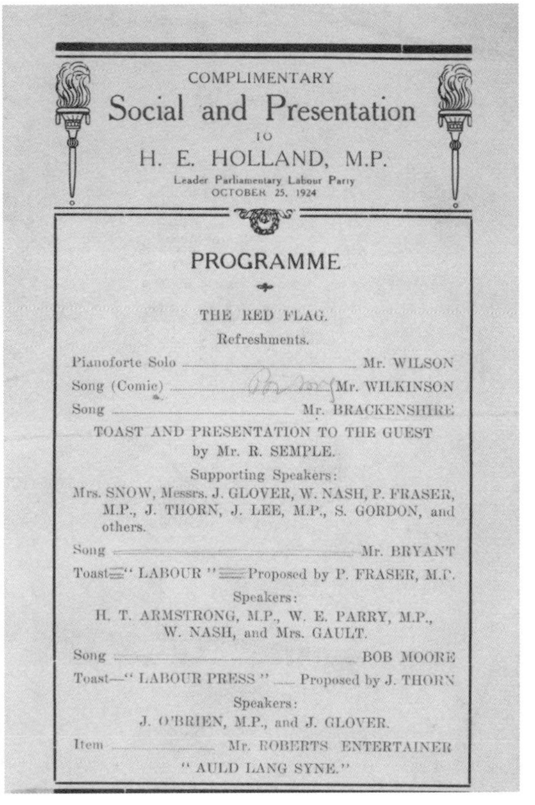

COMPLIMENTARY

Social and Presentation

TO

H. E. HOLLAND, M.P.

Leader Parliamentary Labour Party

OCTOBER 25, 1924

PROGRAMME

THE RED FLAG.

Refreshments.

Pianoforte Solo .... Mr. WILSON

Song (Comic) .... Mr. WILKINSON

Song .... Mr. BRACKENSHIRE

TOAST AND PRESENTATION TO THE GUEST by Mr. R. SEMPLE.

Supporting Speakers:

Mrs. SNOW, Messrs. J. GLOVER, W. NASH, P. FRASER, M.P., J. THORN, J. LEE, M.P., S. GORDON, and others.

Song .... Mr. BRYANT

Toast—" LABOUR " —Proposed by P. FRASER, M.P.

Speakers:

H. T. ARMSTRONG, M.P., W. E. PARRY, M.P., W. NASH, and Mrs. GAULT.

Song .... BOB MOORE

Toast—" LABOUR PRESS " .... Proposed by J. THORN

Speakers:

J. O'BRIEN, M.P., and J. GLOVER.

Item .... Mr. ROBERTS ENTERTAINER

" AULD LANG SYNE."

Above, left: 'The Red Flag' was written in 1889 by Jim Connell, an Irish republican and socialist. It has been the anthem of many English-speaking Labour and socialist parties (the other great socialist anthem, 'The Internationale', has been widely translated from the original French and was adopted by communist parties after 1919). 'The Red Flag' was still sung at conferences of the New Zealand Labour Party in the 1970s, to the dismay of some more conservative figures, and still features in the repertoire of some activists. Wilfred (Bill) McAra papers. MSS & Archives A-139, item 1/2, Special Collections, University of Auckland Libraries and Learning Services

Above, right: Harry Holland was a tireless propagandist for the Labour cause, and as parliamentary leader undertook many speaking tours across New Zealand during the 1920s. Then, as now, a visit by the party leader was an occasion for branch organisations to host members and supporters; this presentation also indicates the high regard in which the party at large held Holland. Wilfred (Bill) McAra papers. MSS & Archives A-139, item 1/2, Special Collections, University of Auckland Libraries and Learning Services

Opposite, top: Labour MPs elected in 1922 and Walter Nash (national secretary). Back row from left: Bob McKeen (Wellington South), Alex Monteith (Wellington East), Dan Sullivan (Avon), James O'Brien (Westland). Middle row from left: Bill Jordan (Manukau), Fred Bartram (Grey Lynn), John A. Lee (Auckland East), Peter Fraser (Wellington Central), Bill Parry (Auckland Central), James Munro (Dunedin North). Seated from left: James McCombs (Lyttelton), Nash, Frank Langstone (Waimarino), Ted Howard (Christchurch South), Harry Holland (Buller), leader, Michael Joseph Savage (Auckland East), Lew McIlvride (Napier), Tim Armstrong (Christchurch South). New Zealand Labour Party. PAColl-1179-07-001, Alexander Turnbull Library

Opposite, bottom: Henry Edmund Holland (1868–1933) was born in New South Wales, and worked as a radical journalist before the Red Federation invited him to New Zealand in 1912 to lecture in support of the striking Waihī miners. Subsequently Harry Holland became editor of the Maoriland Worker from 1913 until 1918 (apart from a spell in prison in 1914). When Paddy Webb was disenfranchised for resisting conscription into the army, Holland succeeded him as MP for Grey, and he held the seat and its successors until his death in 1933. He became leader of the parliamentary Labour caucus in 1919 (apparently defeating James McCombs on the toss of a coin) and remained leader until his death. S.P. Andrew Ltd: Portrait negatives. 1/1-018348-F, Alexander Turnbull Library

TOWARDS THE DAWN!

WHAT Mrs. McCOMBS STANDS FOR

What Labour is working for

The Ideal of Richard John Seddon.

In his **last manifesto** before his death **Richard John Seddon** made a statement which is an exact parallel of the aim of Labour today.

In that manifesto Mr Seddon said:

"I believe, that the cardinal aim of government is to provide the conditions which will reduce want, and permit the very largest possible number of its people to be healthy, happy human beings. The life, the health, the intelligence, and the morals of a nation count for more than riches, and I would rather have this country free from want and squalor and unemployed than the home of multi-millionaires."

These were the words of the last manifesto issued by Mr Seddon, and it is the aim of the Labour Party today to realise this ideal. Labour is carrying on the good work commenced by great statesmen such as Grey, Ballance and Seddon, and will continue until it establishes conditions that will permit all people to be healthy, happy human beings.

The Beauty of a Country is the lives of its Citizens.

LABOUR'S POLICY OF

Restoring Wages, of Work for the Unemployed at Standard Rates and Conditions, of Development of Secondary Industries, of Guaranteed Stabilised Prices for Primary Products, of Control of Banking, Credit and Currency, will increase your Purchasing Power, will enable you to buy what you require in your Homes, and will RESTORE PROSPERITY.

LABOUR WANTS A HAPPY PEOPLE.

VOTE FOR MRS McCOMBS.

Polling Day, Wednesday next, September 13th, 9 a.m. to 7 p.m:

Printed by Christie & Co., Printers and Publishers, 176 Lichfield Street, Christchurch.

Above: For the Labour Party, the 1920s was a decade of building – a decade of developing policy and organisation and expanding its influence across New Zealand. Party conferences devoted much time to discussing these issues. While the conferences were full of enthusiasm, the philosophical debates were sometimes intense and the party was perennially short of money. Discussions about innovative ways of raising funds would have been entirely familiar to later generations in the party. New Zealand Labour Party. PAColl-1179-07-001, Alexander Turnbull Library, Wellington, New Zealand

Opposite, top: What Labour Means to You was a 1938 election campaign booklet comparing the records of the Labour and National parties. The booklet was mainly drawings by 'Fox' (Ivan M. McAnally), the cartoonist for the Standard, Labour's weekly newspaper. New Zealand Labour Party. Eph-A-NZ-LABOUR-1938-01-003, Alexander Turnbull Library

Opposite, bottom left: Elizabeth Reid McCombs (1873–1935) was the first woman elected to New Zealand's parliament. The three formidable Henderson sisters, Elizabeth, Stella and Christina, were Canterbury-born and all became feminists and reformers. Elizabeth was involved for many years in welfare reform and prohibitionist organisations, and she followed Ada Wells as the second woman elected to the Christchurch City Council. Her husband, James McCombs, was Social Democratic and then Labour MP for Lyttelton, 1913–33; when he died Elizabeth fought the by-election and won it convincingly, showing how unpopular the Coalition government had become. Sadly, she had been elected to parliament too late in life to enjoy the sort of career she should have had: she died before the 1935 election and was succeeded by her son, Terry. New Zealand Labour Party. Eph-B-NZ-LABOUR-1933-01, Alexander

Opposite, bottom right: Rangiputangatahi Mawhete (1880–1961, Rangitāne) was born near Palmerston North, and made his living as an interpreter, land agent and dairy farmer. He had political aspirations and stood for Western Māori in 1914 and 1922. From the mid-1920s he was affiliated with the Labour Party; he stood as the party candidate in Western Māori in 1925, and facilitated important meetings between the party leadership and Māori. From the late 1920s he worked to bring the Rātana movement and the Labour Party into an enduring relationship, and in 1936 he was appointed to the Legislative Council, where he was able to work directly with the Rātana MPs. He remained a leading figure in the party's Māori Advisory Council. Gaze, Henry Edward: Negatives. 1/2-174860-G, Alexander Turnbull Library

Above: Michael Joseph Savage (1872–1940) was one of New Zealand's best loved prime ministers. His photograph was widely distributed and became a secular icon in the homes of many working-class families. New Zealand Labour Party collection under regular police surveillance for years. Even in 1926, when Labour led the parliamentary opposition, police reported on Howard's, Armstrong's, Savage's and Lee's political addresses.[21] In the fevered imagination of one policeman, Walter Nash was a 'Socialist, of Bolshevik tendencies'.[22] This seems risible now but the climate of repression was real, and Nash had once been fined for importing proscribed political literature. Even when, as was increasingly the case, the police observer reported that 'no seditious or disloyal utterance or remark came under my notice', systematic police surveillance had its effect. And it was systematic: the orders came from the commissioner himself. The same policeman usually reported on all the meetings in a given locality, a visible presence intended to intimidate.[23]

Organisation

Building a mass organisation was as difficult as constructing a parliamentary majority. As with any political movement, Labour's organisation had a variety of tasks. The most important was recruiting and motivating members and persuading voters with suitable propaganda material. 'Only a strenuous and sustained propaganda campaign can successfully counteract the continuous stream of unscrupulous misrepresentation and senseless abuse to which the Labor movement is subjected by the Press owned and controlled by the Capitalist enemies of the workers.'[24] The party's foundation in the trade unions was both a strength and a weakness: the industrial movement gave invaluable networks and material support, but the dominant place given to unions in the labour representation committees, which were the basic organisation in regions and electorates, could make it difficult for talented individuals to emerge who did not have a union background.

The party expected parliamentarians to devote a good deal of time to speaking and organising work. Most of them met this obligation enthusiastically, but a paid secretary was essential. John Glover, who managed the *Maoriland Worker*, was a voluntary secretary and bluntly told the 1919 conference that the work was more than he could handle. The cost of a full-time appointment and suitable office equipment was an obstacle. Something like £500 a year was needed, and the 1921 conference vainly hoped that a thousand members could each find ten shillings annually.[25] A related question was the structure and location of the executive: while a Wellington-based body would be efficient and cheaper, many party members understandably favoured wider representation, and an executive consisting of a Wellington core with members from other parts of the country was established.[26] Glover acted as secretary from 1916 until 1919; he was followed for a year by Savage, whose Auckland location and parliamentary campaign diminished the time he could devote to the position. Then a radical Methodist preacher, Moses Ayrton, held the position from 1920 until 1922. Ayrton's political formation in the Yorkshire Independent Labour Party was unimpeachable, but his Palmerston North location was one reason why he was not able to fill the position satisfactorily.[27]

Matters improved when Walter Nash replaced Ayrton in 1922. Nash, of course, was a workaholic, and began to develop the office not merely with an emphasis on routine administration but as, he and Fraser hoped, a research and propaganda office 'for the entire Labour movement . . . Industrial as well as political'. In 1922 Nash oversaw the production of half a million leaflets and advice for candidates on policy and campaigning. Continuing on that basis, though, would cost £1000, and although the 1923 conference accepted the challenge, discussions with the transport unions' Alliance of Labour, which was the only effective national labour federation, went nowhere.[28] In September 1924 the party bought Nash's Clarté Book Room, which, under his continuing management, filled the gap and was expected to break even. As well as books and pamphlets, stock included gramophone records of such uplifting material as the 'Red Army March', 'Jerusalem' and talks by the Scottish socialist, James Maxton.[29]

Organising among and for women was sometimes contentious. Women had been far from invisible in the labour movement before 1919, and some well-organised women's branches were formed during the 1920s. Sometimes existing organisations like the Auckland branch of the Women's International and Political League came over as Labour Party branches.[30] The 1918 conference had resolved that delegates to the national conference be appointed by LRCs. The justification was that large conferences were inefficient, but in 1919 the conference agreed to return to the representation of all affiliated bodies. Some speakers pointed to the complete lack of women at the 1919 conference as a reason for larger conferences. Joe Hodgens of Palmerston North was not the only delegate who expressed himself 'surprised, indeed almost shocked' at the suggestion that 'special sex representation [was] necessary in the councils of Labor . . . Men could quite well represent the views of both men and women and vice versa.' Fred Cooke, however, 'asked the delegates to grasp the fact that woman's viewpoint often varied. This was true even of Socialist men and women . . . It was no use some men declaring that they could represent women as well as the women themselves. They simply could not.' Nash, referring to women's domestic sphere, supported Cooke.[31]

Women's branches sometimes insisted on being consulted on matters of interest. In 1922 Savage (who had thought men could represent women at the conference) introduced an Endowment of Motherhood Bill. The Auckland Women's League 'was not favourably impressed by the Bill and thinks the women of the Party might be consulted on a measure of this description'.[32] In 1924 the Wellington Women's Labour Club suggested that the parliamentary party and the national executive should consult women's labour organisations on all matters pertaining to women and children. In 1927 the Wellington women's branch organised a women's conference before the main one. Discussions included the reform of child welfare, extension of the apprenticeship system to girls, nationality issues, education of women in the history and principles of trade unionism, and the need for proper family allowances.[33] These conferences were a feature for some years at least. As the Depression worsened, Elizabeth McCombs appealed to women workers, noting the injustice of taxing them but denying them unemployment relief. At the same time, McCombs appealed to 'the humanitarian ideals of women' to enlist their support for Labour's plans for security and full employment.[34]

By 1925 leading figures within the party were also beginning to think about engaging with Māori, even if this was rather out of their comfort zone. Fraser was a partial exception: in 1922 he had spoken about Māori land grievances, and 'land alienation and the cultural impact it had was something this descendant of Scottish crofters readily understood'.[35] In 1924 Rangi Mawhete took the initiative by writing to Joe Hodgens, the chairman of the Palmerston North LRC. Mawhete had already stood more than once for Western Māori and in 1924 the party adopted him as its candidate. He convened a conference at Parewanui, near Bulls, on 20 December 1924, where he and ten colleagues met with Holland and others from the national executive.[36] Writing afterwards, Mawhete and his colleagues recalled King Tāwhiao's 1882 statement that he had 'pakeha friends . . . in the four corners of these Islands, comprised of shoe-makers, blacksmiths, carpenters and the working classes'. They also recalled the

Sermon on the Mount, and prophecies by Tohu Kākahi of Parihaka and Pāora Te Pōtangaroa of Wairarapa that 'a Pakeha Government would co-operate with a Maori element in uplifting the masses of the people'. All these, they felt, were being fulfilled in the Labour Party.[37]

At least seven Māori attended the 1925 conference. Mawhete and W.D. Barrett, from Kaiapoi, spoke on land grievances, and the conference approved Māori branches and pledged a Labour government to 'appoint a Royal Commission to investigate the Native Land Claims arising out of, and subsequent to, the Treaty of Waitangi', and, as well, a 12-member elected 'Native Council' to advise the government on Māori issues and legislation. Mawhete and his colleagues may, however, have been disappointed by later discussion about continuing purchase of Māori land, with proceeds to be used for pensions and developing other land.[38] James McCombs, paternalistically, thought that Māori desires to manage their own land 'might possibly injure them'. Fraser warned that the past could not be retrieved, and Holland was opposed to anything that implied a separate Māori parliament (the Kotahitanga parliaments of the 1890s were within living memory).[39] The Rātana faith was attracting considerable support among many Māori communities and Mawhete, despite the tensions in his relationship with the party, would be a key liaison between Rātana and Labour, although he was not himself an adherent of the faith. Rātana candidates contested the Māori seats from 1925, and in 1932 Eruera Tirikātene won Southern Māori for the movement. After 1935 he and Toko Rātana, the prophet Tahupōtiki Wiremu Rātana's son, joined the Labour caucus.[40]

Surprisingly, the party paid far less attention to developing a youth organisation, with little discussion at conferences. In 1930 the North Canterbury LRC discussed forming a Junior Labour League. Jock Mathison and Bob Macfarlane, both around 30 years of age, argued that it was 'essential to the future welfare of the Labour Party' and should emphasise political education.[41] In 1932 the national conference was advised that a youth branch would be desirable, but best left to those with the enthusiasm for doing something about it. In the radicalised climate of the Depression this was a strategic error.[42] Some young activists did emerge, but they had to operate within the party's established structures.

Local government was likewise a poor relation during the 1920s. Perhaps this was partly due to a lack of status. City councils and their mayors tended not to be powerful organisations. In the cities smaller boroughs often persisted when a unitary authority might have made more sense. Local government could, however, be a valuable training ground for aspiring parliamentarians, and a Labour mayor could, sometimes, exercise real influence. Dan Sullivan certainly did so as mayor of Christchurch during the Depression: he worked tirelessly to motivate the comfortable to share what they had with the less fortunate. Christchurch had something of a reputation as a 'Labour city' and J.K. Archer, the Baptist minister who won the position in 1925, was the first Labour mayor of a major New Zealand city. Sullivan, a Catholic, replaced him in 1931, and only left office on entering cabinet at the end of 1935. With parliament usually sitting for less than half the year, it was not difficult to combine local authority work with a parliamentary seat.

The party was constantly short of money, as were most of its supporters. Ambitious schemes discussed at the 1919 conference came to little. A fundraising committee proposed a 'fifty thousand half crowns' campaign: the campaign bonds promised 'full Industrial and Political Rights', but in a year only £730 13s 4d was raised, little more than a tenth of the target. As Savage noted, 'the committee had been mistaken in their judgement of the enthusiasm of last conference'.[43] In May 1922 head office was £100 in deficit, and John Glover covered that with an interest-free loan. While the party claimed 25,000 members in branches and affiliated unions, the capitation fee of three halfpence gave only £156 5s. A national campaign fund managed to find £351 18s 6d, but a more modest fifty thousand shillings campaign had an even more modest result than its 1919 predecessor, raising only £138 12s 3d. With the expenses of an election campaign, the national organisation had less than £60 in the bank at the end of 1922.[44]

In 1924 the party's finance committee warned that the party required a political fighting fund of £25,000. All unionists would be asked for a voluntary capitation of ten shillings, and MPs would be asked to canvass for money.[45] While there were branches in all but two North Island and all but seven South Island electorates by 1924, it would be a struggle to raise so much. In 1925 the party membership increased considerably, though, and the party managed to find £9000 for the general election. Total membership was reckoned at nearly 45,000, with 5278 individual members in 105 branches, the rest being members of affiliated unions, whose activity would have varied.[46] Similar sums were raised for the 1928 election. In that year capitation increased from sixpence to ninepence, which gave £900 annually, although that was less than would have been raised if the full sum had been paid. Even at sixpence the revenue should have been £1200 a year, and it cost about £1600 a year to run head office.[47]

The Depression, of course, did the party finances no good at all. During 1929 and 1930 only two things kept the party afloat: a bequest of £500 from Sarah Empson, in Christchurch, and Walter Nash continuing as secretary while living on his parliamentary salary. The 1930 conference resolved 'that at all future Conferences . . . only those organisations which are financial . . . shall be entitled to representation'.[48] By 1933 arrears of levies amounted to £1400.[49] More positively, 28 new branches were established during 1932–33, in places like Hunterville, Norsewood, Martinborough and Karamea as well as larger towns. In the next year another 44 new branches were established.

At least some of this activity reflected Peter Fraser's determination that 'the Labour Party remained the principal vehicle for depression discontents', which involved ongoing contention with communist and other radical organisations.[50] Holland, too, had spent years criticising what he called 'political non-unionism'. While the party generally had good relations with the trades and labour councils and the skilled unions, the relationship with the militant transport unions in the Alliance of Labour was often sour. The New Zealand Workers' Union leadership, likewise, saw industrial action as superior to political, and neither that union nor the alliance co-operated with the party.[51]

James Thorn replaced Nash as national secretary in 1932 and was directed to devote as much time as possible to organising throughout the country. (Appropriately, the party's gift to Nash when he finished as secretary was a filing cabinet.)[52] In the election year of 1935 there were 182 branches (up from 156 in 1934), but a number of smaller unions had folded due to unemployment and the Coalition government's anti-union legislation, and affiliates had declined from 169 to 156. Increasing branch numbers did not translate into massive increases in funds: the 1935 conference was told that the election campaign would require £15,000, but apparently only £4300 was raised.[53] The greater asset was the constant work Labour MPs had done since 1929, in personally supporting the distressed, organising assistance, and in assertive campaigning against the worst of the Coalition policies.[54]

Policy development

Policy development was as important in the years before 1935 as building the organisation and raising money. Most studies have suggested that Labour had to abandon Marxist shibboleths if it was to become electable, and that Harry Holland's ideological rigidity was an obstacle to this.[55] This is rather simplistic, and studies of Labour after 1935 pay little more attention to the intellectual bases of government policy. Walter Nash's biographer wrote that in 1935 'The Red Flag had been furled, replaced by Nash's cornucopia of pink candyfloss', which is a wonderful one-liner but minimises the hard intellectual work which many party members, including Holland, did before 1935.[56]

Certainly there was plenty of radical rhetoric in the early 1920s. Holland reminded parliament that 'all written history from the breakup of primitive tribal communism to the present day is a history of class struggles . . . The workers, through the Labour party, seek to substitute a system that will abolish classes and make class warfare impossible.'[57] The Hastings branch got the national conference to agree in 1921 that 'all candidates . . . shall at all times affirm their belief in the class-struggle', and wanted the party to affiliate with the Third International in Moscow.[58] Conversely, the newly formed Communist Party sought to affiliate with the Labour Party, but Labour's 1925 conference, after hearing a communist, voted to exclude members of any other political party. The communists continued to make overtures, but Labour's attitude was understandable given the communists' general hostility to social democrats, a hostility which Moscow regarded as a fundamental obligation.[59] Some in Labour were equally firm. In 1923 several Dunedin organisations wanted the socialisation objective amended or diluted, the Painters' Union urging that the party 'dissociates itself from the use of the words "Revolutionary Socialism"'.[60] When Lenin died in 1924 the executive sent Moscow a condolence cable. The conference endorsed the cable but deleted, on Nash and Fraser's motion, reference to Lenin as a great Labour leader, and McCombs dissociated himself entirely from it.[61]

Reformist agendas emerged early. The party noted that in wartime the government could 'organize for the housing, for feeding, and the clothing of the people, but when it comes to peace-time you fall back and say "It is causing us great anxiety, but we can do nothing"', and advocated 'a bold and vigorous policy of reconstruction'.[62] On defence policy, in 1924 Fraser argued that while the party should pursue international disarmament, it will 'face the problem of Defence on assuming office . . . in the light of that policy and will be guided by the circumstances prevailing at that time as to the extent to which Disarmament can be achieved or Defence is necessary'. Fraser's prescience was endorsed after considerable discussion.[63] The party also came to accept existing institutions in the electoral system. Proportional representation had been a high priority from 1916, but there were a number of calls to dump the commitment by the late 1920s. Enquiries were made with social democratic parties operating in proportional systems overseas in 1930, but after further years of discussion the 1934 conference resolved that because there was no perfect system of proportional representation the policy should be abandoned.[64]

More visionary was what some disparagingly referred to as Harry Holland's 'Samoa Complex'. Holland 'exhibited an unusual devotion to Samoan affairs'.[65] Humanitarianism and radical opposition to imperialism intersected in Holland's championing of Samoan self-government. His interventions began in 1918 when it seemed likely New Zealand would acquire German, or Western, Samoa in the post-war settlement. Holland argued that foreign meddling had fostered conflict and division among Samoans. Some of his language betrayed a touch of paternalism, and he advocated what would later be called trusteeship, but Holland warned of the serious consequences of New Zealand's increasingly authoritarian approach in Samoa. Holland, and some of his colleagues, championed the nationalist aspirations of the Mau movement, and 'the *New Zealand Worker* was virtually the only newspaper to take the Mau seriously'.[66] Holland's forebodings were all too clearly realised on Black Saturday, 28 December 1929, when New Zealand troops shot and killed 11 unarmed protestors, including one of the Mau leaders, Tupua Tamasese Lealofi III. Holland's continued criticism of New Zealand's record in Samoa may not have contributed much to Labour's electoral fortunes in New Zealand, but it was, and remains, remembered in Samoa. 'Holland heard the distant whispers of the future and realised earlier than any other New Zealand parliamentarian that Western Samoa was destined for eventual self-government.'[67]

Parliamentarians had to do much of the work in policy development. Walter Nash exercised considerable influence in economic policy for some years before his election to parliament in 1929. In land policy, the Wairarapa farmer Ben Roberts was active during the 1920s (he would become MP for Wairarapa in 1935). Parliamentarians, though, had privileged access to resources, and while none of them had formal training in economics (indeed, few had more than a primary school education), they made good use of the parliamentary library to keep up with the latest economic thinking.

Labour's economic arguments emphasised a mixture of developmentalism and underconsumptionist analysis, the latter emphasising the necessity for reasonable wages to maintain demand for expanding production. Labour MPs increasingly argued that low wages were undesirable not merely because they disadvantaged workers, but because they provoked a vicious circle of falling demand, diminished production and rising unemployment. As James Munro said, it was

> an economic fallacy, set on foot by the employers and farmers of this country, to reduce wages at the present time. Reduce wages and you immediately reduce the purchasing-power of the people. Reduce that purchasing-power from an economic standpoint and it immediately kicks along the line to the retailer, the manufacturer and every producer.[68]

Dan Sullivan advocated the development of iron smelting based on the North Island's ironsands, and a pulp and paper industry. Sullivan was

> not prepared to agree that New Zealanders should be hewers of wood and drawers of water or merely growers of food. We want our people to be able to write and produce books, beautiful furniture, and all the other products of art and secondary industries, in order that they should have the opportunity of developing every special attribute and of attaining to the highest possible standard of technical civilization.[69]

James McCombs was the party's principal economic thinker in the 1920s. At least as much as any other parliamentarian he kept abreast of current economic debates and emphasised the importance of demand in the economy. Increasing production, advanced by conservative ministers as the solution to the country's economic problems, was nonsense if demand was not increased at the same time. 'There can be no effective demand . . . unless there is effective purchasing-power . . . Effective demand must precede production.'[70] Among McCombs's reading was the work of two underconsumptionist American economists, William Foster and Waddill Catchings, who warned of the vicious circle of retrenchment and hoped 'for a solution of the problem of unemployment to schemes which will permanently raise wages or, in other words, the effective demand of the working class'.[71]

As the Depression worsened, McCombs buttressed his contention that it was idiotic to reduce wages in a depression with quotations from figures as diverse as Henry Ford and J.M. Keynes as well as Foster and Catchings. Clearly, by 1931 McCombs had read Keynes's *A Treatise on Money*, as well as his journalism in the Liberal periodical the *Nation*. McCombs cited another British Liberal, Reginald McKenna (a former chancellor of the exchequer), to the effect that 'there are times when, judged by the interests of the general economic welfare, thrift may be carried to excess. The present crisis is one of underconsumption.'[72] In 1932 McCombs quoted 'possibly the greatest economist in the British Empire, John Maynard Keynes', that if a single producer cuts wages and others do not follow suit, then that producer gets a greater share of trade, but 'if wages are cut all round, the purchasing-power of the community as a whole is reduced, and no one is further forward'.[73]

McCombs's image was far from that of the socialist firebrand.[74] But Holland, and others usually identified as 'militants', shared his analysis. Holland's own rethinking to a significant extent resulted from the 1925 general election, after which Labour began to court rural voters. Most discussions of the party's agricultural policy emphasise the retreat from land nationalisation. Land policy had, in fact, never been clear-cut. Much of the 1919 policy could have been 1890 radical Liberalism, including the conservation of the national endowment and an emphasis on the 'Securing to the community of all the values created by the community'. What was new was a state bank to provide cheap development finance, thereby weakening the power of private banks and stock and station agencies. More contentious was the creeping nationalisation implied by no transfer of land except to or from the state. This sat uneasily with the vague language of 'tenure based on use and occupancy'. Labour hoped to appeal to 'the small struggling farmer' by these policies, but that was more easily said than done.[75]

Successive conferences debated land policy, often referring the matter to committees which included farmer members. Radical socialists like Rod Ross, from Palmerston North, thought that even the 1919 policy appealed too much to 'an inefficient class of small farmers'; he was obviously thinking of collectivisation.[76] In 1921 the policy was essentially confirmed, with the addition of a commitment to guaranteed prices.[77] In 1925 the state monopoly of transfer was endorsed, but Nash made it clear that inheritance would not be interfered with. In 1926 Ben Roberts and Bill Parry recommended a permanent committee on land policy, representing farmers and rural districts.[78] In 1927 Roberts proposed a farmer section of the party, and argued that Coates's dairy marketing legislation should be supported as 'it is essentially a socialistic measure'. By 1927 the retreat was nearly complete: that year the conference, while nodding to the proposition that 'Public Ownership of Land [is] the only ultimate remedy for the present chaos and muddle', accepted 'Full recognition of owners' interest in all land including tenure, the right of sale, transfer and bequest.'[79] At the same time, Labour placed increasing and excessively optimistic emphasis on land development. In 1929 the national executive advocated 'encouraging as many boys as possible to take up farming occupations rather than professional or commercial vocations . . . farming presents an almost unlimited scope for their employment'.[80]

More constructive were efforts to persuade farmers that they had a vital interest in high wages for urban and industrial workers, as Holland suggested in 1926.[81] In 1932 Armstrong argued that 'the best customer of the farmers is New Zealand itself' and farmers had no interest in constraining domestic demand. Moreover, he pointed out, increased production had not been matched by overseas demand. This meant New Zealand had a direct interest in higher living standards overseas. This perspective would inform the Labour government's advocacy of full employment as an international obligation after 1943.[82]

Holland frequently attacked deflationary policies in the last two years of his life. In one speech he quoted Keynes:

> If we carry 'economy' of every kind to its logical conclusion, we shall find that we have balanced the budget at nought on both sides, with all of us flat on our backs starving to death from a refusal, for reasons of economy, to buy one another's services . . . It is often said by wiseacres that we cannot spend more than we earn. That is, of course, true enough of the individual, but it is exceedingly misleading if it is applied to the community as a whole. For the community as a whole it would be much truer to say that we cannot earn more than we spend. Prices cannot rise, output and employment cannot increase, unless the first stimulant comes from the side of increased spending.[83]

Holland urged the expansion of public works at normal wages and severely criticised the government's reduction of such spending by £4 million, which, again, created a vicious circle. So far as farmers were concerned, Holland foreshadowed the need to develop new markets beyond Britain, not only in the Commonwealth but elsewhere, and advocated price stabilisation for primary producers.[84]

These speeches foreshadowed what the Labour government would do after 1935. Holland would not live to see that government. He died in October 1933, at the age of 65: he suffered a fatal heart attack after insisting on following the cortège of the late Māori king, Te Rata, up Taupiri Mountain near Hamilton, a circumstance that is remembered within Waikato Tainui today. James McCombs also died in 1933, and Nash replaced him as the party's economics specialist. Nash's maiden speech in 1930 was about unemployment, urging that policy makers take an active approach to managing the transitions between old and new industries. Nash went on to advocate equitable distribution as an essential corollary to greater production, and believed that taxation should facilitate that equitable distribution. The present order, he said, leads to 'this astonishing paradox: that because more is created someone has to have less'. Nash quoted the English radical Liberal underconsumptionist John A. Hobson's observation that 'distribution of income more equal and more favourable to the workers would mean that the rising standard of living would keep taut the sinews of production. The difficulty that we are suffering from is unequal, unfair, and unwise distribution of the product.'[85] The essential point of these analyses was that 'enhancing the economic power of the working-class consumer was . . . a constructive and transformative measure, not a cause of further economic disorder'.[86] More generally, it is easy enough to detect particular dimensions of Keynes' thinking that influenced Nash, and McCombs before him. The *Treatise on Money* emphasised the importance of investment, and the role of public authorities in leading investment when necessary. A minority report on the Macmillan Committee (an advisory committee of economists which the British government established late in 1929 to report on banking and finance), signed by Keynes, McKenna and the trade unionist Ernest Bevin, repeated that theme and drew attention to the importance of modernisation as well as demand management. Keynes's criticisms of retrenchment for launching a vicious circle frequently appeared in the *Nation*, and his essay 'Can Lloyd George do it?' foreshadowed the virtuous circle—the multiplier—which public investment could kick off in times of recession.[87]

As Nash developed his thinking, he drew on a number of sources in addition to Hobson and Keynes and other English Liberals.[88] Among his close friends was Allan Fisher, the professor of economics at the University of Otago. Fisher and Nash shared a scepticism about the ability of unregulated markets to satisfy human wants, and Fisher certainly shared Keynes's views on the importance of investment in maintaining employment. Fisher may have reinforced Nash's view that technological progress should be managed in the interests of economic stability and the common good. Certainly, Fisher emphasised that modern capitalism was dynamic and, even if unstable, hardly on the brink of collapse. Whereas some of Nash's colleagues had been naively optimistic about the potential of more intense land settlement to create employment, Fisher emphasised declining agricultural employment under conditions of technological improvement, and Nash certainly accepted that argument, as did Sullivan and John A. Lee. More generally, Fisher's friendship with Nash may have helped the latter to speak in the tones of economists and bankers.[89]

Nash was also distinctly unimpressed by the wave of fervour for social credit, or Douglas Credit as it was often known, which became evident in some party circles, particularly North Island rural branches. It is, as one historian has noted, 'difficult to speak with precision on the degree to which Douglas Credit penetrated the Labour Party'.[90] Social credit diagnoses of the Depression were often expressed in language similar to that used by underconsumptionists, although the formers' hostility to banks amounted to a naive populism. Social credit nostrums were confined to consumption, and paid little if any attention to investment. Moreover, there was very little idea of the redistribution of wealth (which, along with hostility to the modern administrative state, is why the ideology became an alternative conservatism). Nor did social credit have any appreciation that in a boom it might be necessary to limit demand. There were some within the Labour Party whose loose talk of simply printing money to stimulate demand sounded a lot like social credit.

By 1931 Labour's alternative economic perspective remained indebted to earlier traditions of colonial developmentalism, but shaped around an underconsumptionist analysis which urged the necessity of maintaining purchasing power, rather than retrenching, as the proper response to depression. Nash, in particular, was well aware of the importance of foreign trade to the New Zealand economy, but it did not follow that New Zealand's recovery depended on the British. That, for Nash, was 'pure, unadulterated drift'. New Zealand, Nash believed, could control its own destiny if policy makers took more responsibility for economic management. This did not mean autarky. In 1933 Nash specified 15 'affirmations' which would guide the party's economic policy. The first was that 'Economic self-sufficiency and isolation will not accord with the economic and social progress of the Dominion', and indeed Nash, again influenced by Fisher, believed that 'economic self-sufficiency is dangerous to peace'. Economic planning was both inevitable and desirable, and 'must provide for the full utilization of the natural resources of the Dominion, and their distribution to ensure the maximum living standards'. National control of credit and currency were essential, but New Zealand's planned economy would be more successful 'if world trade is regulated through negotiation and co-operation'.[91] The strongest differences (which would lead to problems after 1935) related to financing recovery: some advocated liberal use of central bank credit, some thought taxation would suffice, while some supported internal borrowing.[92]

The 1935 election

It is easy, with hindsight, to view 1935 as a triumph, but the reality was more ambiguous. Labour was not well funded in 1935. Head office spent only £1030 on publicity, although branches spent more.[93] This was partly compensated for by the 'mass union and branch base . . . [Labour] was easily the most effective political organisation'.[94] Neither of the Coalition parties had ever had much of a national organisation; more or less loose electorate or regional committees had been the rule, and by 1935 Davy, having promoted Coates in 1925 and Ward in 1928, was working for the right-wing Democrats. Labour's parliamentarians were the main architects of the party's advertising, and Nash, as president, wrote the manifesto.

Labour went from 24 seats to 53, but did so on just over 45 per cent of the popular vote. That was a considerable improvement on 1931's 34 per cent, but it was hardly a ringing endorsement. Labour would not fall below 45 per cent of the popular vote until 1954; even in 1951 the popular vote was just ahead of 1935. Labour won in 1935 because the right was badly divided.

Official Coalition candidates won 34 per cent, but the Democrats took 7.8 per cent and right-wing independents 8 per cent.[95] Labour won 21 general seats on a split vote, and only two (Eden and Wellington North) were in the cities.[96] All the rest were provincial towns or rural seats: Hamilton, Rotorua, Whanganui, Palmerston (North), Masterton, Tauranga and Invercargill in the former category, and Marsden, Hauraki, Bay of Plenty, Waipawa, Rangitikei, Wairarapa, Ōtaki, Waikato, Manawatu, Wairau, Kaiapoi and Waitaki. In seven of the 21 Labour won less than 40 per cent of the vote, and in Invercargill only 31.7 per cent.[97] Labour may well have won some of these seats in straight fights, but it is impossible to know (the Coalition held 13 seats on split votes, and it is likewise difficult to know what results would have emerged from straight fights).[98] But 1935 gave Labour its chance, a chance for which the party was well prepared. As the great English socialist R.H. Tawney later observed, 'what a Social-Democratic government can do largely depends on the pains it has taken to mature its plans before its advent to office gives it an opportunity of acting on them'.[99]

The years between 1919 and 1935 were very far from an inevitable march to government. Even in 1935, despite a handsome reward in parliamentary seats, the Labour Party could not claim the support of a majority of voters. Despite the enthusiasm of many thousands of members and supporters, the party was always short of money. For many in business and finance, in the press and the police, Labour was even in 1935 scarcely a legitimate part of political society. Despite the obstacles, and some serious errors of political judgement, the party's parliamentarians, members and supporters had by 1935 transformed it into a contender for power. If the moderation of some radical rhetoric was a necessary condition, then that was something that social democratic parties overseas also had to learn. Nor should moderation be equated with surrender. Much of Labour's thinking moved in creative directions and the party actively sought to construct a future. This involved abandoning any notion of capitalism's inevitable collapse and accepting 'the primacy of politics'. As party president James Thorn told the 1930 conference, belief in the inevitability of capitalism's collapse was a

> fatalistic attitude of mind [which] is ruinous to the effort that is required for the construction of a new society . . . Capitalism is intellectually bankrupt but it lived on the people's inertia. If we want a new society we will have to create a public mind that will insist on the application of different economic and social principles.[100]

4

The Welfare State: the Savage Years 1935–40

While Labour got a big majority in 1935, it won only a minority of votes, and was on trial until it won a decisive mandate with its smashing victory in 1938 with 56 per cent. This was a triumph for Labour and for Savage, who was widely revered by the party's supporters. Many of the first Labour government's greatest achievements were made between 1935 and 1940. In these years the party had to adjust to being in government. Ministers had to learn the machinery of state even as they sought to implement wide-ranging reforms, and had to adjust their aspirations to economic reality and a deteriorating international environment. Backbenchers had to learn that social democratic government is often frustratingly incremental, and that negotiation with interest groups and others is essential to embedded reform. These were also issues for the party at large, where membership and affiliation now became a matter of collaboration—however critical—with the party in government, rather than a mobilisation of protest.

The Savage government reversed the Coalition's Depression measures, reduced unemployment through a large public works programme, increased wages and strengthened unions. Labour expanded public education and state housing. A guaranteed price scheme was introduced for dairy farmers and plans made to foster secondary industries. The government's crowning achievement was the Social Security Act, the foundation of the modern welfare state. After the 1938 election it was beleaguered by economic and political problems. John A. Lee and a minority of Labour MPs attacked the government's economic policies as too conservative. Their views, which enjoyed a lot of support in the party, were simplistic and took little account of economic realities. In 1936 and 1937 Labour's membership mushroomed.

Branches were established all over the country, and the number of affiliated union members increased greatly after the introduction of compulsory unionism. After 1938 the party leadership cracked down on internal dissent and Lee and Savage became locked in a struggle to the death. At the 1940 party conference Lee was expelled for disloyalty. Savage died shortly afterwards. While Lee claimed that a third of Labour's branches collapsed because of his expulsion, we argue that the Second World War had much more to do with the atrophy of Labour's organisation in the first part of the 1940s.

Forming the first Labour government

On Monday 3 December 1935 Savage arrived in Wellington. 'Three thousand people cheered him to the echo' as he got off the Auckland train, reported Labour's newspaper, the *Standard*. 'Outside the station another great crowd had gathered and every available vantage point carried its quota of cheering onlookers. The roofs of nearly buildings, taxi-cabs and lorries were all used as grandstands'.[1]

The Labour caucus met that morning. Over half the MPs were new, and Mason and Semple moved that Savage should select the cabinet. He did this in consultation with Fraser and Nash. The new prime minister took the native affairs and external affairs portfolios. Fraser was appointed minister of education, health, marine and police; Nash finance, customs and marketing; Sullivan industries and commerce and railways; Mason attorney-general and justice; and Armstrong labour and immigration. Semple became minister of public works and transport; Parry internal affairs; Webb mines; Jones postmaster-general and defence; Martin agriculture and Langstone lands and forests. Mark Fagan became leader of the Legislative Council and a minister without portfolio.[2]

Lee was appointed under-secretary to the prime minister. He had expected to be a minister and was bitter about his exclusion. Arnold Nordmeyer said Lee 'started immediately almost a vendetta' against Savage.[3]

The new ministers were seasoned party leaders. Their average age was 56. Most had been trade unionists. Six were New Zealand born; five were Australians and former miners; Fraser was a Scot and Nash was English. Savage was careful to ensure geographical balance. Three ministers were from Auckland, three from Wellington, two from Christchurch, one from

Dunedin, two from North Island provincial electorates and one from the West Coast.

Some historians have argued that the Labour government was dominated by Savage, Fraser and Nash and that the rest were 'a gaggle of non-entities'.[4] However, most ministers contributed a lot: for example, Sullivan worked hard to promote industrialisation, Semple led the government's vigorous public works programme, Armstrong carried out major changes in labour laws and Mason was an able law reformer. One eminent economist, a close observer of 1930s New Zealand, would describe the ministry as 'the strongest Cabinet New Zealand had seen for many years'.[5]

A new tone in policy was evident from the beginning. The first cabinet meeting on 6 December decided to pay a Christmas bonus of £100,000 to the unemployed. A week later it voted £27,000 to give relief workers a Christmas holiday and £20,000 to give Christmas bonuses to recipients of charitable aid.[6] This immediate help for the unemployed and poor was long remembered by its recipients. Moving immediately to reverse Depression policies, the government revoked the cuts to award wages. Relief rates were increased and Māori placed on the same scale as Pākehā. Five-year-olds were readmitted to primary schools and teachers' colleges reopened. The hated Unemployment Board was abolished and its duties given to the Department of Labour. The government took control of the railways and sacked the Railways Board, which was loathed by workers.[7]

The government moved quickly to reform the institutions of economic and social policy. The new parliament's first act nationalised the Reserve Bank, which was required to give effect to the government's monetary policy and to regulate and control credit and currency so that 'the economic and social welfare of New Zealand may be promoted and maintained'.[8] To promote economic development, build infrastructure and increase employment, the government announced a three-year public works programme. All public works jobs were to be full-time, with a basic wage of £4 for a 40-hour week. The country's main highways were nationalised and funded centrally, and financial help given to farmers and homeowners.[9] To combat swings in export prices, guaranteed prices were set for dairy farmers, with the state controlling overseas marketing of their produce, giving them 'a degree of security they had never known'.[10] Labour believed that, in the longer term, secondary industries should be extended and new industries established to achieve full employment. The Industrial Efficiency Act 1936 was an effort to do this, but its vision of industry planning was hardly realised. The Second World War shaped industrial development more than this legislation.[11]

While the initial emphasis was on economic policy, Labour took significant steps in other areas. Pensions were increased, rent rises restricted, proficiency examinations for school students abolished, access to tertiary education opened up to all age groups, and there was a major school building programme.[12] The government nationalised radio, setting up a national broadcasting service and a separate commercial service, the latter headed by the flamboyant broadcaster and sometime Methodist parson Colin Scrimgeour. Lee was put in charge of introducing Labour's state housing policy. Reserve Bank credit was used to finance it and 6459 state houses were built between 1936 and 1940.[13]

Although Labour believed in equal treatment for Māori, specific policies for Māori were not part of its 1935 election manifesto. On 22 April 1936 Savage met Tahupōtiki Wiremu Rātana, the founder of the Rātana church. Their meeting sealed a political alliance between the two movements and established a spiritual bond between the two leaders.[14] Rātana reminded Savage of the prophecy of King Tāwhiao in 1869 that 'when the shoemakers, watchmakers, blacksmiths and carpenters rule this country then will the Maori people receive their salvation'.[15]

Labour believed that the overall purpose of government was to bring security to all the people, and that, as Nash said in his 1937 budget, 'when there is security for all who are willing to work the fear of poverty and depression will disappear, and with it the dominant acquisitive instinct will gradually be eliminated'.[16] Central to creating security were policies to increase wages and salaries, a key part of Labour's underconsumptionist policies. Higher wages meant workers needed stronger bargaining power and stronger unions. In April 1936 Labour restored compulsory arbitration, made trade union membership compulsory for workers covered by awards and gave the Arbitration Court the power to include a 40-hour week in awards. Membership of unions registered under the Industrial Conciliation and Arbitration Act more than trebled, from 80,929 in 1935 to 254,690 in 1939. Labour's approach in these areas, though, was firmly based on the traditional idea of the male breadwinner.[17]

A governing party's organisation

The growth of unions and union membership was accompanied by a rapid increase in Labour Party branches and branch membership. By 1937 the party's membership had more than doubled to 67,723 (14,177 branch members and 53,546 affiliated union members). The number of branches rose from 229 to 364 (many of the new ones were in provincial and rural areas) and the number of affiliated unions increased from 184 to 329. Labour was not alone in creating a mass membership party. The National Party, which was formed in May 1936 to unite the remnants of Reform and United, grew by 1938 into a well-organised party with 1000 branches and an estimated 100,000 members.[18]

A bigger party meant a bigger annual conference: 396 delegates representing 409 branches, unions and LRCs attended the 1937 conference, compared to 282 delegates representing 226 organisations in 1936.[19] A larger conference required a tighter structure, and in 1936 it was decided to set up committees to make recommendations on remits before they were debated by the full conference.[20] This streamlined conference business, and gave the leadership an additional lever with which to control conference debates.

One of the main organisational issues discussed at the 1937 conference was Māori structures within the party. The Māori Organising Committee, established at the 1936 conference, set up 160 Māori Labour committees and recruited 9000 members. In October 1936 it organised a Māori Labour conference, attended by 220 delegates, which made a number of recommendations to the government, 'with a strong focus on the Treaty of Waitangi'.[21] The committee was chaired by Eruera Tirikātene and its secretary, Paraire Paikea, was another prominent Rātana member. There was concern that Rātana had taken over the Māori section of the party.[22] A meeting between the Māori Organising Committee and the national executive worked out proposals for future Māori organisation, 'it being understood that members of the Ratana Movement shall not be in the majority'. The organising committee became the Māori Advisory Council, with six members: the chair, Rangi Māwhete (who was not Rātana and who had been appointed to the Legislative Council), Tirikātene, Toko Rātana and three Pākehā Labour MPs. Paikea, who was a talented organiser, became the council's paid secretary.[23]

At the 1938 conference a remit calling for an annual Labour women's conference was narrowly passed with support from Peter Fraser. In practice, however, this was watered down to a Sunday meeting of women delegates before the annual conference.

While Māori and women struggled to find their voice, compulsory unionism and increased union affiliation meant that trade unions became much more influential in the party. This was reflected in the election of Jim Roberts, secretary of the New Zealand Waterside Workers' Federation, as party president in 1937.[24] Roberts, who became known as 'the uncrowned king of New Zealand', held the position until 1950.

The government wanted a disciplined union movement and the *Standard* argued that unions 'should have an effective national executive that would be able to co-operate intimately with the Minister of Labour'.[25] There was much support for a central organisation of unions. Creating one was a harder task: unions were divided nationally between the small craft unions in the trades and labour councils and the large industry-based unions in the Alliance of Labour. The alliance was split between a faction led by Roberts and another by Fintan Patrick Walsh, president of the Seamen's Union.

On 14 April 1937 Fraser, the acting prime minister, opened a national industrial conference which was attended by over 300 delegates representing 212 unions and 178,000 of the 191,000 members of unions registered under the Industrial Conciliation and Arbitration Act. Paddy Webb, who chaired the conference, stressed that industrial and political labour had to act as one: 'We have been sent to Parliament by you to work for you, and we pledge you the loyal services of one hundred per cent of the Government. We on the other hand expect a hundred per cent loyalty from you.'[26] After heated debates over organisation and finance, the conference founded the New Zealand Federation of Labour. Angus McLagan, the former communist secretary of the United Mineworkers of New Zealand, was elected president, Dick Eddy, the president of the New Zealand Workers' Union, vice-president and Fred Cornwell, secretary of the Trades and Labour Councils Federation, secretary. Walsh and Ted Canham, a watersider and 1913 veteran, were elected as the two remaining executive members. Within six months, 150,000 unionists were affiliated to the federation and trades councils had been set up in 12 cities and towns.[27] The growth of unions and the formation of the Federation of Labour gave union leaders such as Jim Roberts, McLagan and Walsh an influence in the labour movement greater than that of most Labour MPs. Fraser, as minister of marine, established a very close relationship with Walsh, who was both the smartest and the most Machiavellian union leader.

The wider party

Histories often focus on leaders. What was happening on the ground in the hundreds of Labour Party branches? Only a handful of branch minute books have survived from the 1930s, but these give a good picture of local activity. In urban areas, political discussions and lectures, particularly on socialism, were a regular feature of branch meetings. Monetary reform was as popular a topic as socialism.[28] The Elizabeth McCombs Club, a Labour women's group in Wellington, had regular speakers on political topics, debated with other Wellington clubs like the Waterside Workers' Union, and had drama, eugenics and home and garden groups.[29] There was less political discussion at branches in provincial areas, but politics was not absent. The St Andrews branch in South Canterbury welcomed four speakers, probably social crediters, from Timaru to its September 1937 meeting to talk about money and banking.[30]

Social activities were an important part of branch life. The Dunedin women's branch's social evenings included songs, recitations, games and competitions, followed by 'a bountiful supper'. The Purakanui branch, near Port Chalmers, held three dances a month and fortnightly card evenings.[31] In preparation for a dance in May 1938, members of the Ōwhango branch, near Taumarunui, agreed that they would donate four large loaves of bread, 3 lb butter, one fowl 'cooked and stuffed', milk, tea, sugar, ballroom powder, a goose to be raffled and 2 lb corned beef. The dance raised £10 for branch funds.[32] Picnics were popular and well attended: the Auckland LRC, for example, held regular picnics at Redwood Park in west Auckland.[33] In 1936 the Auckland LRC established a Labour Club in the Pacific Buildings, Wellesley Street (the home of a number of unions), which held dances, tournaments, card evenings and special functions to host visiting cabinet ministers.[34]

Electoral rolls give some clues about the social composition of party branches, although women were then classified in the electoral rolls only as either 'married' or 'spinsters'. Most of the male members of the Milson branch (Palmerston North) were railway workers. Half the Māngere branch were farmers, the rest mainly labourers or relief workers. Most members of the Ōwhango branch worked at the local sawmill, and others were farmers and labourers. Half the St Andrews branch were labourers; there were several farmers and some railway workers. The Tawa Flat branch included labourers, tradesmen, public servants, clerks and a bookseller. Karori's members were labourers, watersiders, tradesmen and a few white-collar workers, including union officials. Island Bay had a similar composition but more tradesmen and white-collar workers than manual workers. Overall, Labour was very much a working-class party.

Social security and the 1938 election

The national executive's report to the 1937 conference observed that no previous government had done 'so much in such a short period to implement its policy'. The people's feelings were shown on Savage's recent tours of the South and North islands: 'No previous Premier, not even Royalty itself, has received such a right royal welcome . . . The future looks bright, only disunity in our ranks could defeat us, and there is not the slightest indication of anything of that nature, rather the contrary.'[35] However, there were sharp differences within caucus about one of the main planks of Labour's 1935 policy, the introduction of a national health and superannuation scheme to support the sick and the elderly. Gervan McMillan, MP for Dunedin West, who had been a doctor in the impoverished hydro town of Kurow, chaired a caucus committee which in July 1936 proposed universal health insurance. A committee of officials reported in October that universal superannuation at 30s a week and a complete health service would cost nearly £30 million (almost all the government's revenue), greatly alarming ministers.[36]

After many months of work, at a caucus meeting on 10 and 11 February 1938 the cabinet presented proposals for health and superannuation to be means-tested and paid from a fund financed by a flat tax of 1s 6d on wages and other incomes. Pensions would start at 25s a week rising to 30s for those aged 65 and over. Caucus was unhappy with means testing and the idea of a fund. Lee and others on the left, who had little appreciation of the economic realities the government faced, were angry at Savage's reluctance to go to 30s immediately. A caucus committee, chaired by Arnold Nordmeyer, MP for Oamaru, who had been the Presbyterian minister in Kurow, recommended a means-tested pension of 30s a week for men and women at age 60 and a plan for universal free health care. Instead of a fund there would be a tax of 5 per cent on all earners. When the Social Security Bill was introduced into parliament in August 1938, it included a universal superannuation payment at age 65 of £10 a year, rising annually by £2 10s until it reached 30s a week.[37] Introducing the bill, Nash said (with some hyperbole) that it would be

> the first Social Security Act . . . ever written in any statute-book in the world. All those people . . . who today are suffering from circumstances over which they have no control will be . . . as far as it is humanly possible to do it by a Government, freed from the circumstances . . . of dreading where to get the money from which to make provision for their old age; where to find money to pay the doctor . . . how to provide for the youngsters if the father and mother are dead . . . If [the bill] brings the benefits I believe it will bring, then once more this country will be 'God's Own Country'.[38]

Social security and the government's achievements were the main theme of Labour's annual conference in April 1938, at which 443 delegates representing 427 organisations were present. Eighty-eight new branches had been formed, bringing the total to 442. There were 206 Māori Labour committees and 636 union affiliates. Total party membership had risen to 162,157.[39] Three thousand people attended a public meeting during the conference. Savage's speech, which was broadcast over radio, highlighted the social security proposals, which caught the public imagination.[40] Savage astutely decided that introduction of the Social Security Act would be delayed until 1 April 1939, making the October 1938 election a referendum on the legislation. In a riposte to Savage's statement that social security was 'applied Christianity', Adam Hamilton, leader of the opposition, said it was 'applied lunacy',[41] a comment which dogged the National Party for a very long time.

Unlike in 1935, Labour faced a largely united opposition in 1938 which was strongly backed by the daily newspapers. The party pulled out all the stops. Its national campaign included radio broadcasts (shared with its opponents), widespread newspaper and magazine advertising, slides in over 250 picture theatres, posters on nearly 100 large hoardings, a special election film and 2,238,000 pieces of propaganda. There were nearly 900,000 leaflets on unemployment, social security, prosperity and children; 377,000 copies of the prime minister's message which were posted to every household; 200,000 copies of *Constitutional Democracy* (targeted at professionals, farmers and small business people); 80,000 pamphlets on guaranteed prices posted to dairy farmers; and 10,000 pamphlets in Māori of Savage's speech to the recent Labour Māori conference.[42]

Party branches, big and small, worked hard on the election campaign. They set up local committees to canvass door to door, gave money to the national campaign fund and provided cars to take voters to the polls on election day.[43] The party raised over £37,000 for the campaign, nearly five times what it spent in 1935. Over a third of this came from six unions: the Waterside Workers' Union, New Zealand Workers' Union, Hotel Workers' Union, Seamen's Union, Post and Telegraph Association and the Amalgamated Society of Railway Servants.[44] Hundreds of meetings were held throughout the country and thousands came to hear Savage. On 9 October, the Sunday before the election, 80,000 people attended a rally in the Auckland Domain, preceded by a march of 27,000 unionists from the waterfront.[45] The election was bitterly contested. The National Party and the daily newspapers derided the government as socialist and dangerous. John Pell, a tailor and Labour activist since the 1880s, wrote to Lee: 'in all my experience of Politics, I have never seen more class hatred shown than on this Election'.[46]

Labour's victory in 1938 was the greatest in New Zealand's history. In 1935 it won 46 per cent of votes, and 22 of its 55 MPs were elected with fewer than half the votes. In 1938 Labour won nearly 56 per cent of votes and all its 53 MPs won more than half the votes. This percentage of votes was a record for any social democratic party anywhere. Labour lost nine provincial and rural seats and won seven.[47] Paikea's victory in Northern Māori tightened Labour's grip on the Māori seats. Catherine Stewart became Labour's second woman MP by winning Wellington West. Labour supporters were jubilant. In tiny Onekakā in Golden Bay, 'Labour's victory was celebrated in a fit and proper measure, and many a glass of foaming ale was translated into song and rejoicing . . . Sore heads next day? Possibly, but what of it? A small price to pay to welcome Labour's triumph!'[48]

Party strife, 1938–40

For the leaders of the government, the celebrations were short. Labour faced three major problems: Savage's health, an economic crisis and a revolt by backbench MPs, spearheaded by Lee. In February 1938 Savage became seriously ill. He recovered, but collapsed in mid-August after a gruelling speaking tour. He told his closest colleagues he had cancer of the colon and his doctors urged an operation, which Savage refused because he was determined to lead Labour's campaign for re-election. His health continued to deteriorate after the election.[49] This was a major risk for Labour. Savage personified the government to voters, was revered by party supporters and, above all other MPs, enjoyed wide support among party members and unionists.

The economic crisis was caused by a sharp fall in New Zealand's export prices during 1938, while import spending remained high. The country's sterling reserves in London fell from £38 million in 1935 to £8 million in December 1938. The government introduced import and export licensing and exchange controls to deal with the shortage of foreign exchange. It was forced to renew significant loans on the London market and in mid-1939 Nash held acrimonious and protracted negotiations with the British government and the Bank of England, which opposed Labour's industrial development and social security policies. Nash was a determined and dogged negotiator. On the eve of the Second World War the British conceded the loan, but on tough terms.[50]

The backbench revolt after the 1938 election reflected the concern of many party members that the government was too conservative. There was a lot of support for more socialist and social credit policies, for the use of cheap Reserve Bank credit to fund public spending and for nationalising the trading banks. Those who held these views, like Lee, were naive about financial policy. Lee said: 'We will make Walter print and print and print to the limit of commonsense.'[51] Nash had a much greater understanding of both economics and common sense.

There was also a feeling that democracy in the party was under threat. Lee, who played a prominent part in the 1938 campaign, was popular among party members. Shortly before the election, 14 Labour MPs, including Lee, McMillan and Nordmeyer, wrote to Savage calling for cabinet to be elected by caucus.[52] At the first caucus meeting after the election, Lee moved the election of cabinet. After a long and at times bitter debate this was carried 26 to 23. Savage refused to accept the decision, closed the meeting and told the press the membership of cabinet would be unchanged. [53]

The leaders of the large unions watched the backbench revolt with growing anxiety. They generally supported the government's policies, had close ties to ministers, and had their own battles with the Communist Party and other left-wingers in the union movement, particularly in the Auckland Trades Council. Relations between Roberts, McLagan and Walsh had been marred by mutual dislike and suspicion; Lee and the left succeeded in uniting them behind Savage. Walsh reported to Fred Young, the Auckland Hotel Workers' secretary: 'The old man feels quite good and said he had no intention of agreeing to the tripe put up by Lee. The old boy will fight.'[54]

The party's national executive stepped into the argument about election of cabinet. It met caucus on 10 February 1939 and a compromise was worked out. Caucus would elect the leader in election year, the leader would nominate members of cabinet for caucus endorsement, and if anyone was not endorsed, MPs could recommend alternatives. The leader would resubmit nominations for the remaining vacancies for approval and the process would continue until there was agreement. This procedure was unanimously adopted by caucus and the full national executive.[55] Unity did not last long. In December 1938 Lee had written a confidential ten-page letter addressed to all Labour MPs castigating the government for its cautious policies and lambasting Nash, whose finance policy 'is at the real basis of the present dispute in the Party'.[56] Jack Lyon, MP for Waitematā and one of Lee's allies, took a copy to Auckland and it was published in *Smith's Weekly*.[57]

The Labour Party's 1939 annual conference opened on 10 April. There were 580 delegates representing 494 organisations. Party membership had risen to 203,501: 33,408 members of 636 branches and 170,093 members of 788 affiliated unions.[58] The party hierarchy was well prepared for a fight with the caucus rebels. Roberts's opening speech and the national executive report warned of the dangers of disunity. Savage concluded the parliamentary party's report by outlining the agreement on selecting the cabinet. Roberts and Walsh then moved 'complete confidence in the Prime Minister and Cabinet' and endorsement of the agreement, adding that future deadlocks in caucus should be decided by the leader after consulting the national executive or, if practicable, the conference. Lyon and McMillan moved that the second part of the motion be deleted. This amendment was defeated and there was strong support for the motion.[59]

On 12 April Fraser moved that the conference condemn 'in the strongest terms' the Lee letter as 'a breach of Party loyalty and discipline, and unmerited reflection on Mr Nash in particular and the Government in general'. There was a long debate. The letter was read to the conference, which decided that Lee, Nash and Savage would speak before the vote.[60] Lee and Nash each spoke for an hour, with Lee—who was one of New Zealand's best public speakers—having the better of the debate. Savage followed and was uncompromising in condemning Lee. Fraser's motion was carried 285 to 207, but the margin was not decisive and Lee was elected to the national executive.[61]

In a summary report on the conference to branches and unions, the party secretary, David Wilson, played down the differences: 'The "Lee" incident may now be considered definitely closed and it only remains for all members of the Party . . . to give loyal adherence to the decisions of Conference'.[62] However, Lee had no intention of backing down and wrote to Colin Scrimgeour that the conference was 'a great triumph for the so-called Lee faction . . . I have now emerged as a person with a bigger following in the Party than the PM'.[63] Despite his assurances at the conference, he encouraged the wide distribution of the offending letter, which he had separately printed: members of the social credit movement pushed sales around the country and Lee suggested friendly booksellers.[64] Newsagents on Queen Street in Auckland advertised it with placards reading 'Read John A. Lee's famous letter before it is banned.'[65] Labour Party branches read and discussed it and some sent Lee resolutions of support.[66] Lee's supporters—for example, Charles Petrie, MP for Ōtāhuhu, and McMillan—outlined their concerns to party meetings; Young and Walsh's spies took notes which were sent to Fraser.[67] Under the pseudonym 'Spartacus', Lee wrote an article which was published in the fortnightly *Tomorrow* attacking Savage, Fraser and Nash.[68]

On 4 August Savage had the operation that he had put off for almost a year. There were optimistic announcements to cover the truth, but the cancer was terminal. McMillan told MPs that Savage didn't have long to live.[69] 'Your news re the PM is bad', Tom Anderson, secretary of the Auckland Seamen's Union, wrote to Walsh, raising the question of a successor. 'One has got into the habit of thinking he would hang on . . . Fraser has never shown much sign of being a leader. His peculiar talent is the ability to work behind the throne. Yet there is nobody else that I can see'.[70]

Throughout Labour's first four years in office the dark clouds of war hung over the world, with the rise of fascism in Italy and Germany and a militaristic regime in Japan. Previous governments had slavishly followed British policy. Labour strongly supported the League of Nations and collective security. It made tentative steps towards an independent foreign policy: for example, it broke with Britain and opposed the Italian invasion of Ethiopia. From the late 1930s the government stepped up New Zealand's war preparations, a process largely overseen by Fraser.[71]

The declaration of war on 3 September 1939 changed the political climate. The leaders of the government and the Labour Party moved to restrict opportunities for the left. The national executive sent LRCs and branches the 'black circular', which warned that it would take 'drastic action' against any member, branch or committee guilty of assisting or co-operating with another political party or an anti-Labour organisation. No member or party body should assist in any way the Communist Party, the Friends of the Soviet Union or 'any other Communist auxiliary' or publish any resolution not in line with party policy.[72] In Christchurch, Bob Macfarlane, the Labour mayor, called a meeting of 70 'trusted Labour representatives . . . both industrial and political, for the purpose of formulating a plan of campaign against the Comrats'.[73] The Otago LRC protested: 'We object to the Labour Movement being reduced to an echo of reactionary Chamberlain's party'.[74]

The caucus rebels demanded two extra cabinet ministers, one a returned soldier (almost inevitably Lee). Savage refused. At a fractious caucus meeting on 4 November Lee accused him of being mentally and physically ill; Savage told Lee to go to hell and walked out.[75] The two men had pushed each other down a path of mutual self-destruction. Lee and his supporters organised to get nominations for the national executive.[76] Walsh wrote to Reg Brooks, the Canterbury Hotel Workers' Union secretary: 'It is reported that Jack Lee and his colleagues are organising to capture the Executive of the Labour Party . . . We want to take steps to see that the Party is controlled by the Industrial Movement'.[77] Lee wrote to a supporter: 'I shall, directly, start to protest openly about the dictatorship of the poor old fish over Caucus . . . The old chap is today definitely pathological . . . See that every possible delegate comes to National Conference.'[78]

In the greatest blunder of his political life, Lee made a barely veiled attack on Savage in an article entitled 'Psycho-pathology in politics', which was published in *Tomorrow* in December 1939:

> An odd politician becomes physically, becomes mentally sick . . . sycophants pour flattery upon him . . . He becomes vain of mind and short of temper. Wherever this problem of what I call pathology in politics occurred, except that the party managed to cut off the diseased limb, it went down to crashing defeat.[79]

There was outrage at the article and calls for Lee to be expelled from the party. 'He can't possibly be allowed to remain in after such a bastard of an act', Anderson wrote to Walsh.[80] Some of Lee's supporters were appalled. Lyon was so disgusted he 'ripped the damn thing up'. Shortly before Christmas, Lee was sacked as parliamentary under-secretary.[81]

Lee's strongest support was in Auckland and he went to the special LRC meeting called there to discuss the article on 11 January 1940; a record 194 delegates representing 98 branches and unions were present. On behalf of the LRC executive, Young moved that Lee be severely censured and condemned. An amendment complimenting Lee on his article and declaring confidence in both him and Savage was carried by 109 to 85.[82] The meeting became very heated and at one point Winifred Moore, one of Savage's long-time supporters, hit John Banks, a Lee supporter, with her umbrella. Savage was furious at the 'stupid inconsistency' of the LRC's decision, which made him even more determined to remain leader so he could attend the 1940 party conference.[83] Anderson reported ruefully to Walsh: 'Quite clearly, every loyal bonehead present voted for the amendment with the idea of settling a controversy without damage to either side, and it was for that reason the rats got a win.'[84]

The national executive met on 13 and 14 January. Percy Dowse moved that Lee be expelled, supported by Fraser. Roberts showed his political cunning by arguing that Lee should be given one more chance. The next day, Wilson reported that he and Lee had agreed that Lee would submit future articles dealing with the party to the executive for approval, express regret for writing 'Psycho-pathology in politics' and apologise to Savage. Given these promises, the executive voted to withdraw the expulsion motion.[85] Lee soon broke the agreement and in the weeks leading up to the conference both sides worked hard to organise support.

The 1940 annual conference opened on 25 March. A record 740 delegates were present, representing 613 organisations. Party membership had risen to 236,605, with 51,174 members of 630 branches and 185,431 members of 799 affiliated unions.[86] Savage was too ill to attend, but Lee's enemies were well prepared. The national executive's report included a recommendation that national unions be allowed to cast their full card vote provided that those with more than 12 votes were represented by four delegates. This was adopted and increased the voting strength of the large, anti-Lee unions.

Fraser presented the parliamentary party's report on behalf of Savage and explained that it included a confidential addendum, which was the leadership's trump card.[87] In it, Savage said that for the past two years 'my life has been a living hell'. The *Tomorrow* article showed that Lee was trying to destroy him politically.[88] Wilson moved the adoption of the confidential report and the executive report on Lee. Mendaciously, he claimed that Savage had made a marvellous recovery from his operation, and then came the *Tomorrow* article. 'Jack Lee has stabbed Joe Savage in the back. If Mr Lee is fit to be in your party, there are a good few of us who ought to be in a better party.' Lee said that if the conference enthroned dictatorial rule, it would solve no problem. 'If my political life is to go forfeit for fighting for the principles of democratic control in Caucus, I'm under sentence, but I will come again and again.' Fraser remarked, 'It would have been more decent and more honourable for Mr Lee to have taken a revolver and shot the Prime Minister dead than to have tried to destroy him by spreading the idea that he was physically and mentally a wreck.'[89]

The debate carried on into the evening. Barnard, Catherine Stewart, Nordmeyer, Jim O'Brien (MP for Westland) and McMillan defended Lee. Nordmeyer said Lee was being condemned not for his article but for adherence to principles that 90 per cent of the conference adhered to.[90] The reports were adopted on a show of hands 'by an overwhelming majority'. Bill Schramm, MP for Auckland East, and Jock Stewart immediately moved that Lee be expelled from the party. The *Standard* reported that the atmosphere in the conference hall was electric. After a short debate the motion was carried on a card vote by 546 to 344.[91] Lee recorded in his diary that night: 'Exit from the Labour Party, slaughtered . . . the Old Man has beaten me'. Savage, who had been briefed on the outcome, sank into unconsciousness and died early on the morning of 27 March. The conference immediately adjourned.[92]

Savage's body lay in state at parliament for two days. Some 50,000 people filed past. As his body was taken by train to Auckland, thousands gathered at stops on the way. An estimated 200,000 people met the train in Auckland or lined the route to Bastion Point, where he was buried.[93] Under Savage the Labour Party had been transformed into a mass working-class party and become a credible, widely supported government. He was a capable prime minister and one of the party's greatest communicators, with the ability to state Labour's case in clear and simple language. No other Labour leader has been as widely loved as Savage: for years after his death thousands of working-class homes had his photograph on their walls.

Immediately after his expulsion, Lee set up the Democratic Labour Party. While many Labour activists left to join him, Barnard was the only MP to resign from the party.[94] Walsh confidently predicted that 'Outside of a few money cranks, comrats and people the Government did not install . . . in a job, Lee will get no support.'[95] For his part, Lee claimed that 200 branches went out of existence over the following year because he was expelled.[96]

Lee's expulsion was widely discussed following the 1940 conference. The *Standard* reported that over 50 branches had endorsed his expulsion.[97] At other branches and LRCs there were motions opposing it. In New Plymouth, where the Labour MP Fred Frost was a Lee sympathiser, the LRC defeated a motion of opposition, as did the North Canterbury LRC.[98] Motions condemning Lee's expulsion were often linked to calls for a special conference to restore unity in the party.[99] The Otago LRC endorsed the expulsion but only narrowly defeated the call for a special conference.[100] The large unions—the Waterside Workers' Union, New Zealand Workers' Union, Hotel Workers' Union and Amalgamated Society of Railway Servants—voted for Lee's expulsion, as did Walsh's Seamen's Union and the Wellington Clerical Workers' Union, along with many small craft unions. A minority, including the printers', carpenters', Auckland drivers', Canterbury clothing workers' and Canterbury freezing workers' unions, opposed it.[101]

Opposition was strongest in Lee's Grey Lynn electorate, where a large number of members resigned, and Barnard's Napier electorate, although the party re-established its organisation in both places with union support.[102] While the number of Labour Party branches fell from 630 to 555 between 1940 and 1941, branch minute books show that this was not solely because of Lee. Most branches carried on, but Lee's expulsion resulted in 'the significant departure' of members. From the high point of 55,174 in 1939–

40, branch membership fell to 35,481 in 1940–41 and 23,298 in 1941–42. Many of those who left were 'the enthusiasts and the dedicated members who did the hard work in the "grass-roots" organisation of the LP'.[103] In a resolution which reflected the tension in the party between loyalty and democracy, the St Andrews branch urged that

> the National Executive & Cabinet approach the question of dissension in a more tolerant frame of mind than has been evident of late & that they give early & serious consideration to removing the causes of dissension by holding regular caucus meetings at close intervals, the settling of debatable questions in Caucus by democratic vote, and the selection of a Cabinet more representative of the talent available.[104]

The leadership was in no mood to be tolerant. Wilson stated that 'All disruptive elements were to be expelled from the Party and our ranks closed to face the future in a spirit of real unity and comradeship.'[105] A banner headline in red type in the *Standard* read: 'Party Branches Now Getting Rid of Disruptionists'.[106] The surviving branch records that suggest there was regret rather than anger when members resigned. For example, the Tawa Flat branch passed resolutions thanking the members who left for their work for the party.[107] So too did the Island Bay branch, which was furious when the *Standard* boasted about the removal of 'the source of obstructionist tactics' after its president, secretary and five others resigned.[108] Bruce Taylor, who wrote the most comprehensive study of the aftermath of Lee's expulsion, concluded that the Second World War had a much greater impact than the expulsion in ravaging party branches and membership.[109]

Between 1935 and 1940 the Labour Party cemented its place in New Zealand's political landscape. For the first time a working-class party won the Treasury benches and incorporated middle-class liberals, rather than the other way around. The government successfully introduced an economic and social policy regime which lasted until 1984. Labour grew spectacularly into a mass working-class party; but with this growth, and the political fights within the government, the heavy hand of the leadership constricted internal party democracy. The reasons for Lee's failure were summed up by his erstwhile ally Lyon to his LRC secretary:

> Lee will wreck a lot of Party votes but don't forget Joe the workers wage is still a good one, a lot of chaps who had no job for years have seen their kids with decent food and clothes for the past few years . . . No Government has ever been defeated in times of prosperity.[110]

5

War and Recovery: the Fraser Years 1940–49

The years 1940 to 1949 were the most difficult period any Labour government has faced in New Zealand. For the first three years of the war Germany and Japan were triumphant. The Labour government, led by Peter Fraser and Walter Nash, faced many challenges. It had to mobilise troops to join other Commonwealth forces in fighting alongside a beleaguered Britain, and the domestic economy to support New Zealand's own war effort as well as that of Britain and, later, the United States. It had to deal with employer and farmer demands for the dismantling of the welfare state while resisting union demands for pay increases and managing popular discontent with wartime controls and shortages. Determined to emphasise New Zealand's position as an independent nation and to advocate for social justice and economic development, the government embarked on an ambitious foreign policy agenda. After the war there were new challenges. The government had to move from wartime controls to peacetime freedom without the rampant inflation and unemployment that had followed the First World War. Post-war reconstruction was urgent, yet Britain, which controlled our overseas reserves, starved New Zealand of funds to import much-needed capital goods. Despite all the difficulties it faced, Labour was re-elected in 1943 and 1946.

Labour adopted a policy of wartime socialism that was unprecedented in New Zealand's history. The war was funded out of savings, internal loans and hefty tax increases, particularly on the wealthy. Military conscription was followed by civilian conscription and economic stabilisation. The government forged a tight alliance with the Federation of Labour, whose leaders played key parts in economic management. The government adopted a far-reaching rehabilitation programme to ensure servicemen and women had access to education and training and loans to buy farms, businesses and homes. Fraser's leadership of the country through the war and into the peace makes him one of Labour's greatest prime ministers.

Battered by Lee's expulsion and the extraordinary demands of wartime, the party organisation atrophied during the war. There was a major revival of membership and branches after the war, including many new junior and women's branches and Māori Labour committees. However, the heavy hand of the party leadership suppressed democracy within the party, and there was even greater intolerance of dissent once the Cold War between the United States and the Soviet Union began in the late 1940s.

Fraser and wartime government

On 4 April 1940 Labour MPs elected Peter Fraser as leader and prime minister. His victory was decisive but not overwhelming. He won 33 votes, while McMillan got 12 and Clyde Carr three.[1] Fraser faced two immediate problems: unifying the parliamentary caucus, and managing New Zealand's war effort in the face of demands for a coalition government and conscription of manpower. While he lacked Savage's charisma, Fraser was much more adept in dealing with conflict within the party. He quickly conceded the principle of caucus election of cabinet. At the end of May, Nash was elected deputy leader and McMillan elected to cabinet. Fraser sidelined the latter by appointing him minister of marine, scientific research and prisons. At the end of 1940 McMillan resigned from cabinet on the grounds of ill health, as did Lee Martin. They were replaced by two more from the left: James Barclay, who became minister of agriculture, and Nordmeyer, minister of health.[2] Paraire Paikea was also appointed to cabinet; this was important in bringing the government and Māori closer together.[3]

In February 1940 the party's national executive and the Federation of Labour's national council reaffirmed the labour movement's traditional opposition to conscription.[4] After the Nazi assault on Western Europe and the collapse of France, the government came under strong criticism for its conduct of the war effort. There were many calls for a coalition government, conscription and an end to the 40-hour week.[5] In late May the government introduced legislation giving the state wide powers to conscript manpower and wealth.[6] It is said that, in cabinet, Armstrong was the most reluctant to accept conscription, and finally did so on the basis that wealth would be conscripted as well. Outside cabinet, four Labour MPs volunteered for overseas service: Jack Lyon, Gordon Hultquist, C.F. (Jerry) Skinner and Bob Macfarlane. Lyon died on Crete, and Hultquist in Egypt. The emergency legislation allowed the government to override awards and labour laws. An Industrial Emergency Council, with equal numbers of employer and union representatives, was given power to approve changes (such as longer hours) to increase productivity.[7]

As Dunkirk fell, emergency conferences of the Federation of Labour and Labour Party were held to endorse a joint statement by their executives supporting conscription. In an emotional speech, Fraser asked the party conference to give the government a free hand in dealing with the crisis. The joint statement said the government must receive 'the unstinted support of the whole Labour Movement', whose trust and confidence 'must now be vested in the Cabinet and the Parliamentary Labour Party'. The government would ensure that no one profited from the sacrifices made by workers, that other sections of the community would make equal sacrifices, that the sacrifices would only last for the war and that organised labour would be given a voice in the administration of all emergency measures affecting workers. The conference voted by 903 to 100 to adopt the statement.[8] Two days earlier the FOL conference had endorsed it by 275 to 50.[9]

'This question of conscription will split the Labour Party from top to bottom . . . The opposition to it is fanatical', Anderson wrote to Walsh in early 1940.[10] That this did not happen was a testament to the party's confidence in its leaders and to the political skills of those leaders, particularly Fraser and Walsh, who argued that the government's emergency legislation 'will lay the basis for socialism' and insisted on union representation 'on all administrative boards' as a condition of the FOL's support.[11] If conscription was widely accepted, the government's severe treatment of conscientious objectors was justifiably resented in some quarters, particularly in the light of Fraser's and some other ministers' imprisonment in 1917. Some on the left never forgave Fraser for this, or for rigorous wartime censorship, although it has been persuasively argued that he could claim that the First World War was an imperialist war, whereas the Second was a war for the survival of democracy.[12]

While Fraser and Walsh were sympathetic to the idea of a coalition government, the majority view in the party was strongly opposed to it. In July a war cabinet was established, with four Labour (Fraser, Nash, Sullivan and Jones) and two opposition members (Adam Hamilton and Gordon Coates), alongside the existing cabinet, which retained control of domestic policy. The National Party was unhappy with the arrangement, and when Sid Holland replaced Hamilton as leader of the opposition, Hamilton and Coates became increasingly isolated in their own party.[13]

In his first wartime budget, Nash said the government would finance the war out of taxation and savings, rather than Reserve Bank credit or external loans. A 5 per cent national security tax was introduced, the top income tax rate lifted to 77.5 per cent, death and gift duties increased and a tax imposed on excessive profits. Above all, Nash wished to minimise inflation and dependence upon British lenders; his approach reflected Keynes's prescription for wartime finance. In September 1940 the government convened an economic stabilisation conference, which recommended controls on wages and prices.[14]

At the annual conference in April 1941, Roberts and Fraser stressed the importance of unity and discipline. Fraser said the country's war aims must include 'social reconstruction and the building up of a better order in which there shall be no extremes of wealth and poverty and in which men shall be free from the spectre of economic insecurity'.[15] This was a constant theme for the Labour government during and after the war, in domestic and foreign policy alike. The conference unanimously endorsed the government's financial policy and stabilisation and praised Nash, despite calls by Langstone and O'Brien for nationalisation of the trading banks.[16] However, the left was by no means dead. Roberts was narrowly re-elected as president, defeating McMillan by 397 votes to 355, while McMillan was easily re-elected vice-president.[17] 'Big Jim . . . got the shock of his life', Joe Head wrote to Lyon. 'Some of the big unions must have changed their choice & it only needed even a smaller one to have voted for the Doc'.[18] This was the high point of the challenges to Roberts. The following year he defeated McMillan by 457 votes to 209.[19] Nordmeyer, who was elected vice-president in 1942, stood against Roberts for the rest of the 1940s but never came close to defeating him.

Politics became completely overshadowed by the war. The Second New Zealand Division was sent to Greece by the British government in 1941. The fall of Greece and then Crete (where the Allied army was evacuated) threatened the survival of New Zealand's main fighting force and Fraser, who was in Egypt, insisted that the British evacuate as many troops from the island as possible. The division lost over 6000 men killed, captured or wounded. Fraser thereafter insisted that the New Zealand government be fully informed about military operations involving New Zealand forces.[20] Concerned at Britain's weakness in the face of the Japanese threat in the Pacific, the government strengthened ties with the United States, opened an embassy in Washington and appointed Nash as the New Zealand minister (while he remained in cabinet and an MP).[21]

An election was due in 1941. The local body elections in May gave a clear sign that the government was becoming unpopular. Citizens Association tickets (essentially the National Party) trounced Labour in the four main cities. Several MPs lost their seats on local bodies.[22] In a gloomy post-mortem, Karori branch members blamed Labour's defeat on Fraser's leadership, conscription, the government's failure to carry out party policy, the failure of the Price Investigation Tribunal and the lack of a vigorous Labour press.[23] A further warning came when Labour lost the Bay of Plenty by-election, caused by Hultquist's death, in December.

Throughout 1941 the war was going badly for the Allies, and there was a growing public mood to postpone the general election. In October the National Party agreed to Fraser's request to delay it by a year.[24] Japan's surprise attack on Pearl Harbour in December 1941 brought the war much closer to home; with the German attack on the Soviet Union in June, the war was now global. Over the New Year 'a real sense of emergency gripped New Zealand for the first time since the war had begun'.[25] In January 1942 civilian manpower controls were introduced to direct workers to, and retain them in, essential industries. In effect, this was civilian conscription. In April, rationing of essentials, which had begun early in the war, was extended.[26]

In January 1942 union unhappiness with the government's economic policy boiled over in an angry meeting between the Federation of Labour (FOL), the cabinet and the Labour Party executive. The government had waited nearly a year before acting on the recommendations of the stabilisation conference. Prices continued to rise. The FOL had applied for a general wage order; following Pearl Harbour, the Arbitration Court rejected the claim.[27] McLagan told the meeting that the FOL 'were taken for fools . . . we agreed to price stabilisation and took the blame from the rank and file . . . The

Government let us down—they failed in their promise to stabilise.' On the second day of the meeting a shouting match between Fraser and McLagan ended with the prime minister threatening to resign. 'You have a great chance now Peter!' McLagan replied. Nash, Webb and Eddy intervened to calm things down and Fraser concluded the meeting on a conciliatory note, conceding that 'The wave of unpopularity at present comes from war conditions and the blame for everything falls on the Government'.[28]

The immediate result of the meeting was a new application to the Arbitration Court, which gave a 5 per cent wage increase and an increase in the family benefit. The long-term outcome was the expansion and tightening of stabilisation. In December 1942 the government announced a revised scheme, with strict controls on wages, prices, rents and other costs. Wages could only be increased if the wartime price index rose by more than 5 per cent.[29] An Economic Stabilisation Commission was created with wide powers, including the use of subsidies. By the end of the war, subsidies cost £8.9 million. Numerous committees and councils were set up to work with business, farmers and unions. 'The profusion of consultation was no doubt useful in securing consent for the highly managed economy.'[30] McLagan was appointed to the Legislative Council and cabinet as minister of industrial manpower, and Walsh to the Economic Stabilisation Commission, where he played a key role in managing Labour's wartime economic policy.[31] After Armstrong's death in late 1942, O'Brien was elected to cabinet and given transport and marine.

During 1942 the war continued to go badly for the Allies. Japanese forces moved rapidly through South East Asia and into the Pacific. The National Party continued to demand a coalition government, as did the Returned Servicemen's Association, while Labour's annual conference rejected the idea. In June the Labour and National caucuses agreed to form a war administration of seven government and six opposition members with responsibility for the war effort, while the domestic cabinet continued. Holland was appointed deputy chair of the new body and the war cabinet. It was agreed that the election would be postponed again.[32] Many Labour activists were unhappy. Harry Lord, the national president of the Printers' Union, told his party branch, 'he did not know of anything that had caused more discussion and argument in the Labour Movement'.[33]

The war administration lasted only three months. A strike by Huntly miners resulted in prosecutions under the emergency regulations. Several were jailed. There was a threat of a national miners' strike and the Auckland Trades Council pledged its 'whole-hearted support to the Waikato miners in their struggle to maintain working class conditions'.[34] Webb proposed a compromise: the government would take over the mines for the rest of the war, pay the owners a return on their investment and cancel the prosecutions. This was accepted by all ministers except Holland, who claimed that the rule of law had been subverted and that this was a step towards nationalisation of the mines. He persuaded the other opposition members to resign, collapsing the war administration. Coates and Hamilton immediately re-joined the war cabinet. After this, there was no further serious discussion about a coalition.[35]

When parliament met in February 1943, Fraser moved that a general election be held that year. After the Soviet victory at Stalingrad and the Allied victory in North Africa, the tide was turning. In the face of the Japanese threat, Australia withdrew its troops from the Middle East. There were demands that New Zealand follow suit, although Roosevelt and Churchill urged that the Second Division should stay in North Africa. Fraser came to the same view and adroitly manoeuvred to win agreement from caucus, cabinet, the National Party and parliament. Some have regarded this as evidence of colonial cringe, but there were cogent reasons for the decision. The New Zealand troops were now well trained for desert warfare; bringing them home would have been dangerous, and the Allied strategy was to beat Hitler first.[36]

The government faced growing complaints from the public about wartime controls. 'Everywhere there were shortages, occasional electricity blackouts and only intermittent supplies of gas . . . With shipping in short supply, coal was slow to reach its domestic markets . . . New Zealand's over-commitment to the war effort seemed to permeate every neighbourhood and affect every household.'[37] These concerns were echoed within the party. The Otago LRC passed a vote of no confidence in Fraser as 'the rank & file have lost faith in him'.[38] The government lost two key ministers with the sudden deaths in April and May of Paikea and Coates. Paikea had led the mobilisation of Māori support for the war, establishing the Māori War Effort Organisation, based on some 380 tribal committees.[39] Coates, a First World War veteran, had become detached from the National Party and formed a close bond with Fraser, who relied on him heavily for his understanding of military affairs.[40]

The domestic challenges Labour faced were as great as those overseas. In expanding the welfare state, the government endeavoured to deal with its unpopularity, but also to make clear a vision for the post-war order. Presenting the parliamentary party's report to the 1943 annual conference, Fraser focused on the government's plans for rehabilitation of the troops when they returned from the war. 'If millions can be spent in order that we may win the war,' he said, 'then the people . . . have every right to . . . expect that money will be provided for the costs of peace. If democracy can organise itself to wage war successfully, it should organise equally well to give work and security to every citizen'.[41] Major Jerry Skinner, MP for Motueka, who had won a military cross for his conduct during the El Alamein campaign, was brought home and became minister of rehabilitation. The 1943 budget acted on Fraser's promise of social justice. Family benefits were raised from 6s to 7s 6d and pensions increased. The government announced that it would build another 3600 state houses.[42]

The Labour Party went into the election a much weaker organisation than it had been before the war. 'Many branches lapsed for varying periods during the war, or disappeared altogether; between 1939 and 1943 there was a net loss of 240 branches.' The *Standard* admitted that the 'war years have destroyed well-knit units of the Party in numerous places'.[43] For the first time Labour faced a serious challenge on the left from Lee. In 1942 his Democratic Labour Party had collapsed, but it was reformed in 1943 as the Democratic Soldier Labour Party, which stood 53 candidates.

Labour's campaign relied heavily on its record. It said unemployment had been banished, national income more than doubled, social security and health benefits provided for all, dairy farmers rescued from bankruptcy, thousands of state houses built, the 40-hour week established, manufacturing doubled, extensive public works built, better education provided, from kindergarten to university, wages increased from £65 million to £155 million and Post Office savings by 70 per cent.[44] Campaigning, however, was difficult because of wartime restrictions. Lee dubbed it the 'blackout election'.[45] Labour was determined to defeat Lee and Barnard (who stood as an independent). Through its trades councils, the FOL published a hard-hitting leaflet headed 'This Man Apes the Fascists' denouncing Lee, while his reply slated the 'Communist-Controlled Executive of the Federation of Labour'.[46]

On election night, 25 September 1943, it looked as though Labour had lost.

When the votes of the troops overseas were added it had a clear majority, with 45 seats to National's 34. Labour held five seats because of the services' vote, which was also decisive in the re-election of Harry Atmore, an independent MP who supported the government, retaining Nelson.[47] Fraser quipped that 'it was not only North Africa that the Second Division had saved'.[48] National won eight seats from Labour, four because the Democratic Soldier Labour Party split the vote. The 1943 election consolidated National's hold on rural New Zealand and accentuated the urban–rural division in electoral support.[49] Labour's vote fell nearly 10 per cent from 1938, to 48 per cent. It lost two of its three women MPs, Catherine Stewart and Mary Dreaver in Waitematā. (The third, Mabel Howard, had won a by-election early in 1943 for Armstrong's seat of Christchurch East. On the death of her father, Ted, in 1939 she had been beaten for nomination for the seat by Bob Macfarlane.) Fraser was re-elected with his lowest share of the vote since 1918 after a strong challenge from Colin Scrimgeour, whom the government had sacked as head of commercial broadcasting.[50] On the positive side, Labour won back Grey Lynn and Napier and Tiaki Ōmana defeated Āpirana Ngata in Eastern Māori. The Māori Labour committees, many of which had gone into recess, were revived during the election campaign and the national executive applauded the 'splendid effort' of the party's Māori organisation in winning all four Māori seats for Labour for the first time.[51]

After the election, a correspondent in the *Far Eastern Survey* praised Labour's 'remarkably fine' record:

> The mobilisation of one-third of the entire population for war service; the enrolment in the armed forces of one man out of every two of military age; the simultaneous unprecedented expansion of agricultural production, factory output and defence construction to meet New Zealand's own needs, to help feed the people of Britain and to provide for reciprocal aid to the United States on an ambitious scale; the stabilisation of wages, costs and prices to an extent unequalled in any other country; above all, the maintenance, in spite of the war, of a programme of social services and social security recognised as the most comprehensive and liberal in the world, together with a rehabilitation scheme for ex-servicemen, much in advance of the similar measures which most other countries are still only considering—all these are positive achievements.[52]

A few days after the election Fraser fell seriously ill and nearly died. Nash and Sullivan were also unwell. The cabinet was ageing: Skinner, Nordmeyer and Tirikātene (who replaced Paikea) were the only ministers under 50. The government was in need of renewal, but Fraser was loath to replace old comrades (O'Brien, for instance, became a minister in 1942 when already in his late sixties).[53]

Planning for reconstruction

By 1944 it was clear the Allies would win the war and there was increasing emphasis on post-war reconstruction. The Labour government played an active part in the international conferences to plan the new order. The January 1944 Australia–New Zealand Agreement cemented its close relationship with the Australian Labor government, declaring the two countries' common interests in the Pacific (which rather annoyed Washington). Fraser attended a Commonwealth prime ministers' conference in London.[54] Nash represented New Zealand at the International Labour Organisation conference in Philadelphia, which he chaired, and the Bretton Woods conference, which created the International Monetary Fund and the World Bank. Everywhere they went, the Labour leaders emphasised the rights of small countries and the need for full employment and social justice.[55]

While Fraser and Nash were away, caucus supporters of monetary reform were organising. A caucus committee unanimously recommended that the government buy the remaining private shares in the Bank of New Zealand. On the eve of the 1944 annual conference, Fraser and Nash tried to overturn the caucus decision but were defeated.[56] The conference voted unanimously in favour of nationalisation of the bank, with the aim of helping the rehabilitation of returned servicemen and the reconstruction and development of New Zealand.[57] Roberts described the atmosphere at the conference as like a revivalist meeting. There was great applause for Langstone, who said nationalisation would 'make it possible for the sunshine of economic prosperity and progress to shine in even the darkest places'.[58]

Unrealistic though this was, Langstone captured the spirit of optimism in the Labour movement that progressive policies would prevail after the war. The national executive's report to the 1945 annual conference hailed Labour's victory in Britain and asserted that in English-speaking countries the cry of the workers and returned soldiers was, 'If these things can be done in New Zealand, they must be done here!'[59]

In April 1945 the conference to form a United Nations organisation opened in San Francisco. Fraser and Bert Evatt, the Australian foreign minister, played a leading part in arguing for the rights of small countries and for a trusteeship system to help colonies gain independence. They fought unsuccessfully against the great powers having a veto on the Security Council. Fraser earned 'the reputation of being one of the few consciences at the San Francisco conference'.[60] He and Evatt had more success in promoting full employment, which was written into article 55 of the United Nations charter.[61]

Decolonisation applied in New Zealand's own back yard, as Fraser came to realise. In 1944, as minister of island territories, he visited Samoa and 'became aware that his government's policy . . . had been an inadequate one'.[62] If the more oppressive dimensions of the 1920s regime had been mitigated, there was little sense of future development. Nor was Fraser unaware that his idealistic rhetoric at the United Nations would be less credible if he did not address the desire of Samoans for self-government. In 1946, as the government brought Samoa into the UN trusteeship system, Samoan leaders petitioned for independence. Fraser accepted that this was inevitable and desirable, and in 1947 confirmed the appointment of a young historian, J.W. Davidson, to advise on the Samoan situation (Davidson would later advise Samoan leaders on an independent constitution). Fraser's government established a Council of State, consisting of a high commissioner and three Samoan chiefs; early in 1949 Guy Powles, who had had a distinguished career as a soldier and diplomat, was appointed high commissioner. Powles served in that role until 1960.[63]

After the Allied victory in 1945, the government faced the difficult job of moving from the restrictions of war to the freedom people wanted in peace. The government faced some tough economic problems. It was anxious to avoid a repeat of the boom, runaway inflation and slump which followed the First World War. Money supply had nearly trebled during the war and increased production was needed to meet the demand for goods and services and reduce inflationary pressures. The government continued strict price controls, subsidies, rationing and wage controls. The immediate priority was rehabilitation of returned servicemen and women. In short order, £23 million was paid in gratuities for overseas service. 'With subsidised apprenticeships, university study, farm settlement and concessionary loans for business and housing, rehabilitation expenditure peaked at close to £21m in 1947 and averaged £19m between 1946 and 1952.'[64]

Rehabilitation was widely supported, but there was growing resentment at the government's controls. The number of strikes more than doubled in 1944 and increased again in 1945.[65] In February 1946, Walsh presented a report to the Federation of Labour's national council arguing that wage stabilisation should continue and that workers' living standards could be increased only by greater production. This was bitterly opposed by militant unionists and the Communist Party, which had grown in numbers and influence during the war.[66]

Despite the difficulties, Labour pressed ahead with reform. The centrepiece was the Employment Act 1945, which empowered a new employment service to promote and maintain full employment. A universal family benefit paid to mothers of 10s per child per week was introduced in 1946. There were big increases in education and health spending.[67] Two weeks' annual holidays for all workers were introduced in 1944, and a minimum wage and a 40-hour week in all shops and offices in 1945.[68]

The government nationalised the remaining private coal mines and the struggling private airlines. Nationalising the mines was an old ambition, which Paddy Webb was able to see enacted before ill health forced his retirement in 1946, and the government saw both coal and aviation as essential to economic development.[69] More reluctantly, Nash introduced legislation to take over the Bank of New Zealand. Over 10,000 workers, organised by the Wellington Trades Council and the Wellington LRC, marched on parliament to support nationalisation; this was one of the biggest demonstrations in Wellington's history.[70]

The demonstration was a sign of the rejuvenation of the Labour movement after the war. In November 1945 the party and unions celebrated 10 years of Labour in office. In Auckland, 15,000 trade unionists participated in a march through the city to the Domain, where a large crowd was addressed by cabinet ministers, MPs and union leaders.[71] In Wellington, 2000 people took part in a Cavalcade of Labour which marched to parliament.[72] Branch membership revived considerably. In the year to 28 February 1947, 139 new branches were formed (many during the 1946 election campaign), while others came out of their wartime hibernation. The number of branches rose to 620, equalling the record number in 1938–39. Branches had 31,435 members and the 778 affiliated unions 130,620 members. Labour's total membership of 162,055 was a big improvement on the war years, but well down on the 1939–40 peak of 236,605.[73]

Another sign of the party's rejuvenation was the enthusiastically supported campaign for a Labour daily newspaper. After the 1938 election, Savage had been determined that Labour should have its own dailies to counter the conservative press. In 1941 New Zealand Labour Newspapers Ltd was established, with Roberts as chair and Percy Dowse, a member of the national executive, as secretary.[74] At the 1944 annual conference a campaign was launched to raise advance subscriptions and additional share capital.[75] Unions and party branches dug deep to raise money for the *Southern Cross*, which published its first edition in Wellington on 4 March 1946: 186 unions contributed £10 or more. The largest amounts came from the Wellington Hotel Workers' (£4000), the United Mine Workers' (£4459) and the Waterside Workers' (£7121) unions, the New Zealand Workers' Union (£9590) and the Amalgamated Society of Railway Servants (£10,000). Four hundred branches raised £10 or more for shares and subscriptions. Ninety of these gave £100 or more, and four gave over £500: Riccarton (£581), Petone (£589), Epuni–Waiwhetū (£731) and Wellington North (£970).[76] The *Southern Cross* lasted five years. It was praised for its innovative journalism but was hamstrung from the start by inadequate finance and by interference from Labour and union leaders.[77] Jim Thorn said that it was 'an improvisation to meet an emergency'.[78]

Post-war difficulties

Despite the rejuvenation, the Labour Party was a conservative organisation dominated by a small group of leaders reluctant to share power or tolerate new ideas. After the outbreak of war and Lee's expulsion there was little tolerance for dissent. Close co-operation between the executive, the leaders of the parliamentary party and the FOL executive meant that the leadership aggregated power at the expense of the membership. Five men—Fraser, Nash, McLagan, Walsh and Roberts—dominated the Labour movement and held the keys of power.[79]

Labour faced a difficult election campaign in 1946. The party polled badly in the 1944 local body elections; its vote was down in the five by-elections between 1944 and 1946 and it lost one seat, Raglan.[80] In 1945 the government abolished the country quota, which had given rural electorates a 28 per cent population weighting against cities and larger towns. The National Party fought hard against the legislation, which was passed with Labour MPs singing 'The Red Flag' and National MPs 'God Save the King'. The number of rural seats fell from 36 to 31, although one authority doubted that the country quota had ever advantaged the conservatives as much as they thought.[81]

At the 1946 annual conference the government launched an ambitious 'Ten Year Plan', which included greater stimulus for secondary industries and public works and increased social security benefits.[82] Labour ran a vigorous campaign. Over a million pamphlets were distributed, over 60 large hoardings used throughout the country and over 10,000 posters issued. Election advertisements were shown in every picture theatre.[83] As the campaign went on, Labour's message became more negative. It emphasised that a National victory would mean a return to the bad old days of the Depression, a message that still resonated with many voters.[84]

Labour won narrowly, with 42 seats to National's 38. Its vote rose to 537,632, exceeding the 1938 total. Its share of votes increased by nearly 4 per cent to 51.3 per cent. Right-wingers, particularly the *New Zealand Herald*'s cartoonist, Minhinnick, maintained that the four Māori seats gave the government its majority, and played on this theme with a less than subtle racism. There were some close results. Labour won Raglan with a majority of 13 after an electoral petition. It held five other seats by less than 250 votes. Six National seats were in the same position.[85]

After the election there was a renewal of sorts in the government. Two new ministers were elected: Ted Cullen (minister of agriculture) and Fred Hackett (postmaster-general and minister of transport). To Fraser's dismay, Rex Mason was defeated. Fraser kept him in his ministerial posts until he was re-elected by caucus in May 1947 (the caucus had few lawyers and Mason was needed as attorney-general). Also in 1947, after the deaths of Sullivan and O'Brien, Mabel Howard and Terry McCombs were elected. Howard, who was New Zealand's first woman cabinet minister, became minister of health and McCombs minister of education. While Howard was more visible than capable, it was unforgivable to have left McCombs on the back bench since 1935, when he had succeeded his mother in Lyttelton.[86] There were some younger faces in caucus: Alan Baxter, Martyn Finlay, Paddy Kearins,

CIVIL SERVANTS

Under NATIONAL Rule	*Under LABOUR Rule*
Wages cut by 20 per cent. Promotions practically stopped. Thousands of casual employees dismissed. P. and T. Association not recognised. Dismissals, without appeal, for criticising the Government. Grave unrest throughout Civil Service.	Wages cuts restored. Reclassification being carried out. Granted full political privileges. Forty-hour week and five-day week being instituted as rapidly as possible. Thousands of new employees. Anomalies being rapidly rectified.

KEEP LABOUR IN POWER

EDUCATION

Under NATIONAL Rule	*Under LABOUR Rule*
Five-year-old child excluded. Training colleges closed. Schools in disrepair. School teachers on relief. All education grants reduced.	Five-year-old children readmitted. New schools being built everywhere. Reopened training colleges. Teachers' salaries increased and conditions improved. Increased education expenditure of £950,000 compared with 1935.

LET LABOUR FINISH THE JOB

PUBLIC WORKS

Under NATIONAL Rule	*Under LABOUR Rule*
Public Works brought to a standstill, workers dismissed in thousands. Public Works turned into relief camps paying as little as 10/- weekly. Degrading conditions rampant. Wheelbarrow and shovel in general use.	Public Works camps models of convenience and comfort. Best working conditions in history. Minimum wage of 16/- daily. Average wage earned £1 daily. Employees increased by over 8,000. Latest machinery installed.

LET LABOUR FINISH THE JOB

Previous page, What Labour Means to You:

Top: Education. The first Labour government moved quickly to restore the Coalition's cuts in education and Labour capitalised on this in its 1938 election campaign. What Labour Means to You. Eph-A-NZ-LABOUR-1938-01-007, Alexander Turnbull Library

Middle: Public Works. Labour's vigorous public works programme was central to its policies of economic development and reducing unemployment. What Labour Means to You. Eph-A-NZ-LABOUR-1938-01-011, Alexander Turnbull Library

Bottom: Civil Servants. Before 1936 public servants employed by central government, schools, the railways and post office had to resign from their jobs if they stood for political office, and the government placed restrictions on public servants' trade unions. Labour restored the Depression wage cuts and gave public servants full political rights. What Labour Means to You. Eph-A-NZ-LABOUR-1938-01-013, Alexander Turnbull Library

Above: Group photograph outside parliament of delegates and observers attending the 1936 Labour Party annual conference. Wilfred (Bill) McAra papers. MSS & Archives A-139, item 2/39, Special Collections, University of Auckland Libraries and Learning Services

CHANDLER & Co. LTD
No 45.
NOW THEN !
"To Ensure
Social Justice
and Security_
VOTE LABOUR"

Above, left: Catherine Campbell Stewart (1881–1957), MP for Wellington West from 1938 to 1943, was Labour's second woman MP. Born in Scotland, Stewart became active in the labour and women's movements there as a young woman. She was tutored in economics by the socialist John Maclean. After emigrating to New Zealand, she was prominent in the Wellington women's branch of the Labour Party and the co-operative movement. She had strong socialist opinions and was one of a handful of Labour MPs who voted against John A. Lee's expulsion from the party in 1940. R. Holland Collection. PAColl-4415-04, Alexander Turnbull Library

Above, right: Pita Moko (1885–1943) (seated) holding the Paipera Tapu (Holy Bible) and Eruera Tirikātene (1895–1967) holding Te Tiriti o Waitangi (the Treaty of Waitangi). Moko was private secretary to Tahupōtiki Wiremu Rātana. Tirikātene was elected as Rātana MP for Southern Māori in 1932. After the 1935 election, he and Haami Tokouru Rātana (Tahupōtiki's eldest son), MP for Western Māori, joined the Labour Party. Tirikātene held the electorate until his death in 1967. He was a minister in the Fraser government from 1943 to 1949 and the Nash government, 1957–60. New Zealand Labour Party collection

Opposite, top: Backbench Labour MPs in parliament in 1936. Back row from left: Charles Barrell (Hamilton), William Denham (Invercargill), Bert Christie (Waipawa), Ted Cullen (Hawke's Bay), speaking, Morgan Williams (Kaiapoi), Ben Roberts (Wairarapa). Middle row: Joe Cotterill (Whanganui), Len Lowry (Ōtaki), Alex Moncur (Rotorua), Charles Petrie (Hauraki), Robert Coulter (Waikato), Charles Burnett (Tauranga). Front row: Arthur Richards (Roskill), Fred Schramm (Auckland East), Clyde Carr (Timaru). Vera Wood photographs of New Zealand Labour Party and socialist groups. Ref: MSS & Archives Vault 30, Special Collections, University of Auckland Libraries and Learning Services

Opposite, bottom: Labour's popular prime minister Michael Joseph Savage was the face of the party's 1938 general election campaign. This poster was one among three sets of posters displayed on 93 hoardings throughout New Zealand. It was produced by Chandler & Co. Ltd, advertising contractors and designers. New Zealand Labour Party. PAColl-5364-002, Alexander Turnbull Library

Above: In the 1930s, Labour Party branches organised lots of social activities, including card evenings, dances and balls. This photograph was taken at the Labour victory ball in New Plymouth in 1938, held to celebrate the government's re-election and the election of Fred Frost as the first Labour MP for New Plymouth. New Zealand Labour Party collection

Opposite, top: Peter Fraser (1884–1950) standing in front of a group of soldiers from the Sixth New Zealand Infantry Brigade, while visiting New Zealand troops in the Cassino area, Italy in May 1944. Fraser made a particular effort to visit New Zealand troops during his overseas visits in the Second World War. George Robert Bull photograph. War History Branch: Photographs relating to WorldWar 1914–18, World War 1939–45, occupation of Japan, Korean War and Malayan Emergency. DA-05818-F, Alexander Turnbull Library

Opposite, bottom: The joint conference of the Labour Party's national executive and the Federation of Labour's national council on 21 February 1940 reaffirmed the labour movement's traditional opposition to conscription. The fall of France and the Nazi threat to Britain would lead to the party and federation changing their position at emergency conferences in June. Front row: Richard Eddy (FOL vice-president) second from left, Angus McLagan (FOL president) fourth from left, James Roberts (Labour Party president) fifth from left, Michael Moohan (Labour Party acting national secretary) sixth from left, Fintan Patrick Walsh (FOL executive member) far right. New Zealand Labour Party. PAColl-1179-09-03, Alexander Turnbull Library

Above: John Alexander Lee (1891–1982) was MP for Auckland East from 1922 to 1928 and Grey Lynn from 1931 to 1943. He was one of Labour's most gifted speakers and propagandists. His attacks on Savage and Labour's economic policy led to his expulsion from the party in 1940. S.P. Andrew Ltd: Portrait negatives. Ref: 1/4-020175-F, Alexander Turnbull Library

Left: Labour emphasised what it had done for families in This—in Your Hands, one of its main pamphlets in the 1946 election campaign; 400,000 copies were distributed. New Zealand Labour Party. Eph-A-NZ-LABOUR-1946-04, Alexander Turnbull Library

Below: As the 1946 election campaign went on, Labour's message became more negative. This 'Fox' cartoon, published in the *Standard* on 21 November 1946, accuses National of cooking up again the policies of the Depression. A-313-2-052, Alexander Turnbull Library

1935
1945
20,000
FIDO
GOVT. HOUSING
1935
1945
Two & Under
NIL
After Second
2/-
Means Test 65/-
10/- each Child
regardless of Income
FAMILY BENEFIT
1935
1945
17/6 at 65
40/-
at 60
OLD AGE PENSIONS
Secure Your Future—
VOTE LABOUR!
CHRISTIE PRINT
Ten Years'
1935 - 1945
Progress

1935
1945
80,000
NIL
UNEMPLOYMENT
1935
1945
£49,424,000
£113,492,000
Post Office Savings Bank
and National Savings
1935
1945
257
50
BANKRUPTCIES
1935
1945
66 Millions
176½ Millions
WAGES and SALARIES

Above: Peter Fraser addressing the Cavalcade of Labour which marched to parliament carrying banners featuring a photograph of Savage on 1 December 1945 as part of the celebrations of the Labour government's ten years in office. James Roberts (right) and Walter Nash (left) are standing behind Fraser. Fintan Patrick Walsh (president, Wellington Trades Council) is to Nash's left and Jim Collins (secretary, Wellington Labour Representation Committee), standing with his head bowed, is to Fraser's right. New Zealand Labour Party. PAColl-5364-01, Alexander Turnbull Library

Opposite: The Labour government's main achievements in its first ten years were summarised in this 1946 election leaflet, 150,000 copies of which were distributed. New Zealand Labour Party. Eph-A-NZ-LABOUR-1946-03, Alexander Turnbull Library

HOW?

Hardly Eye To Eye!

INDUSTRIES FAIR, NO. 2—THE TIMBER INDUSTRY.

Above: Arnold Nordmeyer (1901–1989), MP for Ōamaru (left), Labour's vice-president, unsuccessfully challenged James Roberts (1881-1967) (centre) for the presidency of the party in the 1940s and finally defeated him in 1950. Michael Moohan (1899-1967) (right) was Labour's national secretary from 1940 to 1946, when he was elected MP for Petone. New Zealand Labour Party. PAColl-1179-02-001, Alexander Turnbull Library

Opposite, top: The Labour government's obsession with communism is captured well in this Neville Colvin cartoon published in the *Evening Post* on 5 May 1949. Angus McLagan (minister of labour) wields the axe, the cat is the police, Arnold Nordmeyer (minister of industries and commerce) holds the eviction order, Walter Nash (deputy prime minister) has the promise not to squeak, Mabel Howard (minister of health) sprinkles salt on the rat's tail, Rex Mason (minister of justice) contemplates making rats illegal, Bob Semple (minister of works) holds a parody of his pamphlet Why I Fight Communism, Peter Fraser (prime minister) looks perplexed and Sid Holland (National Party leader) is sitting reading The Pied Piper of Hamelin. E-549-q-1-023, Alexander Turnbull Library

Opposite, middle: The move by a group of right-wing Auckland union officials to stand candidates against Labour in 1951 was seized on by the press as a sign of divisions in the party. Their plans were squashed by the Federation of Labour and the party. Nash is unfairly characterised as 'neither for nor against'. Neville Colvin, *Evening Post*, 26 July 1951. E-549-q-04-062, Alexander Turnbull Library

Opposite, bottom: Nash and Labour were caught napping by Prime Minister Sid Holland's announcement of a snap election in September 1951. Keith Waite, *Otago Daily Times*, 8 September 1951. E-549-q-05-008, Alexander Turnbull Library

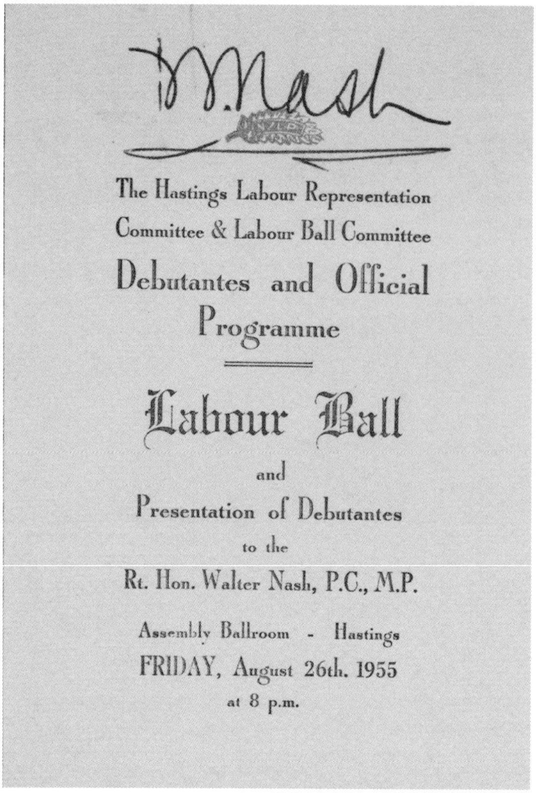

W. Nash

The Hastings Labour Representation Committee & Labour Ball Committee

Debutantes and Official Programme

Labour Ball

and

Presentation of Debutantes

to the

Rt. Hon. Walter Nash, P.C., M.P.

Assembly Ballroom - Hastings

FRIDAY, August 26th. 1955

at 8 p.m.

Above, left: Walter Nash's signed copy of the programme for the Hastings Labour Ball and presentation of debutantes, 26 August 1955. Balls were regular events on the party's social calendar until the 1960s and often included presentations of debutantes. New Zealand Labour Party. Eph-A-NZ-LABOUR-1955-01, Alexander Turnbull Library

Above, right: 'There is a Swing to Labour', the words and music to the party's 1957 campaign song. New Zealand Labour Party. Eph-B-NZ-LABOUR-19587-01, Alexander Turnbull Library

N.Z.L.P.

A cordial invitation is extended to

to celebrate the 50th ANNIVERSARY of the
GREYMOUTH BRANCH OF N.Z. LABOUR PARTY
and the
WESTLAND LABOUR REPRESENTATION COMMITTEE
also the 21st ANNIVERSARY of the
GREYMOUTH WOMEN'S BRANCH OF THE N.Z.L.P.
at a

BUFFET TEA and SOCIAL EVENING

in the LYCEUM HALL on NOVEMBER 25, 1967, at 6 p.m.

Admission: Double $3, Single $2

R.S.V.P. by October 30th — C. S. POWICK, Secretary
P.O. Box 157, Greymouth. — J. E. LAING, President

Right: Invitation to a celebration to mark the 50th anniversary of the Greymouth branch and the Westport LRC and the 21st anniversary of the Greymouth women's branch. New Zealand Labour Party. Eph-A-NZ-LABOUR-1967-01, Alexander Turnbull Library

Previous page: Labour Party annual conference 1950 in Auckland. Front row (left to right): W.J. Butler (press officer), H.E. Combs (national executive), J.D. Davey (*Standard* reporter), J.B. Standring (timekeeper), J.T. Head (timekeeper), Walter Nash (deputy leader), Arnold Nordmeyer (president-elect), James Roberts (retiring president), Peter Fraser (leader), Allan McDonald (national secretary), R.B. McNeill (head office), J.H. Collins (minute secretary), Frank Percy (head office), E. Hutton (Auckland LRC), Ray Boord (assistant national secretary). New Zealand Labour Party. PAColl-1179-08-001, Alexander Turnbull Library

Tom Skinner and Ormond Wilson. They were joined by Warren Freer, who won the Mt Albert by-election in 1947. They often supported Langstone's criticisms of government policy in caucus and had a difficult relationship with Fraser, whose approach sometimes appeared to these more libertarian younger people as 'a purse-lipped culture of censorious rectitude'.[87]

As the war ended, there were hopes among Māori that their contribution on and off the battlefield would be recognised. The Māori Advisory Committee's report to the 1944 conference said: 'The time has arrived for affording to the Maori a greater responsibility and share in the administration of his own domestic affairs.' The committee proposed a raft of remits, most of which were adopted. They included retention of the Māori Emergency War Organisation, replacement of the Board of Native Affairs and a royal commission to investigate all Māori land claims and grievances.[88]

In 1946 Fraser became minister of Māori affairs. He was sympathetic and receptive to Māori concerns, replaced 'Native' with 'Māori' in official usage, and specified that a Māori should be secretary of Māori affairs. In 1948 Tipi Rōpiha was appointed. He and Fraser backed Māori initiatives to manage their own land (for example, on the East Coast), helped the promotion of Māori culture, supported Māori community development in urban areas and encouraged Māori women's involvement in the community.[89] There were settlements of land claims with Waikato, Taranaki and Ngāi Tahu,[90] and Māori benefited from Labour's full employment, rehabilitation and social security policies. However, the government ignored Māori views on the Treaty of Waitangi. The Māori Advisory Committee's report to the 1940 conference called for the treaty to 'be recognised by Statute Law' and a royal commission to be set up 'to assess the amount that should be paid as compensation for alleged confiscation of Maori lands'.[91]

Māori aspirations for a greater role in government, which were strongly supported by their MPs, were not realised. Control remained in Pākehā hands and the Māori Affairs Department was crucial in limiting the possibilities of Māori development.[92] Quite apart from the legitimate desire of Māori to have one of their own as minister, despite his good intentions Fraser was too busy to give Māori affairs the attention it required. Regardless of the limitations of Labour's policies, Māori remained loyal supporters. Labour's Māori organisation was strengthened after the war. In the year to 28 February 1947 there were 257 Māori Labour committees.[93]

In its last three years in office Labour faced a number of challenges in managing the economy. There was an emphasis on production to make up for the shortages of goods and services. While good progress was made, most of the wartime controls were kept. The Control of Prices Act 1947 and the Economic Stabilisation Act 1948 'set up permanent institutional structures to achieve social control'.[94] Imports remained scarce and shortages of capital goods from overseas hindered the country's reconstruction. New Zealand was part of the sterling area, which meant that its overseas funds were managed by Britain. Facing a dire economic situation, the British Labour government coerced New Zealand and other Commonwealth countries into cancelling large amounts of their sterling balances. In March 1947 the government made a 'gift' of £10 million sterling to Britain. It then came under sustained British pressure to restrict spending of US dollars on much needed imports, and even to forego British imports that London could sell elsewhere for dollars.[95]

Rationing continued, to build up food exports to Britain. Shortages were a constant irritation for people: 'In the mind of the public . . . they led to a positive identification of Labour as the party of scarcity and rationing'.[96] Housing shortages were a major problem, with worldwide shortages of materials. Despite great efforts by the construction industry and the government, the building of new houses—both private and state—fell well short of demand and there were significant increases in costs.[97] And despite the government's controls and subsidies, inflation too was a problem. Retail prices rose by 12.2 per cent between 1946 and 1949.[98]

In 1945 the government introduced a new system of general wage orders to allow wages to be adjusted for price increases, but this did little to diminish frustration among workers. Working days lost annually through strikes rose to 218,172 in 1949. In comparison, days lost averaged 34,038 between 1936 and 1939.[99] In late 1946 the Waterside Workers' Union's claim for guaranteed attendance money led to an overtime ban. There was a major clash with the government after the union—led by the militants Jock Barnes and Toby Hill—refused the FOL's assistance. McLagan, who became minister of labour in 1946, settled the dispute on terms favourable to the watersiders. It was 'a significant victory and for a short heady period the militants were riding high'.[100] At the 1947 FOL conference, the militant and Labour Party member Bill Richards beat Walsh for the vice-presidency by one vote. There was a fierce struggle between the left and right wings of the union movement which consumed much energy in the late 1940s. In

1948 Walsh defeated Richards, and the Communist-dominated executive of the Auckland Trades Council, which had been a power base of the militants, was ousted.[101]

In the Labour Party there was a crackdown on dissent. The 1948 annual conference unanimously adopted a national executive recommendation that any party member 'who publicly expresses or publishes statements at variance with the Party's policy in any way calculated to cause dissension or disunity . . . may be expelled'.[102] Annual conferences had traditionally ended with the singing of 'The Red Flag' and 'Auld Lang Syne'. In 1948 the socialist anthem was replaced with 'God Defend New Zealand'. However, the resurgence in Labour's organisation continued. The number of branches rose to 644 in 1948 and 670 in 1949.[103] There was a drive throughout the country to organise young people.[104] The Auckland junior branch had over 300 members.[105] A number of women's branches were formed after 1946. They pressed for a stronger voice in the party, including women's organisers, women's conferences and a women's advisory council. There were meetings of women's delegates before the conference, but the other proposals were rejected.[106]

By the late 1940s post-war optimism had disappeared with the onset of the Cold War between the western Allies and the Soviet Union. There was a pervasive anti-communist mood, encouraged by the press and both major political parties. The communist-led Auckland Carpenters' Union was involved in a dispute over travelling time which led to a lockout. The FOL backed the carpenters, but reversed its position after Fraser publicly denounced their leaders, and proposed that it take over the dispute. The carpenters refused, missing the opportunity to beat an orderly retreat. In March, McLagan deregistered the union. The employers helped form a scab union, which the government registered.[107]

The dispute soured relationships within the Labour movement. Fraser's determination to introduce peacetime conscription made things worse. For all its independence in foreign policy, Labour was firmly part of the Anglo-American camp. Fraser returned home from the Commonwealth prime ministers' conference at the end of January 1949 convinced that New Zealand should introduce peacetime conscription. It has been suggested that, as well as fearing another war and noting the enthusiasm of some Eastern European communist parties for killing social democrats, Fraser was haunted by Crete and determined that in future a citizen army would be properly trained.[108] A caucus committee on defence reported in mid-May, saying that all resources should be used for the defence of New Zealand, including conscription if necessary. However, there was strong opposition from left-wing unions and many trades councils.[109] On 21 May, the first day of Labour's annual conference, Fraser denounced communism at length: 'For the past thirty years the Labour Party has had no illusions about the Communists and has uncompromisingly fought them.' The next day he presented the caucus report on defence. There was a long debate, with over 40 speakers. The Canterbury union leaders Archie Grant and Jack Roberts moved an amendment opposing peacetime conscription. Faced with a stalemate, Fraser proposed a compromise: a referendum on compulsory national service. This was carried with only eight votes against.[110]

During July the government campaigned for conscription. With considerable understatement, Finlay later said: 'Fraser did more than support National Service, he actually manipulated the referendum to secure an affirmative answer.'[111] The government funded advertisements and granted supporters, including the National Party and the Returned Servicemen's Association, greater radio time than opponents.[112] LRCs and branches were urged to support government policy and instructed 'not to use under any circumstances whatsoever their funds to support any agitation against the policy of the Government'.[113] Caucus passed a resolution banning MPs from opposing conscription.[114] Some party branches enthusiastically supported compulsory national service and took part in local campaigns.[115] There was also strong opposition within the party.[116] Jack Roberts, who was one of the most respected union leaders, resigned as chair of the North Canterbury LRC. Norman Kirk later said this made enormous political waves within the party. The referendum, Kirk said, was 'a tactical disaster politically', although he argued that Fraser had no choice because war with the Soviet Union seemed inevitable. 'I was against it, I voted against it, I worked against, very nearly left the Party over it, to be honest . . . but I think in fairness [Fraser] had the invidious task of having to tell the people well I don't like it either but I think we've got to do it'.[117] On 3 August the referendum was carried with 568,427 votes for compulsory military service and 160,998 against. 'Many abstained, and the largest "No" votes were in Labour-held electorates. The Prime Minister had won his battle with the help of his political enemies, but it was soon clear he would lose the war.'[118]

The general election was held at the end of November 1949. Labour's manifesto emphasised security for all, opportunity for all, strong economic foundations and national development.[119] As in 1946, the party and the Federation of Labour hammered the message that a National victory would mean wage cuts, the loss of the 40-hour week and the bad old days of the slump. In its last issue before polling day the *Standard* ran a full-page chronology of the Depression. However, these arguments had lost their strength. For all its promises to abolish controls and make the pound go further, National was committed to stabilisation, price controls and social security. It projected a fresh image, with younger candidates against the government's tired and ageing leaders. Its most effective advertisement said: 'Had enough? Change the Government.'[120]

National won a decisive victory, with 46 seats to Labour's 34. Labour lost eight seats, almost all middle-income urban electorates, four of which were in Auckland. It won 47.1 per cent of votes (a fall of 4.1 per cent), while National won 51.9 per cent (a rise of 3.4 per cent).[121]

In his speech to the 1947 annual conference, Fraser summed up the achievements of the first Labour government. It had transformed social and economic conditions in New Zealand, abolished poverty, given the people economic security and established full employment. Rehabilitation had helped returned servicemen and women to resume a normal life. Despite the accumulated problems of the past, government policy had brought about 'a continuous improvement in the economic, social and cultural conditions of the Maori people . . . The goal for both peoples is the same—equal opportunity for all inside a prosperous democratic nation.' Labour's greatest achievement, he said, was social security:

> Before the Labour Government came into office the system of assistance to needy people was largely based on the old Poor Law conception that penury was mainly due to thriftlessness. Relief of poverty was cramped by this niggardly and hardened attitude . . . Labour established it as a right that all citizens should have freedom from want and fear of want and be enabled to live on reasonable and adequate living standards.[122]

6
Terminal Affluence? Labour in Opposition 1949–57

In the 35 years after it first won office National dominated New Zealand politics. There were only two Labour governments between 1949 and 1984, and each lasted only one term. Between 1950 and 1975 New Zealand was prosperous, with a growing economy and population. After the tough times of the Depression and the Second World War, people were focused on earning a decent income, bringing up their families and acquiring material goods to make their lives easier. There was full employment, and National accepted most parts of Labour's Keynesian economic management and the welfare state. During the 1950s and early 1960s international affairs were dominated by the Cold War between the capitalist United States and the communist Soviet Union. Anti-communism was rife in western democracies, including New Zealand, and social democratic parties found themselves squeezed between conservative governments and communist parties. Labour compounded these difficulties by failing to adapt to changing times. The party's failure to renew its leadership and MPs, and its only belated modernisation of policy and organisation, are major themes of this and the next chapter.

Into opposition, 1949–51

Labour was bewildered by and resentful at its defeat in 1949. Nordmeyer, one of Fraser's most able ministers, lost Oamaru. He wrote to Mick Connelly, a Labour legislative councillor, that the biggest single factor in Labour's defeat was 'the desire for a change . . . Selfishness and in many cases just sheer ingratitude were factors that contributed to our defeat.'[1] Finlay, who was elected Labour Party president in 1960, would tell the 1961 conference that Labour talked too much about the days of the Depression. One of the party's great achievements was persuading National to adopt the welfare state. The battle had been won, but at every election since 1949 'we have gone on fighting it'.[2] The failure to renew the parliamentary party was starkly demonstrated by the election of Nash as party leader in 1951 and his 12-year leadership. Nash was one of Labour's giants, but his long period at the top gave Labour the image of being an old party led by old men.

Fraser had belatedly accepted the necessity of renewal. At the 1950 conference, Nordmeyer (with Fraser's support) defeated Roberts for president by 458 votes to 299.[3] In the face of remits calling for a socialist programme and the nationalisation of most industries, the conference set up a committee to review Labour's programme and another to revise the party's constitution and rules, important parts of which had not changed since the mid-1920s.[4] The 1950 local body elections, which in the main cities had been a graveyard for the party for most of the 1940s, prompted optimism. The party made large gains. Macfarlane was re-elected mayor of Christchurch (he had been mayor from 1938 to 1941) and Labour won 12 council seats. Percy Dowse was elected mayor of Lower Hutt and Labour won all the council seats, and a Labour council was elected in Petone. In Wellington, Frank Kitts was narrowly defeated for mayor, six Labour councillors were elected and the party won a majority on the hospital board. Six Labour councillors were elected in Dunedin. While only three Labour councillors were elected in Auckland City, Labour mayors and councils were elected in Ōtāhuhu, Onehunga and New Lynn.[5] Nash said the swing to Labour 'was the culmination of growing resentment against the Government'.[6] The cost of living rose rapidly in 1950 after the government cut food subsidies.

In late September Fraser's health collapsed. After several heart attacks, he died on 12 December 1950.[7] Fraser was one of New Zealand's greatest prime ministers and one of the party's outstanding leaders. While he never enjoyed Savage's popular appeal, he led the country through the difficult war years and post-war reconstruction. As minister of education, health and Māori affairs he was one of the main architects of the welfare state, Labour's greatest achievement. During and after the war he laid the foundations for Labour's independence in foreign policy. Fraser was a superb political organiser and manager who kept a tight grip on the party. He held it together after the left's challenge to Savage threatened a major split. However, his intolerance of dissent damaged democracy within the party and hindered efforts to renew Labour after 1949.

Walter Nash was unanimously elected leader in January 1951. Jerry Skinner was elected deputy.[8] Fraser had wanted Nordmeyer to succeed him,[9] but there is no evidence that Nordmeyer could have won even if he had been in parliament (having lost Oamaru in 1949, he replaced Fraser as MP for Brooklyn in February 1951). Nash had been one of Labour's most prominent figures since the 1920s. As finance minister and deputy prime minister, he was central to the first Labour government's achievements. He and Fraser had one of the great partnerships in New Zealand's political history, but, at 68, Nash was two years older than Fraser.

Nash was immediately plunged into one of the greatest challenges in his long political life. In February there began the biggest industrial dispute in New Zealand's history, the 1951 waterfront lockout, which lasted for nearly five months and cost the country £42 million and over one million working days lost in industrial action. The lockout ended with the complete defeat of the watersiders and their allies.[10]

The waterfront lockout was significant in Labour's history for three reasons. First, it marked the end of the total unity between the party leadership and the Federation of Labour that had been important to the first Labour government's political success. Second, as John Roberts later wrote, the lockout and the snap election that followed it 'consolidated the National Party's power and completed the disintegration of working-class unity in New Zealand politics. It was in every sense a smashing achievement and the foundation of National's claim to be the party of government.'[11] Third, the dispute was a severe test of Labour's commitment to working people and civil liberties. Nash's statement during the lockout that 'we are not for the watersiders nor are we against them' dogged him for the rest of his life.[12] However, as Bruce Brown, Nash's private secretary during the 1950s, later wrote, in his efforts to get a settlement Nash was 'persistent, consistent and principled'.[13]

In 1950 there was a split in the trade union movement which had a major impact on the lockout. Angry at Walsh's dictatorial leadership and cosiness with the government, the watersiders and 50 other delegates walked out of the Federation of Labour's annual conference and set up a rival Trade Union Congress. By isolating themselves from the majority of unions, the watersiders made it easier for their enemies to attack them.[14]

The dispute began when in January 1951 the Arbitration Court awarded a 15 per cent general wage order. Watersiders refused to work overtime after their employers failed to pass on the full increase; the employers insisted on overtime as a condition of work, which the watersiders regarded as a lockout. The National government offered arbitration. The Waterside Workers' Union refused. On 21 February the government declared a state of emergency. Regulations declared the lockout a strike and made it an offence to be a party to the 'strike' or to support the watersiders.[15] Troops, strongly guarded by police, began unloading cargo in Auckland and Wellington. The Waterside Workers' Union was deregistered and its assets seized. Seamen, miners and Wellington freezing workers went on strike against the regulations. Railway workers and drivers refused to handle goods unloaded by non-union labour.[16] The FOL executive supported the government. Michael Bassett later wrote: 'If it was the Government that erected the scaffold and placed the rope round the watersiders' necks it was the FOL which released the trap.'[17]

A special FOL conference in early March adopted a report by Walsh which supported compulsory arbitration and the defence of democracy against communism, and called on the Waterside Workers' Union to co-operate with the FOL. On 21 March the FOL called on all workers to resume work. A number of unions did so, including the railway workers. By the start of April only the seamen, cement workers, Wellington drivers and freezing workers and most of the miners' unions were still on strike. The cement workers', drivers' and freezing workers' unions were deregistered. On 15 March the prime minister, Sid Holland, announced that there were seven points the watersiders would have to accept before negotiations could take place. These were honouring agreements; settling disputes with conciliation and arbitration; increased efficiency; secret ballots on strikes; open entry to waterfront work (and to the union); full-time permanent work on the waterfront; and ensuring watersiders a just reward for their labours.[18]

For the first month of the dispute the Labour Party lay low. Nash made a statement on behalf of the Labour caucus supporting conciliation and arbitration, calling on the government to convene a compulsory conference on the dispute and saying that the regulations went too far.[19] Labour's position was equivocal. The Labour government had introduced most of the laws National used against the watersiders and their allies. Although the Waterside Workers' Union was one of the party's largest affiliated unions, its leaders had clashed frequently with the Labour government. The caucus was divided. McLagan, the former minister of labour, was ill. Nash was inexperienced in industrial relations. Unlike Fraser, he did not have a close relationship with Walsh. The Federation of Labour pressured Labour to support its stand against the watersiders.[20] Nash also came under pressure from sections of the party that wanted a clearer definition of Labour's policy.[21]

On 29 March Nash and FOL secretary Ken Baxter spoke at a public meeting in Hamilton. It was planned that Baxter would speak first, leaving Nash with no option but to support the FOL. Nash evaded the trap. He was privately furious and wrote a note of the meeting accusing Walsh of trying to line him up.[22] In his speech Nash attacked the regulations for curtailing free speech and said the watersiders disagreed with only one of Holland's seven points, which could be settled by a compulsory conference. The press assailed Nash and Holland accused him of fence-sitting.[23]

Isolated though they were, the watersiders and their supporters remained solid. The government's efforts to organise scab watersiders' unions were largely unsuccessful. Relief committees—in which the union's women's auxiliaries were prominent—organised food, clothes and fuel. Thousands of working people in New Zealand and Australia broke the law by donating money and goods. Sympathetic farmers gave food; businesses in working-class areas of the cities gave goods or credit. Publicity committees produced a vast literature of illegal pamphlets and bulletins which were widely distributed.[24] In small mining towns the unionists resisted constant police intimidation.[25] Labour Party members were active in the relief efforts. Labour women such as Alice Cassie, Pat Lenniston, Ethel Tickner and Eileen Doile took part in the women's auxiliaries, often working alongside Communist Party members.[26]

In April the Labour Party made a determined effort to mediate a settlement. Nash, Nordmeyer and Skinner persuaded the Waterside Workers' Union leaders to write to Holland accepting his seven points.[27] Holland was initially conciliatory. He then rejected the watersiders' proposal and added an eighth point: an end to the national union and the registration of separate watersiders' unions in every port.[28] The government, the Department of Labour and the employers worked overtime to form new unions and screen out 'undesirable' watersiders. Holland rejected Nash's call for parliament to be called to discuss the crisis. The government tightened the emergency regulations. Labour was denied access to the radio, while union leaders who supported the government were given air time to denounce the watersiders.[29]

At the FOL's annual conference in late April, Baxter moved a resolution pledging the FOL's support for the return of a Labour government and calling on unions to support, in selections of Labour candidates, party members who co-operated in furthering the FOL's policy on the dispute. He attacked Labour representatives who were sympathetic to the watersiders. This attack on the party was too much for a majority of delegates. An amendment was carried by 138 votes to 91 that the matter be held over until Nash had spoken. Nash outlined the parliamentary party's steps to get a settlement and said he did not offer one word of criticism of what the FOL had done. Tom Skinner (now out of parliament) and Alex Croskery (the FOL president) then moved a motion of confidence in Nash and the Labour Party, which was carried by acclamation.[30]

In May the Labour Party decided to hold public meetings throughout the country. The Auckland LRC tried to book the Town Hall, but the city council refused the booking. The police told Bill Anderton, MP for Auckland Central, that all political meetings were banned. Labour MPs protested and Bill Fortune, the minister of police, reversed the ban.[31] On 13 May Nash addressed a meeting 7000 people in the Auckland Domain; it was here that he made his 'neither for nor against' remark.[32]

At Labour's annual conference in June, Nash presented a confidential report on the lockout. This repeated Labour's call for a compulsory conference and its support for arbitration. It condemned intimidation, victimisation and the Communist Party. The report attacked the government for prolonging the dispute, called for repeal of the emergency regulations, which were 'a grave breach of the principles of democratic freedom', and criticised the victimisation of watersiders in New Plymouth, the first of the large ports to form a scab union. Nash accused the press of being strongly biased, and attacked the shipowners, who had imposed a 50 per cent surcharge on cargo to and from New Zealand in an attempt to recover some of their losses from the dispute.[33]

The Christchurch unionists Jack Roberts (secretary of the Clothing Trades' Union) and Archie Grant (who was secretary of the Trade Union Congress) moved that the conference congratulate Nash and 'those MPs, party officials and working class people who, at considerable personal sacrifice, are fighting to defend our democracy', and urge 'the liberal minded people of New Zealand to reject the Government and those who are supporting the Government'. This was too strong for the majority of delegates and was rejected by 355 votes to 250. On its final day the conference unanimously adopted a resolution moved by Nash and seconded by Toby Hill reaffirming Labour's opposition to communism and dictatorship, reaffirming its support for democracy, and registering the party's determination to fight all forms of repression, including denial of free speech and free assembly 'as contained in the Emergency Regulations promulgated by the National Government'.[34]

By June the watersiders and their allies were close to defeat. At the request of the Waterside Workers' Union, Nash met the government, but it refused to budge on the union's request that there be no victimisation. On 9 July a meeting of watersiders, seamen, drivers and freezing workers voted unanimously to return to work. The lockout was over.[35] The workers' resistance to the government and the employers was magnificent but the watersiders' leaders had made a series of blunders which allowed their enemies to destroy a strong, militant union.

When parliament finally met at the end of June, Labour went onto the offensive, arguing that inflation had exacerbated industrial tension, the government had turned down four opportunities to settle the dispute, and the emergency regulations were dangerous and too wide. Some Labour MPs noted the fascist overtones in National's anti-union language. On 11 July Holland announced a snap election.[36] The election campaign put Labour on the back foot. The party was perennially short of money and now faced a second general election within 21 months. While prices had continued to rise, the economy was growing on the back of the Korean War boom. At the end of May the government announced that it would pay a bonus of £5 for every child for whom a family (or orphan's) benefit was being paid.[37] National was strongly supported by the press. Bassett comments: 'The morning papers, in particular the *Herald* and the *Otago Daily Times* began to run a series of editorials which, for the savagery of their attacks on the Labour Party, can seldom have been equalled in New Zealand's history.'[38]

The Labour Party scrambled to organise its campaign, raise money and select candidates. Just over a month from election day, the *Auckland Star* reported that a 'powerful group of trade unionists' was considering running their own candidates against the official Labour candidates. They argued that the party was weak in its support for arbitration and the FOL and soft on communism, and complained that not one trade unionist of long standing had been selected as a Labour candidate in Auckland.[39] An anonymous publication, *Who Squeaks in the Dark???*, named the group, who were a motley collection of right-wingers, scabs during the carpenters, and waterfront lockouts and union hacks.[40] They wrote to the FOL outlining their complaints. In his reply, Baxter came down on them like a ton of bricks: 'There is room in New Zealand for only one national union organisation. Similarly there is room in New Zealand for only one national Political Labour Party'.[41] The Auckland Trades Council and Auckland LRC were quick to affirm support for Labour and to dissociate themselves from the group, which beat a hasty retreat, but some damage had been done.[42]

'Never before has the party entered into an election campaign with such enthusiasm', the executive reported to the 1952 Labour Party conference.[43] Unions collected money; the Auckland Hotel Workers gave the party an indefinite loan of £2500.[44] In a move that foreshadowed the regional party structures of the future, all the LRCs and campaign committees in Auckland met weekly to oversee the campaign.[45] Labour promised reduced taxation, extension of social security benefits, to build 100,000 houses in five years, reinstatement of consumer subsidies and effective price controls. The *Standard* observed, 'this really is a cost of living election'.[46] Try as Labour could to avoid the waterfront dispute, National hammered the issue. National candidates repeatedly charged that 'a vote for Labour was a vote for the Communists'. It did not help that the deregistered watersiders and the Trade Union Congress campaigned for Labour. In late July the press widely misreported Pat Potter, the congress's president, as saying, 'Let us put Sid out and Walter in. Then we can line Mr Nash up.'[47]

The general election on 1 September 1951 was a decisive victory for National. Its vote increased from 51.8 per cent in 1949 to nearly 54 per cent. Labour's fell from 47.1 per cent to 45.8 per cent. National won four extra seats—Gisborne, Napier, Lyttelton and St Kilda—taking its total to 50, a 20-seat majority. There was not a significant swing to National, though: its 1952 vote went up by about 20,000 and Labour's fell by 15,000.[48]

When parliament met at the end of September, National introduced two bills to consolidate its victory. An amendment to the Industrial Conciliation and Arbitration Act provided for compulsory secret ballots on strikes, made picketing illegal, imposed hefty fines on strikers, who had to prove their innocence, and required union officials to be elected by secret postal ballot. The Police Offences Amendment Bill widened the definition of 'seditious intention' to include inciting violence or disorder and exciting 'such hostility or ill-will between different classes of persons as may endanger the public safety'. A magistrate or judge had the sole right to decide cases; there was no trial by jury. The onus of proof was shifted to the accused. Picketing, processions, demonstrations and poster displays during strikes were made illegal.[49]

There was strong opposition, particularly to the Police Offences Amendment Bill. Law societies, a hastily formed Human Rights Society, universities, the Methodist and Presbyterian churches, the Federation of Business and Professional Women's Clubs and the FOL joined the Labour Party in criticising it.[50] A number of newspapers attacked the bill. The *Auckland Star* said it was not much different from the 'inquisition of the Middle Ages and the Thought Police of the Fascist State'.[51]

In the face of so much opposition, National toned down the bill, dropping clauses making it an offence to criticise foreign governments and narrowing the picketing provisions. Labour fought the bill vigorously in parliament. Nash described it, in its original form, as 'was one of the most anti-democratic measures' ever introduced to the parliament of an English-speaking country. Mason said there was 'hardly any sort of organisation . . . concerned with freedom of speech . . . that did not voice its fear and alarm'. Jock Stewart, MP for Arch Hill, said the bill was 'an intensification of class warfare' against the workers.[52]

The 1951 waterfront lockout was a momentous event in New Zealand's history. For all its equivocation, the Labour Party, and Nash, showed great courage in refusing to support the government and the FOL in their determination to smash the watersiders. At the 1951 Labour Party conference, Jack Roberts paid Nash and Labour a generous tribute:

> The Party had not joined the hymn of hate and torrent of abuse against the watersiders which had been carried on by the Press, the RSA, the Chambers of Commerce and a section of trade union leaders. Mr Nash had not joined the motley crew of radio stars which had been used to condemn the watersiders.[53]

Years later Nash told an interviewer: 'I had spent my life getting better conditions for the workers and I would not attack them and lose them their gains. I opposed them but I would not attack them.'[54]

Cautious modernisation, 1951–57

Although it was overshadowed by the lockout, the 1951 conference adopted a complete revision of Labour's constitution and rules, which created the foundations of the party's modern structure. This was the work of a committee chaired by Allan McDonald, the party's general secretary. The new constitution retained Labour's hierarchical structure. The party comprised branches (ordinary, women's, junior and Māori), labour representation committees and affiliated unions. The annual conference was the 'supreme governing body of the Party', but the national executive was the governing body when the conference was not in session. LRCs were the 'local governing body, subject to the control of the National Executive'.[55]

There were three important debates about the new constitution. The first was about the traditional socialist objective of Labour parties: 'the socialisation of the means of production, distribution and exchange'. As McDonald pointed out, this was not in the old constitution, but was printed on party membership cards. The committee recommended that the party's purpose be 'to educate the public in the principles of Co-operation and Socialism; to elect competent men and women to Parliament and Local Authorities; and to ensure the just distribution of the production and services of New Zealand'. Len Scorrar (Rodney LRC) and Percy Hansen (Tramways Union) moved an amendment to replace the 'just distribution . . . ' phrase with the socialist objective. This was defeated by 359 votes to 149.[56] Supporters of the amendment argued that if the party was to get out of the doldrums 'it would have to stop running away from Socialism . . . if there was any drifting away from Socialism grave disappointment would be generated within the Party; . . . the dropping of the Socialisation clause would be heralded as an indication that Labour was in retreat'. Supporters of the new clause argued that conditions had changed over the previous 30 years:

> the Labour Party was still a Party of Socialists but it must also be a Party of realists; "the just distribution of the production and services of New Zealand" was applied socialism and was what the Labour Government had sought during its 14 years in office . . . the people had to be educated in the ideals of Socialism before Socialism could be applied.[57]

The second debate was about the national executive. The committee proposed that it should continue to comprise a president, vice-president and secretary elected by conference, five Wellington-based members, elected by conference, and one representative from each of the 12 divisional areas, elected by local branches and affiliates. The parliamentary leader and caucus secretary had the right to attend executive meetings but without the right to vote. The central executive – the officers and Wellington members—had been part of Labour's constitution since 1921 and had long been a bone of contention. Mary Anderson (Westland LRC) and S. Gladstone (Westland Bakers' Union) moved that the national executive be the officers, two parliamentary representatives and 17 divisional representatives. This was defeated by 326 votes to 217.[58]

The final debate was about the selection of parliamentary candidates. Under the old provisions, adopted in 1926, candidates were selected by a ballot of party and affiliated union members in an LRC from a list approved by the national executive. But there were difficulties getting accurate names and addresses of union members and there was often a low return in postal ballots. In 1946, when extensive boundary changes shortened the time for selections, candidates were chosen by the national executive in consultation with LRCs.[59] The committee now proposed that candidates would be selected by a committee of three members appointed by and from the executive and three local members, resident in the electorate, appointed by the LRC. An amendment to retain the old system was defeated by 304 votes to 240.[60]

The 1956 conference would make two changes to the new system. The first was that the executive should give favourable consideration to appointing the local divisional representative as one of its three representatives, and the second that, in the case of multiple LRCs, the local representatives would be elected by LRC delegates resident in the electorate.[61]

The revision of the constitution was followed at the 1952 conference by the adoption of statements of Labour's philosophy on the party's principles, socialism and communism, and war and peace. In the 1950s, the worst years of the Cold War, many social democratic parties found it difficult to find a political space between anti-communist conservative governments and communist parties. The New Zealand Labour Party managed better in this environment than other parties: it regained office in 1957, compared to 1964 for the British Labour Party and 1972 for the Australian Labor Party. The statement of Labour's principles—'Where Labour stands!'—said that capitalism was 'the main enemy of the brotherhood of man' and condemned millions to unemployment, economic exploitation and political oppression. Labour and other socialist parties were 'born as a movement of protest against the diseases inherent in capitalist society'. True socialism could be achieved only through democracy, 'just as democracy can be fully realised only through Socialism'. Labour was opposed to dictatorship. Its objective was to transform the economic system so that 'power over production is placed in the hands of the people as a whole'. Nationalisation was only one of the means of achieving this objective; others were municipal ownership and producers' or consumers' co-operatives.[62]

The statement on international affairs said that world peace was a fundamental aim of the Labour Party. Labour wanted to reduce and remove trade barriers, support the redistribution of the world's wealth, and give all people equality of opportunity and political and economic independence. Collective security through the United Nations was the best way of safeguarding liberty and independence. The statement reaffirmed Labour's support for peacetime conscription. There was a big debate on this, but an amendment to reject conscription was defeated.[63]

At the 1952 FOL conference, McLagan moved to repair the party's relations with the FOL by suggesting the revival of the union/party Labour legislation committee that had existed before Labour won power. As a consequence, the FOL and party conferences voted to establish the Joint Council of Labour, comprised of representatives of each body's national executives.[64] Its first meeting, chaired by Nordmeyer, was on 21 July 1952.[65]

There were further signs of revival in the party in the first half of the 1950s. Over 8000 people had joined since 1949.[66] There were over 600 branches, almost as many as the 1939–40 peak of 630.[67] In 1952 Louise Overacker, an American political scientist, spent several months studying the Labour Party and observing party meetings. She contrasted Nordmeyer's fairness in chairing the party conference with Roberts's 'dictatorial tendencies', but criticised the hierarchical nature of the party, its domination by the parliamentary party (three of the eight central executive members were MPs) and its lack of internal democracy.[68]

Overacker observed that the New Zealand Labour Party, like social democratic parties everywhere, was challenged by the problems we identified at the start of this chapter. The party faced these problems under serious handicaps:

> Divided ideologically at the outset, it has never developed a firm tradition of resolving its internal differences democratically. The morale of the party is undermined by an undercurrent of disaffection which manifests itself in perpetual guerrilla warfare, but is never resolved in a major encounter. Haunted by the ghost of the Lee rebellion and by the fear of Communist infiltration, leaders lack confidence in the good judgement of the rank and file, and members distrust their leaders. Loss of vitality at the rank and file level has left a vacuum which has been filled by the leadership group; at the same time tight control from the centre contributes to the atrophy of the branches . . . Preoccupation with routine business and the tendency of officers to keep a tight rein on discussion and to discourage ventilation of controversial issues have a deadening effect upon meetings of branches and LRCs.

Leadership hostility to criticism and lack of enthusiasm in branches, she observed, created an atmosphere which antagonised rather than attracted young intellectuals and idealists.[69]

Labour made further gains in the 1953 local body elections, but at a national level it struggled to make an impact. Labour was a very weak opposition. Norman Kirk said to Keith Sinclair some years later that the party 'had received such a battering during 1951 that only Nash's doggedness enabled it to recover'.[70] Brown wrote that Nash 'led the band from the front but he led them as a one-man band. Not only did he not organise the PLP [parliamentary Labour Party] himself, he would not delegate authority to anyone to do it.'[71]

Frustration with Nash led to a challenge by Nordmeyer for leadership of the party in 1954. At the 9 February 1954 caucus meeting McLagan moved a vote of confidence in Nash which was carried unanimously. Mason moved that a date be set for selection of the leader. This was also carried.[72] Nash was stunned. In tears, he told Brown: 'Bruce, you may soon have a new boss.'[73] The press ran stories about dissension within Labour. The Labour Party and FOL executives came out strongly in support of Nash. The party executive passed a unanimous vote of confidence in him and deplored 'the treachery which has become evident by the leakage of caucus information to the press'.[74] The FOL backed him publicly, wrote to Labour MPs calling on them to reject any idea of supplanting Nash as leader,[75] and wrote to all trades councils and trade union committees urging them to pass resolutions 'calling for the utmost loyalty to the Labour Party and its appointed leader'.[76] A number of trades councils, unions and party branches did so.[77] There was a lengthy argument between the national executive and the caucus about when the election should be held.[78]

The leadership vote was held on 23 June. McLagan nominated Nash, while Freer nominated Nordmeyer. Nash won by 15 votes to nine; the four Māori MPs abstained. 'While he won the vote clearly enough, [Nash] was shocked by the extent of Nordmeyer's support.'[79] The backing of the party and FOL executives was probably crucial.

Labour campaigned hard in the 1954 general election. It promised stabilisation of food prices, 3 per cent loans for new homes, better housing for state tenants and Māori, support for Māori culture, education, employment and land development, an increased family benefit and pensions, a 40-hour week for nurses, free textbooks in schools, a 'vast public works programme' and support for a ban on nuclear weapons.[80]

The election saw the emergence of a third party, the Social Credit Political League. While it won no seats, it got 11 per cent of the vote. Labour won 44.1 per cent, while National's share fell 10 per cent to 43.9 per cent. Labour gained five seats, but with 45 seats to 35 National still had a comfortable majority.[81] The *Standard* commented sourly: 'The Social Crediters by splitting the vote everywhere . . . kept Labour out of office.'[82] Including those who won by-elections in 1953 and 1954, Labour had 13 new MPs, over a third of the caucus, including one woman, Ethel McMillan, who had won Dunedin North in a by-election in 1953. Seven of the newcomers were to be ministers in future Labour governments.

At the 1955 conference a remit to reinstate the socialist objective was defeated. Addressing the conference, Nordmeyer said Labour sometimes overlooked the fact that the British Labour Party, from which the New Zealand party derived its inspiration, 'was founded and nurtured in a Christian philosophy. The Labour Party early turned its back upon the materialistic Socialism which developed on the continent of Europe and ultimately degenerated in Russia into Communism.' The first Labour government had been 'imbued with a passionate desire to end poverty. The gains here and in Britain were made in response to an appreciation of Christian values.' Referring to Australia, where B.A. Santamaria's Catholic Social Studies Movement, generally known simply as the Groupers, split the Labor Party, Nordmeyer said it was wrong that 'any particular church' sought to gain control of the Labour movement.[83]

Arguing that 'it is not in the interests of our Movement that one man should hold this office for a long period of time', Nordmeyer announced that he was standing down as president. He was succeeded by Michael Moohan. Martyn Finlay was narrowly elected vice-president.[84]

In a significant organisational change, the conference decided that inter-branch councils should be set up in multiple-electorate LRCs to co-ordinate party activities in each electorate, raise money and form new branches, particularly junior branches. These councils would consist of an equal number of representatives from each branch and the local MP or candidate; affiliated unions were not represented. An Auckland provincial office was opened and Arthur Faulkner appointed Auckland organiser.[85]

The 1952 party conference had voted by 253 to 226 to set up a national organisation for junior branches and local area committees.[86] The following year a Junior Advisory Council was established, chaired by R.A. Moore (Papanui).[87] Junior branches held annual rallies, which were 'more social than political'.[88] For example, in 1956, 150 young members spent a week at St Kilda in Dunedin. They held sports competitions, a ball, a Sunday night social and a midnight dance. After listening to addresses by local party luminaries, they visited Larnach's Castle.[89] In 1957 the Māori Advisory Council was reconstituted as the Māori Policy Committee, consisting of the four Māori MPs and four representatives from each of the Māori electorates, with an organising as well as a policy brief.[90]

Women struggled to get their voice heard within the party. While there had been an annual meeting of women delegates to the conference for some years, women's branches wanted a separate women's conference and a women's representative on the national executive.[91] The 1955 conference rejected remits calling for a women's conference and women's, junior and Māori representatives on the executive. Ivy Lambert (Rodney South women's branch) said the time was 'long past due when women should decide that they are not content to go on just raising funds and doing the dishes'.[92] Progress finally came at the 1957 conference, which decided there would be a Māori representative on the executive, chosen by the Māori Policy Committee, and a women's representative elected by the annual conference. P.T. (Steve) Wātene was the first Māori representative. Mabel Howard narrowly defeated Dorothy Fraser by 291 to 263 to become the first women's representative.[93]

After 1954 the Labour Party adopted some new and radical policies. The

1955 conference supported the admission of the People's Republic of China to the United Nations,[94] and in their presidential addresses Nordmeyer and Moohan argued strongly for nuclear disarmament.[95] Compulsory military training was hotly debated at the 1956 conference, which defeated a motion reaffirming Labour's traditional opposition to peacetime conscription by 295 votes to 294. However, the 1957 conference adopted the parliamentary party's recommendation that compulsory military training was 'a waste of time, money and personnel and should be discontinued'.[96]

Labour went into the 1957 general election campaign with a platform that repeated a number of its 1954 policies: 3 per cent housing loans, an increased family benefit, increased social security benefits and free school textbooks. New policies included equal pay for women in the public service, capitalisation of the family benefit so people could pay a deposit on a home or pay off a mortgage, a programme of industrialisation, abolition of compulsory military training and tax concessions.[97] The latter policy became the centrepiece of the campaign.

For several years MPs had discussed the introduction of 'pay as you earn' (PAYE) income tax to replace annual tax payments. National's 1957 budget announced that this would be introduced in 1958. National promised to remit one year's tax so people did not have to pay two years' tax within one year, and offered a rebate of 25 per cent of tax due in the first year of PAYE. Labour promised one year's remission of tax plus a rebate of £100 on tax due in the first year. During the election campaign Labour's advertising included (to Nash's dismay) an open letter to voters from Moohan and McDonald which said that taxpayers would have no tax to pay if their income tax was less than £100. This overlooked the fact that tax demands already included National's 25 per cent rebate. 'The depths were plumbed' by a *Standard* billboard which read: 'Do you want £100 or not?'[98]

National went into the campaign on the back foot. Holland's health was failing and he reluctantly retired, leaving little time for Keith Holyoake, his successor, to establish himself among voters. 'Nash, by contrast, was one of the best known people in the country.'[99] Labour ran a vigorous campaign. In Auckland, one of the key battlegrounds, the LRC set up a metropolitan campaign committee to co-ordinate activity in the 15 Auckland electorates. It organised meetings for visiting speakers, advertising, propaganda and workplace lunchtime meetings. Unions, particularly the Engineers' Union, played an active part. Several non-affiliated unions organised meetings and gave money.[100] The FOL gave £2000 to Labour's campaign.[101]

Nash led from the front. He spoke at 23 major meetings and a number of lunchtime and other workplace meetings. On the Wednesday before election day he spoke to nearly 5000 people in Auckland at a lunchtime meeting of watersiders, a late afternoon factory meeting and three evening meetings in the marginal seats of Roskill, Eden and Tamaki. He 'would have had to go back to the 1938 campaign to find equal enthusiasm and cordiality in the reception given to him', he said.[102]

Labour won 48.3 per cent of the vote, compared to 44.2 per cent for National and 7.2 per cent for Social Credit (which dropped 4 per cent). The party won six new seats: St Kilda, Lyttelton, St Albans, Nelson, Roskill and Tāmaki.[103] The new MPs were a talented group. They included a future prime minister (Kirk), deputy prime minister (Bob Tizard), cabinet ministers (Bill Fraser and Arthur Faulkner), speaker of parliament (Stan Whitehead) and mayor of Christchurch (Neville Pickering). However, it was a narrow victory, because much of the party's popular vote consisted of large majorities in safe seats. Labour won 41 seats to National's 39, giving the new government a majority of one after the appointment of the speaker.

7

Faltering Certainties: Government and Opposition in a Changing World 1958–69

The second Labour government took office committed both to social justice and to economic modernisation. The tension between these goals—hopefully a creative one—is at the heart of social democratic politics. In the decade from 1958 the Labour Party would gradually modernise not only its policy but also its organisation. Labour would seek to position itself as the vehicle for a dynamic and progressive nation. The Labour Party of 1970 would be significantly different from that of 1958, a difference symbolised by—indeed requiring—the gradual passing of the 1935 generation.

The second Labour government included seven ministers who had held office under Fraser. Skinner was deputy prime minister and minister of agriculture; Nordmeyer finance; Mason justice and health; Hackett labour; Tirikātene forests; and Mabel Howard social security. Nash took external affairs and Māori affairs, making Tirikātene his associate in the latter portfolio, to the annoyance of the party's Māori Policy Committee. The newcomers to cabinet were given some important portfolios: Hugh Watt works and electricity; Phil Holloway industries and commerce; and Phil Skoglund education. Bill Fox (housing); Phil Connolly (defence and police); Michael Moohan (railways); Jock Mathison (transport); Ray Boord (customs and broadcasting); and Bill Anderton (internal affairs) were the other ministers.[1]

Nordmeyer and Holloway played important parts in economic policy and several others were capable ministers in their portfolios. However, Nash was the dominant figure, both the government's greatest strength and its greatest weakness. Referring to Nash's inability to move paper, Alister McIntosh, secretary of external affairs, wrote, shortly after Labour took office: 'Walter, like Louis and the other Bourbons of the Restoration, has learned nothing and forgotten nothing when it comes to method.'[2]

Managing economic crisis

The new government was immediately faced with a serious economic crisis. Two weeks before the election Walsh (now FOL president) warned that there was a growing balance of payments deficit. He was ignored.[3] The day Labour took office Treasury told Nordmeyer that export prices had fallen sharply, while import payments were running well above 1956 levels. Nash told the public the trade deficit had increased from £4 million in September to £30 million in December and the country's overseas reserves had fallen from £83 million in October to £45.5 million at the end of December.[4] In January 1958 the government imposed tight import controls and raised £45 million in overseas borrowing. In March the Treasury advised that the situation had deteriorated further and said government action should be 'adequate and rigorous rather than lenient or chance-taking'.[5]

Labour was determined to avoid unemployment and to keep its election promises. Nordmeyer accepted the Treasury's advice to impose substantial increases in income tax and indirect taxes. There are conflicting accounts as to whether the Treasury expected some of its advice to be rejected and overbid to get what it really wanted or whether it advised only what it believed to be necessary.[6] Nordmeyer's 1958 budget quickly became known as the 'Black Budget'. The income tax increases penalised the single and childless. Duties on beer, spirits, tobacco and cars were doubled. Petrol tax was nearly doubled. A tax was introduced on dividends and gifts, and estate duties were raised sharply. Age benefits and the family benefit were increased.[7]

The budget 'received an overwhelmingly hostile reception'.[8] The National Party and the press attacked it strongly, as did Walsh, who predicted that the consumer price index would increase by 5 per cent by the end of September 1958. There were several testy meetings between the Federation of Labour and cabinet ministers. At a special meeting of the FOL national council Walsh argued that the burden of the government's measures would fall heavily on workers and their families. Nordmeyer strongly defended the budget:

> The aim of the Labour Government was to meet the needs of the family man and to endeavour to maintain full employment . . . [the budget] was designed to spread the share of the burden as equitably as possible on all sections of the community as a consequence of the fall in the prices of exports.

At the end of the meeting Walsh remarked that being FOL president was 'a comparatively easy job when a Nationalist Government is in power but he was sure he would get a lot more grey hairs if he continued . . . Loyalties were going to be strained'.[9]

The differences between the FOL and the government have been put down to Walsh's dislike of Nash and Nordmeyer. Melanie Nolan argues, however, that the interests of the party and the FOL had diverged over the way living standards were measured. The FOL had strongly objected to the 1957 revision of the consumer price index to include petrol and liquor because this downgraded the impact of changes in food prices and other 'essentials of life'.[10] Walsh claimed that tax increases on petrol and liquor would intensify inflation and reduce workers' purchasing power.[11] Nordmeyer, however, saw little alternative to raising revenue and deterring importing of luxury goods.

Keith Sinclair argues that the 1958 budget was 'a suicidal mistake' and 'the biggest blunder in Nash's political career . . . It was an economists' budget, a Treasury budget, but it was not what the voters had been led to expect from Labour's fair promises'.[12] An economic historian, however, has praised it for 'courage and responsibility'.[13] Although National ministers had been well aware of the deteriorating economic situation, Keith Holyoake, the National Party leader, repeatedly hammered Nash for his promise in his final campaign speech in 1957 that 'given normal circumstances' there would be no need to increase taxes.[14] Nordmeyer acknowledged this later: 'it wasn't because we increased taxes in 1958, it was because we increased taxes when we had said we wouldn't increase taxes. It was this that the people resented.'[15]

Within the Labour Party there was initial support for the government's handling of the economic crisis. The New Plymouth LRC carried a unanimous resolution on the budget 'commending its courage and realism', while the Christchurch women's branch congratulated Nordmeyer for preventing widespread unemployment.[16] In October 1958 the party's head office circulated a summary of the government's achievements. 'No member of the Party has any need to make excuses for the actions of the Government', it argued.[17] This completely missed the growing mood of anger and resentment within the party. Barry Gustafson says:

> In 1958–59 the party activists at the primary level erupted in fury at their Government's actions. Condemnatory motions were passed at branch and electorate meetings and more letters of protest poured into Head Office than in all the rest of the period 1945–72 put together.[18]

The executive of the Auckland LRC met Nash in January 1959 and criticised the government in blunt terms: 'Arising from insistent demands from Branches and IBCs [inter-branch councils] we are frustrated and at a loss to understand certain measures that strike most unfairly at the lower paid group . . . Party members are alarmed at the Government's failure to attack our political enemies'. Nash discussed the executive's concerns 'fully and frankly', but there was no change.[19] He was seen as out of touch by many backbench MPs as well as party members. The cabinet did not consult the caucus and Nash's habit of making important policy announcements without forewarning MPs left them scrambling to answer questions from constituents. The cabinet was divided. Moohan invited MPs to his office to make free toll calls home on his ministerial phone and undermined Nordmeyer by criticising his 'Presbyterian Wowser' budget.[20] At the 1959 annual conference there was an unprecedented amendment proposed to Nash's report deploring 'the fact that the Parliamentary Labour Party is completely out of touch with the rank and file of the Labour Party'. This was defeated, but the debate on it was only ended by a card vote of 277 to 253.[21]

Economic development and social justice

Economic conditions, particularly export earnings, rapidly improved after 1958.[22] The following year's budget reduced income taxes in two steps, bringing them back to 1957 levels. Taxes on petrol, tobacco and cars were reduced in the 1960 budget.[23] Having weathered the economic crisis, the Labour government emphasised industrial development. This policy was designed to reduce New Zealand's dependence on primary product exports and foreign imports. However, it was not as novel or radical as its main advocate, W.B. Sutch, secretary of industries and commerce, later claimed. The expansion of manufacturing had been a concern of the first Labour government, and the Nash government's measures enjoyed a large measure of bipartisan support.[24]

In June 1960 the government held a widely representative Industrial Development Conference. The following month, Holloway said that new capital investments in industry exceeded £73 million.[25] Agreements were signed with overseas companies to establish a steel mill, a glassworks, a gin distillery, an oil refinery, an aluminium smelter and a cotton mill. The last two projects were controversial. The government was criticised for agreeing to a very cheap price for electricity for Consolidated Zinc Proprietary to establish the Tīwai Point smelter to manufacture aluminium from alumina mined in Queensland. There was widespread concern about environmental damage from raising the levels of lakes Manapōuri and Te Anau for the huge hydroelectric project required to provide electricity to the smelter. There was another outcry after the government negotiated with a British company to build a mill in Nelson to process imported cotton. This project, which would have given the company a virtual monopoly, was scrapped by the National government.[26]

While the second Labour government's record was overshadowed by the Black Budget, it introduced a number of changes in social policies promised in the 1957 manifesto. It increased old-age pensions and introduced universal superannuation without a means test for everyone over 65. The family benefit was increased by 50 per cent to 15s a week tax free. The benefit could be paid in a lump sum of up to £1000 for a deposit on or to repay a mortgage on a family home. Three per cent housing loans were introduced for people whose needs were greatest.[27] These loans and capitalisation of the family benefit 'greatly extended the possibilities of the not so wealthy acquiring a home'.[28] There was a big increase in home building under Labour. The total number of new houses and flats rose from 18,955 in 1958 to 24,397 in 1961.[29]

In education, the government introduced free textbooks in schools, increased university and school teachers' salaries, and commissioned the Hughes–Parry report, which made recommendations for the 1960s expansion of universities.[30] Compulsory military training was abolished and the oppressive clauses of the Police Offences Act repealed. Arts funding was expanded. Equal pay for women was introduced in the state services.[31]

Nash was widely criticised for the government's failure to achieve much in Māori affairs. He lacked Fraser's instinctive rapport with Māori, and, like Fraser, was far too busy to be able to give Māori affairs due attention. At the 1958 annual conference, Steve Wātene, the chair of the Māori Policy Committee, criticised the government for failing to implement its 1957 policy. The committee asked, pointedly, when it could expect the 'time-honoured privilege' of a Māori minister of Māori affairs. It appealed to the conference 'to give your Maori colleagues what is a fair return from the Labour Movement commensurate with the weight and force of the Maori membership'.[32] The following year Wātene assured the conference of Māori allegiance to Labour, 'but my committee cannot . . . placidly accept the inaction and lack of real implementation of its reports unanimously adopted by the conferences of 1957 and 1958'.[33] Labour had promised to make 6 February a public holiday to commemorate the signing of the Treaty of Waitangi. However, the 1960 Waitangi Day Act only provided for the day to be declared a public holiday in substitution for another.[34]

In June 1959 the New Zealand Rugby Union announced that Māori players would not be selected for the All Black team that was to tour South Africa. A few days later Tirikātene spoke out against the tour, and was joined by two of the other three Labour Māori MPs.[35] One of the biggest protest movements in New Zealand's history sprang up to oppose the tour. The Citizens' All Black Tour Association organised a petition signed by 153,000 people which called for the tour to be abandoned. The National Council of Churches, the FOL, many Māori leaders and some Labour Party branches opposed it.[36] Nash refused to take a stand. After an approach from the Rugby Union, he told caucus that MPs should not raise the tour as a political issue. Many took this as an order.[37] He was supported by Labour's national executive, which felt the party 'should not be associated in any way with the controversy'.[38] In April 1960 Nash defended the Rugby Union's decision to go ahead with the tour. For a man who had long been a critic of apartheid, it was a stand which dismayed many within the party.[39]

As external affairs minister, Nash travelled widely, attended a number of international conferences and met world leaders to promote peace and disarmament. He was often criticised for his absences. Nash's willingness to pursue an independent foreign policy fluctuated. On some matters he was careful not to get out of step with the United States: for example, he prevaricated on Labour Party conference decisions to recognise the People's

Republic of China. Sometimes, however, he was more forthright. In 1959 there was a crisis in Laos. The pro-western government accused North Vietnam of aggression and there was fighting between government forces and the pro-communist Pathet Lao. In the United States there was talk of intervention under the SEATO (South-East Asia Treaty Organisation) treaty. In October Nash attended the ANZUS council meeting in Washington and was 'extremely outspoken' against American views; Dag Hammarskjöld, the United Nations secretary-general, expressed appreciation for his stand.[40] Norman Kirk later said the war in Indochina would have started eight to ten years earlier but for Nash: John Foster Dulles, the US secretary of state, 'pushed hard for intervention under SEATO and Nash painstakingly went through all the documents, he reported to caucus about them, said he could find no evidence whatever of external aggression and refused to change that view'. At the ANZUS meeting Nash 'hung out against quite substantial pressure and . . . was instrumental in having the Australians change their views'.[41] Nash regarded his resistance to United States intervention in Laos as 'one of his most important deeds'.[42] In a very different context, Nash was also an important advocate of international co-operation in the Antarctic and the Antarctic Treaty of 1959 owed much to his advocacy.[43]

The Hamilton by-election in May 1959 showed that the political tide was running against Labour. National retained the seat with a much bigger majority. McDonald told the national executive that reports from Hamilton showed that workers felt 'they had been called upon to shoulder more than their share of the burden to resolve a situation which they themselves had not created'.[44] In June 1960 Nash was re-elected as Labour's leader 'but there was widespread dissatisfaction with his leadership'.[45] The National Party had campaigned vigorously against the government throughout its term in office. In 1960 Holyoake attracted record crowds on a nationwide speaking tour.[46] National won the general election easily, with 47.6 per cent of votes and 46 seats. Labour's vote fell nearly 5 per cent to 43.4 per cent and it lost seven seats. Ten per cent of the electorate did not vote. With the exception of 1943 and 1951, it was the lowest turnout since 1935. Many of those who didn't vote were wage and salary earners.[47]

A weakened party

The second Labour government successfully managed an economic crisis and maintained full employment. It introduced significant reforms in social policy. Nash's vigorous personal diplomacy built on Fraser's achievements in foreign policy. Labour was successful in governing for three years with only a one-seat majority. However, it also left the party in a weakened state and underlined its failure to modernise sufficiently after 1949. In Auckland, in the two years after the 1957 election the number of branches fell from 110 to 80 and total membership more than halved.[48] The *Standard*, Labour's newspaper, ceased publication in 1959 because of financial difficulties.[49] Nationally, branch membership fell from 37,749 in 1955 to 17,810 in 1965.[50]

The malaise within the party was reflected in the Wellington City branch's discussion after the 1960 conference. Gerald O'Brien, the branch delegate to the conference, bemoaned 'the inability and unwillingness of Ministers to face up to criticisms', while Ethel Harris criticised the conference's failure to discuss the women's report and felt that 'expediency still tended to be regarded as of greater importance than principle and that the rank and file of the party have lost control of the hierarchy'.[51] There was a widespread feeling that Labour was suffering from 'Fraseritis', the domination of the party by the old and conservative parliamentary leadership. When Stan Rodger attended his first annual conference in 1961, 'it was just a sea of grey heads. In retrospect I have come to the view that the Party could have died in that era.' What saved it, in his view, were the new social and political movements of the 1960s which meant new agendas could be formed on Labour's platform.[52]

Some steps were taken to address rank and file disenchantment with the parliamentary party. The 1961 conference approved an executive report which recommended the establishment of a permanent policy committee representing the parliamentary party and the executive. In 1960 Nash had drawn up the election manifesto without convening a meeting of the ad hoc election policy committee.[53] However, the new committee 'would be consultative and advisory only—as the MPs elected by the people cannot be subjected to any extra-parliamentary fetter'.[54] These claims of parliamentarians' absolute supremacy would be stated in almost identical language in the late 1980s.

A more fundamental reform of the party's organisation was initiated in

Auckland. After the 1960 election, the Auckland Metropolitan Campaign Committee adopted proposals by Colin Moyle, the party's Auckland organiser, to establish an Auckland Regional Advisory Council to co-ordinate the party's activities and to be 'a pattern for the reorganisation of the Labour Movement throughout New Zealand'.[55] The proposal was supported by the Auckland and other local LRCs and the national executive.[56] At the same time the party in Auckland launched a monthly newspaper, the *New Zealand Statesman*, edited by Bill Anderton, who retired as MP for Auckland Central in 1960.[57] In less than six months the paper had a circulation of over 81,000.[58]

The leaders of the new regional organisation, such as Moyle, Roger Douglas (who chaired the Regional Advisory Council from 1964 to 1969) and George Broad, a boilermaker and trade unionist, believed that the party's traditional structure was no longer fit for purpose. In his comprehensive study of the Labour Party in the Auckland region in the 1950s and 1960s, Barry Gustafson analysed the decline of Labour as a mass-based party. Between 1946 and 1970 the number of branches in Auckland fell from 100 to 71, average branch membership from 81 to 41 and total branch membership from 8193 to 2659. Branches became more narrowly focused on election activity and lost interest in social activities, solidarity and community affairs. Fundraising fell markedly.[59]

There were a number of reasons for the fall in membership. The members of the 1930s started to die off, but an ageing leadership meant the party had difficulty attracting younger people. Labour's messages failed to resonate with the electorate. Changing social habits meant that people stopped going to dances, cinemas and socially oriented political party meetings. Urban renewal and motorways in Auckland destroyed traditional working-class areas that had supported strong party branches.[60] Last but not least, frustration and resentment at the second Labour government 'led to an exodus from the NZLP and a decline in the intensity of commitment of many of those who remained'.[61] The reformers believed a strong regional organisation with professional staff could undertake large-scale fundraising, strengthen electorate activities, concentrate resources on marginal seats and mobilise activists during election campaigns. They were viewed with increasing suspicion by traditionalists in the party, including the national executive and many affiliated unions, who believed in a mass-based, working-class party, despite the fact that the Labour Party itself was now hardly mass-based, and despite evidence that society itself was changing.[62]

The 1962 annual conference adopted a statement on Labour's aims and objectives which said the party stood for 'the brotherhood of man and the greatest good for the greatest number'. Democratic socialism had achieved much but greater tasks lay ahead. 'A fair distribution of wealth required an extension of public ownership and control and other legislation to curb private monopolies, undertake a radical reform of the tax system and protect consumers.' Labour repudiated alike 'the soulless tyranny of communism and the wasteful inhumanity of capitalism'. Freedom and equality were essential to human happiness.[63] It was hard, however, to convince enough people of such ideals; the early 1960s were generally comfortable and Holyoake astutely cultivated a liberal and humanitarian image where it counted.

In 1962 Nash, who had turned 80, came under pressure to retire as leader. In February he told the national executive he would step down by the end of the year. In April Skinner died. Nash had second thoughts because he was reluctant to give up and didn't want Nordmeyer, his obvious successor, to replace him. In June Hackett defeated Nordmeyer for deputy leader (the party's problem was not just its octogenarian leader: Nordmeyer, Hackett and Skinner were all in their early sixties, older indeed than Holyoake). Alister McIntosh observed that Nordmeyer had been 'fixed' by Nash and the Auckland trade unionists and had nearly resigned as a result.[64] Martyn Finlay, the party president and a Nordmeyer supporter, wrote to caucus saying the party had done nothing to grapple with its problems, was 'totally unfitted to govern' and couldn't win under Nash. While there was a great deal of criticism of this letter, Nash finally got the message. He announced that he would resign as leader. Hackett, who was ill, said he would not stand (and died a few weeks later). On 26 February 1963, Nordmeyer was elected unopposed as Labour Party leader.[65] He was 62, Labour's first New Zealand-born leader and the first university graduate to lead the party.

Nordmeyer set out to modernise the party. He upset traditionalists in the Federation of Labour by saying there was no place 'for what used to be known as the class struggle'.[66] There was wide support in the party for Nordmeyer's position. At the 1964 annual conference a move to reinstate the socialist objective was defeated by 354 votes to 93. McDonald said that adopting it would 'turn the clock back for over a quarter of a century'.[67] The party and the Federation of Labour, led from 1963 by Tom Skinner, moved further apart. The 1930s and 1940s image of a united Labour movement no longer suited the interests of either the FOL (which had to develop working relations with National governments) or the party (which wanted to be seen as free from union domination).

Norman Kirk: a new generation and party reorganisation

Labour campaigned at the 1963 election on a 'New Look' programme. The *Statesman* proclaimed that Labour's proposals were 'the world's boldest incentives to sky-rocket production and export income'.[68] National won the election comfortably. Its vote fell slightly to 47.05 per cent and it won 45 seats. Labour's vote rose slightly to 43.76 per cent and it won 35 seats. Social Credit won 7.95 per cent.[69] But the election brought a number of key figures in the third Labour government into parliament. Among the party's new MPs in Auckland were Phil Amos and Colin Moyle, both teachers by profession, and Finlay. Finlay, a highly-trained lawyer (he had a doctorate and had studied at the London School of Economics under Harold Laski) had been in parliament in the last Fraser term, and would go on to be a reforming minister of justice and attorney-general. Bob Tizard returned after a 1960 loss. Bill Rowling had won the Buller by-election in 1962, and Matiu Rata had won Northern Māori in a by-election when Tāpihana Paikea died early in 1963. Tiaki Ōmana retired from Eastern Māori and was replaced by the sadly short-lived Steve Wātene.

Many people in the party believed Labour could never win under Nordmeyer: for the National Party the Black Budget was the gift that kept on giving, and it featured in their 1963 campaign. The rising star was Norman Kirk, who won Lyttelton for Labour in 1957. Defeated by one vote for deputy leader in 1963 by Hugh Watt, Kirk was elected party vice-president that year and president in 1964 after Finlay stood down.[70] Kirk worked hard to strengthen the party's organisation. He and McDonald went on a nationwide tour, visiting LRCs and speaking at lunch-hour and factory meetings.[71] In his speech at the 1965 annual conference Kirk staked out his position, emphasising equality of opportunity and nationhood along with a continued commitment to the welfare state. Labour, he said,

> does not accept that fear and greed are the only motives people will respond to.

> It plans for the future. It plans to build a better nation . . . Through equality of opportunity, particularly in higher education, we can throw open the gates to the future, we can create a stronger sense of national purpose and of pride in the nation . . . The society which we want to build is outward-looking, based on justice, freedom and a pride in our country.[72]

While there was little difference in substance between Kirk and Nordmeyer, Moohan, Fox and Freer started canvassing support for Kirk as leader. Nordmeyer ignored warnings that his position was under threat.[73] On 9 December 1965, Kirk defeated Nordmeyer by 25 caucus votes to 10. 'There are some members of the party who believe the public will never forgive or forget the Budget of 1958', Nordmeyer told journalists.[74] It was a sad end to the political career of one of the architects of the welfare state and one of the party's outstanding intellectuals. Michael Cullen said in 1999: 'Banned from the top by Nash's one-man gerontocracy, [Nordmeyer] got there too late and in the wrong circumstances to succeed. He was, I still believe, the best Prime Minister we never had'.[75]

At 42, Kirk was Labour's youngest leader to that date. His potential as a future leader had been recognised by Moohan and Mabel Howard after he led a Labour ticket to victory in Kaiapoi and was elected mayor in 1953.[76] Born into an impoverished working-class family, he had left school at 12, followed a variety of manual occupations and educated himself through voracious reading. With his solid working-class and trade union credentials, Kirk was at first seen as a party traditionalist. However, he was strongly committed to reforming Labour and changing its image.[77] His politics emphasised a progressive and humanitarian nationalism. He told the 1968 annual conference:

> The New Zealand Labour Party is the NEW ZEALAND party. The words New Zealand are as important as the word Labour. We are for New Zealand—we aim to strive for opportunities for New Zealanders in every field. We demand that New Zealanders should be allowed to run their own affairs—we are in strong opposition to all those who demonstrate by word or action that they intend to sell New Zealand short.[78]

In 1966 Labour celebrated its 50th anniversary. Kirk told the annual conference its task was not 'to bask in the reflected glory of our past. Our task is to organise for the next three years, the next 10 years, the next 50 years.'[79] Apart from the conference celebrations, the party's main recognition of its history was the publication of a golden jubilee edition of the recently established *New Zealand Labour Party Journal.* While including much interesting material, this was nostalgic and contained little analysis.[80]

In May 1965 the National government announced that it would send an artillery unit to support the United States in the Vietnam War. This military commitment put Labour in a difficult position. On one hand, the party had a strong tradition of independence in foreign affairs, sympathy with independence movements and support for peacekeeping through the United Nations. Opposition to the war was an important factor in the big increase in party membership among students and white-collar workers in the 1960s.[81] On the other hand, Labour supported New Zealand's alliances with the United States and was strongly anti-communist. Nordmeyer carefully analysed these issues in his speech to the 1965 annual conference. He emphasised Labour's tradition of independence in foreign policy, rejected the argument that military intervention could defeat communism and concluded that New Zealand should refuse to become involved.[82] His position was clear and principled. Kirk, on the other hand, feared that Labour would be tarred by association with communist opponents of the war. The FOL's strong opposition was crucial in determining Labour's position. Before the 1966 annual conference, the Joint Council of Labour made a statement on Vietnam which opposed sending New Zealand troops and called for their withdrawal. This was adopted by the conference, which defeated by 360 to 64 an amendment moved by Finlay and supported by Kirk to replace the artillery unit with a non-combatant force.[83]

The National government capitalised on the pro-American, anti-communist public sentiment in the early years of the war. It campaigned strongly on the issue in the 1966 general election, claiming Labour was dominated by the Federation of Labour. Kirk told candidates to avoid Vietnam, but attempts to equivocate only made the party look shifty.[84] Like Nordmeyer in 1963, Kirk had little time to establish himself as an alternative leader to the popular National prime minister, Holyoake. One journalist cruelly described him as having 'the mien of a jewelled cherub and build of an out-of-training wrestler'.[85] Labour won New Plymouth and lost Miramar. Its vote fell to 41.21 per cent. National's vote fell to 43.40 per cent. Social Credit jumped to 14.4 per cent. It won one seat (Hobson),

Labour won 35 and National 44. Only 86.59 per cent of electors voted, the lowest turnout since 1935.[86]

In the second half of the 1960s the New Zealand economy ran into difficulties. The National government introduced the toughest economic measures since 1958 after a crash in wool prices at the end of 1966. Consumer subsidies were removed, a number of government charges increased and, belatedly, the New Zealand dollar devalued by 20 per cent.[87] Unemployment jumped from 500 to 13,000 in 1967 (Nordmeyer couldn't resist 'bestowing the charity of his silence' on the government).[88] The sudden death of Harry Lake, the minister of finance, in February 1967 gave Labour an opportunity to capitalise on the bad economic news. His Fendalton seat was blue-ribbon National. Labour's Bruce Barclay won on election night, only to lose by 286 on the final count. There was a 7 per cent swing to Labour.[89]

The parliamentary party used this success to argue for improvements in Labour's election organisation. In a report adopted by the national executive, Auckland MPs and former party organisers Arthur Faulkner and Colin Moyle recommended that the party concentrate its efforts on new seats and marginal seats, appoint paid organisers in selected areas, institute systematic fundraising across the country, organise a nationwide membership drive, select candidates in key seats as soon as possible and prepare suitable publicity for distribution.[90] They also promoted a new method of election organisation, outlined by Moyle in a pamphlet, *Organising to Win*, in which canvassing data was collected and analysed to target potential Labour voters on election day, when scrutineers' reports from polling booths would be used to identify supporters who had not voted so they could be visited by the party's canvassers.[91]

There could be little disagreement about improving the party's election methods. However, there was fierce debate about Labour's organisation and changes to its constitution. The central issue was regional organisation and the main battleground was Auckland. The Auckland Regional Advisory Council's success in fundraising, organising educational seminars and promoting new ways of electioneering meant it trod on the toes of the traditionalists. This was particularly so after it appointed Jim Anderton, a gifted organiser with experience in the Catholic Youth Movement, as its first paid secretary/organiser in late 1965. Roger Douglas observed, 'Jim Anderton gave us real oomph, particularly in the fundraising area.'[92] Broad, the Auckland LRC president, was candid about the tensions. He told the

LRC's annual meeting in 1966 that for Labour to win nationally, 'a strong centre in Auckland is vital'. However, there was considerable suspicion of 'Auckland power seeking' by some on the national executive and some leading members of the LRC had deliberately undermined the Regional Advisory Council's efforts.[93]

The 1967 annual conference focused on constitutional issues. The reformers in the Auckland Regional Advisory Council came up with a plan for a complete revision of the party's constitution. The Red Book, as it became known, was 'forthright in our criticisms and sweeping in the changes we suggest'. It proposed that multiple-electorate LRCs be abolished and replaced with LRCs (consisting of branch and union delegates) in each electorate. Regional councils, made up of four delegates from each LRC, would be formed in Auckland, Waikato, Wellington, Christchurch and Dunedin. The national executive would consist of the president and vice-president, elected by the annual conference, three representatives of the parliamentary party (with no right to vote) and eight to ten regional representatives. The Wellington-based central executive would be abolished. Regional conferences would discuss remits from LRCs and send them on to the annual conference. Representation at the annual conference would be from regional councils and LRCs only. Branches and affiliated unions would no longer be represented in their own right.[94]

The reformers overreached themselves with these proposals. Kirk and Norman Douglas, MP for Auckland Central (who replaced Kirk as party president), came down on them hard.[95] The Regional Advisory Council had organised a study weekend to discuss its plans. This was cancelled on the instructions of the national executive, which ordered that the Red Book be recalled.[96] Unions were furious at its proposals. Dave Isbey, a maritime worker who succeeded Broad as Auckland LRC president, said: 'whatever changes there are going to be . . . the Trade Union Movement must have its proper representation and equal voice or we shall be doomed to a political wilderness'.[97] The 1967 conference 'resulted in a crushing, though temporary, defeat for the reformers on almost every issue'.[98] To counter the Auckland plan, the New Zealand executive (as the national executive was renamed in 1967) proposed that divisional area councils could be formed by two or more LRCs. This was carried. Anderton (representing the Manukau LRC) and Trevor de Cleene (Palmerston North LRC) moved an amendment to establish regional councils. This was defeated by 457 votes to 102.[99]

'[W]e went to conference like lambs to the slaughter', Anderton later said. He was attacked publicly by Norman Douglas and McDonald and resigned as Regional Advisory Council secretary/organiser.[100]

Although it took until the 1970s for the reformers to win the argument for regional organisation throughout the country, their set-back was only temporary in Auckland. The traditionalists' base was the Auckland LRC. By the late 1960s it was a shadow of the organisation it had once been. It included only half the Auckland electorates, some of which were the inner-city seats, whose branch membership was falling fast, and attendances at LRC meetings were low. Its financial position was deteriorating, and in 1968 three of the eight electorates in the LRC decided to break away.[101] In contrast, the Regional Advisory Council had an income of about $30,000 a year.[102] A special LRC meeting in November 1968 set up a committee, chaired by Gordon Dryden (Labour's publicity officer in 1966) and including reformers and traditionalists, to review party organisation in Auckland.[103] The Regional Advisory Council's leaders wisely kept their distance. Submissions were invited from party organisations and most supported change. The subcommittee recommended that the LRC and Regional Advisory Council be merged into a new Auckland Labour Regional Council, which would be the central campaign committee in Auckland and the 'main centre for strengthening the ties between the Party, the unions and the other key sections of society'. It would have two delegates from each electorate, trade union representation on the same basis as the Auckland LRC, and one delegate each from the women's branch, Auckland Labour youth council, university branch and the industrial Quay Street branch.[104] The report was unanimously adopted by the Regional Advisory Council and the LRC.[105] The new organisation came into being on 1 May 1969.

Barry Gustafson has documented the changes in the occupational composition of party branch members in Auckland. Between 1949 and 1969, those in semi-professional and professional jobs increased from 1.5 per cent to 14.5 per cent. Those in semi-skilled and unskilled manual jobs fell from 34.6 per cent to 21.1 per cent.[106] These changes, which partly reflected wider social changes, were symbolised by the emergence of a strong youth movement in the party in the second half of the 1960s. The New Zealand executive's report to the 1968 annual conference welcomed 'the resurgence of activity within the junior section of the party. Branches have been formed in a number of areas'. It recommended that in future they be called youth branches.[107] A conference of youth delegates held the weekend before the conference recommended that a Youth Advisory Council be elected to co-ordinate activities.[108] The 1969 annual conference voted to elect a youth representative on the New Zealand executive. Mike Moore, an Auckland printer, defeated Michael Hirschfeld, a Wellington university graduate, by 261 votes to 237 for the position.[109] The importance of these developments was not lost on women within the party. Throughout the 1950s and 1960s the annual meetings of women delegates had argued for a greater say. The 1969 women's meeting unanimously recommended a Women's Advisory Council: 'New Zealand Labour women are not playing as full a part as is desirable, and positive leadership and encouragement from the Party would do so much in this connection', it said in its report to the conference.[110]

The youth branches of the late 1960s were different from the junior branches of the 1940s and 1950s. They were interested in policy rather than social activities and sports. The university branches, in particular, were active in proposing remits to the annual conference and organising their members to attend (often as delegates from other branches). The Princes Street branch, the Auckland university branch formed in 1960 on the initiative of Norman Douglas, was the leader in promoting new policy. It published pamphlets on its policy ideas and pushed for educational reforms.[111] David Butcher, the interim Youth Advisory Council president, told the 1969 youth conference that 'although issues of economic welfare remain important, the Party must recognise that a growing percentage of people are most concerned with moral issues'. The youth conference said, somewhat tongue-in-cheek, that Labour 'must continue to speak out fearlessly on moral issues'.[112] Remits on moral issues, civil liberties and foreign policy had a mixed fate at annual conferences. In 1969 there was support for abolishing corporal punishment in schools, but remits to disband the Security Intelligence Service, support homosexual law reform and oppose regional defence alliances were defeated.[113] Tensions over these issues reflected differences within New Zealand society and the party leadership's concern that Labour should not be distracted or get too far out of step with provincial conservatism in an election year.

Labour approached the 1969 general election with a good deal of confidence. Kirk had established himself as a credible leader. At the 1967 conference the New Zealand executive, at his prompting, had pushed through a constitutional change requiring MPs over 70 to retire.[114]

Nordmeyer, Howard, Bob Macfarlane, Ritchie Macdonald and Iriaka Rātana retired in 1969 (some reluctantly). Mason had stood down, or been eased out, in 1966; Tirikātene had died in 1967 and Nash in 1968. The old guard was gone. After 1966 Kirk reorganised the party's front bench and caucus committees to develop greater policy expertise and more effective opposition in parliament.[115] Joe Walding's victory in Palmerston North in December 1967, the first time an opposition party had won a by-election since 1946, was a boost for Labour.[116]

The 1969 election campaign was closely fought between National and Labour. Holyoake faltered in a televised debate with Kirk, who campaigned strongly. A poll published nine days before the election showed the parties were neck and neck. A long-running industrial dispute involving Auckland seafarers was seized on by the government and the media in the last days of the campaign. Labour MPs felt this cost the party the election.[117] National won 45 seats to Labour's 39, but there was a difference of only 12,707 votes between them. National won 44.89 per cent, Labour 43.95 per cent, and Social Credit slumped to 8.96 per cent.[118] Among the new MPs was a young Auckland accountant, Roger Douglas, who joined his father Norman in caucus; a rare pairing.

By 1969, as Jim Eagles and Colin James have written, Labour had changed significantly. It was:

> a modern party, subscribing to the fundamental principles of 1935 in relation to social justice, but fully in tune with 1960s materialism . . . It was still attentive to workers' needs in industrial law but it was also pitching its appeal to the increasing proportion of white-collar workers in the workforce, to manufacturers through its programme for expanding production by private enterprise. It was shedding the image of regimentation that had dogged it since the 1940s. Now it looked to increase the cake rather than redivide it, and it was trying to project itself as the party of the man of initiative.[119]

8

Ruined Optimism: The Kirk Years 1970–75

By 1970 the Labour Party had largely changed from the mass-membership party of the 1930s and 1940s which was dominated by the parliamentary leadership, into a smaller but more democratic and modern party which attracted activists from the growing anti-apartheid, environment, peace and women's movements. This engagement with 'new social movements' was increasingly a hallmark of social democratic parties at the time. Kirk and Labour's front bench outshone the National government, which looked old and tired. However, there was growing economic instability, the world economy was changing and the post-war settlement was beginning to fracture.[1] Following the Arbitration Court's 1968 'nil wage order', the arbitration system came under increasing pressure and there was a big increase in strikes. It was the party's misfortune to finally win office just before the worst recession in 40 years hit the world economy.

Labour swept into office in 1972 winning over 48 per cent of votes and a 23-seat majority, although it had small margins in a number of electorates. It seemed Labour would be in power for a long time. The third Labour government endeavoured to refurbish the welfare state. It instituted a number of important reforms, particularly in education, Māori affairs, social welfare and superannuation. Kirk changed New Zealand's foreign policy from one subservient to the western alliance to one which emphasised independence, cultivated relations with Asia and Africa and vigorously opposed racism and nuclear weapons. However, Labour struggled to manage the economy, which was booming when it took office. Inflation was rising sharply and the government's price control measures were a failure. Although Britain's accession to the European Economic Community in 1973 had long been foreseen, and a workable arrangement made for New Zealand exports to the EEC, trade diversification remained an urgent priority. Following the October 1973 Arab–Israeli war, the Organization of Petroleum Exporting Countries (OPEC) sharply increased oil prices. There was a global economic downturn in 1974 and New Zealand's terms of trade fell sharply. Kirk's untimely death in August 1974 robbed the party of its popular and dominant leader. The Labour government was successful in avoiding a depression and mass unemployment, but politically it was no match for a resurgent National Party led by Robert Muldoon, which won a sweeping victory in 1975.

Organising in a new society

Labour's shock victory in the February 1970 Marlborough by-election, only two months after the general election, put the government on the back foot. Labour had run an effective advertising campaign in 1969, women and young people had a growing voice in the party, and a quarter of Labour's 40 MPs were new.[2] To bolster the party's finances, membership subscriptions were doubled and a $200 levy on electorates introduced.[3] The decline in branch membership was halted at 13,193 in 1970. Over the next five years there was an 8 per cent increase to 14,247.[4]

Bill Rowling, MP for Buller since 1962, was elected unopposed as party president in 1970.[5] He had been narrowly defeated for vice-president by Henry May in 1966, 1967 and 1968, before beating May in 1969.[6] Rowling epitomised the new breed of Labour MP elected after 1960. He had a degree in economics, had served in the army and was a teacher. He came from a strong Labour family in Motueka.[7] Charles Bennett, a commander of the Māori Battalion during the Second World War and former diplomat and senior public servant, who had contested Rotorua for Labour in 1969, was narrowly elected vice-president with strong support from Kirk.[8] John Wybrow, a former Treasury officer, replaced McDonald as general secretary in 1971.[9] These leaders, and new executive members such as Stan Rodger and Gerald O'Brien, were much more open to reform of the party than the executive of the 1960s. The 1970 conference established a permanent standing committee of executive members and MPs to review the constitution.[10]

The changes in the party were also reflected in the increasing influence of Māori, women and young people. Since 1936 Labour had had a Māori

Advisory Committee or Māori Policy Committee. After 1969, when Matiu Rata, MP for Northern Māori, became its chair, the Māori Policy Committee had a greater focus on policy and became a stronger voice within the party. There was a substantial increase in Māori delegates to the party conference.[11] The committee's strong attack on sporting contacts with South Africa was important in encouraging the party leadership to propose a resolution opposing the All Black tour of South Africa to the 1970 conference.[12] In 1972 150 people attended a Māori Policy Committee convention at Te Poho-o-Rāwiri marae in Gisborne.[13] The Māori Policy Committee's reports argued consistently for maintaining a distinct Māori identity and developing institutions that could strengthen the place of Māori in New Zealand society.[14] At the 1971 conference Rata said the National government's legislation alienating Māori land had given rise to discontent and 'one of the greatest needs is to ratify the principles contained in the Treaty [of Waitangi]'.[15]

The importance of these developments was not lost on women. The Women's Advisory Committee struck a radical note in its report to the 1970 conference:

> We have a new and revolutionary situation as regards women. For the first time in the history of civilisation, women can control their own fertility and . . . it is going to have undreamed of changes in society . . . we must make it crystal clear that Labour not only believes that women have a point of view . . . but that it is prepared to promote such a viewpoint by reflecting them in policy.

The report noted that in 1969 many of the non-voters were women. 'We warned the Party about this last conference and we are convinced that had the same amount of money been expended on enlisting the support of women as was for younger voters, Labour would be the Government today.'[16]

The women's representatives on the national executive in the late 1960s and 1970s were mainly trade union women, such as Sonja Davies, Eileen Crawford, Mary Batchelor, Dorothy Jelicich, Connie Purdue and Maureen Gibbons. A number of more radical women who were active in the Women's Advisory Committee, such as Margaret Shields, Lois Welch and Sue Kedgley, were critical of the party's treatment of women members.[17] At the 1972 conference Welch said women were largely ignored; Shields complained that the women's report was 'merely an act of super tolerance by the party and means very little'.[18] However, women's concerns were becoming more visible in the party. Feminist women had a noticeable impact on the views of older women delegates. For the 1972 election, Batchelor was selected for the safe Avon seat and Jelicich for a winnable Hamilton seat, and the party published a special campaign leaflet directed at women.[19] Already, too, a young Whetū Tirikātene-Sullivan had succeeded her father in Southern Māori.

The youth section had the most fractious relationship with the party hierarchy. The number of delegates to the annual conference under 25 years of age increased from fewer than 10 in the early 1960s to about 60 in the early 1970s.[20] About half the delegates to the annual youth conference were university students. Youth delegates were on the left of the party, although most were moderate, not radical left-wingers.[21] Many were active in the anti-apartheid and anti-Vietnam War protest movements. In a 1975 interview, Helen Clark, an activist in the Princes Street branch and leader of the Youth Advisory Committee, explained why she and other young radicals had joined the Labour Party:

> After the [1969] election it seemed clear to me that unless you had a political party pushing your ideas you would forever be knocking your head against a brick wall . . . The youth section of the party acts in a way as the conscience of the party . . . Most people in the youth section would call themselves Socialists, whereas the main body of the party would not always be happy with that label.[22]

The 1970 youth report was critical that policies passed by the annual conference were not included in Labour's election manifesto.[23] The 1971 report complained that the parliamentary party and the executive were overcautious on issues of vital concern to youth and had failed to co-operate with the Vietnam peace movement and groups opposing racist South African sports tours.[24]

Co-operating with protest groups was the last thing the party leadership wanted to do. Kirk, in particular, was sensitive to the point of paranoia about Labour's connections with radicals.[25] As the 1972 election approached, and Labour's lead in the polls over National fell, the leadership was anxious to distance itself from the left. The Socialist Action League, a small Trotskyite organisation, was proscribed by the executive, so its handful of members in the Labour Party were forced to resign.[26] The Victoria University Labour Club protested that this decision was 'unwise and a bad precedent'. It did not sympathise with or support the Socialist Action League, but argued that if it was ignored it would have little influence in the party.[27]

At the 1972 annual conference there was a major row about the youth report. Rowling insisted that resolutions passed by the youth conference be deleted. These included resolutions expressing support for the National Liberation Front in South Vietnam and for non-violent protest to disrupt the proposed 1973 South African rugby tour of New Zealand.[28] The leadership got its way, but the report presented to the conference pulled no punches. It criticised the majority of Labour MPs for failing to realise that 'bold statements of conviction would help change public opinion to our way of thinking'. The report concluded that unless Labour stated 'clearly, courageously and firmly the position of democratic socialism', the people would undoubtedly choose once again the philosophy of self-interest proclaimed by National.[29]

In September 1972 the Wellington LRC held a study conference to strengthen contacts between the party and members of pressure groups and to suggest that these groups would get a better hearing from a Labour government than from National. Pressure from the leadership resulted in the organisers dropping Kay Goodger, a prominent feminist and Socialist Action League member, from the speaking list. The speakers included several academics and a number of Wellington Labour candidates.[30] It was a respectable line-up, but Labour MPs were strongly opposed to the conference being held close to the election and tried, unsuccessfully, to stop it.[31]

The major debates at Labour Party conferences in the early 1970s were on foreign policy and moral issues. Supporters of an independent foreign policy had some success, with conference decisions that New Zealand withdraw from SEATO and to prohibit New Zealand companies and individuals from investing in South Africa.[32] However, they were defeated on remits to set a date for the withdrawal of New Zealand troops from Malaysia and Singapore and to ban trade with South Africa.[33] The 1971 conference rejected remits calling for the abolition of the Security Intelligence Service and reform of the cannabis laws, but supported homosexual law reform.[34] The 1972 conference debated a remit that a Labour government give favourable consideration to liberalising the law on abortion. Kirk, ultra-conservative on that issue, made a lengthy speech at the end of the debate to ensure the remit was defeated.[35]

Despite heavy-handed interventions like this, the Labour Party of the 1970s was a far cry from the leadership-dominated party of the 1940s, when most cabinet ministers sat on the platform and made lengthy speeches, particularly during debates on remits.[36] Richard Northey's comprehensive study of the party's annual conferences from the mid-1950s to the early 1970s shows that, while the parliamentary party dominated policy formation, rank-and-file opinion, as expressed by conference decisions, was influential. About 40 per cent of policy resolutions endorsed by the conference eventually reached the party's manifesto in some form.[37] The conference was the largest and most representative gathering of Labour's supporters and MPs gave its views 'considerable respect for that reason'.[38]

Labour was often accused by National of being dominated by trade unions. Northey's study rejected this claim. Union delegates were only a quarter of those present at conferences. While they had over 50 per cent of the voting entitlement, card votes were infrequent and union delegates were often as divided as the conference as a whole. Unions did tend to vote as a block on changes to the constitution that they thought affected their status in the party, and their votes were influential in the executive elections.[39] Union votes were decisive in Kirk's elections in the 1960s as vice-president and president and in delaying Rowling's rise to the presidency.[40] Michael Hirschfeld, a leader of the left, was narrowly elected to the executive in 1971;[41] lobbying by conservative union leaders was crucial in ensuring his defeat a year later. The political scientist Keith Jackson described this as 'naked machine politics'.[42]

Northey argued that the conference's format had not been adapted 'to make it principally a show-piece for the Party leadership'. It was mainly 'an avenue for the expression of those sections of the Party's rank and file that are present'. While the conference was not 'the supreme governing body of the Party', as Labour's constitution stated, it provided 'a very important forum within the movement', which helped initiate, demonstrate and influence 'major trends of thinking within the Party'.[43]

The surviving branch records show that a number remained focused on social activities and fundraising. For example, the Horowhenua women's branch held bazaars, regular sales of sewing and knitting and well-attended Christmas parties. It raised substantial amounts of money.[44] The Tākaka branch raised funds through dances and street stalls.[45] The Blenheim branch held an annual cabaret. In 1970 its social committee approved the following items for catering: 25 chickens, two large hams (approximately 30 lbs), four gallons of curry and rice, $10 worth of cheerios, one good-sized hogget, pastry for savouries, $4 worth of chippies and 8 lbs of peanuts; the profit of $98 was slightly less than expected, it was reported, because 'some of the liquid refreshments had gone astray'.[46] Provincial branches did not ignore policy issues, but tended to be conservative. After the 1971 conference debate on cannabis, the Tākaka branch passed a resolution deploring any action to reduce penalties for pushing or taking drugs.[47] The Allenton branch in Ashburton called for more severe penalties for crimes committed by young people.[48] The Blenheim branch complained about stoppages on the Cook Strait ferries and called for the deregistration of maritime unions.[49]

Time for a change: the 1972 victory

Labour went into the 1972 election campaign with policies that reflected the party's continued commitment to the welfare state and struck an uneasy balance between progressive urban youth and provincial conservatism. Kirk told the 1972 conference that a Labour government would 're-establish that the family is the base unit of our society . . . and the key to its happiness and fulfilment'.[50] To the dismay of liberals, Labour campaigned hard on law and order. It said the growth of gangs and violence was one of the country's most serious social problems and promised to take bikes off the bikies and send 'selected first offenders' to 'rigorous and Spartan corrective work camps'.[51] Radical policies included abolishing wage controls, introducing a wage-related compulsory contributory superannuation scheme, preventing the raising of lakes Manapōuri, Te Anau and Wānaka, providing major government assistance for regional development, lowering the voting age from 20 to 18, overhauling local government, increasing government assistance to exporters and introducing an independent foreign policy. Labour promised sweeping changes in education, health and housing and increased welfare benefits. It pledged to support the retention of Māori land in Māori ownership, support Māori land incorporations and trust boards, and consider confirming the principles of the Treaty of Waitangi in law.[52] The manifesto promised 'something for everyone'.[53] The party adopted the Australian Labor Party's campaign slogan, 'It's Time'. Its overarching campaign theme was Kirk's promise that a Labour government would 'create the climate in which New Zealand can grow to strong, independent, self-reliant nationhood'.[54]

Labour's campaign was hamstrung by money: its advertising budget was only $50,000, compared to more than $100,000 for National and $45,000 for Social Credit. Its campaign was concentrated on South Island marginal seats (particularly the Otago and Southland seats, where there was strong opposition to raising lake levels to generate more electricity for the Comalco aluminium smelter) and the marginal provincial city seats in the North Island (where there was resentment that National had neglected the regions).[55] Kirk campaigned hard. In 23 days 'he criss-crossed the country . . . making up to eight speeches a day . . . working 16–18 hour days'.[56] He modestly told the 1973 party conference that Labour's victory was 'the victory of thousands of people not of one man'.[57] However, his leadership was central to the party's success. During the election campaign Kirk dominated Jack Marshall, who had replaced Holyoake as prime minister in early 1972.

Labour won a landslide victory. It won 15 seats: Awarua, Invercargill, Otago Central, Ōamaru, Rangiora, Kapiti, Whanganui, Hastings, Taupo, Hamilton East, Hamilton West, Gisborne, Eden, Waitematā and Whāngārei. Batchelor and Jelicich were elected, doubling the number of women Labour MPs to four. Labour won 48.37 per cent of votes and 55 seats, National 41.5 per cent and 32 seats. Social Credit's vote fell to 6.65 per cent. The Values Party, New Zealand's first green party, which was formed only six months before the election, won nearly 2 per cent. However, Labour's majority was not impregnable. It held 14 seats by majorities of less than 7 per cent.[58]

Most of the members of the new cabinet had a lot of political experience, although only Watt had been a minister in the Nash government. Kirk was minister of foreign affairs; Watt deputy prime minister, minister of labour and minister of works; Freer trade and industry and energy resources; Rowling finance; Finlay attorney-general and justice; Rata Māori affairs and lands; Mick Connelly customs and police; Faulkner defence; Norman King social welfare; Tizard health and state services; Moyle agriculture; Fraser housing; May internal affairs and local government; Basil Arthur transport; Amos education and Pacific Island affairs; Tirikātene-Sullivan tourism; Joe Walding overseas trade and environment; Fraser Colman immigration; Tom McGuigan railways and electricity; and Roger Douglas broadcasting. Rata was the first Māori to hold the Māori affairs portfolio since Sir Āpirana Ngata in the 1930s.[59]

Above: Although women were active in the party from its inception and Māori from the 1920s, Labour's national executive was all male until the constitution was changed in 1957 to provide for women and Māori representatives. This photograph is of the 1952–53 national executive. Stand from left: Ray Boord (assistant national secretary), R.A. Keeling (Gisborne), H.E. Combs (Wellington), J.H. Collins (Wellington), C.R. Palmer (New Plymouth), G.A. Hansen (Kaiporoporo), F.J. Kitts (Wellington), J.A. Stead (Dunedin), J.J. Lynch (Southland), R.F. Barter (Auckland), A. Hallyn (Whāngārei), E.A. Waters (Hamilton), H.L.J. May (Wellington), T. Martin (Christchurch) and Michael Moohan (Wellington). Seated from left: Walter Nash (leader), James Roberts (vice-president), Arnold Nordmeyer (president), Allan McDonald (national secretary), Rex Mason (parliamentary representative). New Zealand Labour Party. PAColl-1179-09-002, Alexander Turnbull Library

Below: Tapihana (Dobbie) Paraire Paikea, Te Uri-o-Hau and Ngāti Whatua (1920–1963), was a Rātana minister and Labour MP for Northern Māori from 1943 to 1963, succeeding his father, Paraire Karaka Paikea. The Paraire whānau's close association with Labour and Rātana was continued by Dobbie's grandson, Tapihana Shelford, who provided constant support and advice to Helen Clark. New Zealand Labour Party collection

Above: Walter Nash (1882–1968) was criticised for the amount of time he spent overseas while he was prime minister. He is met at the airport by Rex Mason (1885–1975) (minister of justice), left, and Jerry Skinner (1900–1962) (deputy prime minister), centre. New Zealand Labour Party. PAColl-1179-05-001, Alexander Turnbull Library

Left: Tiaki Ōmana, Ngāti Kahungunu (1891–1970), Labour MP for Eastern Māori from 1943 to 1963, was a successful sheep farmer and runholder who joined the Rātana movement in the 1930s. He defeated Sir Āpirana Ngata in 1943 to give Labour and Rātana all four Māori electorates. New Zealand Labour Party collection

Opposite, top: Bill Rowling (1927–1995) narrowly won Buller in a by-election in 1962. He was one of a group of young, university-educated MPs who helped revitalise the party in the 1960s and 1970s. Sonja Davies Collection. PAColl-9354-5-011, Alexander Turnbull Library

Opposite, bottom: Ethel McMillan (1904–1987) was Labour MP for Dunedin North from 1953 to 1975. She was married to Gervan McMillan, MP for Dunedin West, from 1935 to 1943. Ethel McMillan also had a long career in local government as a member of the Otago Hospital Board and the Dunedin City Council (where she was the first woman councillor). New Zealand Labour Party collection

Above: The Labour Party national executive in 1966 when the party celebrated its 50th birthday. Back row: L.T. Fischer (Napier), B.J. Landers (Wellington), R. Waishing (Pukekohe), L.C. Hair (Wainuiomata), N.J. Callaghan (Tauranga). Third row: W.G. Kenyon (Motueka), B.A. Manson (Invercargill), B.G. Barclay (Christchurch), J.H. Collins (Wellington), E.A. Waters (Hamilton). Second row: A.L. Leaming (Kaukapakapa), E.J. Hemmingsen (Palmerston North), J .McLaffery (New Plymouth), Norman King (parliamentary representative), J. Dalziel (Dunedin), A.E.P. Boorman (Auckland). Front row: Sonja Davies (women's representative), Fraser Colman (assistant national secretary), Jim Bateman (vice-president), Norman Kirk (president and leader), Allan McDonald (national secretary), Ralph Love (Māori representative), Ethel Harris (women's representative). New Zealand Labour Party. PAColl-1179-09-001, Alexander Turnbull Library

Opposite, top: The second Labour government after being sworn in at Government House, 1957. Standing from left: Bill Anderton, Philip Skoglund, Philip Holloway, Hugh Watt, Eruera Tirikātene, Philip Connolly, Jock Mathison, Ray Boord, Michael Moohan and Bill Fox. Seated from left: Fred Hackett, Arnold Nordmeyer, Walter Nash, Viscount Cobham (governor-general), Jerry Skinner, Rex Mason and Mabel Howard. New Zealand Labour Party collection

Opposite, bottom: Iriaka Matiu Rātana, Te Āti Haunui-a-Pāpārangi (1905–1981), was Labour MP for Western Māori from 1949 to 1969. She won the seat after the death of her husband, Matiu, the younger son of Tahupōtiki Wiremu Rātana, who had succeeded his elder brother, Haami Tokouru Rātana. The photograph shows Iriaka, with her niece Mīria Veuger, meeting Indira Ghandi, prime minister of India, on 28 May 1968. New Zealand Labour Party collection

Above, left: Puti Tīpene (Steve) Wātene, Ngāti Maru and Te Arawa (1910–1967), was the first Māori representative on Labour's national executive. As chair of the Māori Policy Committee he expressed the frustration of Māori in the party at the lack of progress under the second Labour government. He was elected MP for Eastern Māori in 1963. A Mormon, he was the first non-Rātana Labour Māori MP. Wātene died of a heart attack at Parliament Buildings in 1967 while cross-examining a witness in a hearing on the controversial Māori Affairs Amendment Bill. New Zealand Labour Party. PAColl-1179-03-001, Alexander Turnbull Library

Above, right: Martyn Finlay (1912–1999) was Labour MP for North Shore, 1946–49 and Waitākere and Henderson, 1963–78. One of Labour's outstanding intellectuals, he was a strong advocate for party reform as party president from 1960 to 1964. New Zealand Labour Party collection

Opposite: Norman Kirk (1923–1974) speaking at Civic Square Wellington, 1972 election campaign. John Miller photograph

EUROPA
OUR COUNTRY
CLEAR WEAPONS FREE

HOA BINH VIETNAM LOVE IT or LEAVE IT!!
PEACE
US MONOPOLIES THRIVE ON US AGGRESSION
STOP THE
LABOUR PARTY.
AGAINST THE WAR

Above: Norman Kirk had a great affinity with Māori. This photograph shows him meeting local children during coronation celebrations at Tūrangawaewae marae in May 1973. John Miller photograph

Opposite, top: Members of CANWAR (Campaign Against Nuclear Warships) aboard the yacht Phoenix at the Port Nicholson Yacht Club in Wellington harbour, 13 August 1976. They are about to sail to Seatoun to stand watch for the arrival of the American nuclear warship USS Truxtun. There was a series of one-day strikes by the port unions in protest at ship's visit. Protests like these helped build public support for a nuclear-free New Zealand, a policy adopted by the Labour Party in the early 1980s. *Evening Post* photograph. EP/1976/2841/26a-F, Alexander Turnbull Library

Opposite, bottom: A Labour banner in an anti-Vietnam War mobilisation in Auckland in 1972. Opposition to the Vietnam War led many young people to become involved in politics in the 1960s and 1970s and the anti-war movement was an important recruiting ground for Labour Youth. John Miller photograph

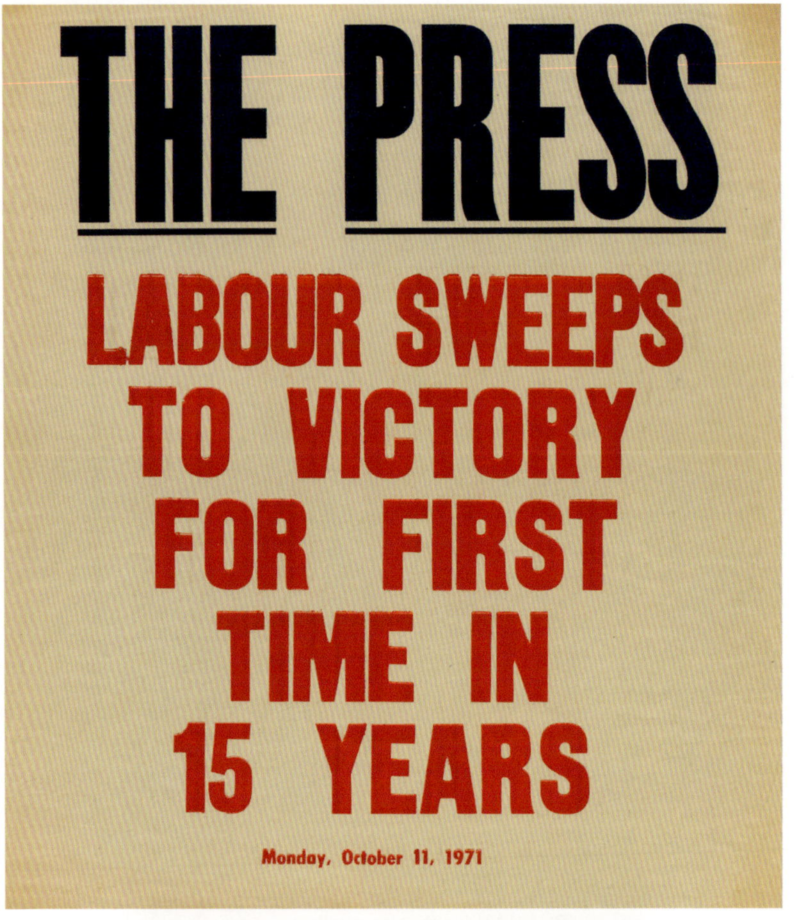
THE PRESS
LABOUR SWEEPS TO VICTORY FOR FIRST TIME IN 15 YEARS
Monday, October 11, 1971

Above: Most of the people in this photograph of the 1972–73 executive of the Auckland Labour Regional Council were key players in the debates about reforming Labour's organisation in the 1970s. From left: George Broad, Dave Isbey, Philip Holloway, Jock Stewart, Richard Prebble, Ken Hastings (secretary), Michael Bassett (president), Les Ritchie (vice-president), Fred Gerbic, Brian Lythe and Chris Pickett. New Zealand Labour Party, Auckland Regional Council records. MSS & Archives A-161, Special Collections, University of Auckland Libraries and Learning Services

Opposite, top: Neville Pickering was elected Labour mayor of Christchurch in 1971 and Labour won the council by 12 seats to seven. Labour's success in the local body elections foreshadowed the party's general election victory in 1972. Press Collection. Eph-D-LOCAL-Christchurch-1971-0 Alexander Turnbull Library

Opposite, bottom: Colin Moyle, MP for Manukau and Māngere, 1963–77 and Hūnua and Ōtara, 1981–90, played a leading role in the revitalisation of the Labour Party after its 1960 defeat. He was a party organiser from 1960 to 1963 and initiated the formation of the party's Auckland Regional Advisory Council. He and Arthur Faulkner (MP for Roskill) were the party's main election organisers in the 1960s and early 1970s. Moyle was a cabinet minister from 1972 to 1975 and 1984 to 1990, and was Labour's longest-serving minister of agriculture. New Zealand Labour Party collection

Above: Matiu Rata (1934–1997) (minister of Māori affairs) and Bill Rowling (prime minister) meeting the 1975 land march at parliament. Phil Amos (minister of Pacific Island affairs) is to Rowling's right; Ralph Love, one of Labour's most prominent Māori leaders, is next to Amos. Robert Muldoon (leader of the National Party) is to Rata's left. John Miller photograph

Opposite, top: Tiria Asher, a member of the Tawa–Linden branch, the Women's Advisory Council and the Māori Policy Committee, places a flower on Norman Kirk's casket as it is carried into parliament by his colleagues. Matiu Rata, Bill Rowling and Hugh Watt are on the left and Mick Connelly, Colin Moyle, Norman King (obscured), Martyn Finlay and Warren Freer (obscured) are on the right. John Miller photograph

Opposite, bottom: Bob Tizard (1924–2016) became a Labour activist as a school boy. He was MP for Tāmaki, 1957–60 and for Ōtāhuhu, Pakuranga and Panmure, 1963–90. Tizard was one of Labour's most able MPs, serving as minister of health, state services and finance and deputy prime minister in the third Labour government and as minister of energy and defence in the fourth. New Zealand Labour Party collection

Above: Bill Rowling on the campaign trail in 1978. Glen, his wife, is to his right. After Labour's big defeat in 1975, Rowling led the party to a moral victory. It won more votes than National in 1978 (as it did in 1981) but lost the election. New Zealand Labour Party collection

Left: Cath Tizard was mayor of Auckland from 1983 to 1990 and New Zealand's first woman governor-general, 1990–96. One of the few Labour candidates to be elected to the Auckland City Council after the 1950s, she was a councillor from 1971 to 1980. This leaflet is from her first mayoral campaign in 1980. New Zealand Labour Party, Mt Albert Electorate Committee records. MSS & Archives 2015/3, folder 4/7. Special Collections, University of Auckland Libraries and Learning Services

Opposite: The New Zealand Council and party staff, 1980–81. Front from left: Bill Rowling (leader), Jim Anderton (president), David Lange (deputy leader). Second row from left: Alan O'Neill, Barry Brown, Reg Boorman, John Wybrow (general secretary), Fred Anderson, Joan Sim, Arch Philpott. Third row from left: unidentified, unidentified, Stewart McCaffley (senior vice-president), unidentified. Fourth row from left: Helen Clark, unidentified, Jim Kebble, Nick Barnett, unidentified, Jack Elder. Fifth row from left: Bill Jeffries, Mike Williams, Dave Vallely, unidentified. Sixth row from left: Jock McChesney, John Hercus, Pam Nuttall, Pete Hodgson, Paula Clark. Seventh row from left: unidentified, unidentified, Stan Rodger. Back row from left: Murdo Macmillan (assistant general secretary), Aubrey Begg, John Thew, Simon Walker, unidentified. Stan Rodger collection

Above: Richard Prebble, MP for Auckland Central, 1975–93, speaking at a meeting of Labour's Pacific Islands Advisory Council. To his left is Louisa Crawley, who was a founding member and president of PACIFICA, the nationwide Pasifika women's organisation. Prebble was minister of Pacific Island affairs, transport, railways, works, state-owned enterprises and police and associate finance minister in the fourth Labour government. New Zealand Labour Party collection

The new government moved quickly. It paid a Christmas bonus equal to one week's benefit to pensioners, and received 7000 letters of thanks. It announced that Lake Manapōuri would not be raised, removed wage controls and set up rent appeal boards. The remaining New Zealand troops in Vietnam were withdrawn. New Zealand recognised the People's Republic of China and Kirk announced that embassies would be opened in Beijing and Moscow.[60] Michael Bassett, the newly elected MP for Waitematā, wrote in 1976: 'It is impossible to over-emphasise the goodwill that existed towards the new Labour Government.'[61] On Waitangi Day 1973 Kirk won much public regard when he took the hand of a young Māori boy, Moana Priest, a member of the Ngāti Pōneke concert party, as he walked to the platform to announce that the day would become a public holiday.

The government faced a major political challenge with the South African rugby tour. There was strong support for the tour among rugby fans, and growing opposition to contacts with South Africa's apartheid regime. The protest organisation Halt All Racist Tours promised to use non-violent methods to disrupt the tour. Labour had said that it opposed it but would not stop it, but Kirk became convinced the tour would damage New Zealand's foreign policy and cause unacceptable civil strife at home (he must also have been mindful of the threat a tour would pose to the 1974 Commonwealth Games, which were to be held in Christchurch). The government asked the New Zealand Rugby Union to call off the tour; it refused. Kirk cleverly manoeuvred between both sides, playing the issue out slowly over two months before telling the Rugby Union the tour must be cancelled.[62] Bob Tizard later described Kirk's handling of the issue as an example of his consummate political skills.[63]

Labour protested at French nuclear tests in the South Pacific by taking a case to the International Court of Justice with Australia and sending the frigate *Otago* to the test zone, with Fraser Colman on board, as a sign of its opposition.[64] At the Commonwealth prime ministers' conference in August 1973, Kirk won much support for his leadership on nuclear tests, apartheid and other issues. At home, however, Labour was running into problems. The economy was expanding quickly and inflation rose on the back of an international commodity boom.[65] The government tried ineffectually to hold prices and to deal with industrial unrest. In August it reimposed wage controls.[66]

Labour's economic and social agendas were ambitious. The 1973 budget increased health and education spending significantly, relaxed the criteria for capitalisation of the family benefit for housing, and cut income tax for the majority, while increasing it for the higher paid. Industrial development councils were established and given money for subsidies and incentives to encourage manufacturers to set up in the regions. The Development Finance Corporation was nationalised, the Rural Bank established as a state-owned agency for farm finance and the Export–Import Corporation set up to promote trade development.[67]

A state-owned shipping line was established, broadcasting reorganised into three public corporations, and the law amended to speed up the implementation of equal pay in the private sector. A major reform provided for regional, district and community councils, to streamline local government. Guardians were appointed for lakes Manapōuri, Te Anau and Wānaka and environmental impact reports introduced as a check on development projects. Teacher–pupil ratios were reduced in primary and secondary schools. The Accident Compensation Act 1972 was amended to include non-earners, and the Industrial Relations Bill (largely the work of the Federation of Labour and the Employers' Federation) amended to remove most penalties for industrial action. There were substantial increases in social welfare benefits, including payment of half of a beneficiary's phone rental and television licence fee, as well as rates relief.[68]

At the 1974 conference there was a major overhaul of Labour's constitution. This was the culmination of the moves to reform the party's structures which began with the formation of the Auckland Regional Advisory Council in 1961. The path to reform continued to be difficult. At the 1973 conference, the constitution remit committee had recommended that the future structure of the party be general or special branches, single electorate LRCs, regional councils and the New Zealand executive. Unions saw this as an attempt to undermine their influence and the recommendation was defeated by 353 votes to 289. However, the conference voted to abolish the Wellington residential qualification for the central executive, and directed the standing committee on the constitution to call for submissions and circulate a complete revision of the constitution for debate the following year.[69]

The new constitution was adopted with little fuss. It streamlined the party's structure by abolishing inter-branch councils and divisional area councils. The party would consist of ordinary and special branches, union affiliates, Labour electorate committees, Labour regional councils, the New Zealand Council (as the executive body) and the annual conference. In a nod to union concerns,[70] provision was made for Labour metropolitan representation committees where there was an existing multi-electorate LRC. Branches gained the right to communicate with each other and with affiliates. The New Zealand Council was made up of a president, senior vice-president, junior vice-president, general secretary and five other members, all elected by the annual conference; other members were the chairs of the regional councils (elected locally) and two women's representatives, one youth representative, one Māori representative and one Pacific Island representative, all elected by the conference. The council would meet six times a year, with an executive, meeting monthly, consisting of the officers and the five 'at large' members. In another important change, the conference voted that the policy committee would be made up of an equal number of MPs (chosen by the parliamentary party) and party representatives (elected by the conference). Candidate selection remained largely unchanged, although 'for guidance in its deliberations' a selection committee would hold a preferential secret ballot of financial members of the party present at selection meetings.[71]

An unlucky government

In 1974 the Labour government's luck started to run out. The sharp increase in oil prices following the Arab–Israeli war contributed to political and economic instability around the world. The New Zealand economy deteriorated rapidly. Inflation reached double figures. The major industrial economies went into deflation and demand for New Zealand's exports dropped. Import prices rose and New Zealand's terms of trade fell by 23 per cent in the year to June 1974.[72] The economy fell into the worst crisis since the Depression, a crisis that was all the more severe for its suddenness. As Roger Douglas later recalled, when Labour was elected the economy 'was going like a fast train . . . and . . . we added a hell of a lot more fuel . . . All of a sudden we hit a brick wall and we didn't know how to handle that as well.'[73]

Kirk's health deteriorated in early 1974 and a strong 'sense of drift' hung over the government.[74] Its attempts at wage and price controls continued to be unsuccessful, and a long-running dispute between the drivers' and seamen's unions and an anti-union Auckland ferry owner flared into a major confrontation. The Supreme Court granted the company an injunction to force the unions to supply fuel to the ferries. Bill Andersen, the Drivers' Union secretary and a prominent communist, was arrested and jailed for defying the injunction. Between 40,000 and 50,000 workers stopped work and threatened a general strike.[75] Kirk contemplated declaring a state of emergency, and attacked unions: 'The public has had a gutsful and so have we.' Watt and Skinner negotiated a compromise, the ban on fuel supplies was lifted and Andersen was released.[76] The crisis passed, but it left a sour taste for many Labour supporters.

Kirk's health got worse. He died of heart disease on 31 August 1974, aged only 51.[77] There was a huge outpouring of public grief; in his 20 months as prime minister he had won the affection and respect of many New Zealanders. His death was a devastating blow to the Labour government and the party. Don Milne, who was the Wellington bureau chief of the *New Zealand Herald*, later described it as the worst day in New Zealand politics.[78]

Kirk played a major part in revitalising and modernising the party after 1960. He welded the parliamentary party into an effective team: he was a strong leader but, unlike Nash, was not an autocrat. His vision of nationhood captured the imagination of people who wanted an independent New Zealand. Many of the changes he made in New Zealand's foreign policy endured, and the government's opposition to nuclear weapons testing paved the way for the major changes that took place under the Lange government in the 1980s. Kirk was a mixture. A social conservative, he had little patience for demands for women's rights to control their fertility and strongly opposed homosexual law reform (although David Grant suggests that he may have been becoming more open-minded on the latter).[79] These views reflected those of many Labour supporters and party branches, particularly in provincial New Zealand. A child of the Depression, Kirk was determined to protect and rebuild the welfare state, but he had a poor grasp of economic policy. He regarded protest movements with suspicion but was a radical on race relations; strongly opposed to apartheid and strongly committed to a better deal for Māori. He understood, too, the anti-materialistic philosophy of the emerging counter-culture and, with Matiu Rata, hoped to support these aspirations through the generally short-lived experiment of ohu, intentional communities on marginal Crown land.[80]

On 6 September caucus elected Bill Rowling as leader and Labour's fifth prime minister. Tizard was elected deputy leader and Ron Bailey elected to cabinet. Rowling took foreign affairs; Tizard became minister of finance; Faulkner labour; Fraser defence; McGuigan health; and Douglas housing.[81] Colin Moyle urged Rowling to call a snap election and tell voters the country's economic problems meant that Labour couldn't fulfil all its promises, 'but with the goodwill for Kirk still there and straight honesty about the problems, I said, we'll win'.[82] Cabinet agreed. However, Rowling dithered and wanted consensus. He insisted on consulting backbenchers and those anxious about losing their seats argued against the idea.[83]

Labour's approach to the recession was to maintain full employment and ensure that those on lower incomes did not experience undue hardship, to encourage a continuing reorientation towards exporting and to control inflation.[84] Incomes policy was tightened in December 1974 and the government borrowed heavily overseas to avoid cutting public and private spending and reducing domestic production, which, Bryan Philpott estimated, would have resulted in very high unemployment of at least 50,000.[85] The 1975 budget increased spending on health, housing and education, increased taxes on petrol and duty on luxury imports, left food subsidies and postal, rail and electricity charges unchanged, reduced taxes on lower incomes and increased them on higher ones.[86] During 1974 and 1975 the government developed a new, contributory superannuation scheme. It would have significantly increased the level of savings, and eventually provided a degree of certainty around retirement income. Its major flaw, however, in a period when many women were only intermittent participants in the paid workforce, was linking payments to contributions from wages and salaries.

Rowling told the 1975 annual conference that the Labour government had achieved the lowest unemployment rate in the western world, one of the highest rates of growth and lower inflation than most developed nations.[87] However, the government was on the back foot. Robert Muldoon, who ousted Marshall as National Party leader just before Kirk's death, was a much more effective opposition leader, who succeeded in convincing many that the entire blame for the country's economic difficulties rested on the Labour government. Labour also faced some other difficult issues. Gerry Wall, Labour MP for Porirua and a social conservative, introduced (with Kirk's encouragement) a private member's bill to try to close down a privately owned abortion clinic in Remuera (the clinic was taking advantage of a lack of precision in the law about the circumstances under which abortion was permissible). The Labour Women's Council (formerly the Women's Advisory Committee) pressed for a royal commission on abortion.[88] The government agreed to this, but a police raid to seize the clinic's records, prosecution of some of its doctors and the passing of Wall's bill resulted in a lot of ill feeling (from both sides of the abortion debate) towards Labour.[89]

At the 1974 party conference women delegates held a picket to protest because the women's report was not discussed.[90] The following year the report of the Labour Women's Council was the first item on the conference agenda after the New Zealand Council's report. That year the Labour Women's Council adopted a new structure to ensure that it represented Labour women throughout the country.[91] The government funded activities for International Women's Year and Rosslyn Noonan was engaged as International Women's Year organiser. A select committee was established on the role of women in New Zealand. While this was, incongruously, chaired by the 65-year-old Norman Douglas, *Femina*, the Labour Women's Council newspaper, praised the committee's report as 'one of the most comprehensive and detailed ever to be prepared in the history of the women's movement in New Zealand'.[92] Margaret Wilson says the report was a template for the changes Labour women achieved in the 1980s: for example, the Working Women's Charter.[93]

In contrast to the Nash government, the third Labour government worked hard to carry out its promises to Māori. Rata consulted widely and held conferences of Māori trust boards and Māori land incorporations to involve Māori in decision-making.[94] There was a royal commission on Māori reserved lands, many of which were administered by officials on long, perpetually renewable leases. The 1974 Māori Affairs Amendment Act gave statutory recognition to the Māori language. It abolished the Board of Māori Affairs, established the Māori Land Board with increased Māori representation, amended the law on the alienation of Māori land and provided for land taken under the 1967 Māori Affairs Amendment Act to become Māori land again.[95]

Māori had long wanted the Treaty of Waitangi recognised by law. This was an early Labour promise which was disregarded by the first Labour government. The Treaty of Waitangi Act, passed in 1975, recognised the principles of the treaty. It established the Waitangi Tribunal to make recommendations on claims against any act or government policy which was inconsistent with the treaty, although claims could not be retrospective (Rata accepted this as the cost of caucus support for the legislation). At least as important, in time, was the fact that the tribunal was empowered to discern the Treaty's principles from the two, non-identical language versions of the document.[96] Rata told parliament that Māori had 'always regarded the treaty as a charter which protects their interests'. The legislation acknowledged its importance to both Māori and the country.[97] Koro Wetere later said Kirk had played a crucial part in shaping the bill.[98] National MPs attacked it as 'pretentious political nonsense'[99] and 'only window dressing'.[100] However, there was growing discontent among Māori, which was symbolised by the 1975 hīkoi from Te Hāpua at the top of the North Island to parliament; on 13 October about 5000 marchers presented Rowling with a petition signed by 60,000 people calling for the end of the alienation of Māori land.[101]

From late 1974 the Labour government looked under siege. Property investors and landlords, infuriated by Labour's tax on property speculation, formed the Capital Club, which ran a series of advertisements attacking the government and viciously abusing its leaders. A young Wellington speculator, Bob Jones, was a prominent figure in this agitation and he subjected Rowling to particularly nasty personal denigration, which Muldoon happily echoed.[102] Following the trial of the prominent left-wing intellectual W.B. Sutch, who was acquitted of charges of passing secrets to Soviet diplomats, the right-wing newspaper *New Zealand Truth* ran a series of articles claiming that Sutch was part of a group, with Kirk, Gerald O'Brien and the public servant Jack Lewin, that had hatched a sinister plot to socialise New Zealand. It has been suggested that there was an 'obvious link' between *Truth* and the Security Intelligence Service, on whose dubious information the articles were based.[103]

As Holyoake had done in 1960, Muldoon held a series of well-attended meetings throughout the country in the months leading up to the 1975 general election to rally National's supporters. National's well-funded campaign was its most aggressive since 1938. It denounced Labour's economic management. Its 'Dancing Cossacks' television advertisements claimed that Labour's superannuation scheme (which had come into operation on 1 April 1975) was a plan to nationalise the whole economy. The centrepiece of National's policy was a promise to replace Labour's scheme with superannuation paid out of current revenue, giving everyone over 60 a benefit calculated at 80 per cent of the average weekly wage for a married couple. National assailed trade unions and scratched every itch of prejudice against the poor, particularly the brown poor.[104]

Kirk was able to 'flatten' Muldoon in parliament, but Rowling was no match for National's leader.[105] As the economy showed no sign of a swift recovery, Labour was on the defensive. David Exel, a former television journalist, initiated the Citizens for Rowling campaign. He recruited a number of prominent people, including Edmund Hillary, Bishop Paul Reeves, the industrialist Sir Jack Harris, educationalist Walter Scott, and a young Wellington law professor, Geoffrey Palmer. The campaign tried to capitalise on the widespread dislike of Muldoon among Labour supporters and university-educated people but it backfired, as Muldoon was able to portray its supporters as elitists out of touch with 'ordinary New Zealanders'.

National won a smashing victory in November 1975. It gained 55 seats and 47.44 per cent of votes. Labour lost 23 seats and its vote tumbled nearly nine points to 39.7 per cent. Social Credit won 7.43 per cent and the Values Party 5.19 per cent. Five ministers—King, Amos, McGuigan, May and Walding—were defeated and almost all the newcomers of 1972 lost their seats.[106] In Michael Bassett's words, 'The Party had been decimated.'[107] Although the percentage of those who voted fell from 89.25 in 1972 to 82.67 in 1975, the election was held on an unchanged roll. Bassett rejected the argument that Labour lost because its supporters failed to vote: he said that taking into account the 'real' non-vote, National would have won by a 15-seat majority.[108]

The third Labour government was kneecapped by similar economic problems to those that undermined the second. The recession made life tougher for most people and the government got the blame. The government was successful in maintaining full employment in the face of a severe economic crisis, but it failed to get this message across to voters. In 1975, as in 1960, Labour was decisively outmanoeuvred by National. As a one-term government, Labour had a number of plans and reforms that were never passed or were reversed. These included superannuation, reforms of the transport and health systems, and a new satellite city at Rolleston, near Christchurch. Radical reform of local government had to wait for a future Labour government.

Nevertheless, the third Labour government's achievements were considerable. It doubled the number of children in preschool education, expanded community education and technical institutes, increased opportunities for Māori and Pacific Island students and for learning Māori, reduced class sizes and introduced a standard bursary for tertiary students. Its greatest accomplishment in education was the integration of private schools, particularly the financially struggling Catholic schools, into the state system (the Dunedin Catholic newspaper the *Tablet* was, however, singularly ungrateful).[109] As well as increasing the real incomes of beneficiaries, Labour carried out major reforms in social welfare, implementing and sometimes going beyond the recommendations of the visionary McCarthy commission on social security, which had reported in 1972. It introduced the domestic purposes benefit to give independence to solo parents, gave financial support to day care centres, increased the availability of suitable accommodation for the aged and expanded assistance for disabled people through grants to voluntary organisations such as the IHC. Child welfare law was reformed and humanised by the Children and Young Persons Act 1974.[110] Taken together, these reforms helped refurbish the welfare state. While the government struggled to get on top of demand for houses, the total number of houses built increased from 22,400 in 1971–72 to 31,000 in 1973–74.[111]

Labour lowered the voting age to 18, expanded and reorganised state funding for the arts, established the Ministry of Recreation and Sport to encourage healthier lifestyles (fulfilling some of Bill Parry's physical welfare and recreation visions of the first Labour government). It passed the Commerce Act 1975 to consolidate the law on competition, price controls, monopolies and takeovers, established a national urban fire service and increased paid holidays to three weeks a year. Its successful negotiations with the private sector resulted in the Māui gas field agreement, the largest single infrastructure undertaking by the state in New Zealand's history.[112] Its changes to policies on the environment, Māori affairs and foreign affairs were important forerunners for the future. For all its shortcomings and bad luck, it was 'a good Government'.[113]

9
Recession, Crisis and Social Tension 1975–84

The nine years of National Party rule between 1975 and 1984 were a tough time for the Labour Party. Muldoon, one of New Zealand's most polarising politicians, dominated parliament and, for most of his time in office, enjoyed much popular support. Although Rowling was tireless in opposing National's divisive policies, he was overshadowed by Muldoon. The parliamentary Labour Party was initially demoralised and became factionalised. A growing number of MPs came to the view that Labour had to ditch its traditional policies to regain economic credibility. The election of David Lange as party leader in 1983 saw Roger Douglas become finance spokesperson, and by the 1984 election Douglas had become a convert to the free-market policies later known as Rogernomics.

Unlike 1960, when Labour's defeat saw a big decline in party membership, 1975 resulted in a revival of the party. A determined effort to rebuild its membership, modernise its organisation and bolster its finances—led by Rowling and Jim Anderton (who was elected president in 1979)—saw major growth in party branches and membership. In Steve Maharey's words, by 1984 Labour 'had become the party of choice for almost anybody who wanted changes in New Zealand' and was 'an incredibly broad-based coalition'.[1]

Painful rebuilding

The savage defeat of 1975 left Labour activists reeling. Phil Goff says it was 'probably the hardest election result I've ever had to handle. I just couldn't believe that New Zealanders had turned against the Labour government in the way they had.'[2] There was a widespread feeling that the parliamentary party was out of touch. Mollie Clark, a Christchurch Labour city councillor, said that when she tried to talk to Labour ministers and MPs, 'they had a glazed look in their eyes, they weren't really interested in what you were saying. They knew the answers and you were just a silly little rabbit.'[3]

After 1975 there was 'a steady and spontaneous increase in Party membership'.[4] The first reason for this was Muldoon and National: the new government sharply attacked public spending, imposed a wage freeze and made anti-union changes to industrial laws. In 1976 the number of working days lost through strikes was the highest since 1951.[5] There was a series of confrontations with unions throughout Muldoon's nine years in office. National's attacks on civil liberties and support for sporting contacts with apartheid South Africa and American nuclear warship visits caused much public opposition.

The second reason was a concerted move by the party leadership to rebuild Labour's organisation. Head office was strengthened by the appointment of South Island organiser Murdo Macmillan as assistant general secretary, David Exel as director of communications, Eleanor Roy as Rowling's press secretary, and a number of regional organisers.[6] Jim Anderton initiated new types of fundraising and J.B. Munro, the former Labour MP for Invercargill, was appointed fundraising director.[7] The Labour supporters' fund they established raised over $500,000 by 1979.[8] Rowling threw himself into the campaign to rebuild the party, speaking at dozens of rallies and challenging the party to increase branch membership to 100,000.[9] Labour's branch membership doubled to 30,000 by mid-1976.[10]

Despite the growth of the party outside parliament, Labour was a weak opposition between 1975 and 1978. Caucus could ill afford the loss of so many younger members. One of only two new ones was a young lawyer, Richard Prebble, who took over Norman Douglas's Auckland Central seat. One of the few of the 1972 intake who held his seat was Russell Marshall, MP for Whanganui. A Methodist minister before he entered politics, Marshall was regarded as a keeper of the party's progressive conscience. The parliamentary party's difficulties were compounded by scandals concerning two MPs. In July 1976, Gerald O'Brien, MP for Island Bay, was accused of indecently assaulting two youths in his Christchurch motel room. The charges were dropped after a magistrate rejected the youths' evidence, but there was growing pressure on O'Brien not to stand again and a new selection was held for his seat, which resulted in Frank O'Flynn, MP for Kapiti between 1972 and 1975, being chosen as Labour's 1978 candidate.[11] Then, on 4 November 1976, in a particularly bad-tempered parliamentary debate, Muldoon accused Colin Moyle, the MP for Māngere, of having been 'picked up' by the police for homosexual activity. Rowling led a walkout by Labour MPs in protest. An inquiry by retired Appeal Court judge Sir Alfred North attacked Moyle for giving three different explanations of his late-night meeting with an undercover police officer in June 1975. North was strongly criticised for refusing Moyle the right of legal representation. In any case, it was constitutionally improper for an outside body to inquire into parliamentary proceedings and the matter should have gone to the Privileges Committee. North's report dealt 'a devastating blow' to Moyle's political career and in December 1976 he resigned from parliament.[12]

Moyle, who has always denied Muldoon's accusation and was seen by some as a future leader, believes Muldoon did it to remove a political rival. National MPs told him the prime minister quipped, 'That's got rid of Moyle', as he walked into a caucus meeting.[13] Senior National ministers were privately appalled at Muldoon's behaviour.[14] Moyle planned to stand in the by-election to vindicate himself; however, when Mike Moore, Labour's junior vice-president and MP for Eden in 1972–75, announced his nomination, Rowling persuaded Moyle, a close personal friend, to withdraw.[15] Eighteen people contested the Labour selection in Māngere, including Moore and Dorothy Jelicich, the former MP for Hamilton West. Another candidate was David Lange, an Auckland barrister who had contested Hobson in 1975. Lange, an untidily dressed man of imposing bulk, had had some involvement in civil liberties groups; his legal practice, which concentrated on criminal defence in the Auckland Magistrates' Court, was not lucrative, and he was a Methodist, although not, as often believed, a lay preacher. Faulkner, the party president, had endorsed Moyle as the candidate, so he withdrew from the selection panel. Stan Rodger, as the senior executive member, chaired the panel. Joe Walding and John Wybrow were the other New Zealand Council representatives. The three local members of the panel were committed to Moore. Before the panel deliberated the candidates addressed a packed meeting of party members. Lange was the final speaker. Faulkner introduced him as the man who had had the longest wait. 'Mr President, not only have I had the longest wait but I am of the greatest weight,' began Lange, who went on to give a brilliant speech.[16]

Rodger was determined that Labour should have a new face: 'The Party was in terrible trouble. It had been through the O'Brien affair and now had the Moyle business.' The straw poll among party members was overwhelmingly for Lange. The panel deliberated and the choice came down to Lange or Moore. Rodger remarked, 'wouldn't it be good if the outgoing member could endorse the incoming candidate'. Everybody agreed.

> I looked at the local people and said do any of you believe that Mr Moyle would endorse Mr Moore. And I watched one of their eyes flicker and I said, 'well the Party's got the habit of declaring the candidate elected unanimously out of a selection process . . . What's say I go out and declare Mr Lange the candidate'—just like that. I waited a moment and nobody said anything . . . I flicked my papers together and said, 'very well, that's what I'll do'. I don't know whether I had a majority or not . . . I came back in to the main hall . . . stood up and said 'your panel has decided that the candidate for Māngere will be Mr David Lange'. Wild applause, absolutely wild applause.[17]

Lange won the by-election with a majority of 4294, compared to 1604 in 1975.[18] His election was to be an ill wind for both Rowling, whom he overshadowed and eventually replaced, and Muldoon, whom he decisively defeated in 1984.

The 1977 conference adopted a bland statement that Labour believed in democratic socialism and was working towards a society in which 'co-operation is more important than competition'. After it also voted for an amendment put forward by Vicki Buck, the youth representative on the New Zealand Council, that the party restore the socialist objective to its constitution,[19] Rowling expostulated that this was 'a bloody great step backwards'.[20] The issue was settled at the 1979 conference, which decided that Labour's 'democratic socialist principles' included support for democratic elections, community ownership of natural resources, equality of access 'to all social, economic, cultural, political and legal spheres' regardless of wealth, co-operation rather than competition to ensure a just distribution of wealth, the right to work, the right to have wealth and property (although people were always more important than property), international peace and social justice, and human rights for all 'regardless of race, sex, marital status, sexual orientation, age, religious faith or belief'.[21] An amendment to recognise that 'the natural resources of New Zealand belong to the Maori people' was defeated.[22] This statement has remained largely unaltered since 1979. The most significant amendment, in 1991, added: that 'Te Tiriti o Waitangi/The Treaty of Waitangi is the founding document of New Zealand, and that the Treaty should be honoured in the Party, government, society and the whanau.'[23]

Debates on foreign policy and moral issues continued at party conferences.[24] The most controversial issue was abortion. The Royal Commission of Inquiry into Contraception, Sterilisation and Abortion resulted in legislation in 1977 that made it more difficult for women to get abortions. There was much public debate and protest about the issue and, after much discussion, the 1978 conference voted by 708 to 238 in support of motions by Ann Hercus and Helen Clark that 'while respecting the individual consciences of candidates and Party members', Labour advocate the repeal of the 1977 act and recognise the right of every woman to have an abortion without state interference. The conference also supported a motion by Richard Prebble and Arthur Faulkner that any legislation on abortion should consider the rights of the unborn child.[25]

During 1977 there was a major controversy over the National government's legislation to strengthen the powers of the Security Intelligence Service to conduct surveillance on the order of the minister (by convention, the prime minister). Muldoon refused to refer the bill to a select committee, so Labour's caucus committee on justice held its own hearings. 'Public reaction was intensely angry—fifteen thousand people protested in the streets of Wellington, meetings and marches were held up and down the country.'[26] Labour promised to repeal the bill. However, the 1978 conference defeated an amendment to make SIS surveillance of New Zealand citizens illegal by 473 votes to 327.[27]

Labour went into the 1978 election as the underdog. The Rangitīkei by-election in February 1978, won from National by Social Credit's popular leader, Bruce Beetham, with 48 per cent of the vote compared to 11 per cent for Labour, showed that New Zealand's two-party system was breaking down. Rowling struggled to foot it with Muldoon in parliament and in the news media. Three weeks before the election, a poll showed National was seven points ahead of Labour. Rowling, however, campaigned strongly, holding 20 major meetings and adopting 'a "whistle stop" style, which included many calls at small towns, strolls down the main streets and factory meetings. He regularly covered three or more towns in one day.'[28] Two thousand people attended his Christchurch Town Hall meeting, and 1900 a meeting in the Auckland Town Hall. Three thousand people took part in an outdoor rally at Woolston Park near the end of the campaign. Labour's campaign theme was unity, with the slogan 'Together we'll make it'. Rowling pitched himself as the leader who would heal the country's divisions.[29]

There was a 5 per cent swing to Labour, larger than in 1972. The party won 691,076 votes, or 40.4 per cent, compared to 680,911 or 39.8 per cent for National. Social Credit won 274,756, 16.1 per cent. Labour won a moral victory, but National was re-elected with 51 seats to 40 for Labour and one for Social Credit.[30] The caucus was strengthened with the return of Walding, Moore, Kerry Burke and Bassett, and the election of Rodger, David Caygill, Ann Hercus and David Butcher, among others. Geoffrey Palmer's election in the 1979 Christchurch Central by-election gave the caucus another able new member. Caygill and Hercus, like Palmer, were lawyers and represented Christchurch seats. Caygill had already had some years on the city council; Hercus had worked in the Commerce Commission, and Palmer attracted attention with his manifesto of constitutional reform, *Unbridled Power?*, published in 1979. All in their thirties, the three were a new, modernising face for Labour in Christchurch.

At a New Zealand Council seminar in September 1979, Professor Bob Chapman of the University of Auckland gave the party some grim messages. Social Credit's 1978 advance cost Labour victories in provincial towns and severely damaged its support in rural and farmer seats. 'The threat now posed by Social Credit is that Labour could lose its claim to be a truly New Zealand-wide party.' The New Zealand Council recognised that Labour had to re-establish itself in rural areas and strengthen its position in the provincial towns with the sort of organisation it had in marginal city seats.[31] This meant a stronger and more professional party organisation. The man who was determined to achieve this was Jim Anderton, who was elected party president in 1979, defeating Joe Walding by 586 votes to 527. Anderton was strongly supported by Helen Clark and John Hercus, who were elected to the executive, and Margaret Wilson, who was elected as one of the women's representatives on the New Zealand Council.[32] Clark says they were intent on shaking the party up and getting 'some proper modern organisation'.[33] In the first issue of Labour's new paper, *New Nation*, Anderton outlined a number of the initiatives taken since his election. The New Zealand Council had formed a strategy committee with the parliamentary leadership, and a marginal seat strategy committee chaired by Clark. Rowling had appointed a shadow cabinet. Labour Week activities were organised to promote the party. The president and executive members had visited all electorates, organisational seminars were held in seven regions, and a national meeting of all union affiliates improved liaison with them.[34] The 1980 conference voted to set up a Victory 81 fund and to increase branch membership fees to $2 a year, and by $1 a year over the following three years to $5.[35]

The party organisation was strengthened with the appointment of the first women's co-ordinator, Pam Nuttall, and education officer, Mike Williams. Regional organisers were an important link between the party leadership and the grassroots. They travelled around their areas attending branch and Labour electorate committee meetings and reporting on the New Zealand Council's plans, mediated disputes within party organisations, visited large worksites and local unions and ran raffles to raise money.[36] They also organised and ran Labour's election campaigns in marginal seats.[37] By December 1979 Labour had 55,218 branch members and 53 per cent were outside the four main cities. Sixteen electorates had more than 1000 branch members: Nelson (1038), Hastings (1059), Palmerston North (1071), Napier (1073), Onehunga (1087), Eastern Hutt (1100), Timaru (1127), Lyttelton (1144), Auckland Central (1157), Western Hutt (1166), New Plymouth (1268), Wellington Central (1348), Tasman (1684), Horowhenua (2048), West Coast (2134) and Marlborough (2196).[38]

Women activists were at the forefront of many of Labour's resurgent branches and were making their voices heard. By 1980 the Labour Women's Council had become a major force in the party, and it was instrumental in the annual conference adopting the Working Women's Charter, whose articles included the right to work for women, equal pay for work of equal value, elimination of discrimination in the workplace, family friendly policies, and the removal of impediments to safe contraception, sterilisation and abortion.[39] Mary Thomas reported to the Hastings women's branch that the 1980 conference was 'really significant with its accent on women'.[40] Joan Caulfield recalls that 'the women in the Party were very strong and determined in those days, it was really fantastic'.[41]

After the Second World War, New Zealand governments encouraged migration from Pacific Island countries because of labour shortages, and in the 1960s and 1970s many Pacific people came to work in manufacturing. From the mid-1970s governments cracked down on Pacific people who overstayed their visas; this began under Kirk and was intensified under National. Dawn raids aroused a lot of public opposition, including the formation of the American Black Panther-inspired Polynesian Panther Party.[42] There was a long affinity between Pacific peoples and Labour: Albert Henry, the first premier of the Cook Islands, had been a party and union activist in Auckland in the 1940s. The growing involvement of Pacific peoples in the party saw the formation of a Pacific Island Council in 1979.[43]

The big increase in branch membership challenged the unions' traditional influence in the party. The unions' share of votes at annual conferences fell from 43 per cent in 1975 to 34 per cent in 1979.[44] After the 1976 conference voted the Engineers' Union's Brian Landers and Fred Anderson off the executive, the union withdrew from the party in a huff, although it later re-affiliated.[45] A background paper by Dave McDonald, the Federation of Labour's research officer, analysed some of the reasons for declining union influence in the party. The growth of membership and proliferation of new branches was 'very healthy'; however, many of the new members 'do not have strong industrial experience' or 'appreciation of the role played by industrial unions'. Despite their financial support for the party, unions were criticised because the active participation of unionists in branches, electorate committees and the annual conferences was 'not as strong as it should be'. Another reason for the decline in union influence was that the growing white-collar unions—shop employees, clerical workers, public servants and teachers—did not have a tradition of support for Labour.[46]

After Anderton was elected president and union leaders Stewart McCaffley and Dan Duggan elected senior and junior vice-president respectively, there was a concerted effort to strengthen the party's relations with unions. A union affiliates council was established to improve liaison between unions and the party, increase union support for Labour and encourage more unions to affiliate.[47] The 1979 conference voted by 548 to 418 to include two union affiliate representatives, elected by conference, on the New Zealand Council.[48]

This conference also made constitutional changes to streamline Labour's remit process and give local members more voice in candidate selection in electorates where the party was well organised. In future, remits would be considered first by regional conferences and only those adopted would go to the annual conference. The conference decided that the New Zealand Council would continue to have three representatives on selection committees, and that where membership was 20 per cent of the Labour vote, the locals would have four members of the selection committee, where it was 10 per cent they would have three and where it was less than 10 per cent there would be only two; the result of the ballot of party members at the selection meeting would count as one vote on the selection committee.[49]

The rise of David Lange

Within two months of the 1978 election the Iranian revolution provoked the second oil shock, and New Zealand's economic difficulties intensified. Inflation remained above 12 per cent, unemployment continued to increase and the trade and budget deficits grew significantly.[50] Labour should have been able to capitalise on the country's economic woes, but it seemed to a growing number in the parliamentary party that its leadership was unable to do so. In November 1979 David Lange replaced Bob Tizard as deputy leader in a vote of 20 to 18. After Lange's elevation, Rowling moved Matiu Rata off the front bench. Rata had earlier been upset when Rowling took over his position as convenor of the Māori Policy Committee and now he resigned from the Labour Party.[51] His reasons for doing so were more than personal pique. Rata was frustrated at his inability to achieve more for Māori within Labour at a time of growing Māori grievances and protest, particularly over land issues.[52] In his last conference report on behalf of the Māori Policy Council, Rata said Māori had 'never felt more let down, more insecure and more economically and socially deprived than we are today'.[53] Rata resigned from parliament in April 1980 and formed a new Māori party, Mana Motuhake, to contest the by-election, which Labour's Bruce Gregory won by 991 votes.[54]

In late June 1980 the tensions within the parliamentary party were heightened when Roger Douglas, Labour's shadow minister of transport, released an alternative budget, a few days before Muldoon's budget. This proposed changing the tax system by shifting from company tax to an assets tax and death duties to gift duties, supplementing income tax by a 10 per cent sales tax on most goods and services, removing subsidies and tax incentives to industry and farming and charging them the full cost of government services, and devaluing the dollar by 20 per cent. Rowling sacked Douglas from the shadow cabinet and demanded his resignation from the party's Policy Council, giving Douglas's document much more publicity than it might otherwise have received.[55] While much of Douglas's budget anticipated the policies that became known as Rogernomics, Russell Marshall says that Rowling was more concerned with party discipline than differences over economic policy, which did not emerge until 1983.[56]

Rowling's decisions to discipline Rata and Douglas were a failure of leadership and personnel management, and highlighted divisions within the party. In the September 1980 East Coast Bays by-election Social Credit's Gary Knapp won a safe National seat and Labour was beaten into 'a humiliating third place'.[57] A number of Auckland Labour MPs decided radical changes were needed, including a new leader. Lange, who rated above Rowling in the polls, was the obvious alternative: his imposing presence and oratorical skills recalled, for some, Norman Kirk at the height of his powers.[58] In October, Douglas and Prebble told Rowling he should step down. After a poll in early December showed that Labour had fallen to third place behind Social Credit,[59] Bassett, Douglas, Prebble and Moore began organising to get Lange elected leader. Within two days they had pledges of support from 22 of the 40 Labour MPs.[60] Anderton and others in the party leadership mobilised party branches and electorate committees to rally behind Rowling, and the Engineers' Union threatened to disaffiliate again if Rowling was replaced.[61]

At a special caucus meeting on 12 December there was a vote by show of hands on whether there should be an election for party leader. Three MPs were absent. The motion was defeated by 19 to 18 after two MPs, Fraser Colman and Koro Wetere, changed sides.[62] Rowling denounced his opponents as 'nakedly ambitious' and 'has-beens' and a special New Zealand Council meeting threatened disciplinary action against 'party members whose actions bring the party into disrepute'.[63] Rowling had survived, but his leadership was fatally weakened.

Despite the divisions over the leadership, the party continued to grow. Anderton told the 1981 conference that Labour's membership—he claimed 80,000 branch members and 190,000 affiliated members—was the highest ever. The party had 584 branches and 95 affiliated unions.[64] While the Labour Women's Council continued to grow, however, Labour Youth was flagging and the Māori Policy Council struggled to rebuild after Rata's defection.[65]

Unemployment was rising sharply and Labour's 1981 election policy was focused on restoring full employment. It countered National's 'Think Big' programme of large energy projects with a plan for government investment to assist small and medium enterprises to create jobs in a range of industries. Labour also proposed tax cuts and social welfare improvements.[66] Douglas thought the party's policies were completely unrealistic and two months before the election decided not to stand again. He was talked out of this by his electorate committees and by Lange, who promised he would be finance spokesperson if Lange became leader.[67]

Between July and September 1981, the Springbok rugby tour of New Zealand took place. Opposition to playing sport with racially selected South African teams was an important part of the international campaign against apartheid. Labour opposed the tour, but Muldoon refused to take action to stop it. Thousands of people took part in protests. There was a heavy police presence at demonstrations and brutal behaviour by police riot squads. There was also much support for the tour, particularly in provincial New Zealand, and the country was bitterly divided.[68] Allowing the tour to go ahead was a cynical move by Muldoon to gain political advantage.

Labour raised over $1 million for the election campaign.[69] The party began the four-week campaign trailing badly behind National in the polls; as in 1978, it made a 'dramatic surge' but failed narrowly to win.[70] Labour again won the most votes—702,630, or 39 per cent. National won 698,508, 38.8 per cent, and Social Credit 372,056 or 20.6 per cent. National won 47 seats, Labour 43 and Social Credit two. Labour lost Taupo and won Hūnua (where Moyle returned to parliament), Kapiti, Miramar and Wellington Central, as well as Nelson, where Mel Courtney, elected as a Labour MP on Stan Whitehead's death in 1976, had become an independent. It was beaten in four seats by margins of 200 or less.[71] There were 12 new Labour MPs and the number of women MPs doubled to six. The 1981 intake were a talented group. They included a future prime minister, Helen Clark; deputy prime minister, Michael Cullen; and party leader, Phil Goff. All three were from academic backgrounds. Clark and Goff, 31 and 28 respectively, had taught in Auckland University's politics department; Cullen, 36, in Otago's history department. Clark and Goff had years of experience in the party's organisation, and Cullen's superb analytical mind had been sharpened by a doctorate from the University of Edinburgh. Eight of the others of that intake also became ministers in the fourth Labour government.

The Springbok tour was a major reason Labour failed to win key marginal seats in the provinces. Anderton also blamed Labour's internal divisions.[72] The party was criticised for advocating unrealistic policies given the economic crisis. FOL president Jim Knox said it had failed to put up a cohesive economic strategy and made promises 'more in keeping with Father Christmas' (a criticism also made by Roger Douglas).[73]

In his comprehensive study of the debates on economic policy within Labour, Hugh Oliver says that the 1981 defeat was an important turning point in Douglas's thinking. Douglas argued that it was contradictory for Labour to say the economy was in deep trouble while promising tax cuts and more social spending, and came to the view that political parties were irresponsible in responding to voters' demands for improved living standards: social goals should be subordinated to economic policy and Labour should promise little but a responsible economic policy. Mike Moore complained that there was a perception that Labour wanted to 'reward the lazy and defend bludgers'.[74]

The 1982 conference began in an upbeat mood. After Peter Fraser died, the party had undertaken to build Fraser House in memory of him and his wife, Janet, as a new home for head office in Wellington. It took over 30 years to achieve this. Conference delegates marched to the party's new headquarters in Willis Street, which Rowling opened on 10 May 1982. At the conference, Anderton noted Labour's achievements despite the election loss. Branch membership was over 100,000, a new fundraising scheme—Victory for Labour—would provide adequate funding at national and regional levels, and there was an able team of regional organisers.[75] However, there was a good deal of uncertainty about Labour's future direction. Nick Barnett reported back to his branch that Rowling's future and replacement were 'a major topic during social activities at conference'.[76] On the Friday before the conference opened, Douglas released a statement criticising the party's unrealistic election promises and there was a sharp clash between him and Tizard, Labour's shadow finance minister, on the conference floor.[77]

The main issue at the 1982 conference, however, was not economic policy but trade union affiliation to the party. Under the leadership of the 1951 veteran Jim Knox and FOL secretary Ken Douglas (a prominent member of the communist Socialist Unity Party), the union movement took a more militant approach than it had under Tom Skinner. Unions got a bad press and Muldoon targeted the Socialist Unity Party as the source of industrial strife.[78] In February 1982 Rowling told the Labour regional conference in Timaru that the system of union affiliation had outlived its usefulness. Only 15 per cent of unions were affiliated and they contributed only 8 per cent of Labour's revenue. Rowling said 'We are reformers, not revolutionaries', who reject 'the Fascism of the Left' as well as the right. Anderton replied with an article in the *Auckland Star* defending affiliation.[79]

Rowling's attempt to distance the party from the unions fell flat. Most of the regional conferences supported continued union affiliation. The New Zealand Council set up a working party to report to the annual conference. The working party acknowledged that there was a lack of effective communication between unions and the party and proposed measures to address this. It also acknowledged there was insufficient union involvement at electorate and regional levels. The working party rejected the idea that the party's rules should allow individual unionists to opt out of affiliation; decisions to affiliate were made democratically and union rules allowed members to request ballots on affiliation. More unions should be encouraged to affiliate, it said, and Labour's rules, particularly the party pledge, prevented other organisations from influencing its policy. The working party's report then buried the issue by recommending further discussion and consultation,[80] and union affiliation continued unchanged.

In December 1982 Rowling announced that he would not stand again, and on 3 February 1983 David Lange was elected Labour's leader, defeating Russell Marshall by 33 votes to nine. There was a close contest for deputy leader. Geoffrey Palmer, a loyal Rowling supporter, defeated Moore by 22 to 21. Douglas was appointed finance spokesperson.[81] Bill Rowling had led the Labour Party for over eight years. He was a determined and able politician, a reforming party president and a more than competent finance minister and prime minister, who worked tirelessly to protect working people in hard economic times. Marshall observes that Rowling 'suffered . . . the treble misfortune to be preceded by Kirk, opposed by Muldoon and to have Lange breathing down his neck—three of all-time larger-than-life Prime Ministers . . . But he was also instinctively cautious, never really comfortable unless he was thoroughly prepared, and he lacked a killer instinct.'[82]

Towards 1984

Lange's election was a sea change in the party's history. The change of leadership largely united the caucus. Led by Lange and Palmer, Labour was a much stronger opposition, its MPs were younger and more dynamic than Muldoon and his tired government, and Lange was a superb communicator and debater. One critical party member wrote: 'A benchmark of Lange's conservatism within the labour movement can be seen in his conception of equality. Lange argues for equality of opportunity even though he acknowledges that this inevitably results in inequality of outcomes.'[83]

The supporters of traditional Labour policies, personified by Anderton, were increasingly on the back foot. In December 1982 a group of party activists in Auckland, including Peter Davis, Jack Vowles, Keith Leonard, Peter Etchells, Val Scott and Anna Green, launched *Labour Network*, a journal 'providing a forum for comment and debate' among party members.[84] This was an attempt to strengthen the left in the party, although *Labour Network* was anxious not to be seen as the organ of a left-wing faction.[85] Attacked by the party's Auckland Regional Council for creating divisions, *Labour Network* replied that while it sometimes published critical articles, there was 'nothing destructive and nothing which has not already become known as a focus of debate within the party'.[86] Its critics had no such scruples: a paper probably written by the historian Jim Holt, who was close to Douglas and Bassett, sneered at the 'Limousine Liberals' within the party who had comfortable lifestyles and supported traditional left-wing Labour economic policy.[87]

The divisions within the party were spelt out by a *Labour Network* article shortly before the 1983 conference which said that the nomination of Peter Tapsell, MP for Eastern Māori since 1981, against Anderton for president was 'part of a concerted challenge to the current direction and stewardship' of the party: 'The question is will the present broadly-based liberal/Left continue to hold sway on the Executive, or will more conservative office-holders take their place? The choice is over to you!'[88] The article was seized on by the press and Lange denounced it as 'inaccurate and self-defeating'.[89] The elections were largely a victory for Anderton and his supporters. He defeated Tapsell by 978 votes to 259, while Margaret Wilson beat Dan Duggan for the junior vice-presidency by 657 to 650. John Hercus, Helen Clark and Fred Anderson, who were, like Wilson, close allies of Anderton, were re-elected to the executive.[90]

Anderton told the conference there were 'very real dangers' in Labour trying to be seen as middle-of-the-road: 'We want to bring about equality and social justice. We want the spirit of "Robin Hood" rather than the "Sheriff of Nottingham".'[91] In his leader's speech Lange riposted that it wasn't just a choice of being Robin Hood or the Sheriff of Nottingham. Labour's principles were as relevant as they were in 1916, but 'diabolical economic forces' made their implementation much more difficult. To win power, Labour had to be credible and show that it could be a better economic manager than National. 'And let's say it again and again—there are no quick fixes.'[92] Lange was telling an unpalatable truth; perhaps both sides could have worked harder to understand each other and develop agreed positions.

National's policy of allowing nuclear-powered and -armed US warships to visit New Zealand ports sparked protests which led to a broad-based anti-nuclear movement. Labour's policy was to oppose these visits. Early in his leadership Lange tried to water this down to one which would accept nuclear-powered ships, but ran into strong opposition within the party.[93] At the 1983 conference there were remits calling for Labour to withdraw New Zealand from all military alliances, including ANZUS. It was Rowling, now Labour's foreign affairs spokesperson, who steered a compromise: the next Labour government would renegotiate New Zealand's association with Australia and the United States, with basic requirements being Labour's 'unconditional anti-nuclear stance', a nuclear weapon-free South Pacific, equal partnership and unanimous decisions, and an absolute guarantee of New Zealand's sovereignty. He said: 'If . . . our allies are not prepared to accept our anti-nuclear position as the bottom line, it will be they who have to do the withdrawing from existing arrangements.'[94] In another portent of the future, the conference carried a remit that the Waitangi Tribunal be empowered to investigate 'any Maori grievances associated with the Treaty'.[95]

After the 1981 election, Muldoon's economic management became more interventionist and more intransigent. In June 1982 he imposed a wage and price freeze which lasted until 1984.[96] After 1981 there was wide support in the Labour caucus for economic restructuring, even among MPs not in particular sympathy with Roger Douglas. This included support for trade liberalisation, radical reorganisation of the economy and closing inefficient industries, even at the cost of social dislocation.[97] There was also wide support for corporatism, 'the formulation and implementation of government policies through . . . a negotiated and consensual alliance of labour, capital and the state'. Oliver argues that restructuring and corporatism were incompatible because the latter would have allowed unions to effectively oppose restructuring. However, they were not seen as contradictory until very late in the process of formulating policy for the 1984 election.[98]

By the end of 1983 an 'enormous change' had taken place in Douglas's thinking. His shift towards the free-market economics advocated by the Treasury was influenced by Doug Andrew, a Treasury advisor seconded to Lange's office, and Geoff Swier in Labour's parliamentary research unit. However, before the 1984 election Douglas was not fully committed to the Treasury programme.[99] His views were severely at odds with those of the supporters of corporatism, of which Mike Moore was a leading proponent. In Australia the Labor government elected in early 1983 negotiated an accord with the Australian Council of Trade Unions. Within Labour's caucus economic committee, Rodger, a former Public Service Association president, strongly opposed the idea of a New Zealand accord, arguing that the decentralised structure of unions and the weakness of the FOL meant that unions would not be able to deliver on any agreements reached. Rodger also objected to an accord on principle, maintaining that it would dilute the government's ability to make meaningful reform, which was exactly the line taken by neo-liberals. The 'corporatist tendency' in the caucus declined, and the major beneficiary was Douglas.[100]

By the end of 1983, an economic policy package written by Douglas, Swier and Andrew had been accepted by the caucus economic committee and sent to the Policy Council, where 'the debate was extremely polarised' and 'factions formed around antagonistic positions'. That of Douglas and the dominant caucus grouping 'was based on restructuring and elitism'. The other position, set out in what became known as the Harris/Rowling/Hercus papers, written by Public Service Association economist Peter Harris, 'retained corporatism and advocated an economic policy that would not impose the high social costs of restructuring'.[101] The clash between the two positions led to a deadlock on the Policy Council.

In January 1984, FOL economist Gary Bevin wrote a report on Labour's economic strategy based on his discussions with Andrew. It said that Labour believed a complete 'shake out' of the economy was required. Labour would devalue the dollar, get the budget deficit down as quickly as possible, constrain growth in money supply and reform import licensing and tariffs. Labour would means-test superannuation, bring electricity prices up to cost, eliminate the general medical services benefit and charge for pharmaceuticals. Bevin commented:

> The overall thrust of the package is to return to the market to sort out the economic problems of efficiency and equity . . . For the suggested devaluation to be effective in reducing the external deficit would require a substantial adjustment to the exchange rate. Real wage loss for workers would be considerable and . . . would mean a deterioration in living standards.[102]

The Bevin report caused a furore; many FOL executive members, including Knox, did not want to believe it.[103] Ken Douglas wrote to Wybrow requesting an urgent meeting between the FOL, the Combined State Unions and the party 'as the package reported to the national executive is impossible for the Federation of Labour to endorse'.[104] The FOL and CSU tabled their own proposals for Labour's policy, and on 22 February the Joint Council of Labour established a working party to discuss the party's economic strategy.[105] Devaluation was clearly unacceptable to the unions and Douglas removed it from his proposed policy (in any case, no sensible aspiring finance minister would go into an election promising devaluation).[106] On 14 June, before the working party's deadline to report back,[107] Muldoon called a snap election. To break the deadlock, Geoffrey Palmer wrote a bland, compromise economic policy, which was approved by the Policy Council and the Joint Council of Labour.[108]

Oliver rejects the argument that the final policy was contrary to Douglas's proposals. The policy was 'vague to the point of offering almost no information' on the actual content of economic policy. The only policy advocated by Douglas that was explicitly ruled out was privatisation of state-owned enterprises. The major concessions he made to secure agreement on the Policy Council were abandoning devaluation and 'the inclusion of assurances that change would be gradual, planned, and done after securing agreement through negotiation'. The final policy was

> a form of words forced on both sides by the pressure of external events. The election was near and the Labour Party had its best chance in a decade to form a

government. The vote was unanimous in favour of Palmer's final version and the two sides agreed to disagree on what a Labour Government should actually do.[109]

When he called the snap election, Muldoon slurred that it didn't give his opponents much time. There were only two working days to get people on the electoral rolls before they closed. Labour was well prepared for the election and was greatly helped by trade union support, which was co-ordinated by a union/party liaison committee, with Mike Smith as the party's union liaison officer. Union organisers pulled out all the stops to enrol workers and unions organised job meetings for Labour speakers; over 200 attended by up to 60,000 workers were held in Auckland. The FOL, the Engineers' Union and others paid for national newspaper advertisements supporting Labour, while some CSU unions also ran extensive national advertising: for example, the Post Primary Teachers' Association on education. A large number of unions and some trades councils provided organisers in marginal seats. Unions donated tens of thousands of dollars and provided printing, vehicles and use of their offices.[110] The Waterside Workers' Federation donated over $81,000 to the party and the Hotel Workers' Federation $10,000.[111]

Labour won a decisive victory, with 56 seats to National's 37 and Social Credit's two. One dimension of Labour's victory showed how the party had changed: ten of the 56 MPs were women; a record. In its report on the election the New Zealand Council said:

> We owe our victory in no small way to the very effective work of a large number of women who took key organisational positions right throughout the country during the last few years culminating in a tremendous effort by so many women both as candidates and organisers in the 1984 election campaign.[112]

Otherwise, it was an ambiguous victory. Labour won only 43 per cent of the popular vote. National won 35.9 per cent. New Zealand's two-party system had been fracturing since at least 1978, and in 1984 a fifth of voters supported smaller parties. Third parties are wild cards under simple plurality voting, and the New Zealand Party, founded by the right-wing property speculator Bob Jones, was particularly wild in 1984. That party was a protest vehicle for disaffected National voters and delivered a number of seats to Labour. Labour won 36 of its 56 seats with absolute majorities, and another 12 with better than 45 per cent of the vote. That would have given it a bare majority in the House. Labour's other eight seats were won with 45 per cent or less, and in all those seats the New Zealand Party won more votes than Labour's majority over National. These seats were Hamilton East, Waitaki, Horowhenua, Hawke's Bay, Wairarapa, Glenfield, East Cape and (most spectacularly) Ōhariu, where a 29 per cent vote for Jones allowed Peter Dunne to win with a paltry 38 per cent. The same arithmetic applied in Hamilton West, Wellington Central, Miramar and Eden. We cannot say that Jones handed all 12 seats to Labour, for it is impossible to know what those who voted for his party would have done in its absence, but Labour's parliamentary majority was inflated by splits on the right.

The fourth Labour government took office in the context of widespread public feeling that economic and social policy had to change. There was much less consensus about the direction of that change, and these tensions in New Zealand society at large would be reflected in the new government.

10

Labour and Neo-liberalism 1984–93

The 1984 election was an ambiguous victory in another sense. While the fourth Labour government would enact much significant reform, the economic direction would alienate many party members and supporters. After defeat in 1990 the party's viability was sometimes doubted.

The fourth Labour government has been subject to more analysis than any other administration in New Zealand's history. Most accounts emphasise economic policy and the anti-nuclear policy, but there were significant reforms in many other areas. Social and foreign policy reflected Labour's progressive traditions, but economic policy became increasingly deregulatory and market-oriented. There had always been a tension in Labour, as in many other social democratic parties, between economic modernisation and social justice. While Roger Douglas and his close colleagues had a disposition to liberalise in 1984, their agendas changed over time. For much of the first term, ministers and senior party officials endeavoured to maintain a working relationship between caucus and the wider party, even as many ministers were less than enthusiastic about the wider party having much input into policy. Their attitude reflected the enduring tension between activists' reformist zeal and the constrained reality of making policy. Real problems for party and government alike emerged in 1987, when Douglas and his allies took neo-liberalism far beyond what the party, and David Lange, were prepared to accept. The party's tragedy was that Lange did not have the political skills necessary to shape the government's direction after 1987.

Lange's first cabinet has been described as one of the best-educated in New Zealand's history. It included four veterans of the Kirk–Rowling cabinet: Fraser Colman (works); Colin Moyle (agriculture, fisheries); Bob Tizard (energy, science); and Roger Douglas (finance). The novices, apart from Lange (who also took foreign affairs) and Palmer (justice, attorney-general), were Mike Moore (trade); Richard Prebble (transport, railways); Koro Wetere (Māori affairs, lands, forests); David Caygill (trade and industry); Russell Marshall (education, environment); Frank O'Flynn (defence); Michael Bassett (health, local government); Ann Hercus (social welfare, police, women's affairs); Stan Rodger (labour, state services); Jonathan Hunt (broadcasting, postmaster-general); Kerry Burke (employment, immigration); Margaret Shields (customs, consumer affairs); Peter Tapsell (internal affairs); and Phil Goff (housing). All but Tapsell, Shields and Goff had been in parliament since before 1981.[1] The inner circle, however—Lange, Palmer, Moore, Douglas, Prebble and Caygill—were all, with the exception of Douglas (who was 47), under the age of 43, and thus represented a new generation, one which, as Colin James has emphasised, was socially liberal, and at least open to economic liberalism as well.[2]

Economic policy, 1984–87

Debates over economic policy had not been resolved when Muldoon called the early election. Douglas and his caucus allies emphasised deregulation; some preferred corporatism, a managed approach to reform, with consultation among unions, employers and other sector groups. Vague language bridged the differences. Anticipating a substantial devaluation after the election, currency traders rapidly unloaded New Zealand dollars. 'Foreign exchange', as then deputy Reserve Bank governor Roderick Deane later recalled, started 'going out the door like there's no tomorrow', but Muldoon refused to discuss devaluation. In the 30 days before 14 July the Reserve Bank lost $1.4 billion in overseas exchange, and had to borrow $1.7 billion to compensate. On the day after the election, Treasury and the Reserve Bank presented Lange and his senior colleagues with the grim news and advised an urgent 20 per cent devaluation. Officials and prospective ministers met in person on the 16th, a Monday, and the advice was repeated. Lange accepted it but, despite his heavy electoral defeat, Muldoon refused, on the technical grounds that he remained prime minister until the writs were returned. An economic crisis thereby became a constitutional one. After hours of manoeuvring within the National caucus, Muldoon complied.[3]

Lange excelled at capturing the public mood in a crisis, and his and Douglas's measured demeanour gave the new government much political capital. Lange later said that the July crisis fundamentally set the government's direction: if the election had been in late November, as usual, ministers would have 'celebrated through December, gone on holiday, come back and had a formal opening of Parliament and tried out our new seats . . . The first Budget would have been drawn up in circumstances of great party orthodoxy and we would have had a very different Government.'[4] This is doubtful. Pressure for devaluation and the run on the dollar would have been as intense in November. In the weeks after the July election Douglas concentrated on significant if unspectacular measures of financial liberalisation that could be achieved by regulation; there is no reason to suppose that his approach would have been any different in December. Economic policy was driven by the 'troika'—Douglas, Prebble and Caygill—and they were all seized with some sense of urgency. They would hardly have deferred their discussions about economic directions for the sake of a Christmas dinner.[5]

Some suggest that Douglas orchestrated the crisis to get a favourable climate for the deregulation he planned to push through. This cannot be sustained. One consequence of Muldoon's freeze was an end to the managed and gradual adjustment of the exchange rate, the 'crawling peg', which Muldoon had introduced in 1979. The Reserve Bank warned in 1982 that when the freeze ended, immense pressure for a devaluation would quickly emerge. This is exactly what happened.[6]

The government's first public economic initiative was to hold an economic summit. Hundreds of representatives of business and farming organisations, trade unions and community groups convened to discuss the country's economic direction. There was apparently much common ground, especially on Muldoon's disastrous record, but debate over terminology; for instance, the FOL and the Manufacturers' Federation meant very different things by 'tax reform'. It was easy to elide differences over means, and the priority of each goal.[7] It would be unduly cynical to suggest that the summit was a sham (even if Douglas later fostered that view with his 1987 remark about the danger that some people would expect too much participation).[8] The summit reflected the tension at the heart of the government's approach: the rhetoric of consensus alongside the reality of an elitist approach to policy making.

During the first term, cabinet and caucus were generally cohesive. Cabinet cohesiveness was natural enough; almost all ministers had significant reform agendas. Most of the caucus supported the general direction, partly because it was more moderate than it later became, and partly because Douglas and the other economics ministers liaised with the back bench, indicating the direction through informal seminars on economic policy. Conversely, backbenchers who questioned the economic direction, including Helen Clark, were largely ignored and had weak links to cabinet, if any.[9]

Douglas's first budget removed many agricultural and export subsidies, and imposed an income tax surcharge of 25 per cent on additional income in excess of $100 weekly for national superannuitants. The former measure had been urged by many economists (by no means all hard-line neo-liberals). The latter drew vociferous objection from superannuitant lobby groups, even though it applied to only a quarter of recipients. However, whatever the flaws in Labour's 1975 superannuation scheme, Muldoon's replacement, funded only from current revenue, was poorly conceived.[10] More generally, the government's economic priorities were reducing inflation and the budget deficit. These had been implicitly endorsed by most at the summit, including the FOL. Aware of the difficulties many lower-income people were facing, Douglas included in the budget an enhanced child support payment, known as Family Care.[11]

The government sought to increase the New Zealand economy's exposure to global market forces, believing that this would foster greater efficiency and prosperity. A major step was floating the dollar, in March 1985. Caygill later called it the most important thing the government did. It was also very far from established Labour thinking about a managed economy.[12] The Treasury supported the idea, while the Reserve Bank was initially cautious. As late as February 1985 something less than a complete float seemed likely, but another run on the dollar at the end of that month pushed Douglas to an unconditional float. Thereafter, international currency markets, not the government, would set the value of the New Zealand dollar. Arguments for the float emphasised the changing international monetary system, and the destabilising effect of major devaluations (or, more rarely, revaluations). Yet the government's reliance on high interest rates to attack inflation made the floated dollar an attractive proposition to international investors and currency speculators, and the July 1984 devaluation was soon reversed, which damaged exporters.[13]

The 1984 budget foreshadowed major changes in state sector organisations and in taxation, changes which contrasted fundamentally with the party's traditional views, although both were defended as facilitating economic modernisation. The government significantly reduced the higher rates of income tax and introduced a universal consumption tax, known as goods and services tax (GST). There had been widespread arguments that high marginal rates of income tax were a disincentive to increased work and increased productivity, while many of the wealthy were able to find ways of avoiding tax. Douglas and his closest colleagues came to accept this view, and argued that a universal consumption tax, as well as being easy to collect, would encourage saving and investing. Critics of the 10 per cent GST, as it was proposed, argued that its effects would be more noticed by the lower-paid, and it was to that extent regressive. Legislation was introduced in 1985 and the new regime came into force in April 1986.

State sector reform was even more far-reaching. The first major change was transforming state trading organisations into state-owned enterprises, which would be required as far as possible to operate according to normal commercial practice. The radical departure was not the idea of a public corporation, but the principle that state-owned enterprises should operate at a distance from ministerial control.[14] This legislation having been passed in 1986 'without electoral retribution, the Government turned its attention to the "core" Public Service'. Here the general principles were shaped by the criteria of 'accountability, responsibility, and efficiency'. There was 'increasing . . . pressure to adopt the best of private sector management practice', which itself had become far more professionalised in the previous 20 years.[15] The government appointed Roderick Deane as state services commissioner, with a brief for reform, and the State Sector Act 1988 replaced permanent heads of departments with 'chief executives' on five-year contracts, who replaced the State Services Commission as the employer of staff in their departments. Ministers, in turn, now became involved in the appointment of their chief executives and in negotiating performance agreements. Although it has been suggested that there was considerable support for the reforms among public servants themselves, 'the human costs of redundancy and disruption of expected career patterns [were] very large'.[16] In the new state-owned enterprises many thousands of workers were laid off, with vast disruption to their own lives and those of their communities.

Business groups and some in the Treasury lobbied for deregulation to extend to labour relations; this the government largely refused. The government's approach owed something to the work done by a committee of Department of Labour officials and employer and union representatives established under Muldoon in 1982. Stan Rodger's role was of fundamental importance: he consulted widely and, with the support of Lange and Palmer, steered a middle course between deregulation and a return to the old order.[17] Rodger's 'model of trade unionism [was] large, democratic, effective, and self-reliant'.[18] The 1987 Labour Relations Act required a minimum of 1000 members that unions choose between awards of the court or enterprise bargaining (pursuing both, known as second-tier bargaining, had been a fruitful source of employer complaint); and continued unqualified preference.

Social policy

Much of the economic reform of the 1984–87 term was justified as overdue adjustment, necessary means to traditional Labour ends. The government also placed a high priority on social services and social policy. Michael Bassett, for instance, worked hard to increase the subsidy paid to general medical practitioners, and introduced funding for union health clinics. Phil Goff significantly expanded state support for home ownership, increased rental support and reformed tenancy law. Russell Marshall secured significant increases in education spending (even after taking into account large pay rises for teachers). He sought to shift the focus of later secondary schooling from the assumption that it was only about preparation for university, and also increased support for early childhood education.[19]

As promised, a Ministry of Women's Affairs was established to advise the minister on the differential impact on women of any dimension of government policy, to promote and initiate measures for equality, to facilitate the appointment of qualified women to public entities, and to undertake or commission research on matters of concern to women. In its first years the focus was on matters like health, housing, violence, paid work and voluntary work. There were hopes that the ministry would be a bridge between communities and policy makers.[20] Its work programme drew heavily on 21 women's forums, held across the country and attended by 12,000 women and by Ann Hercus, the first minister of women's affairs, and other women MPs. These gatherings, a 'brave exercise in participatory democracy', attracted considerable controversy, were targeted by conservative Christians and reflected 'ugly divisions . . . within the Labour Party and society as a whole'.[21]

One of the most far-reaching social reforms came through a private member's bill. In March 1985 Fran Wilde, the MP for Wellington Central, introduced a bill to remove criminal penalties for sex between consenting male adults and prohibit discrimination on the grounds of sexual preference. Wilde had been liaising with gay and lesbian communities for some time and took care to ensure that the bill accorded with their wishes and priorities.[22] The bill proceeded through parliament over the next 16 months and attracted intense public controversy. Many Christian organisations campaigned against the bill, some in exceptionally bigoted language (their attacks on the women's forums were a preliminary to this assault). Two Labour MPs, Geoff Braybrooke and Allan Wallbank, joined National's Norman Jones and Graeme Lee to lead opposition; few National parliamentarians supported the bill and many vociferously opposed it. The bill's advocates did their best to mobilise public support among heterosexuals as well as gays and lesbians. It was crucial that the age of consent be equal and compromise on that point resisted.[23] In the end, decriminalisation passed by five votes (only three National MPs voting in favour), but the human rights dimension had to wait until 1993.[24]

The Waitangi Tribunal, established in 1975, had not met the hopes Matiu Rata and others had had for it. In 1983, however, a new membership began to move the tribunal in a more meaningful direction, first in a case concerning industrial discharge from the Motunui synthetic petrol plant off the coast at Waitara. There had been increasingly intense protest at Waitangi and elsewhere, while Māori had long campaigned within the party for recognition of the treaty. Palmer and Wetere persuaded cabinet to extend the tribunal's jurisdiction to 1840. They were no doubt mindful of Māori aspirations, although the balance of political advantage was debatable. Palmer, in particular, insisted that it was the right thing to do, even as few could have appreciated the extent of historical wrong that would be dealt with in ensuing decades.[25]

Nuclear politics

Labour's policy on nuclear disarmament was clear in 1981 and did not change before the 1984 election: no ship or aircraft carrying, or likely to be carrying, nuclear weapons would be permitted into New Zealand. That applied as a matter of logic to nuclear-powered warships, for 'if a . . . ship was nuclear powered, it was likely to be nuclear armed'.[26] As we have seen, Lange's pre-election ruminations about the acceptability of nuclear-powered vessels did not go down well, although Lange was never inclined to compromise on weapons. By 1984 there was considerable public support for Labour's position. That this would complicate New Zealand's diplomatic relationship with the United States was widely appreciated, although less widely welcomed.

The issue was highlighted immediately after the 1984 election. An ANZUS council meeting had been scheduled for 16 July. Lange, as prime minister elect, found himself in a rather awkward meeting with US secretary of state George Shultz. While Shultz and his department thereafter maintained that Lange had indicated that he would seek to change the policy, Merwyn Norrish, New Zealand's secretary of foreign affairs, who was the only other person present, did not believe Lange had given any such undertaking and suggested that Shultz had 'convinced himself . . . Mr Shultz heard what he wanted to hear'.[27] The Australian Labor government had reversed its own policy and that 'led the Americans to take it for granted that New Zealand too would recant'. The Australian prime minister, Bob Hawke, pressured Lange to do just that.[28]

Lange and Shultz did agree that officials would try to find a solution that would allow United States ships to visit without breaching New Zealand's nuclear-free policy.[29] This proved impossible. In January 1985 the Americans requested a visit by the USS *Buchanan*, a rather elderly diesel-powered destroyer. The Americans hoped that the New Zealand government would accept that the *Buchanan* was unlikely to be carrying nuclear weapons, but there was an element of 'don't ask, don't tell'. The proposal became public knowledge when Australian sources leaked it: there is reason to suspect that Hawke hoped to force the New Zealand government's hand into diluting the policy. The ambiguity on which American hopes rested was, as Palmer and the defence minister, Frank O'Flynn, recognised, unacceptable. Lange was out of reach, in Tokelau, when the news broke; when he was back in contact with Wellington he received a recommendation from Norrish that the request be agreed to and one from Palmer that it be declined. Once the proposal was public knowledge the wider party reinforced Palmer; Lange later wrote that the leak 'made the visit a public issue and put the decision beyond diplomacy'.[30] On returning to Wellington he met with cabinet, who agreed that the request must be declined, and that Lange 'should see the American ambassador the next day to ask him to send a ship which complied with the policy, an invitation he declined'.[31] Soon afterwards, the American government announced New Zealand's effective suspension from ANZUS, a decision Lange received at the end of February, en route to Britain for the Oxford Union debate.[32]

This engagement, at the University of Oxford on 1 March, in which Lange debated the morality of the nuclear deterrent with an influential American fundamentalist preacher, Jerry Falwell, allowed Lange to take the government's policy onto the world stage. Some senior foreign affairs officials had profound misgivings; Lange later described it as 'not the best speech I ever made but it was the one which mattered most'.[33] Lange's case was that nuclear weapons were irrational and of themselves had a corrupting influence on those states which possessed or relied on them. His performance was a remarkable oratorical and political success. Even more crucial in linking the anti-nuclear policy with New Zealand nationalism was French secret service agents bombing the Greenpeace protest ship the *Rainbow Warrior* in Auckland harbour on 10 July 1985. Fernando Pereira, the ship's photographer, was killed. French ministers obfuscated, but once the truth emerged two agents were imprisoned for manslaughter and eventually ransomed.

For Lange the *Rainbow Warrior* was 'the defining moment . . . that was the end of any New Zealand commitment to the so-called Western Alliance. It was not when it sunk that I knew. It was when we knew who'd sunk it that I knew.'[34] Nevertheless, Palmer visited the United States in September 1985 in a fruitless effort to seek an accommodation on ship visits, but made it clear that there was a fundamental political commitment: 'we cannot retreat from the policy and to do so will destroy the Government'.[35] Before the 1987 election, the New Zealand Nuclear Free Zone, Disarmament, and Arms Control Act was passed, providing that no nuclear weapon or nuclear-powered vessel would be accepted in New Zealand territory. It has often been suggested that the anti-nuclear policy ensured that traditionally minded Labour supporters continued to adhere to the government despite the heresies of Rogernomics. This is too simple an explanation.

Party and government, 1984–87

The government's economic policy provoked widespread concern, and some outright opposition, within the party. That an open split was avoided was due to a number of factors. There was widespread acceptance that the Muldoon years had been economically disastrous, and that a degree of adjustment was necessary. To an extent the government sought to mitigate the consequences of that adjustment. Certainly, social and foreign policies were generally popular in the party. The party as a whole accepted the necessity of unity and discipline in the interests of maximising the chances of re-election; few were unaware of the dismal record since 1949.

The key figure in the liaison between party and government was Margaret Wilson, party president from 1984 to 1987. Wilson was a legal academic and a socialist feminist, committed to what some called the 'long march through the institutions'. Walking away was never an option for her.[36] Wilson sought to 'deal with the government and work towards solutions that, if they were not ideal, were at least acceptable', and she experienced 'increasing irritation with those who wished only to stand and criticise and not deal with the reality with which they were faced'. Her vehicles were a close working relationship with Palmer, weekly meetings with Lange, the Joint Council of Labour, and ministerial commitment to at least a degree of debate.[37] Sometimes, of course, the best of intentions can be misunderstood. Wilson later wrote that careful plans for an honest discussion about economic policy at regional conferences in 1985 were undermined when the government introduced the GST legislation before the national conference. According to one minister, this was done precisely so that the conference could be properly informed of the government's intention.[38] In fact, most of the 1985 regional conferences and the annual conference supported GST, the annual conference thanks to the votes of the Hotel Workers' Federation.[39]

As Wilson told the 1985 conference, '[I]t is the Party's role to keep the Government in touch with what is happening in the community. We are the early warning system for the Government.' A close relationship between government and party was all the more important when the economic situation required unpopular policies that provoked 'much unease and criticism within the Party'.[40] Palmer spoke in almost identical terms.[41] Debates on economic policy, Wilson said, if risky, were overdue.[42] She was, however, distinctly lukewarm about the Economic Policy Network, a loose group that emerged around Jim Anderton and some trade unionists.[43] Wilson advised the wider membership to judge new policies with an open mind, but warned cabinet that the unexpected economic direction was 'a political problem that could threaten the unity of the Party and . . . the next election'.[44] Lange emphasised that economic recovery was fundamental to social goals, and that the government had 'attempted to ensure that the burden of that recovery does not fall too heavily on those least able to bear it'.[45] Not all ministers appreciated Wilson's efforts, but it is political common sense to keep the base on side.[46]

There had been an unwelcome loss in the Timaru by-election in June, following the death of the speaker, Basil Arthur. The loss was usually explained as a rejection of the government's economic policies, combined with an unacceptably liberal and feminist candidate. In fact, National won the seat with only 42 per cent; the New Zealand Party increased its share of the vote from 8 to nearly 14 per cent, and Social Credit went up too, as did abstentions. By-elections can be strange. However, the 1985 conference demonstrated significant trust in the government, avoiding blanket condemnations and contenting itself with a resolution that economic policy had to involve consultation.[47] In 1986 one candidate for the New Zealand Council, who would later build a career as a 'left-wing commentator', noted the concern within the party over economic direction and averred that it was

> vital that the lines of communication are kept open between the Party, the Caucus, and the Trade Unions. Having abandoned the quick-fix, ad-hoc solutions of the Muldoon era we must all strive to increase the levels of political and economic understanding throughout the entire Labour Movement. If we fail in this task we will be unable to convey to Labour's supporters the 'new means to old ends' being employed by our government.[48]

Dave Vallely, the central North Island organiser, warned that favourable opinion polls were giving 'a false sense of security . . . There are a lot of people out here in the field hurt and angry . . . a lot of them are our traditional supporters . . . young working class people being screwed with home loan interest rates of 20 per cent plus leaving them little or nothing for food and clothing for kids'.[49] Vallely emphasised that the Timaru by-election had been a severe warning, and more warning was evident in the total muster. At the end of 1986 branch membership was 26,262, having been around 40,000 in 1984. (The latter figure, incidentally, was much lower than was often claimed: higher figures were based on inadequately managed records, and when central billing was introduced in 1984 a truer picture emerged.)[50] Regional organisers were well placed to comment on grassroots feeling, and how sparse those roots often were. Peter Beyer, in Waikato, undertook 'rocky journeys over confiscated land, slowly establishing a Labour presence and signature in party branch meetings, smoko rooms, public meetings, stopworks, shops and businesses, local newspapers and pubs'. Many branches relied on a handful of members, and in provincial towns National politicians often enjoyed unquestioned legitimacy. In Thames the National incumbent was 'conducting a series of "non-political" town and country meetings where a chorus of Federated Farmers reps, MAF flunkies and accountants gang up on the township's retailers with dire threats of "cold winds"'.[51] In Auckland, Andrew Beyer (Peter's brother), in his report to the New Zealand Council, referred to 'the many (and now familiar) problems of an electorate long-held by Labour and with ageing and diminishing membership . . . this and other similar electorates which can guarantee a Labour MP but very little contribution to the Party as a whole'.[52] This was the local face of the fragile 1984 election victory.

The 1986 conference, marking the party's 70th anniversary, was an uneasy celebration. Jim Knox, delivering what he called the hardest speech he'd ever had to make, said that the unions wanted a Labour government, but 'this mindless purism, this ideological straitjacket, this market madness, it is tearing our country apart'. He warned that the government had a great deal of work to do if it was to restore its integrity.[53] Lange addressed such sentiments in a masterly speech. He recalled that the party had been

> founded to serve the interests of women and men who had been told that they did not belong. The economic and social order had excluded them. It had measured them and found them worthless . . . This party is founded on the

> worth of the individual and the right of all the members of the community to a share in the resources of the community.

He went on to declare that 'this Labour government is unashamedly a promoter of the public sector. It is only through the intervention of the state that fairness can be restored to people whose lives would otherwise be ravaged by the turbulence of forces outside their power to influence.'[54] Lange would express himself in very similar terms in 1987 when he rejected Douglas's more extreme proposals. Palmer also reassured members that the government had listened very carefully to their unease and promised 'a year of consolidation, finetuning and implementation of changes already announced'.[55]

Second term: division and collapse

Despite the tensions, the party held together until the 1987 election. One reason was that ministers frequently emphasised that their unorthodox means were directed towards traditional Labour ends. Another was the general desire that there not be a third one-term Labour government. Behind the scenes, though, pressures were building that would explode after 1987.

The most serious divergence was between Lange and Douglas and it began to emerge, in private, in April 1987. With an election due by September, the budget needed to foreshadow the government's direction for a second term. Douglas was under pressure to reduce debt, the budget deficit and inflation, but was becoming committed to further reductions in income tax, and to privatising state-owned enterprises. Then and later, privatisation would be justified in terms of reducing debt and allowing 'more for health, education and welfare', but Douglas himself has said that debt was only the easiest political argument.[56] Douglas floated various options, the most radical of which 'would emphasise asset sales, pursue expenditure cuts vigorously, and signal a flat tax scenario for the longer term'.[57] Neither of the associate finance ministers, Prebble and Caygill, was enthusiastic (Prebble, apparently, had no commitment to privatisation at that time). That plan was more radical than anything that Treasury had been working on, and it seemed that a rather austere budget, cutting spending by up to $1 billion, would result.[58]

Lange rapidly became concerned at the direction of Douglas's thinking and made it clear that he regarded such proposals as unacceptable. As Lange put it, 'people who support us are people who depend on the government. Their lives are enriched by it. Tax cuts mean little to them.'[59] Douglas would later insist that his intention in putting forward radical proposals was to have a comprehensive debate on how to achieve desired ends, and that an efficient welfare state would deliver to the people about whom Lange was concerned.[60] Lange's comments should not have been a surprise after what he had said at the 1986 conference. He wished to defer further major change until the Royal Commission on Social Policy had reported. The commission, established in 1986, had been a manifesto commitment, and while Lange wanted it to serve as a counterweight to the Treasury, he also noted that rapid social and economic change made a review of social policy essential. While Lange has been criticised for moving slowly to establish the commission, he recalled a wearing bureaucratic war with the Treasury, which was 'implacably opposed' to it. Douglas and some of his ministerial allies were dismissive of the commission, then and later, arguing that it would unduly slow the pace of reform. Not for the first time, elitism and consensus were in conflict.[61] For the time being the differences were shelved.

The election was called for 15 August. Behind the scenes there was increasing tension between the dominant cabinet group and the party organisation, particularly as a number of trade union-aligned candidates were selected for vacant safe seats, such as Graham Kelly in Porirua, Larry Sutherland in Avon, Elizabeth Tennet in Island Bay and Sonja Davies in Pencarrow. The party organisation saw such selections as a means of moderating policy, but there were some ructions from disgruntled contenders.[62]

Lange felt that he campaigned poorly in the 1987 election. His health was causing trouble, his personal life was in turmoil, and he remained apprehensive about Douglas's future direction. His apprehensions were reinforced by the fact that business leaders were making large donations to Douglas to distribute as he saw fit, rather than to the party.[63] Labour won two more seats and increased its percentage of the popular vote to 48. This victory—the first time an incumbent Labour government had been re-elected since 1946—was notable, but the result was at best highly ambiguous. The National Party's vote increased by much more, admittedly from a historic low, and abstentions increased significantly. Labour's vote declined in safe electorates, and particularly in ministers' seats. 'There was thus a sizable element of warning.'[64]

Immediately after the election, Lange sought to slow the pace of reform and to emphasise the language of consensus. This influenced portfolio allocation in the new cabinet, to which Helen Clark, Michael Cullen, Bill Jeffries and David Butcher were elected. Clark got housing and Cullen social welfare. Lange removed Douglas's associate ministers from those roles, putting Cullen and Butcher in there instead; Caygill replaced Bassett in health (to the latter's great disappointment) and Prebble took state-owned enterprises. This did nothing to diminish Prebble's power; if Lange thought it would, he miscalculated.[65] Lange judged better with Caygill, whose ability to distinguish between economic and social policy was demonstrated when he quietly shelved the 1988 Gibbs report, which would have imposed market models on the public health system. Similarly, Clark doggedly defended public housing. The other very disappointed minister was Russell Marshall, moved from education to foreign affairs. Lange's characterisation of Marshall as too close to the teacher unions was ungenerous: Marshall had championed Labour's progressive approach to education, and he proved to be a successful foreign minister. Lange took education himself, to, he hoped, defend it from neo-liberalism while overseeing a measure of reform. Combining a major ministry with the prime minister's position is risky, for a prime minister needs to exercise strategic oversight of the government.[66]

On 20 October 1987 world share markets slumped, and New Zealand's fell further and faster than most. Douglas regarded the crash as requiring further radical 'reform' in order, as he said, to reinforce business confidence.[67] The Treasury's post-election briefing, prepared well before the crash, had foreshadowed Douglas's agenda. If the 1984 briefing 'was about restructuring the economy [the 1987 briefing] was about restructuring the state': privatising state-owned enterprises and turning major areas of social services over to the market.[68] Even before the crash, Douglas had resurrected his radical option of April, proposing a flat rate of income tax at 22 per cent, an increase in GST to 12.5 per cent and a guaranteed minimum family income. Douglas was convinced that the package would leave very few people worse off, although the explanations were complex. He continued to work on these ideas through November. Lange was becoming increasingly uneasy, but unable or unwilling to take control of the government's direction (having to come to grips with a major social portfolio did not help).[69]

On 17 December ministers announced a package including a flat rate of income tax, increased GST, a guaranteed minimum family income, more rigorous targeting of transfer payments (benefits) and extensive privatisation. Lange had advised Douglas of his opposition to increasing GST and a flat-rate income tax about three weeks earlier, and warned that it was important not to pre-empt the Royal Commission on Social Policy. Inexplicably he allowed matters to proceed. Ministers differed, at the time or later, about whether the package was a concept or a set of specific policies.[70] Lange insisted that it was 'a statement of possibility rather than of firm intention'.[71]

Lange became increasingly concerned that the package would not deliver what was promised and would increase inequality to an unacceptable degree. On 28 January 1988 he announced at a press conference that it would be unlikely to proceed. Much political damage resulted, not least because Lange had not discussed his intentions with either the full cabinet or the party caucus. This was a breach of collective responsibility so far as cabinet was concerned (as Lange later admitted). Douglas, understandably, felt betrayed.[72] One minister later said that Lange's action was unnecessary because cabinet would inevitably have come to the conclusion that the numbers didn't work.[73] Lange had been stung by a critical analysis in an influential Auckland magazine by his old friend Bruce Jesson which suggested that, lacking any philosophical core, he was merely Douglas's frontman. Bassett emphasises the influence of Margaret Pope, the prime minister's speechwriter, and of some within the union movement and wider party. Lange and Pope were already, clandestinely, pursuing a romantic relationship, and they would later marry. Above all, though, Lange's attitude was consistent with his own Methodist social conscience, as well as a wider feeling in the party that reform had been necessary, but within limits.[74]

In April 1988 the income tax scales were greatly flattened to two steps of 24 and 33 per cent (the top rate had come down to 48 per cent when GST was introduced). The Royal Commission on Social Policy felt that the December package had irrevocably compromised its work, and issued a lengthy but incomplete report in April. The 1988 budget announced sweeping privatisations, including of Government Property Services, the New Zealand Shipping Corporation, the Tourist Hotel Corporation, Landcorp's financial assets, the Bank of New Zealand, Postbank (the former Post Office Savings Bank), the Rural Bank and substantial forestry assets.[75] If Douglas regarded privatisation as good in itself, Caygill, like others, thought the most important justification was the urgent need to repay debt.[76]

The 1987 budget had included only the sale of minority shareholdings in a few state-owned enterprises; more had not been foreshadowed in the 1987 election campaign and many voters inevitably felt deceived.[77]

By the end of 1988 the government was dysfunctional. Lange's and Douglas's offices engaged in open warfare. Douglas discussed radical options in public. Lange was isolated, needing support from more traditional elements in the party whom he had alienated with his sharp tongue and support for Douglas over the previous few years.[78] Some MPs repeatedly offered to support Lange in changing the policy direction, but he seemed unable to take up these offers. In November, after a dispute over privatisation process, Lange removed Prebble from the state-owned enterprises portfolio. Prebble then made unflattering remarks on television about Lange's mental health and was dismissed from cabinet. A month later, after Lange refused to renew the contract of Douglas's press secretary, Douglas informed him that he could no longer serve in a Lange ministry, and this was taken as resignation.[79] Douglas's replacement was Caygill, who had worked closely with him but followed Lange in being 'not prepared to rely on the market to provide education or health', and he had no interest in major labour market deregulation.[80]

One Douglas policy which Caygill did take over became the Reserve Bank Act 1989. This innovative legislation largely confined monetary policy to price stability. It assumed that monetary policy could not satisfactorily influence other areas such as employment and investment, the promotion of which had been specified in New Zealand's central banking legislation as in other countries. All that monetary policy could do was 'provide a stable background for the economy—keep the machine well oiled' by creating an expectation of price stability and by itself being stable rather than erratic.[81] The act specified that inflation targets would be agreed with the minister of finance and that the governor of the bank was accountable for achieving those targets. The merits of this purist approach remain controversial.

The fractures between the wider party and caucus intensified. Wilson retired from the presidency in 1987 and was replaced, for a year, by the Engineers' Union's national secretary Rex Jones. He in turn was succeeded by Ruth Dyson, who won an intensely fought contest with Jim Anderton. Ironically, cabinet supported Dyson, whose instincts were with the broad left of the party. President until 1993, Dyson sought to emulate Wilson's approach of ensuring consultation between party and government. As privatisation gathered momentum, this became increasingly difficult. The 1988 conference established a mechanism for representatives of cabinet, caucus and the New Zealand Council to discuss measures that contravened party policy, but this had little real effect. Ministers were committed to privatisation; the council's commitment was the opposite, and in any case few ministers, if any, were willing to accept limits on their discretion.[82]

Dyson inherited a party in disarray. Several electorate committees had condemned the December package. The Wellington Amalgamated Watersiders' Union disaffiliated 'with regret' over port reform.[83] One member of the New Zealand Council resigned, having 'lost faith in the Government's will to represent the principles of the Party . . . The Government is destroying the social fabric which I am committed to preserving and enhancing.' Remaining would have no result 'other than compromising my own personal integrity'.[84] The South Island organiser, Pete Hodgson, reported in May that 'the Party is not available to be organised . . . there is widespread anger, confusion and torpor'. While some of this was 'post-election malaise or our penchant for always wanting to be first to criticise the government', there were 'deep and serious misgivings about political direction'.[85] The party was in debt, and some nominally large donations had been in shares that became worthless after the stock market crash. Parts of Fraser House were sold to ease the financial situation.[86] Public fights about the standing of particular branches in Prebble's Auckland Central electorate did nothing to help matters, and one of the few policy areas where the government could claim a progressive record, Treaty of Waitangi claims, had some members 'confused, lost, even angry'.[87]

During 1988 Anderton abstained on some privatisation votes. Caucus suspended him, but the council continued to oppose privatisation and implicitly supported Anderton. On one level the question was whether Labour candidates' pledges to support party policy were more or less binding than their pledges to vote in accordance with caucus decisions.[88] Anderton resisted, strenuously and at length, the proposition that caucus had the right to suspend him. Palmer defended caucus, maintaining that by failing to vote in accordance with a caucus resolution Anderton had automatically removed himself, and that the ministry must be assured of a parliamentary majority, which meant a solid caucus (that, in fact, was and is only true of confidence and supply). Although Dyson brokered Anderton's return to caucus, he left the party in April 1989.[89]

The NewLabour Party which Anderton almost immediately formed took many Labour activists, but none of the other left-wing MPs joined. Anderton announced his resignation from Labour on the eve of the union affiliates' conference. Pat Kelly, who had been a vocal trade union opponent of the government's direction, noted that had Anderton's intention not been leaked he would have made his announcement at the conference itself, which would have done even more damage. Kelly criticised two people at the conference who 'use[d] our meeting to grandstand', which was 'destructive, and intended to be so'. He warned that while the council was loyal to the party, the government had to 'turn the economy away from the disastrous course it is on . . . [or] the government will be history'.[90]

Kelly deserved more credit for his loyalty than he got. He warned that any suggestion of returning Douglas and Prebble to cabinet in the interests of 'reconciliation' was 'naïve . . . and out of touch with reality'. He was correct: when caucus returned Douglas at the end of July it was the final straw for Lange, who resigned on 7 August.[91] Lange's successor was Palmer, with Helen Clark as deputy. Clark's rise was remarkable. Two years previously she had not been in cabinet, but she had managed major portfolios and was persuaded to stand for deputy as the alternative to Douglas.[92] Palmer knew that he 'got a hospital pass from David Lange—it was really a question of holding the place together as long as possible'.[93] He later wrote that his inheritance was 'scorched earth in the Labour Party that [Lange] and Douglas together had created'.[94]

In different circumstances Palmer might have been regarded as a successful prime minister. Since 1984 he had overseen the modernisation of parliamentary services, established a more predictable sitting year and funded offices in electorates (which relieved members' wives of a huge unpaid burden). Whatever his missteps, he had, with Koro Wetere, brought the government to engage with the Waitangi Tribunal process. He was an eloquent advocate for constitutional reform, ensured that a royal commission investigated the electoral system, and would finally see a non-binding Bill of Rights Act passed in 1990. Even as he oversaw major economic restructuring, on social policy his approach was measured, thoughtful and in keeping with Labour's social democratic traditions. He spoke of the universal need for 'friendship, companionship and love . . . security . . . to feel self-reliant . . . hope for the future', and reaffirmed the importance of 'equal access to the social, economic and cultural assets of this country'. As prime minister he emphasised a collaborative approach and deprecated the 'drift to a presidential style'.[95] In all this he was like his mentor, Bill Rowling. Palmer was also the most environmentally aware prime minister New Zealand had yet seen; almost a third of his speech to the 1989 conference addressed environmental issues.

Any hope of a fresh start was brief and illusory; too much damage had been done. Caygill's more moderate approach as finance minister might have made a difference to the government's fortunes if Lange had appointed him in August 1987. The Palmer government's significant achievements in social policy, such as pay equity, made little impact despite their importance (Clark, the architect of pay equity, was the subject of a good deal of right-wing populist sniping over her anti-smoking initiatives). Some initiatives, as when Goff oversaw the introduction of fees for tertiary education, were widely resented. The Resource Management Bill, finally passed after 1990, integrated planning and environmental legislation and was innovative, but necessarily lengthy and complex rather than the stuff of soundbites (to which Palmer was in any case allergic).

Palmer's political judgement was sometimes lacking. In January 1990, aware that six ministers were intending to retire at the election, he asked them to resign, believing that voters deserved to see some of the faces of the future and that a later Labour government would benefit from the experience in cabinet office these new ministers would gain. However, it created ill feeling.[96] More seriously, although caucus, not Palmer, then re-elected Prebble to cabinet, Palmer returned to him his old portfolio of state-owned enterprises; Prebble promptly privatised Telecom. Whatever the merits of privatisation (and Palmer reluctantly concluded that 'our economic credibility' required it), selling Telecom and some other state-owned enterprises could hardly have reassured anyone that Rogernomics had been consigned to the past. Almost as politically inept was giving Bob Jones a knighthood; a deeply hurt Rowling quietly resigned from the party.[97]

By August 1990 the polls were quite unforgiving. Most ministers thought electoral damage might be reduced if Moore replaced Palmer. Palmer could probably have rallied a caucus majority but, understandably, decided to walk away. He found being prime minister less satisfactory than being deputy. As deputy he had effectively run the government, but 'when I was prime minister I was the front man. I didn't have time to run the show—you are spending your life at functions or with the Queen for three

Above: Māngere MP David Lange (1942–2005) (Labour's deputy leader), speaking, and Frank O'Flynn (1918–2003) (MP for Island Bay) at The Great Debate, Auckland Town Hall, October 1980. This was part of Labour Week, a programme of social and educational events organised to promote the party. New Zealand Labour Party, Mt Albert Electorate Committee records. MSS & Archives 2015/3, folder 4/7. Special Collections, University of Auckland Libraries and Learning Services

Left: In its 1984 general election campaign Labour promised to bring the country together after the divisions of the Muldoon years. Labour Party ephemera. MSS & Archives 2015/22, Special Collections, University of Auckland Libraries and Learning Services

COBB & CO.
New Zealand
Labour Party
WOODCRAFT
Come into the...
crows nest
COFFEE HOUSE
KB 1303

Above: The Labour caucus after the 1987 election. Front row from left: Allan Wallbank (Gisborne), Jenny Kirk (Birkenhead), Ross Robertson (Papatoetoe), Annette King (Horowhenua), David Lange (leader, Māngere), Peter Dunne (Ōhariu), John Terris (Western Hutt), Margaret Shields (Kapiti), Sonja Davies (Pencarrow), Graham Kelly (Porirua). Second row from left: Mike Moore (Christchurch North), Fran Wilde (Wellington Central), Judy Keall (Glenfield), Trevor Young (Eastern Hutt), Bob Tizard (Panmure), Geoffrey Palmer (deputy leader, Christchurch Central), Noel Scott (Tongariro), Whetū Tirikātene-Sullivan (Southern Māori), Geoff Braybrooke (Napier), Elizabeth Tennet (Island Bay), Colin Moyle (Ōtara), Larry Sutherland (Avon), Koro Wetere (Western Māori), Anne Collins (East Cape), Richard Prebble (Auckland Central), Margaret Austin (Yaldhurst). Third row from left: Trevor Mallard (Hamilton West), David Caygill (St Albans), Stan Rodger (Dunedin North), Peter Tapsell (Eastern Māori), Phil Goff (Roskill), Bill Sutton (Hawke's Bay), Roger Douglas (Manurewa), Peter Simpson (Lyttelton), Harry Duynhoven (New Plymouth), Jack Elder (West Auckland), Dave Robinson (Manawatū), Jim Sutton (Waitaki), Michael Cullen (St Kilda), Jonathan Hunt (New Lynn), Russell Marshall (Wanganui), Ralph Maxwell (Titirangi), Bruce Gregory (Northern Māori), Fred Gerbic (Onehunga), Michael Bassett (Te Atatū). Back row: Ken Shirley (Tasman), Bill Jeffries (Heretaunga), Clive Matthewson (Dunedin West), Richard Northey (Eden), David Butcher (Hastings). Absent: Jim Anderton (Sydenham), Kerry Burke (West Coast), Helen Clark (Mt Albert), Trevor de Cleene (Palmerston North), Bill Dillon (Hamilton East), Peter Neilson (Miramar), Philip Woollaston (Nelson). Sonja Davies Collection. PACoII-9354-6-051, Alexander Turnbull Library

Opposite, top: Roger Douglas (left) and David Lange (right) meeting Bill Hayden, minister of foreign affairs in the Australian Labor government, in Canberra on 12 September 1983. Australian Information Service. New Zealand Labour Party collection

Opposite, bottom: The Labour Party conference marching up Willis Street, Wellington to open Fraser House, the party's new (and present) headquarters, on 10th May 1983. In the front row are, from left, Bill Rowling (leader), Jim Anderton (president), unidentified, David Lange (deputy leader) and John Wybrow (general secretary). New Zealand Labour Party collection

Above: David Lange addressing Labour's victory conference, September 1984. To his right are Jim Anderton (president), Naomi Lange, Margaret Palmer and Geoffrey Palmer (deputy prime minister). New Zealand Labour Party collection

Left: Mike Moore at the launch of his book The Added Value Economy in 1984. He was MP for Eden, 1972–75 and for Papanui, Christchurch North and Waimakariri, 1978–99. Moore was the first youth representative on the party's national executive, and was very influential in the party and caucus after his re-election in 1978. He was minister of overseas trade, tourism, recreation and sport, external relations and trade and deputy minister of finance in the fourth Labour government. He was elected Labour leader and prime minister in September 1990, just weeks before the general election. In 1993 Moore was defeated by Helen Clark as leader. He was later director-general of the World Trade Organisation (1999–2002) and New Zealand ambassador to the United States (2010–15). New Zealand Labour Party collection

Opposite: By the 1980s the Labour Women's Council was a powerful force in the party. This photograph is of the 1985–86 council. Standing at rear: Whetū Tirikātene-Sullivan, Ngāi Tahu (1932-2011; MP for Southern Māori, 1967–96). Fourth row: Helene Ritchie, Judy Keall (MP for Glenfield, 1984–90 and Horowhenua and Ōtaki, 1993–2002), Rae Julian, Kathleen Mary. Third row: Tala Cleverley, Gail Jackson, Denise Yates, Elizabeth Tennet (MP for Island Bay, 1987–96). Second row: Jan Walker, Ruth Dyson (Labour Party president from 1988–1993 and MP for Lyttelton, Banks Peninsula and Port Hills since 1993), Lois Welch. Front row: Sandi Beattie, Maryan Street (Labour Party president, 1993–95 and list MP, 2005–14). New Zealand Labour Party collection

Above: Geoffrey Palmer and Helen Clark were elected as Labour prime minister and deputy prime minister in August 1989 following David Lange's resignation. As deputy prime minister Palmer had effectively run the government, but by the time he replaced Lange the government was terminal. He said later: 'What I got from Lange was a hospital pass.' New Zealand Labour Party collection

Opposite, top: Julie-Ann and Dennis Pyatt canvassing for Fran Wilde. New Nation, June 1987, New Zealand Labour Party collection

Opposite, bottom: Margaret Wilson (president, 1984–87), Rex Jones (president, 1987–88), centre, and Tony Timms (general secretary, 1985–94) at the 1987 party conference. Wilson was a key figure in liaising between the party and the fourth Labour government. Jones was national secretary of the Engineers' Union and subsequently the EPMU, Labour's largest affiliated union, from 1983 to 2000. Timms played a central role in holding the party together during a very difficult period. New Zealand Labour Party collection

Above: Jonathan Hunt (MP for New Lynn and list MP, 1966–2005, minister of broadcasting and tourism and leader of the House, 1984–90 and speaker of parliament, 1999–2005) after Helen Clark had presented him with life membership of the Labour Party in 2001. Hunt is shaking hands with Steve Maharey (MP for Palmerston North, 1990–2008 and minister of social development and employment, broadcasting and education, 1999–2007); immediately behind them is Vui Mark Gosche, New Zealand's first Pasifika cabinet minister and list MP and MP for Maungakiekie, 1996–2008. At the back is Michael Cullen. Carol Gosche is standing next to Clark. John Miller photograph

Opposite, top: Judith Tizard (left), Jill Amos (centre) and Helene Ritchie at the 2001 Labour Party conference. Judith Tizard succeeded her father, Bob, as MP for Panmure in 1990 and was MP for that electorate and Auckland Central until 2008. She was a minister outside cabinet in the fifth Labour government. Amos was a Manukau city councillor for a number of years and also served on the Auckland Hospital Board and the Auckland Regional Council. Ritchie is a long-serving Wellington city councillor and member of the Capital and Coast District Health Board. John Miller photograph

Opposite, bottom: Parekura Horomia, Ngāti Porou, Te Aitanga-a-Hauiti, Ngāti Kahungunu and Ngāi Tahu (1950–2013), was MP for Ikaroa–Rāwhiti, 1999–2013 and minister of Māori affairs, 2000–08. This photograph shows him speaking during the national hui on the foreshore and seabed at Ngahuitoitoi marae, Paeroa on 12 July 2003. A thousand people attended and almost all were strongly opposed to the Labour government's policy. Jason Ake, Horomia's press secretary, 'said Parekura's performance on the marae that day was stellar and the best delivery he had seen him give on any marae anywhere.' (Wira Gardiner, Parekura Horomia, 'Kia Ora, Chief!', Huia Publishers, Wellington, 2014, p.205).
John Miller photograph

"MY COMMITMENTS ARE":

1. **Create jobs through promoting New Zealand industries and better support for exporters and small business.**
2. **Focus on patients not profit and cut waiting times for surgery.**
3. **Cut the cost to students of tertiary education, starting with a fairer loans scheme.**
4. **Reverse the 1999 cuts to superannuation rates. Guarantee superannuation in the future by putting a proportion of all income tax into a separate fund which cannot be used for any other purpose.**
5. **Restore income related rents for state housing so that low income tenants pay no more than 25 per cent of their income in rent.**
6. **Crack down on burglary and youth crime.**
7. **No rise in income tax for the 95 per cent of taxpayers earning under $60,000 a year. No increases in GST or company tax.**

Above: Murdo Macmillan (Labour's assistant general secretary), Mark Peck (MP for Invercargill, 1993–2005), Ron Bax, Ross Robertson (MP for Papatoetoe and Manukau East, 1987–2014) and Michael Cullen (MP for St Kilda and Dunedin South and list MP, 1981–2009, minister of finance, 1999–2008 and deputy prime minister, 2002–08) campaigning for Marian Hobbs, Labour candidate for Selwyn, 1994. New Zealand Labour Party collection

Opposite, top left: A Labour Women's Council leaflet encouraging women to become active in the party. Eph-A-NZ-LABOUR-1995-01, Alexander Turnbull Library

Opposite, top right: Taito Phillip Field was New Zealand's first Samoan (and Pasifika) member of parliament. He was MP for Ōtara and Māngere, 1993–2008 and was a minister outside cabinet in the fifth Labour government from 2003 to 2005. In 2009 he was jailed after being convicted of bribery and corruption. Labour Party ephemera. MSS & Archives 2015/22, folder 2, Special Collections, University of Auckland Libraries and Learning Services

Opposite, bottom: Labour's 1999 pledge card. After the broken promises of successive Labour and National governments, Labour campaigned heavily on a promise that it would deliver on its policies. Peter Franks collection

The Labour caucus after the 2005 election. Front row from left: Parekura Horomia (Ikaroa–Rāwhiti), Pete Hodgson (Dunedin North), Annette King (Rongotai), Steve Maharey (Palmerston North), Margaret Wilson (list), Helen Clark (leader, Mt Albert), Michael Cullen (deputy leader, list), Phil Goff (Roskill), Trevor Mallard (Hutt South), Ruth Dyson (Banks Peninsula), Mark Burton (Taupō). Second row from left: Ross Robertson (Manukau East), Harry Duynhoven (New Plymouth), Clayton Cosgrove (Waimakariri), Chris Carter (Te Atatū), David Parker (list), Darren Hughes (Ōtaki), David Benson-Pope (Dunedin South), Georgina Beyer (list), Nanaia Mahuta (Tainui), David Cunliffe (New Lynn), Rick Barker (list), Ann Hartley (list). Third row from left: Dianne Yates (list), Sue Moroney (list), Darien Fenton (list), Russell Fairbrother (list), Moana Mackey (list), Ashraf Choudhary (list), Jim Sutton (list). Fourth row from left: Mark Gosche (Maungakiekie), Martin Gallagher (Hamilton West), Marian Hobbs (Wellington Central), Jill Pettis (list), Judith Tizard (Auckland Central), Lynne Pillay (Waitakere), Maryan Street (list), Steve Chadwick (Rotorua). Fifth row: Mita Ririnui (list), Lianne Dalziel (Christchurch East), George Hawkins (Manurewa). Sixth row from left: Mahara Okeroa (Te Tai Tonga), Dave Hereora (list), Winnie Laban (Mana), Tim Barnett (Christchurch Central), Shane Jones (list). Back row from left: Taito Phillip Field (Māngere), Dover Samuels (list), Paul Swain (Rimutaka). Absent: Damien O'Connor (West Coast–Tasman). New Zealand Labour Party collection

The 2000s saw a renaissance of Young Labour as a political force among students and as an influence within the party. This photograph shows Young Labour activists with Prime Minister Helen Clark. New Zealand Labour Party collection

Above: At the 2014 general election Labour increased its number of Māori MPs to seven. From left: Louisa Wall, Ngāti Tūwharetoa, Waikato (MP for Manurewa), Rino Tirikātene, Ngāi Tahu, Ngāti Hine, grandson of Eruera Tirikātene and nephew of Whetū Tirikātene-Sullivan (MP for Te Tai Tonga), Nanaia Mahuta, Waikato–Maniapoto, Ngāpuhi (MP for Hauraki–Waikato), Peeni Henare, Ngāti Hine, Ngāpuhi (MP for Tāmaki Makaurau), Kelvin Davis, Ngāti Manu (MP for Te Tai Tokerau), Meka Whaitiri, Rongowhakaata, Ngāti Kahungunu (MP for Ikaroa-Rāwhiti) and Adrian Rurawhe, Ngāti Apa, Ngāti Hauiti, Whanganui, Ngā Rauru Kitāhi, Ngāti Ruanui (MP for Te Tai Hauāuru); Rurawhe's grandparents, Matiu Rātana and Iriaka Rātana, were Labour MPs for Western Māori. Alison Bell photograph

Opposite, top: Phil Goff (MP for Roskill, New Lynn and Mt Roskill, 1981–90 and since 1993) and Annette King (MP for Horowhenua, 1984–90 and Miramar and Rongotai since 1993) were elected leader and deputy leader of the Labour Party in 2009. They stepped down after the 2011 election. King was re-elected deputy leader in 2014. They were ministers in the fourth and fifth Labour governments. Goff's portfolios between 1984 and 1990 included housing, employment and education; between 1999 and 2008 he was minister of foreign affairs, justice, Pacific Island affairs, defence and trade. King was minister of employment, 1989–90 and minister of health, state services, police, transport and justice, 1999–2008. New Zealand Labour Party collection

Opposite, bottom: There were five Pasifika MPs in the Labour caucus after 2014. From left: Poto Williams (MP for Christchurch East), Carmel Sepuloni (MP for Kelston), Su'a William Sio (MP for Māngere), Kris Faafoi (MP for Mana) and Jenny Salesa (MP for Manukau East). Alison Bell photograph

Above: Andrew Little (list MP since 2011 and Labour leader since 2014) speaking at the dinner held at parliament on 27 November 2015 to celebrate the 80th anniversary of the election of the first Labour government. Alison Bell photograph weeks or some bloody thing'.[98] Only 48, he had a long and distinguished career ahead of him.

Mike Moore's seven weeks as prime minister could only be a postscript to the fourth Labour government. Whether his elevation made any difference cannot be known; the election was devastating. Labour was reduced to 29 seats and 35 per cent of the vote. Outside the four largest cities, the only seats held were Napier, Palmerston North and Nelson. Otherwise, the party lost all its provincial seats, as well as many in the middling suburbs of Auckland and Wellington. Some maintain that had Lange and Douglas not fallen out, and Douglas been able to continue his increasingly radical policies, the party would have won in 1990. This may be doubted. National won by campaigning on the impression that the pace of change would slow, and when instead Jim Bolger and Ruth Richardson intensified the neo-liberal direction, National in its turn was almost defeated in 1993.

In only one dimension was there much for the party to celebrate in the late 1980s. Michael Bassett had driven through a sweeping reform of local government, amalgamating a very large number of small territorial local authorities.[99] Labour or Labour-identified candidates secured some notable victories in both the old and new administrations. In Wellington, Jim Belich came from a successful advertising career to win the mayoralty in 1986 and brought the city council's first Labour majority with him. Cleaning up a dysfunctional sewage system was a major achievement, along with developing amenities around the waterfront. Belich won the mayoralty in 1989 and retired three years later.[100] He was succeeded by Fran Wilde. In Auckland, Cath Tizard won the mayoralty in 1983 (as an independent with strong Labour support), resigning in 1990 to become New Zealand's first female governor-general. And in Christchurch, Vicki Buck, who had been a city councillor since 1974, won the mayoralty of the enlarged city in 1989 with a considerable number of Labour-aligned councillors behind her. When Buck stepped down in 1998 she was replaced by another Labour-aligned mayor, Garry Moore.

Mike Moore brought considerable energy and tireless work to the party leadership, but some handicaps were acknowledged at the time. Having helped promote Lange to the leadership, and having worked in cabinet with Douglas for five years, despite some more moderate instincts Moore now had something of a credibility problem in maintaining that the party under his leadership was returning to more traditional Labour values.[101] More generally, as even one of his close colleagues noted, Moore's approach to politics was characterised by 'a mixture of grand ideas, good salesmanship, gut philosophy and bullshit'.[102] Unfortunately, Moore's approach to the party leadership became increasingly personalised, to the point that he oversaw the establishment of Mike Moore supporters' clubs, which he wanted affiliated to Labour electorate committees.[103] Something of a praetorian guard emerged, which made itself unpopular in some quarters.

In any case, Moore would have had an almost impossible task restoring the party's fortunes in a single parliamentary term. The party launched a 'Labour Listens' exercise which discussed aims and values. Any such undertaking would have needed time to show results. The party's organisation was gravely weak: the youth council had fallen apart with infighting and affiliated union membership fell because private sector unions were decimated by the Employment Contracts Act 1991.[104] The party was nearly bankrupt, and, as the general secretary noted early in 1992, only able to 'continue to operate at the whim of our bankers'.[105] One response was to significantly reduce the size of New Zealand Council, with regional representatives now responsible for much larger areas.[106]

The fourth Labour government requires more than a simplistic analysis. It was always torn between social reform and economic reform. Even in 1984 those tensions were daunting enough. We generally share the views of critics who argue that the pace and direction of economic reform were increasingly unwise, even accepting as we do that much needed to change. Some of the government's lasting legacies—in more enlightened attitudes to sex and gender, in a more independent foreign policy, in an integrated approach to conservation and resource management—should have been broadly acceptable. But the elitism of economic reform and, more, economic policies increasingly driven by market fundamentalism did the party lasting damage. Labour would face a decade of rebuilding.

11

Rebuilding Social Democracy in a New Globalisation: The Clark Years, 1993–2008

When Helen Clark was elected Labour Party leader in 1993, the party was in a parlous state. This was made worse by the coup in which she defeated Mike Moore, as the caucus was left badly divided. Labour and Clark polled badly in the early 1990s, and there was an attempt to remove her only months before the 1996 election, the first to be under held mixed-member proportional representation (MMP). During the election campaign Clark came to be recognised as a credible and capable leader. Between 1996 and 1999 she united the party, eliminated factionalism in the caucus, built a strong team with a credible social democratic programme and established a coalition with the new Alliance. Labour's victory in 1999 began nine years of centre-left coalition governments, with Labour in coalition first with the Alliance and, after 2002, with Jim Anderton's Progressive Party. The government corrected the worst excesses of neo-liberal policies, ran a strong economy, introduced important social reforms which benefited low-income families, including Māori and Pasifika, encouraged arts and culture to flourish and emphasised New Zealand's independence in foreign policy. Clark was Labour's longest-serving leader to date and one of its greatest prime ministers. The biggest shortcoming in these years was the failure by the leadership inside and outside parliament to rebuild the party by increasing its membership and putting its finances on a sound footing.

Rebuilding, 1993–96

The party entered the 1990s in a very weak state. Its financial membership had fallen to 9500, it had only a handful of union affiliates and it had a deficit of over $280,000. Since the 1987 election the party had funded its deficits by an advance of $1 million from Fraser House, but that funding had run out.[1] Remarkably, Labour almost pulled off an upset victory at the 1993 general election. National was punished by voters for breaking its promises and continuing with neo-liberal policies. Its majority fell from 37 seats to only one. Labour achieved a net gain of 16 seats, and with 45 seats was only five behind National. Taito Phillip Field, who won Ōtara, became Labour's first Pasifika MP. Labour's share of the popular vote, however, marginally decreased. The parliamentary ground regained was entirely due to the emergence of two strong minor parties. Anderton had brought his NewLabour Party into the Alliance, which included the recently formed Green Party, the social crediters (now known as the New Zealand Democratic Party), and a couple of dissident National MPs. Bolger had expelled the neo-Muldoonist Winston Peters from cabinet in 1991 and Peters then established New Zealand First, a party of conservative populist nostalgia. These parties polled 18 per cent and 8 per cent respectively, winning two seats each and delivering many more to the other parties on minority votes. For the Alliance, Anderton held his Wigram seat and, in a significant upset, Sandra Lee defeated Prebble in Auckland Central; for New Zealand First, Peters held his Tauranga seat and Tau Hēnare defeated Bruce Gregory in Northern Māori. Many of Labour's new or returned MPs would help shape a rural and provincial base for the party under MMP, under which party votes were crucial. While Moore claimed, with some justification, that he had taken the party to the verge of victory, a 1993 Labour government would have been a government without a mandate.

The real winners in 1993 were those voters who wanted to put a brake on the power of errant governments: 54 per cent supported MMP in the referendum on the electoral system which was held at the same time as the election. Under MMP, which was implemented from 1996, the number of seats each party had in parliament was determined by its percentage of the party vote. Parties had to reach a 5 per cent threshold to be represented, although all their party votes counted if they won an electorate seat. In the new system, the Alliance and New Zealand First were clearly a threat to both Labour and National. This parliamentary term would be transitional, not least as other MPs sought to maximise their own advantage in the new regime. In late 1994 Peter Dunne, the MP for Onslow, who had been aligned with Roger Douglas, left Labour and formed his own Future New Zealand party. In 1995 two other Labour MPs, Margaret Austin and Clive Matthewson, also deserted and, with four National MPs, joined Dunne in what became United New Zealand. The declared aim was to operate as a centrist party. Outside parliament, Roger Douglas and other neo-liberals had formed the Association of Consumers and Taxpayers, or ACT.

Immediately after the election, supporters of Helen Clark launched a coup against Moore, who was criticised for blurring Labour's messages rather than branding it clearly as a centre-left party, and for having a poor grasp of policy.[2] Moore had a bad relationship with the leadership of the extra-parliamentary party, which saw the Mike Moore Supporters' Club, set up in 1992 to boost support for both the party and Moore, as a challenge to the existing party organisation.[3] A senior colleague has said that, although talented and energetic, Moore did not inspire confidence as leader, and irritated many, if not all, the women in caucus. Clark was seen as reliable, consensus-seeking and willing to make a clear break from Rogernomics. She had broad support in the party organisation and a good understanding of policy, and was seen as better equipped to deal with the challenges of MMP.[4] Most of the new MPs elected in 1993 (as opposed to those defeated in 1990 who were re-elected) supported her. The challenge became public on 25 November. Angry that he had not been informed, Moore accused the challengers—'chardonnay socialists', he called them—of being out of touch with Labour members and supporters.[5]

Maryan Street, who had replaced Ruth Dyson as party president in 1993, asked Moore to stand down voluntarily. Moore called for a 'peace conference' between him and Clark.[6] Behind the scenes, the leadership of the Council of Trade Unions (formed in 1987 by a merger of the FOL and Combined State Unions) supported Clark, who declared her intentions on 27 November. From then until the caucus vote on 1 December it was a very public fight.[7] In the final days before the vote 'the animosity between the two camps continued to intensify'; in a fax to Street, Moore said, 'I will not serve in any position in a Helen Clark shadow cabinet if that were to ever happen'.[8] Jonathan Hunt, Labour's senior whip, advised Moore that there wasn't a majority for a 'spill' motion (a vote to hold a leadership election). To Hunt's astonishment, Moore seconded David Lange's motion for a spill. Clark defeated Moore by 26 votes to 19. David Caygill was elected deputy leader, beating Michael Cullen by 23 to 21.[9]

There was much criticism of the challenge within the party. According to Street, majority support in the party was for Moore but majority support in the caucus was for Clark.[10] The challenge left Labour MPs badly bruised and deeply divided; Goff recalls that it was 'a pretty traumatic experience'.[11] Clark's first three years as leader were, in Street's words, 'a hideously difficult time'.[12] Clark, Street and Dyson were subject to offensive vituperation by some of Moore's supporters. Clark herself struggled to win public support and Labour continued to slide in the polls, while the Alliance surged.[13] The August 1994 Selwyn by-election (following Ruth Richardson's resignation) was a disaster for Labour. National had a narrow victory over the Alliance (whose candidate was a social crediter), and Labour's vote plummeted from 37.4 per cent in 1993 to 10.3.[14]

Labour's polling recovered, and Clark and Caygill were re-elected unopposed in early 1995. However, in October Labour fell to 16 per cent, while Clark had only 3 per cent support as preferred prime minister. There was controversy over Labour's party list for the 1996 election which was released that month, as it ranked five Māori and Pasifika newcomers—Dover Samuels, Mark Gosche, Nanaia Mahuta, Joe Hawke and Tariana Turia—above some sitting MPs (who would be expected to hold their electorate seats). The working party, chaired by Street, which devised the rules for party list selections had endorsed affirmative action but rejected quotas.[15] The new rules required Labour's moderating committee, which selected the party list from lists decided on by regional conferences, to produce a list that fairly represented women, Māori and Pasifika peoples and other ethnic groups, and had regard to the geographical spread of the population.[16] Moore said the list was a 'suicide note' and continued to snipe at his successor and the party, calling it a 'toxic waste dump' and 'a bit of a poisoned chalice'.[17]

At the 1995 party conference, Clark signalled Labour's return to its traditional positions, such as universal provision of social services.[18] The following year she told Labour's election congress that mistakes had been made during the fourth Labour government, but the party had learned from them and changed the policies that were wrong.[19]

Labour continued to languish in the polls, and on 28 May 1996 five front-bench MPs—Phil Goff, Koro Wetere, Jim Sutton, Annette King and Cullen—asked Clark to stand down. Labour MPs had been asked to sign a letter calling on her to do so, but there wasn't a majority in favour of a change and the letter did not say who should replace her, although Moore was the obvious candidate.[20] Supported by Hunt, Larry Sutherland (the junior whip), Lianne Dalziel and Trevor Mallard, Clark stared them down. Her supporters contacted the media and appealed to the party organisation for support. As in 1993, the Council of Trade Unions leadership strongly backed Clark, as did Michael Hirschfeld, who was elected party president in 1995, and the New Zealand Council.[21] There was intense lobbying by both sides; recalls Mallard, 'it was quite heavy . . . a few of us thought that the future of the Labour Party was at stake'.[22] At a caucus meeting on 11 June, Clark challenged anyone who wanted to move a spill motion to do so; nobody did. Caygill resigned as deputy, Cullen was elected in his place and the five MPs pledged their loyalty to Clark.[23] There was much anger in the party about the attempted coup. The Wellington Central Labour campaign committee wrote that members felt 'used, abused and disempowered'. Clark replied that this was 'an excellent way to describe how activists have felt about a lot of PLP actions!'[24]

The failed attempt to oust Clark, and Cullen's election as deputy, marked the end of the divisions over Labour's leadership and Clark united the caucus by retaining the five in their front-bench positions. Labour and Clark picked up in the polls, but the party went into the 1996 election campaign on only 22 per cent.[25] Clark campaigned strongly and won the first television leaders' debate. After Winston Peters publicly offered him a cabinet post in a New Zealand First 'Ministry of All Talents', Moore mended his rift with Clark and agreed to become Labour's shadow foreign minister.[26] When Clark was speaking at a Labour rally at the University of Otago, a mature student picked up a bunch of flowers, walked across the quadrangle and gave them to her; the crowd went wild. Patricia Herbert, a *New Zealand Herald* reporter, turned to Pete Hodgson, the Dunedin North MP, and said, 'she has become the phenomenon of the campaign'.[27] Peter Aimer later wrote: 'In a nutshell, Helen Clark stole the first MMP campaign.'[28]

The 1996 election result was bad for both National, which won 33.8 per cent of party votes, and Labour, which won 28.2 per cent. New Zealand First won 13.4 per cent and all the Māori seats. The Alliance won 10.1 per cent and ACT 6.1 per cent, and the deserters in United lost all but Dunne's seat.[29] After eight weeks of tortuous negotiations with National and Labour, New Zealand First decided to form a coalition with National. Poor though the 1996 result was, the election was a turning point for Labour and for Clark. The party had run third behind both the Alliance and New Zealand First in different polls in the first half of the 1990s and the election cemented Labour's position as the main centre-left party. Hodgson comments that the campaign was one of the factors in Clark becoming a strong leader. Others were her ability to learn on the job, her hard work, her travelling throughout the country to meet people, and 'that she got forged in the heat of the caucus discord'.[30] Clark herself thought New Zealand First's decision not to go into coalition with Labour was 'a very lucky break'.[31] Because Peters had campaigned strongly against National in 1996, the coalition government was seen by many as another betrayal of voters.

Cullen told the 1997 conference that there had been 'a dramatic transformation' in Labour's position.[32] Membership was up by a third, the party's net financial position had gone from minus $27,472 in 1994 to $84,035 in 1996, and 563 delegates attended the conference, the largest number since 1988.[33] The main business was the report of a working party on structural reform which considered whether Labour electorate committees, rather than branches, should be Labour's primary organisational unit. Opinion at the regional conferences was divided, and the conference decided to keep the status quo but allow electorate committees to apply to become membership-based and dispense with branches.[34] The 1998 conference supported remits to enhance the status of Labour's Māori Policy and Advisory Council (later renamed Te Kaunihera Māori) and provide for increased Māori representation on the New Zealand Council and the Policy Council.[35]

A major obstacle to Labour forming a government was its relationship with the Alliance. After Jenny Shipley seized the National leadership from Bolger, there was a by-election in Taranaki–King Country in May 1998. Admittedly in a safe National seat, Labour and the Alliance each got about a sixth of the vote. Subsequently, the leadership of both parties realised that continued feuding was self-defeating. Clark credits Sandra Lee, the Alliance's deputy leader, with getting them talking.[36] After Anderton persuaded the Alliance council that the party had to work with Labour, Clark addressed the 1998 Alliance conference and received a very warm reception. Agreement was reached that Labour and the Alliance would form a coalition if they could in 1999,[37] and a strong working relationship was established behind the scenes.[38] Not the least significant dimension was the personal reconciliation between Clark and Anderton.

Into government, 1999–2002

Labour's 1999 election manifesto was deliberately modest. Borrowing from Tony Blair's successful campaign in Britain in 1997, Labour's seven main promises were published on a credit card-sized commitment card. They were: to create more jobs, cut the cost of tertiary education for students, cut waiting times for surgery in public hospitals, reverse the cuts in superannuation payments, restore income-related rents for state house tenants, crack down on burglary and youth crime, and no tax increases for the 95 per cent of taxpayers earning less than $60,000.[39] Increasing the top tax rate from 33 per cent to 39 per cent for those earning over $60,000 had been Labour policy since 1994.

Labour won 38.7 per cent of the party vote in 1999 and 49 seats. (Among its new members, on the list, was Luamanuvao Winnie Laban, who was parliament's first Pasifika woman member.) National fell to 30.5 per cent and 39 seats. The Alliance won 7.7 per cent and nine seats, and ACT 7 per cent and nine seats. The Green Party, having left the Alliance, scraped in after special votes were counted with 5.2 per cent and seven seats. New Zealand First won 4.3 per cent and five seats and United one seat. Labour won back all six Māori seats.[40] New Zealand First only held on because Peters survived in his Tauranga seat; some thought Labour would have been better served if the liberal Katherine O'Regan had taken it for National.[41] Labour and the Alliance moved quickly to negotiate a coalition agreement and form a new government. Anderton became deputy prime minister and Cullen finance minister. There were 20 ministers in cabinet, 16 Labour and four Alliance, five ministers outside cabinet and one under-secretary. Eleven ministers were women, four Māori, and Mark Gosche became the first Pasifika cabinet member as minister of housing. Clark herself took arts, culture and heritage; Steve Maharey, a sociologist who had been identified with 'Third Way' rethinking of social democracy, oversaw social policy; Margaret Wilson, a new list MP, became minister of labour. These appointments were clear signals that a degree of progressive reform was planned, as were Anderton's appointment to economic development, Annette King's to health and Mallard's to education. Phil Goff's appointment as justice minister, however, was a nod to more conservative views (Goff was heavily committed, being also foreign minister, in which role he was much more in tune with Labour's progressive traditions). Other members of the full cabinet were Sandra Lee (conservation); Jim Sutton (agriculture and overseas trade); Hodgson (energy and science); Dover Samuels (Māori affairs); Matt Robson (corrections); Lianne Dalziel (immigration); George Hawkins (police); Mark Burton (defence); Paul Swain (commerce); Marian Hobbs (environment); and Laila Harré (women's affairs). The Greens supported the government on confidence and supply. Unlike the prescriptive National/New Zealand First coalition agreement, the Labour/Alliance agreement was brief and included a 'party distinction' clause to allow them to take different positions in parliament.[42]

The new government increased the minimum wage, repealed the 1991 Employment Contracts Act, passed the Employment Relations Act 2000, which gave greater support to collective bargaining and unions, and renationalised Accident Compensation Corporation workplace coverage. An $800 million cultural recovery package increased funding for the New Zealand Symphony Orchestra, the Royal New Zealand Ballet, the Historic Places Trust, the national museum, Creative New Zealand and Māori arts and culture, and saw the establishment of the New Zealand Music Commission.[43] A 'Closing the Gaps' programme addressed the economic, social and educational needs of Māori and Pasifika peoples.[44]

The Labour/Alliance government's honeymoon came to a sudden end in the 2000 'winter of discontent'. Business leaders attacked its policies on employment relations and the ACC, the economy went flat, and polling showed Pākehā discontent with the government's Māori policy. In June, Clark sacked Dover Samuels, the minister of Māori affairs, who was embroiled in allegations about his private life (of which he was later cleared). He was replaced by Parekura Horomia, MP for Ikaroa–Rāwhiti. National jumped ahead of Labour in the polls. Clark acted quickly. The emphasis of Closing the Gaps was shifted to addressing all inequalities and the name abandoned, while a charm offensive with business repaired relations there. Labour's polling improved.[45]

There were a number of elements to Labour's philosophy and approach in government. The first was an acceptance of most of the 1980s economic reforms: for example, the government was conventionally neo-liberal on monetary policy. The second was a recognition that globalisation placed limits on governments and that 'love it or hate it, you can't stop it', as Clark told the 2000 party conference.[46] The third was that the role of the state remained critical, although it had changed from the 1930s and 1940s model. Speaking to the London School of Economics in 2002, Clark acknowledged the influence of 'Third Way' social democratic thinking on her government. It was essential to maintain the confidence of business for the nation's economic health and to carve out a competitive edge in the global economy. This called for sound macroeconomic policy, and for the state to act as a leader, facilitator, co-ordinator and broker in economic development and a funder of education and skills development.[47] The state had to safeguard the nation's social health, 'and in New Zealand's case, it cries out for considerable improvement'.[48]

The fourth element was sound, stable and progressive government. Cullen told the 2003 Labour conference that this meant sound budgets, promoting economic growth and avoiding rushed and ill-informed policy making. Delivering progressive government that improved people's lives was 'the heart of the Labour mission. We exist to change things for the better, lift up the downtrodden, give hope to the excluded and strengthen the foundations of family, community and society.'[49] The fifth element was inclusion. The government worked hard to develop partnerships and relationships. It held regular forums with local government, trade unions, business, non-government organisations and Māori. Nanaia Mahuta says that Māori greatly appreciated being able to meet and discuss issues with Clark and cabinet ministers.[50]

The sixth element was to win voters' trust. Clark told the 2000 party conference that of all the lessons she had learned in politics, 'the most important is to promise only what you can deliver and then to keep your word'.[51] The final element was unity, discipline and strong leadership. Cullen told the 2003 conference that unity and discipline had to be maintained at every level of the party if Labour was to be a successful, long-term government.[52]

Much of the Clark government's approach was, in fundamentals, consistent with older social democratic thought, which, after all, had always been about managing a capitalist economy, modernising it, and mitigating inequality. The Clark government enjoyed very strong support within the Labour Party throughout its nine years in office. Membership grew modestly to between 11,000 and 12,000 in 2001, when 633 delegates attended the national conference.[53] While Labour was 'basking in the glow of power',[54] however, the Alliance was in trouble. Its poll ratings fell below 5 per cent in early 2000 and never recovered. After the terrorist attack on the United

States on 11 September 2001, the government sent a small military force to support the US-led war against the Taliban government in Afghanistan. While there was unease within the Labour Party,[55] there was open rebellion in the Alliance, which started to fall apart.[56] Convinced that some of his colleagues wanted to destroy the government, Anderton made the 'hard-headed decision' to walk away from the Alliance and form the Progressive Coalition to support the government. Looking back, he argued that the gains the Alliance had made were well worth the compromises.[57]

Consolidation, 2002–05

By the end of its first term the government had a long list of achievements. It had come to power when overseas prices for New Zealand exports were booming. Cullen's prudent fiscal policy resulted in low government debt and large budget surpluses. Inflation was low and unemployment fell to 5.4 per cent, the lowest since 1987.[58] More than 81,000 people were in industry training and over 2000 young people in the Modern Apprenticeships programme. The government froze tertiary education fees, removed interest on student loans for full-time students and abolished bulk funding of schools.[59]

The government boosted health spending, promoted mental health services and primary health care, and established the New Zealand Superannuation Fund to ensure superannuation would be affordable in the future given the projected large rise in the number of those aged over 65. Income-related rents meant state house tenants paid less; thousands of state houses were improved through a major maintenance programme and new state houses built.[60] The minimum wage was increased by 14 per cent between 2000 and 2002, and 12 weeks' paid parental leave introduced from 1 July 2002. The government invested heavily in research and development, and transport. It bought a majority share in Air New Zealand to prevent the airline failing. Anderton persuaded Labour ministers to agree to his proposal for a new publicly-owned bank with cheaper fees: Kiwibank, owned by New Zealand Post, was launched in September 2001.[61] The government launched a biodiversity strategy to protect endangered species, ended logging of native timber on the West Coast, signed the Kyoto Protocol on climate change and set up a royal commission on genetic modification.[62]

In response to the royal commission's report, the government proposed a two-year moratorium on the release of genetically-modified organisms. The Greens said that if a minority Labour government allowed the moratorium to expire, they would vote with opposition parties to bring the government down. Clark called an early election for 27 July 2002. Labour's strong polling was as big a reason for doing so as the difficulties with the Alliance and the Greens, and Labour seemed on track to form a majority government.[63] Early in the campaign, however, Clark came under fire when a police report was released criticising her for (while in opposition) signing a painting for a charity auction that she hadn't painted. On 10 July the genetic modification issue blew up. Clark was ambushed by broadcaster John Campbell in a television interview over claims the government had covered up the release and planting of genetically-modified corn. The next day, investigative journalist Nicky Hager published a book making the same claims (Campbell had obviously been well briefed). The government scrambled to respond. 'Over the next few days it became clear that government scientists and those working for the companies concerned had concluded that the episode had been a false alarm and that initial tests had indicated a "false positive".'[64]

The issue, and Clark's angry response to Campbell, diminished the party's standing. Labour slipped in the polls and after 'Corngate', as it became known, the term 'majority government' became a dirty word.[65] The beneficiary was not National but United Future, whose leader, Peter Dunne, performed strongly in television debates.[66] If the election campaign was difficult for Labour, it was disastrous for National, which fell to 20.9 per cent of party votes and only 27 seats. Labour won 41.3 per cent and 52 seats. New Zealand First won 10.4 per cent and 13 seats; ACT 7.1 per cent and nine seats; the Greens 7 per cent and nine seats; United Future 6.7 per cent and eight seats; and the Progressive Coalition 1.7 per cent and two seats. The Alliance won only 1.3 per cent. Turnout fell from 84.8 per cent in 1999 to 77 per cent.[67]

The 2002 election was a clear endorsement of Labour's policies. For only the fourth time since 1938 a governing party increased its share of votes and seats after its first term.[68] A new government was formed quickly: the minority Labour/Progressive government signed a support agreement with United Future, giving it a majority on confidence and supply, and a co-operation agreement with the Greens. Cullen replaced Anderton as deputy prime minister.[69]

A continuing important theme in Labour's policies in this term was asserting New Zealand's national identity. It supported local music, the arts and film, cultural institutions outside Wellington such as the Auckland and Canterbury museums, Puke Ariki in New Plymouth (opened in 2003) and the Christchurch Art Gallery, and historical projects, including the new digital encyclopaedia, Te Ara.[70] In the teeth of opposition from some lawyers and law societies, the government established the Supreme Court as the country's highest court, replacing the right of appeal to the Privy Council in London.[71] In early 2003 the United States led an invasion of Iraq, based on spurious arguments about the Iraqi regime's links to terrorism and possession of weapons of mass destruction. New Zealand refused to join the 'coalition of the willing', which did not have United Nations approval. Clark's 'wise decision not to sign up to the "war on terror" kept New Zealand out of a war that became another Vietnam for the US'.[72]

There were important debates on moral issues during Labour's second term. Most Labour MPs supported Tim Barnett's private member's bill to decriminalise prostitution. The government's Civil Union Act allowed same-sex (and heterosexual) couples to enter into a legal relationship akin to marriage.[73] This reflected the influence of the 'Rainbow' sector within the Labour Party. Chris Carter, New Zealand's first openly gay MP, strongly promoted the establishment of Rainbow branches and the 2003 party conference voted for a Rainbow representative on the New Zealand Council.[74] By 2006 Labour had five Rainbow MPs: Barnett, Carter, Georgina Beyer, Maryan Street and Charles Chauvel.[75]

December 2003 was the tenth anniversary of Clark's election as Labour leader. From being a leader with a badly divided caucus and little public support, she had become a prime minister who commanded the political landscape like no other since Muldoon.[76] However, in January 2004 Labour faced its greatest political challenge since 1999, when Don Brash, the newly elected leader of the National Party, made a speech at Ōrewa attacking so-called special privileges for Māori and calling for 'one law for all'. The speech struck a chord with non-Māori and National soared in the polls, overtaking Labour for the first time since October 2000.[77]

The government was vulnerable because of the controversy over ownership of the foreshore and seabed. In June 2003, in the Ngāti Apa decision, the Court of Appeal ruled that the Māori Land Court could decide whether iwi and hapū had valid claims to the foreshore and seabed, thereby questioning the official assumption that land below the high-water mark was the domain of the Crown. The government proposed legislation to make the foreshore and seabed part of the 'public domain' not owned by anyone. Māori opinion was overwhelmingly hostile to the government's position, and 15,000 took part in a hīkoi to parliament. Tariana Turia, a minister outside cabinet, resigned from Labour and parliament and formed the Māori Party. Against no serious opposition she won the resulting by-election. Labour's remaining Māori MPs came under a lot of pressure to join her, but remained loyal while pressing for changes to the legislation.[78] To pass it Labour had to turn to New Zealand First for support and drop the reference to the 'public domain'. Under the Foreshore and Seabed Act 2004 ownership of the foreshore and seabed was vested in the Crown, with full access guaranteed to all New Zealanders.[79]

At the 2004 party conference Cullen strongly defended the government's action. Its record on Māori issues was, he claimed, 'second to that of no government in New Zealand's history'. The rate of historical treaty settlements was increasing, the Māori fisheries settlement had been successfully concluded, freeing up massive assets to support Māori development, and the newly established Māori Television Service had got off to a good start.[80] In its report, Te Kaunihera Māori pointed out that, under Labour, Māori unemployment had fallen to 8.8 per cent, 40,000 more Māori were in work than in 1999, Māori enrolments in tertiary education had doubled and Māori life expectancy had improved.[81] Parekura Horomia, minister of Māori affairs, was greatly respected by Clark for the esteem in which he was held among Māori and his powerful advocacy for the government on marae.[82]

In its second term Labour took major initiatives in social policy. In the 2004 budget Cullen announced Working for Families, a combination of family support payments and tax credits, aimed at ensuring that low- and middle-income households had adequate incomes and reducing child poverty. The budget gave three- and four-year-olds 20 hours' free early childhood education a week.[83] The 2005 budget introduced KiwiSaver, a work-based retirement savings scheme, to start from 1 April 2007. KiwiSaver provided for automatic enrolment of new workers, with the ability to opt out, a $1000 government contribution to workers' accounts and contributions from both workers and employers. The scheme allowed people to withdraw savings to put towards buying their first home and gave a first home deposit subsidy.[84] The government had already brought in retirement savings schemes for public servants and teachers.

A difficult third term, 2005–08

Labour went into the 2005 election with the economy prospering. Economic growth was 4.2 per cent in the year to March 2005 and all regions were doing well.[85] Unemployment had fallen to 3.9 per cent.[86] Apart from pratfalls by a few ministers and MPs, the government was well run and competent and its coalition and support agreements had worked well. However, it faced a resurgent National Party, which led in the polls, emphasised the racist appeal of Brash's attacks on Māori, and promised large tax cuts skewed to the better off. Labour countered with a promise to write off all interest on student loans for those who stayed and worked in New Zealand.[87] It then announced an extension of Working for Families which meant nearly all families (with children) earning less than $70,000 would get a tax break and those on $35,000 a year or less would get an extra $199 a week.[88]

Colin James observes that this election was 'the hardest fought campaign for a quarter of a century'.[89] Brash was badly compromised when it was revealed that, contrary to his initial denials, he had met members of the ultra-conservative Exclusive Brethren church, which funded a campaign of anonymous pamphlets attacking the Greens and Labour to assist National.[90] Labour worked hard to its identify supporters who hadn't voted in 2002 and established a 'Labour Factory' of volunteers who processed 600,000 targeted letters to non-voters, focused on state house tenants, students and other core constituencies.[91]

The election was very close. Labour's share was virtually unchanged at 41.1 per cent of party votes and 50 seats. National leapt to 39.1 per cent and 48 seats. New Zealand First won 5.7 per cent and seven seats; the Greens 5.3 per cent and six seats; the Māori Party 2.7 per cent and four seats; United Future 2.7 per cent and three seats; ACT 1.5 per cent and two seats; and the Progressives 1.2 per cent and one seat (Anderton's own). Labour lost 14 electorate seats, 10 to National and four to the Māori Party, but made up the ground on the list. In the party vote, Labour did better than National in Auckland, Wellington, Christchurch and Dunedin, while National did better in the provinces and the general electorates as a whole. Labour won

54.6 per cent in the Māori seats, compared to 4.3 per cent for National.[92] It took four weeks to form a new government. Labour formed another coalition with Anderton and negotiated confidence and supply agreements with New Zealand First and United Future. Winston Peters became foreign minister and Dunne revenue minister, both outside cabinet, and their parties had much greater scope than earlier coalition or support agreements to disagree publicly with the government. Neither party would support a government of which the Greens were a part. The Greens' consolation prize was a co-operation agreement giving them a say in government policy in specific areas.[93]

Why did Labour win an historic third term in 2005? It ran a very effective campaign and successfully mobilised the party's base. Clark and Labour were trusted more than Brash and National. Brash's hard-line stance on the Treaty of Waitangi cost National votes among liberal Pākehā, Māori and Pasifika peoples, although it played well in some rural and provincial areas.[94] Foreign policy was also important. Brash wavered on Iraq and his comment to a United States congressional delegation that, if National won, New Zealand's nuclear-free policy would be 'gone by lunchtime' was thrown back at him by Labour. National Party polling 'showed foreign affairs and tax issues scared many women voters'.[95]

After the election, an inquiry by the auditor-general found that seven parties had wrongly used parliamentary funds for their election campaigns. In Labour's case this was the $826,524 it spent on its 2005 commitment card. After saying for months that it would not repay the money, looking arrogant and unwilling to play by the rules, the party backed down[96] and Labour launched the 'big whip round' to raise the money from MPs, party members and supporters. This fundraising was successful, but Labour was left in a weakened financial position. It already had a deficit of over $600,000 in 2005 and the 'big whip round' emptied electorate committee and branch bank accounts.[97] In the past, party members might have revolted over such a debacle; that they didn't was a testament to the party's strong support for the government, Labour's internal discipline and the leadership's tight grip on the party. Although large numbers attended the 2006 (684 delegates) and 2007 (735) conferences, membership plateaued.[98]

Labour faced a number of difficulties after 2005. National replaced the abrasive Brash with the much more astute John Key. Controversies about the behaviour of two ministers led to the resignation of David Benson-Pope and the expulsion from caucus of Taito Phillip Field. Field was later convicted of corrupt practice. The government's Electoral Finance Bill, aimed in part at preventing anonymous campaigns like that run by the Exclusive Brethren, was widely attacked for denying free speech and resulted in a confusing law. This 'shambles called into question the government's competence'.[99]

A private member's bill introduced by Green MP Sue Bradford proposed removing the legal defence of 'reasonable force' from parents facing charges of assaulting their children. There was strong public opposition led by conservative groups. Labour supported the bill, and while National did so too, the government got the political backlash and lost ground among socially conservative supporters.[100] Key began to reclaim the support of moderate women voters for National. For the first 18 months after 2005, Labour and National were evenly balanced in the polls. From May 2007 National had a large lead over Labour, and there was little change up to the 2008 election.[101]

For all its political difficulties, Labour went into the 2008 election with a solid record of achievements in its third term. Over 800,000 people had joined KiwiSaver, vastly exceeding predictions; 370,000 families were receiving assistance under Working for Families; and superannuation was increased as part of Labour's agreement with New Zealand First, which also saw the introduction of a Gold Card giving concessions for those over 65, including some free public transport. There were cheaper doctors' charges for every age group, and more than 130,000 parents benefited from enhanced paid parental leave, which was extended to 14 weeks' paid leave and to the self-employed. The minimum wage continued to increase, and four weeks' annual leave was introduced for all workers in 2007. Twenty hours' free early childhood education was introduced, there were 600 more teachers above what was required by roll growth, there were 15,000 on the Modern Apprenticeships programme and interest-free student loans were implemented. Labour's reforms in social policy largely helped students, workers and the retired. But the government did not restore National's 1991 cuts to benefits (an omission of which the party was often reminded when it later criticised National Party policies in this area).

Economic growth had averaged 3.4 per cent since 1999, there were 373,000 new jobs and unemployment was at 3.9 per cent. The government continued to run budget surpluses and government debt was below 20 per cent of GDP. In 2008 Labour cut company tax, increased funding for research and development, continued to invest heavily in infrastructure and public transport, brought Kiwi Rail back into public ownership and ended Telecom's monopoly. In April 2008 New Zealand became the first western country to sign a free trade agreement with China.[102] In October 2007 the government announced a comprehensive emissions trading scheme to help tackle climate change.[103] This was passed by parliament just before the 2008 election.

In 2008 National 'systematically eliminated' any policy differences between it and Labour which might be seen negatively by voters,[104] making it difficult for Labour to portray National as too scary for voters to trust. The election was a big victory for National. It won 44.9 per cent of party votes and 58 seats. Labour fell to 34 per cent and 43 seats, losing another nine electorate seats. The Greens won 6.7 per cent and nine seats; ACT 3.7 per cent and five; the Māori Party 2.4 per cent and five; Jim Anderton's Progressive Party 0.9 per cent and one; and United Future 0.9 per cent and one. New Zealand First won only 4.1 per cent and no electorate seats, so was not returned to parliament.[105] National formed a new government with support from the Māori Party, ACT and United Future. The main reason Labour lost was 'a persistent and widespread feeling that it was "time for a change"', along with the impression that this would be cost-free.[106]

The Clark government was the longest serving and most successful Labour government since 1949. It won three elections, giving it the opportunity to make major changes, particularly in social policy. Working for Families, and other policies, resulted in a significant redistribution of income and Labour was 'the first government for decades to reduce inequality.'[107] Between 2004 and 2008 the incomes of low- to middle-income households grew more quickly than those of higher-income households and the percentage of children living in poverty dropped by eight points.[108]

After the radicalism of 1984–93, the Labour government moved economic policy back to the centre while retaining most of the fourth Labour government's reforms. Cullen's conservative fiscal strategy meant the next government was well placed to deal with the effects of the global financial crisis of 2007–08 and the 2010 and 2011 Canterbury earthquakes. National accepted many of Labour's policies, particularly Working for Families, KiwiSaver and the New Zealand Superannuation Fund. Although some of its environmental policies, such as the emissions trading scheme, did not last, the Clark government was New Zealand's most environmentally friendly government, making substantial acquisitions to the conservation estate and adopting a comprehensive sustainability programme.

The government's greatest political failure was its handling of the foreshore and seabed issue, which severely strained its relations with Māori. Adrian Rurawhe has called this a 'huge blight' on Labour's record; Nanaia Mahuta says, 'we handled it badly all the way through'.[109] Cullen says that in hindsight the government could have handled the foreshore and seabed issue differently, although 'people have forgotten that within 24 hours of the release of the Ngāti Apa decision the great bulk of the public, both Māori and Pākehā, had made up their minds the court had determined that Māori owned the foreshore and seabed', which was not the case.[110] Brash had already positioned National as firmly anti-Māori and National reaped much political benefit. Without the political skills of Cullen and Horomia, the fallout would have been much worse. Then, in 2007, the armed police operation in Tāneatua and Rūatoki against an alleged terrorist group infuriated Tūhoe and other iwi; the point that ministers do not authorise such operations was hardly appreciated.[111]

Like other low- to middle-income groups, Māori and Pasifika peoples benefited from Labour's economic and social policies, as well as its policies to promote Māori and Pasifika languages and culture. The government completed a number of treaty settlements and was in negotiations with 27 claimant groups when it left office. Labour's victory in 2005 ended Brash's anti-Māori policy, and, in this respect, it was a very different National Party which won in 2008. Labour's support for local music, arts and culture and its continuation of the party's independence in foreign policy were important in promoting the country's national identity, and the government's apologies to Samoa, New Zealand's early Chinese settlers and Vietnam War veterans helped heal past injuries.

Those who criticise the fifth Labour government for not being radical ignore two things. Labour campaigned on a moderate social democratic programme that did not seek to reverse all the changes of the past, and it was always a minority government. The Clark government made MMP work. It was a stable government which moved from a model of strict cabinet collective responsibility to flexible support agreements that allowed partners a voice in government and the right to disagree.

Helen Clark was Labour's longest serving leader to date, the only one to win three elections, and was a fine Labour prime minister. She kept a tight grip on the government, ably supported by Heather Simpson, her chief of staff. The partnership between Clark and Cullen, one of New Zealand's best finance ministers, was central to the government's success, as was the government's core of competent senior ministers, particularly Anderton, Maharey, Goff, King, Mallard and Hodgson. Mallard comments that he was

> probably one of the few in the Cabinet who would argue with [Helen]. Generally I lost the arguments but the thing that I appreciated about her was that we could have those arguments and then move on to the next issue . . . but there weren't many ministers who were prepared to do that because she did have a sharp tongue.

Cullen says Clark

> wanted to have a very large level of control and knew how to organise and effect that control . . . I've always thought of Helen as being Peter Fraser's true successor as prime minister . . . The most admirable thing in many ways, given her own Fraserian instincts in terms of being leader, [was her being] extraordinarily supple and subtle in dealing with other parties within an MMP environment. That's what basically enabled us to govern successfully.[112]

Unity and discipline were the government's watchwords. While party members largely accepted this and supported the government's policies, the party outside parliament did not prosper. The party leadership did not use the good years between 1999 and 2008 to strengthen the party, particularly its membership and finances. In 2001 the party had around 12,000 members and 292 branches. In 2008 it had 7500 members, 193 branches[113] and a deficit of over $700,000,[114] although the number of affiliated unions had increased, Young Labour became a strong voice within the party, and Chinese, Indian, Korean and general ethnic branches formed, mainly in Auckland.[115] According to Anderton, the Labour Party suffered from the 'huge amount of control exercised out of the prime minister's office'.[116] The Clark years cast a long shadow over the party as it struggled to rebuild after 2008.

12

A Painful Transition? Opposition, 2008–16

Opposition is usually difficult for a political party, especially after a lengthy and successful period in government. Labour's problems after 2008 reflect this truism, and have been compounded by the difficulties inherent in a generational shift, a shift not only in the party but in the wider society.

Helen Clark resigned as party leader on election night 2008 and Michael Cullen resigned as deputy. They left parliament in April 2009. Their decisions, though understandable, were not in the party's best interests. In particular, the swift replacement of Clark and Cullen by Phil Goff and Annette King deprived the party of a necessary period of reflection and debate about the future direction, a problem exacerbated by the lack of a leadership contest. Leftist critics outside the party complained about a stitch-up. The *New Zealand Herald*—not among the Clark government's left-wing critics—pointed out that the sudden resignations 'allow[ed] Labour no time to find a promising successor . . . the party might have found it kinder had [Clark] waited long enough for a potential successor to emerge'.[1] In the party organisation, the departure of Mike Williams and Mike Smith as president and general secretary and their replacement by, respectively, Andrew Little and Chris Flatt was less publicly visible.

Goff and King were, and are, politicians of considerable talent and experience, and they had had senior roles in the Clark governments. Some commentators noted, however, that they were of the same generation as Clark and Cullen, and had been in parliament almost as long. In some quarters there was a perception that Goff and King were caretakers. On the other hand, a pool of younger MPs moved to the front bench: Ruth Dyson and Maryan Street were only in their early 50s, while Clayton Cosgrove and Nanaia Mahuta were not yet 40, and Darren Hughes just 30. David Cunliffe, 45, was already there (he and Dyson had had major cabinet posts under Clark).[2] More generally, the rapidity of the handover meant that it took place while the news organisations were bestowing all their attention on the incoming prime minister; there was no media honeymoon for Labour's new team.[3]

In the medium term Labour's problems were compounded by the Clark government's very success. Just as with Fraser and Nash, the National Party was only able to displace Labour by adopting many of the Labour government's popular policies, and promising very little substantive change except a more relaxed approach. Key, like Holland, combined this with a few rhetorical flourishes around the edges, issuing a few kicks to the middle class's folk demons (militant unionists in 1949, feckless recipients of welfare in 2008) and a pitch to immediate gratification (an end to rationing in 1949, the illusory promise of tax cuts in 2008). Michael Cullen's fiscal prudence, which spared his successor in finance from having to adopt drastic measures to deal with the financial crisis, ironically made it much easier for the National Party to maintain these policies of mainstream appeal, while only gradually introducing anything more right-wing. For all that, Key had emerged as an extremely astute politician, and underestimating him was a very bad mistake.

Perhaps Labour misunderstood the reasons for Key's victory. In our analysis the primary reason was not that Labour's core policies were unpopular but, as we have said, that National adopted most of them, thus outmanoeuvering Labour. Thus, we argue, the 2008 election result was not a wholesale rejection of Labour's policies; it reflected a certain boredom among a portion of the electorate, a susceptibility to the rhetoric of 'time for a change', along with a reasonable certainty that nothing very much would in fact change. It follows that Labour's soul-searching and defensiveness about policy was overdone, particularly as four-term governments have been rare in New Zealand.

If the conclusion that defeat was the result of unpopular policy was largely mistaken, an exercise in rethinking policy could look like, or be caricatured as, rootlessness or lack of conviction. It is always a difficult balance. On one level—and this is to make a virtue out of necessity—as the British Labour politician Tony Crosland observed many years ago, a period in opposition can be used like a sabbatical: a chance for some longer-term thinking. And Labour MPs and the Policy Council put a good deal of effort into this sort of thinking after 2008. Much of this got little immediate traction during Key's extended political honeymoon. Some in the wider party might have thought that the party's post-2008 language was not helpful. The post-election survey of members sought their 'views on the Labour brand'. But social democratic politics should be about more than a 'brand'; it is not, or should not be, like selling soap.[4] Perhaps this contributed to a certain fractiousness.

It was all a recipe for a good deal of frustration, and frustration can all too easily breed indiscipline. While Goff worked enormously hard to provide stable leadership, he naturally wished to place his own stamp on the party. Some of his centrist instincts were, so the analysis went, exactly what was required in reconnecting with 'middle New Zealand'—the voters, mostly white and either in the cities' mortgage belts or in provincial towns, who had stayed with Labour for two, if not three, terms but had then switched. Thus, in November 2009 Goff delivered a speech on 'nationhood' in which he criticised the Māori Party, particularly its agreement with National ministers to compensate iwi for loss of value in forestry assets that resulted from new carbon trading policies, as well as some of Te Tai Tokerau MP Hone Harawira's more colourful observations. Rightly or wrongly, some within the party saw this as an unhelpful pitch for conservative votes, and some of the criticism became public.[5] Then, in the middle of 2010, there was a media beat-up over ministerial expenses, in which journalists indulged their most prurient instincts. Shane Jones and Chris Carter were targets, and when Carter failed to display abject contrition, Goff—perhaps feeling obliged to show 'strength'—publicly reprimanded him. Carter then delivered around the parliamentary press gallery an unsigned letter calling for Goff to step aside because he was incapable of leading the party to victory. One of Goff's allies publicly described Carter as unbalanced. Carter remained in parliament until 2011, but was dismissed from the party, a sad end to long service.[6] Labour received more bad publicity when Darren Hughes felt obliged to resign from parliament in March 2011.

This sort of public feuding did no good. Key's image of steadiness was to the fore when disastrous earthquakes hit Canterbury in 2010 and 2011. More positively, the 2011 election campaign was immediately preceded by the Rugby World Cup, hosted in New Zealand for the first time since 1987. Clark and her ministers had worked hard to secure the tournament, and may have regretted that they had done so, as the All Black victory was hardly likely to sour the public mood against a prime minister who took good care to follow the victors around the country.[7] In any event, it was always going to be extraordinarily difficult to make Key's government a one-term administration: there had not been a one-term government since 1975, and only two since 1930 (both of them, as many were no doubt aware, Labour). The 2011 election 'was never Labour's (or Goff's) election to win; it was always National's (and Key's) to lose', and Key was far too astute to put the voters off by taking unnecessary risks with his personal popularity.[8]

While the National campaign emphasised Key, Labour's advertising had Goff almost invisible, which was interpreted as an implicit vote of no confidence. As such, it was not only a big mistake; it was unfair, as Goff campaigned well: he 'showed real fight and a level of energy'.[9] Some of Labour's advertising, particularly about removing GST from fresh fruit and vegetables, was unclear, and such policies appeared to be mere tinkering.[10] Much of Labour's campaign emphasised opposition to government proposals, especially the partial privatisation of state assets. While privatisation was, on the face of it, unpopular, National astutely pitched it as meaning selling only minority shareholdings, and their focus groups showed that at worst the policy did little damage.[11] Arguably, too, National got points for honesty, openly declaring its intentions before the election; those with long memories would recall that Labour had apparently deceived the voters on this point in 1987. In the months after the election, Labour, with the Greens and others, devoted much time and effort to a petition against the sales. Given that opposition was hardly intense, this effort may have been better spent, to say nothing of the risk that the plebiscitary strategy might come back to bite a future Labour government. In blunt terms, Key, having been open about his intentions, was entitled to claim a mandate; it was hardly accurate to accuse him of failing to listen to 'the people' as represented in a petition signed by far fewer than had voted National. Further, and worse, it was far from inconceivable that moral conservatives—think vengeful hardliners on penal policy—might in due course muster a petition against the declared progressive policy of a Labour government and similarly complain that 'the people' were being ignored.[12]

Other policies were more robust. A capital gains tax had been widely advocated to dampen property speculation; gradually increasing the eligible age for superannuation had also been widely discussed, and strengthening

KiwiSaver also reflected the opinion of responsible economists. One journalist described the policy approach as 'courage born of desperation', but the campaign was a little muted.[13] Annette King's work on child-centred social policy was 'a major innovation', but was 'barely mentioned during the campaign because of worries about how the cost and its timing would affect the numbers contest with National. The same went for the dozens of other policy releases.'[14] Thus, Labour implicitly accepted both National's narrative of the importance of a fiscal surplus and the implication that the Clark government had been profligate. This meant denying both that Cullen delivered nine consecutive surpluses in relatively easy times, and that counter-cyclical spending in recession has long been accepted as necessary. Goff stumbling over Key's 'show us the money' line in a televised debate should have been avoided; that, after all, is the oldest line in the Tory songbook.[15] All up, it was easy for National, and many journalists, sceptical at best about Labour, to characterise the party as knowing what it was against, but not what it was for.

Labour's party vote declined significantly in 2011, falling by 180,000 from 2008, to 27.5 per cent. Indeed, the air of a foregone conclusion may well have contributed to the appalling turnout, the lowest percentage of eligible voters in all the years of universal suffrage, as well as prompting a fair number of Labour supporters to give their party vote to the Greens or New Zealand First.[16] The Greens got their best ever result, at 11.4 per cent, and New Zealand First came back into parliament. (Between them the Greens and New Zealand First accounted for Labour's drop.)

Goff and King announced their resignations from the leadership—although not from parliament—three days after the election. Their rapid departures compounded the negative consequences of Clark and Cullen's sudden resignations, and set a dangerous precedent that electoral defeat should automatically mean the leader's resignation. That, in the past, would have deprived the party not only of Clark, but also of Norman Kirk. The leadership was contested by David Cunliffe, David Parker and David Shearer. The former two had been ministers under Clark, but Shearer was a novice, having won Clark's seat in June 2009 when she departed for the United Nations. It was a surprising candidacy, attributed to both caucus antipathy to Cunliffe and the hope that Shearer's career before parliament, as a humanitarian troubleshooter for the United Nations in some of the world's more dangerous places, would provide a compelling alternative to

Key's 'state house boy made good' narrative. Parker withdrew and Shearer was elected. Once again, the organisational leadership changed too. In 2011 Andrew Little had resigned as president to stand for parliament; he was elected as a list MP. Moira Coatsworth, the party's senior vice-president, was elected president. In mid-2012 Flatt resigned to become general secretary of the Dairy Workers' Union and Tim Barnett, MP for Christchurch Central from 1996 to 2008, became general secretary.

Following the 2011 election the party began an organisational review, with the aim of modernising the party. It was a thorough and carefully considered exercise, with over a thousand members taking part in the consultation. Key recommendations were to emphasise political and social activity rather than routine business in branches and electorate committees, and to create regional hubs. This was necessary and drew much engagement from party members, although one recommendation, to emphasise electorate rather than branch membership, did not survive the 2012 conference.

The 2012 conference was a watershed in a number of ways. For nearly 20 years party conferences had been unified and disciplined under the eagle eye of the leadership, which kept a firm lid on dissent. At the 2012 conference, which debated the review's recommendations, the lid blew off in a spectacular manner. The review had recommended that the parliamentary leader be elected by the party at large, with individual members and caucus having 40 per cent of the vote each and affiliated unions 20 per cent.[17] An additional recommendation was that caucus could trigger a leadership election if 50 per cent of MPs plus one voted for a spill. An amendment proposed that 40 per cent of caucus could trigger a spill. This was advocated on the strange logic that caucus had 40 per cent of the votes for the leader under the new rules. The debate was chaotic and many delegates were alarmed to see MPs on both sides attacking each other. The amendment, however, was carried.[18]

Fuelled by commentary on *The Standard*, a left-wing internet blog, calling for Shearer to quit and promoting Cunliffe, journalists made the main story of the conference whether Cunliffe would challenge.[19] Cunliffe, unwisely, refused to rule out a challenge, and Shearer, also unwisely, later demoted him to the back bench. Shearer's election had been preceded by a series of party meetings around the country in which Cunliffe appeared to draw more support from the party at large. There was therefore some annoyance when caucus elected Shearer. The latter's sometimes halting public performances further increased Cunliffe's support in the party and had the pundits suggesting that the experiment with Shearer had not been a success.[20] While many social democratic parties include the whole membership in electing the parliamentary leader, the fractiousness of the 2012 conference did Labour no good at all. One journalist summed up the public relations disaster of the conference with the acerbic comment that Labour could teach lemmings a few things about self-destruction.[21]

During 2013 the party struggled to rise above the low 30s in the opinion polls and, under pressure from key members of the caucus, Shearer resigned the leadership in August. The leadership election which resulted took place under the new rules, and the three candidates—Cunliffe, Grant Robertson and Shane Jones—addressed meetings around the country. One positive consequence, along with a high level of engagement by party members, was a significant increase in membership, in some cases the return of people who had left years before in protest at Rogernomics.[22]

Cunliffe won with 51.15 per cent of the vote, and subsequently David Parker was elected deputy. While Cunliffe took 60 per cent of the vote of the membership at large, and 71 per cent of the union affiliates, he won only a third of the caucus (Robertson, the caucus favourite, took 47 per cent).[23] A lack of support among caucus need not have been fatal; what damaged Cunliffe was the active dislike of a number of his colleagues, who blamed him for deliberately undermining both Goff and Shearer. For instance, there was criticism from within caucus about Cunliffe taking a pre-campaign school holiday break in July 2014.[24] This sort of thing was unhelpful, but also unhelpful was Cunliffe's failure to capitalise on his early victory. While he delivered powerful speeches emphasising Labour's egalitarian traditions to the candidates' meetings and the 2013 party conference, this tone was not persistently maintained during 2014.[25] He did, however, make a crucial decision in appointing as his chief of staff Matt McCarten, a veteran and extremely talented organiser. McCarten had been president of the Alliance, and had gone on to a leading role in the Unite union, organising previously unorganised workers.

Cunliffe had been a talented and effective minister in the later Clark governments, and a degree of ambition is no bad thing in an aspiring prime minister. Unfortunately, Cunliffe's ambition was often represented by hostile commentators as palpable insincerity. Certainly, Cunliffe made his own mistakes, including hoping that a trust fund to support his leadership campaign would remain unknown.[26] But he was also subjected to some underhand attacks. Supposedly responsible media organisations colluded in a National Party set-up in June 2014 involving a Chinese businessman who claimed to have made large donations to the Labour Party. There was no evidence to support this claim, but an Official Information Act request by *New Zealand Herald* journalists for paperwork relating to the businessman's application for permanent residence was processed with unusual speed. Primed, these journalists asked Cunliffe if he had advocated for the businessman. Cunliffe replied that he had not. In fact, he had written a form letter a decade previously; unsurprisingly enough, he did not remember having done so, and by sheer mischance the relevant papers had been misfiled in his office, so were not found when he checked. This trivial affair was regarded by the *Herald*'s commentators as a resignation matter.[27]

This affair reflected what became one of the talking points of the 2014 election campaign with the publication, five weeks before polling day, of a book detailing the close connections between National ministers, business lobby groups and some unsavoury bloggers. Despite this reflecting badly on the National Party, the author of *Dirty Politics*, Nicky Hager, was no particular friend of Labour. Winston Peters later observed that if Hager had been intending to influence the election he should have drip-fed his revelations; others noted that the volume of the material proved to be beyond the attention span of many voters, and the book's allegations were easily spun into the line 'all politicians do that sort of thing', a cynicism which plays into conservative hands. In the end the book probably reinforced committed Labour supporters' visceral dislike of John Key, but that population was too small to dislodge him.[28]

Other dimensions of the 2014 campaign also damaged Labour. The 2011 vote was too low a base from which to begin with any sense of comfort. A Labour–Green government, if that were possible, would probably have required other support in parliament. Winston Peters' agreement on this could not be taken for granted, so on that point alone Labour had difficulty projecting itself as the leader of a stable alternative government.[29]

There was worse. The Māori Party had fractured: Hone Harawira in Te Tai Tokerau had revolted over the party's close relationship with National and established his own Mana Party. Mana hoped to attract left-wing Pākehā voters, particularly with such luminaries as Sue Bradford, a former Green MP, and the veteran activist John Minto. In January 2012 a German-born internet entrepreneur, Kim Dotcom, who had been living in New Zealand since 2010, was arrested by armed police in connection with American charges of copyright infringement. Schmitz (to give him his original name) naturally contested the extradition proceedings initiated by the United States, and in March 2014 he established his own Internet Party. Subsequently this party merged with the Mana Party. It was never made clear to left-wing voters why they should have any interest in a multi-millionaire whose first foray into New Zealand politics had been a very large donation to John Banks, whose political views—often expressed in blunt, sometimes offensive, terms—combined antediluvian moral conservatism and simplistic free-market economics.[30] While Cunliffe sought to distance the Labour Party from this strange beast, the result was a bit like the neighbour's smelly mongrel rolling around on your best carpet in front of visitors whom you badly need to impress. Labour, in other words, was tainted by unsought association, and the effect seemed 'to have been . . . to persuade National-leaning potential non-voters to vote'.[31]

Nor did Labour's own publicity help. 'Vote Positive' was widely derided as a meaningless slogan, and certainly the billboards placed insufficient emphasis on the party vote. The party was badly short of money, having received just under $1 million in election donations (National had four times as much). The result was a morale-shattering 25 per cent of the vote, and the involuntary departure of several talented MPs, including Maryan Street and Moana Mackey. (The latter had, for a time, shared the parliamentary benches with her mother, Janet Mackey, certainly a first for the New Zealand parliament, if not any.) About the only bright dimension was re-establishment in the Māori seats, although the actual shift was not big, as the party vote there had always been Labour. In Te Tai Tokerau, Kelvin Davis ran explicitly against Dotcom, portraying him as inimical to northern pride; Harawira had asked for that by taking Dotcom's money. In Te Tai Hauāuru, Adrian Rurawhe had distinguished connections, being a grandson of Matiu and Iriaka Rātana and the great-grandson of the prophet. Likewise, Peeni Henare in Tāmaki Makaurau is a great-grandson of the esteemed northern kaumātua Sir James Henare. Only partly was Labour's success to be explained by the retirement of the Māori Party founders.[32]

A few commentators pointed out that even in the best of circumstances it would have been difficult to displace National. Two-term governments are as rare as one-term governments; the only one since 1935 was the fourth Labour government. It is not entirely cynical to suggest that, in those circumstances, Shearer should have been allowed a gallant try. As one political scientist noted, not giving him one was 'an impressive display of division and disloyalty'.[33] David Lange would have described it as the action of poll-driven fruitcakes. In fact, UMR polls through most of 2013 suggested that a Labour–Greens combination might have had the numbers to govern; in hindsight, one may wonder why caucus didn't hold its nerve.[34]

After some hesitation, Cunliffe accepted that his position was untenable. Labour's second leadership election in 14 months returned, by the narrowest of margins, the former Engineering, Printing and Manufacturing Union general secretary and party president, Andrew Little, as leader. Little asked Annette King to serve as deputy, which she willingly did.

Labour approaches its centenary, therefore, where it began: in opposition. Some commentators are keen enough to suggest that, like most centenarians, the party will receive a telegram from the queen before quietly shuffling off this mortal coil. However, as Mark Twain said of himself, the reports of a demise are greatly exaggerated. The fortunes of political parties go down and they go up. It became evident during 2015 that the caucus was prepared to unite behind Andrew Little and give him the loyalty that a leader requires and should expect. Little himself is an able advocate for Labour's core values.

Perhaps, as one of New Zealand's most astute political commentators notes, Labour's future looks a bit better. A new generation is finally in place: Little, Robertson, Carmel Sepuloni, Jacinda Ardern, Chris Hipkins, David Clark, Nanaia Mahuta and Megan Woods, among others. In 2014 Labour was 'still in the long shadow of Helen Clark's "third-way" modification of market liberalism (though it did make some substantial modifications reminiscent of the 1940s–70s mixed economy) and was still stamped with the Clark-era image as the party representing disparate minorities'.[35] Yet New Zealand society includes many disparate minorities and Labour must remain the party of tolerance and of diversity. In 2013 Louisa Wall, the Labour MP for Manurewa, piloted a private member's bill into law which provided for marriage equality. Whereas in 1986 National MPs had fallen over themselves to denounce Fran Wilde, 27 years later they queued up to proclaim their commitment to tolerance and diversity.

Thirty years after the neo-liberal policy regime supplanted the post-war settlement, dramatically increased inequality is a serious problem in many democratic societies, including New Zealand. The Labour Party was formed in 1916 to challenge inequality and to improve the lives of working people. This meant redistributing wealth, building universal public education and health services, and ensuring that all had adequate housing. It also meant guiding economic development so that these needs could be met. In the middle of the most destructive war yet seen, Labour's commitment to international co-operation was marginalised, but this commitment shaped the party's foreign policy in the succeeding decades. A harder lesson for many in the party to learn was that New Zealand's future was one of cultural diversity, and one in which Māori communities would be able to restore and develop their cultural and economic foundations. Over the decades, too, Labour became an important vehicle for women's equality and advancement, and this was not always welcomed by Labour men. Nor was Labour's agenda confined to material well-being. The right of all to enjoy meaningful leisure, to create and enjoy art and culture, to engage in and enjoy sport and recreation were seen as essential components of a civilised society.

Much can be said about how the world has changed since 1916. Yet the issues which Labour was established to address are still with us. Most people still have to support themselves through work, however much the structure and definition of 'work' have changed, and the right to secure, meaningful and adequately compensated work is no less than it was in 1916. Housing, education and health remain fundamental human rights, and art, culture, leisure and recreation no less important. There are dimensions in economic modernisation unthought of in 1916, especially in terms of environmental sustainability, but the need for democratic public authorities to shape economic direction is as important as it was in the 1920s and 1930s. If social democracy has itself developed and changed as a political philosophy, some fundamentals remain. As Labour's second century begins, a social democratic vision is as essential in Aotearoa New Zealand as ever it was.

Notes and References

Abbreviations:

AJHR: *Appendices to the Journals of the House of Representatives*
ATL: Alexander Turnbull Library
NZPD: *New Zealand Parliamentary Debates*
UAL: University of Auckland Libraries

Preface

1 Sheri Berman, *The Primacy of Politics: social democracy and the making of Europe's twentieth century*, Cambridge University Press, New York, 2006.
2 This necessarily brief comparative discussion draws, broadly, on two outstanding surveys: Donald Sassoon, *One Hundred Years of Socialism: the west European left in the twentieth century*, Fontana, London, 1997 and Geoff Eley, *Forging Democracy: the history of the left in Europe, 1850–2000*, Oxford University Press, New York, 2002.
3 Jim McAloon, 'Unsettling recolonisation: labourism, Keynesianism, and Australasia from the 1890s to the 1950s', *Thesis Eleven*, 92, 2008.
4 Peter Gourevitch, *Politics in Hard Times: comparative responses to international economic crises*, Cornell University Press, Ithaca, 1986.
5 At the time of writing, of course, Senator Bernie Sanders, a self-described democratic socialist, is making a credible bid for the Democratic Party nomination for the United States presidency. His policies are mainstream social democracy, and particularly adventurous only in the American context.
6 Timothy A. Tilton, 'A Swedish road to socialism: Ernst Wigforss and the ideological foundations of Swedish social democracy', *American Political Science Review*, 73 (2), June 1979, p.509.
7 C.A.R. Crosland, *The Future of Socialism*, Jonathan Cape, London, 1956.
8 Barry Gustafson, *The First 50 Years: a history of the New Zealand National Party*, Reed Methuen, Auckland, 1986.
9 Barry Gustafson, *Labour's Path to Political Independence*, Auckland University Press, Auckland, 1980; Bruce Brown, *The Rise of New Zealand Labour: a history of the New Zealand Labour Party from 1916 to 1940*, Price Milburn, Wellington, 1962.
10 Malcolm McKinnon, *Treasury: the New Zealand Treasury, 1840–2000*, Auckland University Press, Auckland, 2003; Margaret McClure, *A Civilised Community: a history of social

security in New Zealand, 1898–1998, Auckland University Press, Auckland, 1998; Malcolm Templeton, *Standing Upright Here: New Zealand in the nuclear age 1945–1990*, Victoria University Press, Wellington, 2006.

11 P.J. O'Farrell, *Harry Holland: militant socialist*, Australian National University Press, Canberra, 1964; Keith Sinclair, *Walter Nash*, Auckland University Press, Auckland, 1976; Erik Olssen, *John A. Lee*, University of Otago Press, Dunedin, 1977; Barry Gustafson, *From the Cradle to the Grave: a biography of Michael Joseph Savage*, Reed Methuen, Auckland, 1986; Michael Bassett with Michael King, *Tomorrow Comes the Song: a life of Peter Fraser*, Penguin, Auckland, 2000; Mary Logan, *Nordy: Arnold Nordmeyer: a political biography*, Steele Roberts, Wellington, 2008; Raymond Richards, *Palmer: the parliamentary years*, Canterbury University Press, Christchurch, 2010; David Grant, *The Mighty Totara: the life and times of Norman Kirk*, Random House, Auckland, 2014.

12 Rosemary Jamieson, *In Command: Phil Connolly*, Steele Roberts, Wellington, 2009; John Dunmore, *Norman Kirk: a portrait*, New Zealand Books, Palmerston North, 1972; John Henderson, *Rowling: the man and the myth*, Australia and New Zealand Book Co., Auckland, 1981; Vernon Wright, *David Lange, Prime Minister: a profile*, Unwin Paperbacks, Port Nicholson Press, Wellington, 1984; Brian Edwards, *Helen: portrait of a prime minister*, Exisle, Auckland, 2001.

13 Michael Bassett, *Working with David: inside the Lange cabinet*, Hodder Moa, Auckland, 2008.

14 Margaret Hayward, *Diary of the Kirk Years*, Cape Catley and A.H. & A.W. Reed, Wellington, 1981.

15 Warren Freer, *A Lifetime in Politics: the memoirs of Warren Freer*, Victoria University Press, Wellington, 2004; David Lange, *My Life*, Viking, Auckland, 2005; Geoffrey Palmer, *Reform: a memoir*, Victoria University Press, Wellington, 2013; Mike Moore, *Hard Labour*, Penquin Books, Auckland 1987; Mike Moore, *A Labour of Love*, MMSC, Wellington, 1993.

16 John A. Lee, *Political Notebooks*, Alister Taylor, Wellington, 1973, p.114.

17 Margaret Clark (ed.), *Peter Fraser: master politician*, Dunmore, Palmerston North, 1998; Clark (ed.), *Three Labour Leaders: Nordmeyer, Kirk, Rowling*, Dunmore Press, Palmerston North, 2001; Clark (ed.), *For the Record: Lange and the fourth Labour government*, Dunmore Publishing, Palmerston North, 2005.

18 J.D. Salmond, *New Zealand Labour's Pioneering Days: the history of the labour movement in N.Z. from 1840 to 1894*, ed. D.W. Crowley, Forward Press, Auckland, 1950.

19 E.P. Thompson, *The Making of the English Working Class*, Gollancz, London, 1963, p.12.

20 Brown, *The Rise of New Zealand Labour*, p.41.

21 One of the authors asked Professor O'Farrell in 1992 whether he still had such a negative view. O'Farrell confirmed that he did, and that he blamed Holland for Labour not winning the 1931 election and so not being able to mitigate the Depression.

22 Dougal McNeill, 'Labouring feeling: Harry Holland's political emotions', *Journal of New Zealand Studies*, 21, 2015. Len Richardson has suggested in conversation that Holland has been misjudged.

23 Keith Sinclair, 'The Lee–Sutch syndrome: New Zealand Labour Party policies and politics, 1930–1940,' *New Zealand Journal of History*, 8 (2), Oct. 1974.

24 W.B. Sutch, *The Quest for Security in New Zealand*, Oxford University Press, Wellington, 1966, pp.335, 337, 343. One of us has dealt with this in more detail: Jim McAloon, *Judgements of All Kinds: economic policy-making in New Zealand 1945–1985*, Victoria University Press, Wellington, 2013.

25 For instance, Jim Tomlinson, *Democratic Socialism and Economic Policy: the Attlee years, 1945–51*, Cambridge University Press, Cambridge, 1997.

26 Robert Chapman, 'The response to Labour and the question of parallelism of opinion', in Robert Chapman and Keith Sinclair (eds), *Studies of a Small Democracy: essays in honour of Willis Airey*, Paul's Book Arcade for the University of Auckland, Auckland, 1963.
27 Roy McLennan, 'The Last Years of the First Labour Government, 1945–1949', MA thesis, University of Auckland, 1963.
28 Barry Gustafson, *Social Change and Party Organisation: the New Zealand Labour Party since 1945*, Sage Publications, London, 1976.
29 Brian Easton, *The Nationbuilders*, Auckland University Press, Auckland, 2001, ch.11.
30 Peter Hebblethwaite, *Paul VI: the first modern pope*, Paulist Press, New York, 1993, p.3, n.1.

Chapter 1: The Democratic Tradition, 1840–1905

1 Herbert Roth, 'Parnell, Samuel Duncan', from *The Dictionary of New Zealand Biography*, Te Ara—the Encyclopedia of New Zealand, http://www.TeAra.govt.nz/en/biographies/1p7/parnell-samuel-duncan.
2 Kerry Taylor, 'The ambiguous legacy of Samuel Duncan Parnell: the eight hour day in New Zealand', in Julie Kimber and Peter Love (eds), *The Time of Their Lives: the eight hour day and working life*, Australian Society for the Study of Labour History, Melbourne, 2007.
3 John E. Martin, *Honouring the Contract*, Victoria University Press, Wellington, 2010, p.37.
4 Generally, Martin, *Honouring the Contract*, ch.2.
5 Constantine Dillon, *The Dillon letters: The letters of the Hon. Constantine Dillon*, 1842–1853, ed. C.A. Sharp, A.H. & A.W. Reed, Wellington, 1954, p. 65; R.E. Wright-St Clair, *Thoroughly a man of the world: A biography of Sir David Monro*, M.D, Whitcombe & Tombs, Christchurch, 1971, p. 84.
6 Jim McAloon, *Nelson: a regional history,* Cape Catley, Whatamongo Bay, 1997, pp.25–9, 37–9.
7 Martin, *Honouring the Contract.*
8 *New Zealand Gazette & Wellington Spectator*, 13 Apr. 1842, p.2, 18 Apr. 1842, p.1.
9 Ibid., 28 Dec. 1840, p.2. For Davis, see Martin, *Honouring the Contract*, p.40.
10 *New Zealand Gazette & Wellington Spectator*, 16 Feb. 1842.
11 Ibid., 9 Mar. 1842, p.3.
12 Ibid., 17 Aug. 1842, p.2.
13 *Daily Southern Cross*, 11 Sept. 1849, p.2, 18 Sept. 1849, p.2.
14 *Nelson Examiner*, 30 Dec. 1848, p.175; *Daily Southern Cross*, 20 Jan. 1849, p.3; *Wellington Independent*, 3 Feb. 1849, p.3, 3 Mar. 1849, p.3, 29 Aug. 1849. The advertisement for the March 1849 banquet in Wellington is reproduced in John E. Martin, *The House: New Zealand's House of Representatives*, Dunmore Press, Palmerston North, 2004, p.8.
15 *Nelson Examiner*, 11 Jan. 1851.
16 Ibid., 30 Nov. 1850, p.158.
17 *Wellington Independent*, 23 Apr. 1851, p.3.
18 *Lyttelton Times*, 10 July 1852, p.9.
19 Martin, *The House*, p.11, says it was 'almost universal adult male suffrage'; Neill Atkinson, *Adventures in Democracy: a history of the vote in New Zealand*, Otago University Press, 2003, p.35, suggests about half the white male population was registered, though more were eligible.
20 *Wellington Independent*, 4 May 1853, p.3; *Lyttelton Times*, 3 Sept. 1853, p.6.
21 *Nelson Examiner*, 27 Aug. 1859, p.2.
22 *Wellington Independent*, 27 Jan. 1860, p.3; see also 4 Nov. 1859, p.5.

23 *Otago Witness*, 9 Nov. 1861, p.5.
24 *Press*, 19 Nov. 1864, p.2.
25 *Daily Southern Cross*, 15 May 1867, p.5, 16 May 1867, p.4.
26 *Press*, 23 Dec. 1865, p.2; *Lyttelton Times*, 27 Dec. 1865, p.2, 1 May 1866, p.2.
27 Ibid., 18 Apr. 1866, p.2, 1 May 1866, p.2, 12 June 1866, p.2.
28 Herbert Roth, 'Marx and New Zealand', *New Zealand Monthly Review*, July 1983, p.3.
29 *Daily Southern Cross*, 19 Jan. 1871, p.2; *New Zealand Herald*, 20 Jan. 1871, p.3. For Gillies see Hugh Rennie, 'Gillies, Thomas Bannatyne', from *The Dictionary of New Zealand Biography*, Te Ara—the Encyclopedia of New Zealand, http://www.teara.govt.nz/en/biographies/1g9/gillies-thomas-bannatyne.
30 *Evening Post*, 19 Jan. 1871, p.3.
31 *Wellington Independent*, 20 Jan. 1871, p.2.
32 *Evening Post*, 20 Jan. 1871, p.2.
33 Ibid., 24 Jan. 1871, p.2.
34 Ibid., 18 Dec. 1875, p.2, 22 Dec, 1875, p.2.
35 *Otago Daily Times*, 30 July 1877, p.3; *Otago Witness*, 11 Aug. 1877, p.5.
36 Edmund Bohan, *To Be a Hero: a biography of Sir George Grey 1812–98*, HarperCollins, Auckland, 1998, p.259.
37 *New Zealand Herald*, 20 Aug. 1879, p.5.
38 Ibid., 29 Aug. 1879, p.3; Grey's advice is in the *Oamaru Mail*, 12 Aug. 1879, p.2.
39 Martin, *The House*, p.81.
40 *Star*, 17 Sept. 1881, p.3, 24 Sept. 1881, p.3.
41 Ibid., 3 Oct. 1881, p.4; *Press*, 28 Sept. 1881, p.3, 11 Oct. 1881, p.3.
42 *Hawke's Bay Herald*, 20 Aug. 1879, p.2.
43 Edmund Bohan, 'Andrews, Samuel Paul', from *The Dictionary of New Zealand Biography*, Te Ara—the Encyclopedia of New Zealand, http://www.TeAra.govt.nz/en/biographies/2a9/andrews-samuel-paul.
44 *Star*, 24 Nov. 1881, p.4, 30 Nov. 1881, p.2.
45 *West Coast Times*, 3 Sept. 1879, p.2.
46 *New Zealand Herald*, 19 Nov. 1879, p.3.
47 *Star*, 22 Oct. 1879, p.3.
48 The Working Men's Political Association's progress is traced in the *New Zealand Herald*, 27 Sept. 1879, p.4, 4 Oct. 1879, p.6; *Auckland Star*, 4 Oct. 1879, p.2, 10 Oct. 1879, p.2, 22 Oct. 1879, p.3, 17 Jan. 1880, p.2, 14 Apr. 1880, p.2, 24 Aug. 1880, p.2.
49 *Press*, 23 Nov. 1880, p.2. The royal commission's report is in *AJHR*, 1880, Sess I H–22.
50 *New Zealand Herald*, 11 Nov. 1881, p.4.
51 *Star*, 29 Nov. 1881, p.2.
52 Ibid., 15 Nov. 1881, p.3, 30 Nov. 1881, p.2.
53 *Otago Daily Times*, 23 Nov. 1881, p.3. For Green see *Otago Daily Times*, 21 May 1880, p.2.
54 F.R.J. Sinclair, 'Fish, Henry Smith', from *The Dictionary of New Zealand Biography*, Te Ara—the Encyclopedia of New Zealand, http://www.TeAra.govt.nz/en/biographies/2f8/fish-henry-smith
55 *Auckland Star*, 30 June 1883, p.2.
56 *New Zealand Herald*, 23 May 1884, p.5; *Star*, 14 June 1884, p.3, 30 June 1884, p.3, 1 July 1884, p.3.
57 *Otago Daily Times*, 2 June 1884, p.4, 4 June 1884, p.4.
58 Jebson in St Albans and Dorney in Stanmore.
59 *Hawke's Bay Herald*, 16 May 1884, p.3; *Otago Daily Times*, 23 May 1884, p.3.
60 *Star*, 23 May 1884, p.3, 16 June 1884, p.3, 7 July 1884, p.3.

61 The most important study for our purposes is Erik Olssen, *Building the New World: work, politics and society in Caversham, 1880s–1920s*, Auckland University Press, Auckland, 1995, quote at p.166.
62 *Otago Daily Times*, 9 Jan. 1885, p.2.
63 Ibid., 14 Jan. 1885, p.3, 12 Jan. 1885 p.3.
64 *Auckland Star*, 26 Jan 1886, p.3.
65 Ibid., 29 Jan. 1886, p.3, 30 Jan. 1886, p.8.
66 Ibid., 29 Jan. 1886 p.4, 1 Feb. 1886, p.6.
67 *Star*, 24 Sept. 1887, p.3.
68 Len Richardson, *Coal, Class and Community: the United Mineworkers of New Zealand, 1880–1960*, Auckland University Press, Auckland, 1995, p.21. Burns's great-uncle, the Scottish bard, would have turned in his grave.
69 Richardson, p.30
70 Richardson, pp.32–6.
71 *Otago Daily Times*, 20 Oct. 1888, p.3.
72 Ibid., 22 Jan. 1889, p.3; see also 24 Jan. 1889, p.3, 28 Jan., p.3.
73 Ibid., 30 Jan. 1889, p.2.
74 Ibid., 8 June 1889, p.2, 14 June 1889, p.2, 12 July 1889, p.2, 28 Aug. 1889, p.2, 29 Aug. 1889, p.4, 2 Sept. 1889, p.3.
75 The strike was reported virtually every day in November 1889 by the *Star*. *Star*, 5 June 1889, p.2, 5 June, p.4, 18 Oct., p.4, 19 Oct., p.3, 24 Oct., p.3, 29 Oct., p.3, 1 Nov., p.2, 2 Nov., p.3, 4 Nov., p.3, 6 Nov., p.3, 11 Nov., p.3, 12 Nov., p.3, 13 Nov., p.3, 14 Nov., p.3, 22 Nov., p.3, 23 Nov., p.4, 25 Nov., p.2.
76 Barbara Fill, *Strike: trouble at t' mill*, GP Books, Wellington, 1989. See also *Evening Post*, 10 Mar. 1890, p.4.
77 *Star*, 30 Apr. 1890, p.2.
78 Ibid., 27 Jan. 1890, p.2.
79 *Otago Daily Times*, 30 Jan. 1890, p.2.
80 *Star*, 10 Mar. 1890, p.3, 21 Mar. 1890, p.4, 5 May 1890, p.4.
81 Ibid.,, 29 May 1890 p.4, 30 May 1890, p.3, 2 June 1890, p.3.
82 Ibid., 31 Mar. 1890, p.2; the paper noted omitting 50 bookbinders, 1 Apr. 1890, p.3. Miles Fairburn, *The Ideal Society and its Enemies: the foundations of modern New Zealand society, 1850–1900*, Auckland University Press, Auckland, 1989, p.122. A larger estimate is 40 per cent: Mark Derby, 'Strikes and labour disputes', Te Ara—the Encyclopedia of New Zealand, http://www.teara.govt.nz/en/strikes-and-labour-disputes/page-2.
83 This discussion of the Knights largely relies on Robert Weir, *Knights Down Under: the Knights of Labour in New Zealand*, Cambridge Scholars Publishing, Newcastle upon Tyne, 2009. See also J.D. Salmond, *New Zealand Labour's Pioneering Days: the history of the labour movement in N.Z. from 1840 to 1894*, ed. D.W. Crowley, Forward Press, Auckland, 1950, pp.136–46.
84 *Star*, 31 Mar. 1890, p.4.
85 Ibid., 19 May 1890, p.4.
86 David Grant, *Jagged Seas: the New Zealand Seamen's Union 1879–2003*, Canterbury University Press, Christchurch, 2012, ch.2.
87 Gavin McLean, *The Southern Octopus: the rise of a shipping empire*, Wellington Maritime Museum/New Zealand Ship and Marine Society, Wellington, 1990, p.107.
88 Ibid., p.110.
89 Richardson, pp.43–4.
90 Ibid., p.44.

91 *Lyttelton Times*, 8 Aug. 1890, p.6.
92 Erik Olssen and Len Richardson, 'The New Zealand labour movement 1880–1920', in Eric Fry (ed.), *Common Cause: essays in Australian and New Zealand labour history*, Allen & Unwin/Port Nicholson Press, Wellington, 1986, p.4.
93 Olssen, *Building the New World*, p.177.
94 Ibid., p.188.
95 See, for instance, Daphne Patai (ed.), *Looking Backward, 1988–1888: essays on Edward Bellamy*, University of Massachusetts Press, Amherst, 1998. Debs quoted in Franklin Rosemont, 'Bellamy's radicalism reclaimed', in Patai, p.163. See also Herbert Roth, 'Bellamy societies abroad', in Sylvia E. Bowman (ed.), *Edward Bellamy Abroad*, Twayne, New York, 1962.
96 Norman D. Stevens, 'Labour candidates for the New Zealand House of Representatives 1890–1916, part 1: 1890–1896', *Political Science*, 7 (1), 1955, p.39 makes this point. Does one confine the definition to 'working men' or expand it to include 'whether or not the candidate was endorsed by any section of the working-class movement', and even further to include self-definition as 'standing in the labour interest'?
97 *Timaru Herald*, 11 Aug. 1890, p.3.
98 *Press*, 26 June 1891, p.5.
99 Olssen, *Building the New World*, pp.180–1; *Star*, 25 Aug. 1890, p.4.
100 *Lyttelton Times*, 9 July 1890, p.4, 2 Oct., p.5, 8 Oct., p.5, 28 Oct., p.6; *Star*, 6 Dec. 1890, p.3.
101 Stevens.
102 *Press*, 26 June 1891, p.5.
103 *Otago Daily Times*, 28 May 1891, p.3; see also Olssen, *Building the New World*, pp.188–90.
104 *Star*, 26 Aug. 1893, p.6. The *Star* counted Pinkerton, Earnshaw, Hall-Jones, Tanner, Sandford, Buick and James Kelly.
105 *Evening Post*, 18 June 1891, p.2, 22 June 1891, p.3, 23 Jun 1891, p.4.
106 The strike is extensively covered in the *Auckland Star*: 20 Mar. 1891, p.4, 26 Mar., p.12, 4 Apr., pp.2, 5, 6 Apr., p.3, 7 Apr., p.5, 11 Apr., p.5, 23 Apr., pp.3, 9, 4 May, p.4, 6 May, p.5, 11 May, p.3, 16 May, p.2, 2 June, p.5, 19 June, p.4, 22 June, p.4, 18 July, p.5, 5 Aug., p.5, 16 Sept., p.4, 19 Oct., p.5.
107 Olssen, *Building the New World*, p.184.
108 Quoted R.T. Shannon, 'The fall of Reeves', in R.M. Chapman and Keith Sinclair (eds), *Studies of a Small Democracy: essays in honour of Willis Airey*, Paul's Book Arcade for the University of Auckland, Auckland, 1963, p.129.
109 *Auckland Star*, 8 Feb. 1893, p.2, 6 June 1893, p.2.
110 Olssen, *Building the New World*, p.191.
111 Ibid., p.193.
112 D.A. Hamer, *The New Zealand Liberals: the years of power 1891–1912*, Auckland University Press, Auckland, 1988, p.144.
113 e.g. *New Zealand Herald*, 9 Feb. 1895, p.5.
114 Tom Brooking, *King of God's Own: the life and times of New Zealand's longest serving prime minister*, Penguin, Auckland, 2014 makes the best possible case for Seddon's continuing sympathy for labour.
115 As we noted above, the 'contract' has been extensively discussed by John E. Martin.
116 Hamer, *The New Zealand Liberals*, p.146.
117 Olssen, *Building the New World*, p.202.
118 Jim McAloon, 'Cooke, Frederick Riley', from *The Dictionary of New Zealand Biography*, Te Ara—the Encyclopedia of New Zealand, http://www.TeAra.govt.nz/en/biographies/3c29/

cooke-frederick-riley. For Clark see Mark E. Dunick, 'The Clarion Settlers: a socialist migration to New Zealand', BA (Hons) dissertation, Victoria University of Wellington, 2014, p.40.

119 *Evening Post*, 29 July 1901, p.6.

120 *Star*, 22 Jan. 1902, p.1.

121 James Taylor, '"To me, Socialism is not a set of dogmas but a living principle": Harry Atkinson and the Christchurch Socialist Church, 1890–1905', MA thesis, Victoria University of Wellington, 2010.

122 Herbert Roth, 'The New Zealand Socialist Party', *Political Science*, 9 (1), Mar. 1957, p.55.

Chapter 2: Labour Parties 1904–19

1 *Star*, 2 Apr. 1904, p.4.

2 Ibid., 8 Apr. 1904, p.3.

3 *Press*, 27 Sept. 1904, p.4.

4 *Star*, 9 Apr. 1904, p.4.

5 *Wairarapa Daily Times*, 14 Jan. 1905, p.4.

6 *Auckland Star*, 25 Oct. 1904, p.3; *Evening Post*, 5 Jan. 1905, p.6.

7 *Otago Daily Times*, 27 Jan. 1905, p.6; *Star*, 8 Feb. 1905 p.4.

8 *Evening Post*, 26 Apr. 1905, p.5.

9 *Auckland Star*, 9 Mar. 1905, p.3; *Evening Post*, 26 Apr. 1905, p.4, 27 Apr. 1905, p.2, 28 Apr. 1905, p.2.

10 *Star*, 31 May 1905, p.2, 2 June 1905, p.2; *Press*, 15 July 1905, p.2; 28 July 1905, p.6. The league claimed 1000 members in Christchurch: *Evening Post*, 5 Sept. 1905, p.3.

11 *Press*, 14 Oct. 1905, p.10.

12 *Evening Post*, 24 Nov. 1905, p.2.

13 *Otago Daily Times*, 8 Dec. 1905, p.6; *Star*, 7 Dec. 1905, p.4.

14 *Star*, 14 Dec. 1905, p.3.

15 Ibid., 17 Apr. 1906, p.3.

16 Erik Olssen, 'The origins of the New Zealand Labour Party: a reconsideration', *New Zealand Journal of History*, 21 (1), Apr. 1987, p.82.

17 Ibid., pp.84–5.

18 Ibid., p.86.

19 *Evening Post*, 2 Jan. 1908, p.3; *Otago Daily Times*, 7 Feb. 1908, p.6.

20 The matter is discussed by David Hamer, 'The second ballot: a New Zealand electoral experiment', *New Zealand Journal of History*, 21 (1), Apr. 1987: see especially p.105.

21 Barry Gustafson, *Labour's Path to Political Independence*, Auckland University Press, Auckland, 1980, pp.19, 27.

22 *Evening Post*, 18 Nov 1908, p.2, 25 Nov. 1908, p.3.

23 *NZPD*, vol.147, 1909, p.286; vol.146, 1909, appendix, p.51; vol.146, p.121.

24 Ibid., vol.146, 1909, pp.124, 194

25 *Evening Post*, 25 Apr. 1912, p.3.

26 Jack McCullough, quoted in Melanie Nolan, *Kin: a collective biography of a New Zealand family*, Canterbury University Press, Christchurch, 2006, p.72.

27 *Auckland Star*, 19 July 1910, p.6; Jim McAloon, 'A Political Struggle: Christchurch Labour Politics 1905-1913', *New Zealand Journal of History*, 28, (1), 1994.

28 e.g. *Auckland Star*, 27 May 1910, p.5.

29 Ibid., 21 July 1910, p.5.

30 Ibid., 20 July 1910, p.5.

31 Ibid., 19 July 1910, p.6.
32 Melanie Nolan (ed.), *War and Class: the diary of Jack McCullough*, Dunmore Press, Palmerston North, 2009, pp.100–3.
33 Nolan, *War and Class* has details of the relationship.
34 Nolan, *War and Class*, p.122.
35 Gustafson, *Labour's Path*, p.39.
36 Ibid.
37 Olssen, 'Origins', p.89. Gustafson, above, suggests that the New Zealand Labour Party was advocating 'practical reforms' rather than 'radically changing society'. His analysis of each electorate contest is, however, very valuable.
38 *Horowhenua Chronicle*, 2 Dec. 1911, p.4; Gustafson, *Labour's Path*, p.165 for biography.
39 Barry Gustafson, 'Payne, John', from *The Dictionary of New Zealand Biography*, Te Ara—the Encyclopedia of New Zealand, http://www.TeAra.govt.nz/en/biographies/3p18/payne-john. The figures for Payne and Robertson are from the *Maoriland Worker*, 22 Dec. 1911, p.11.
40 Kerry Taylor, 'Hindmarsh, Alfred Humphrey', from *The Dictionary of New Zealand Biography*, Te Ara—the Encyclopedia of New Zealand, http://www.TeAra.govt.nz/en/biographies/3h28/hindmarsh-alfred-humphrey.
41 Nolan, *War and Class*, p.203.
42 As Gustafson noted in *Labour's Path*, p.47.
43 *Maoriland Worker*, 15 Mar. 1912, p.10; *Dominion*, 11 Apr. 1912, p.6.
44 Erik Olssen, 'Mills, Walter Thomas', from *The Dictionary of New Zealand Biography*, Te Ara—the Encyclopedia of New Zealand, http://www.TeAra.govt.nz/en/biographies/3m54/mills-walter-thomas; Thomas J. Morgan, 'Walter Thomas Mills: his record', *The Socialist*, 350, 2 Nov. 1907, p.3, www.marxisthistory.org; Olssen, 'W.T. Mills, E.J.B. Allen, John A. Lee and socialism in New Zealand', *New Zealand Journal of History*, 10 (2), Oct 1976.
45 Gustafson, *Labour's Path*, p.45; Nolan, *War and Class*, p.166.
46 W.T. Mills, *Proposals for Securing the Industrial and Political Union of all the Labour Organisations of New Zealand, New Zealand Worker*, Auckland, 1911.
47 Erik Olssen, 'Bennett, Henry Gilbert Scott', from *The Dictionary of New Zealand Biography*, Te Ara—the Encyclopedia of New Zealand, http://www.TeAra.govt.nz/en/biographies/3b30/bennett-henry-gilbert-scott.
48 *Report of Debate between Mr H. Scott-Bennett and Professor Walter Thos. Mills, M.A.: which took place at the Choral Hall, Auckland, on December 8th, 1911*, Voice Publishing, Auckland, 1912.
49 Gustafson, *Labour's Path*, pp.49, 51, 54, 57.
50 Nolan, *War and Class*, p.219.
51 Drawn from Gustafson, *Labour's Path*, pp.54–5 and Olssen, 'The origins of the New Zealand Labour Party'.
52 There are detailed accounts in Erik Olssen, *The Red Feds: revolutionary industrial unionism and the New Zealand Federation of Labour, 1908–14*, Auckland University Press, Auckland, 1988, from which this paragraph largely draws, and also in Stanley Roche, *The Red and the Gold: an informal account of the Waihi strike, 1912*, Oxford University Press, Auckland, 1984. H.E. Holland et al., *The Tragic Story of the Waihi Strike*, Hocken Library, Dunedin, 1975 should not be ignored either.
53 Olssen, *The Red Feds*, p.133.
54 e.g. *Lyttelton Times*, 17 Aug. 1912, p.16; 20 Aug. 1912, p.8.
55 Telegram by McCullough, quoted H. Roth, 'Buying a Labour Party: Fowlds, Mills, and the ULP', *Political Science*, 20 (1), Sept. 1968, p.30.
56 Olssen, *The Red Feds*, p.164.

57 *Maoriland Worker*, 6 Dec. 1912, p.3.
58 Ibid., 17 Jan. 13 p.4; *Otago Daily Times*, 7 Dec. 1912, p.7, 21 Dec. 1912, p.7.
59 Conference reports in successive issues of the *Maoriland Worker* from 31 January 1913. See also Olssen, *The Red Feds*, ch.13; Michael Bassett with Michael King, *Tomorrow Comes the Song: a life of Peter Fraser*, Penguin, Auckland, 2000, pp.52–7; Gustafson, *Labour's Path*, pp.57–8.
60 *Maoriland Worker*, 31 Jan. 1913, p.4.
61 P.H. Hickey, *Red Fed Memoirs*, Wellington Media Collective, Wellington, 1980, p.62.
62 McCullough to McCarthy, 1 June 1913, McCarthy Papers McIII, Hocken Collections.
63 The figures are in Hickey, p.70 and the quote is Olssen, *The Red Feds*, p.171.
64 Petterd to Arthur McCarthy, 2 May 1913, McCarthy Papers VIII, Hocken Collections.
65 Olssen, *The Red Feds*, pp.171–4.
66 No doubt McLaren, Paul and their ilk thought the platform was a jack-up. Gustafson, *Labour's Path*, p.67 also described it as such.
67 Massey sacked the Auckland police superintendent, John Mitchell, who was inclined to enforce the law without fear or favour.
68 Melanie Nolan, 'Introduction', in Melanie Nolan (ed.), *Revolution: the 1913 great strike in New Zealand*, Canterbury University Press, Christchurch, 2006, p.25.
69 *Lyttelton Times*, 7 Feb. 1913, p.4.
70 Ibid., 8 Aug. 1913, p.5.
71 Wellington Strike Committee minute book, 22 Oct. 1913, MS-Papers-11367-191, ATL; Olssen, *The Red Feds*, p.186.
72 *Lyttelton Times*, 8 July 1913, p.8; Olssen, 'The lessons of 1913', in Nolan (ed.), *Revolution*, p.44.
73 Olssen, *The Red Feds*, pp.210–1. The non-striking majority is discussed in Peter Franks, '"Arbitrationists out and out": the involvement of the craft unions', in Nolan (ed.), *Revolution*.
74 Gustafson, *Labour's Path*, pp.78–9.
75 Fraser moved this, and, remarkably, Paul advocated such a restoration, Fraser saying that he 'believed [Paul] to be more revolutionary than he got the credit for': *Maoriland Worker*, 15 July, p.4. Fraser's remark may be construed as an olive branch to Paul and the ULP/LRC holdouts; cf Gustafson, *Labour's Path*, p.73.
76 *Maoriland Worker*, 15 July 1914, p.4, 22 July 1914, p.4.
77 Ibid., 2 Dec. 1914, p.16, 9 Dec. 1914, p.8. See also Gustafson, *Labour's Path*, pp.82–5.
78 Olssen, 'Origins', p.87.
79 This discussion of the results relies on Gustafson's careful analysis. See also *Maoriland Worker*, 16 Dec. 1914, p.8.
80 Olssen, 'Origins', p.86.
81 Ibid., p.96.
82 *Maoriland Worker*, 21 July 1915, p.4.
83 *Maoriland Worker*, 1 Dec. 1915, p.7. The parlous state of the Social Democratic Party is discussed by Gustafson, *Labour's Path*, ch.8 and Jack Vowles, 'Ideology and the formation of the New Zealand Labour Party: some new evidence', *New Zealand Journal of History*, 16 (1), Apr. 1982.
84 *Maoriland Worker*, 15 Sept. 1915, p.1.
85 Ibid., 11 Aug. 1915, p.4.
86 Ibid., 1 Sept. 1915, p.5. Vowles stresses Paul's importance.
87 *Maoriland Worker*, 26 Jan. 1916, p.5. See generally Gustafson, *Labour's Path*, ch.10, especially pp.109–12.

88 *Maoriland Worker*, 2 Feb. 1916, pp.4–5
89 *NZPD*, vol.175, 1916, pp.877–85.
90 Ibid., pp.542–4 (Hindmarsh), pp.547–50 (McCombs), pp.502–66 (Webb).
91 *Maoriland Worker*, 12 July 1916, p.4, 14 June 1916, p.5.
92 Ibid., 12 July 1916, p.4, 26 July 1916, p.7.
93 Ibid., 19 July 1916 p.2.
94 E.W. Plumridge, 'Labour in Christchurch 1914–19', MA thesis, University of Canterbury, 1979, p.62; Vowles, pp.44–5; *Sun*, 11 Apr. 1916, p.12.
95 Quoted Bassett and King, p.67.
96 *Maoriland Worker*, 12 July 1916, p.5. Alexandra Hall was at 56 Abel Smith Street, and had been leased by the SDP for headquarters at the beginning of 1916 (ibid., 2 Feb. 1916, p.7). Previously the building had been a Presbyterian church, before being converted to a hall in 1904: http://www.nzhistory.net.nz/media/photo/scots-memorial-church.
97 Vowles; Gustafson, *Labour's Path*, pp.94, 114.
98 Minutes, 9 July 1916, New Zealand Labour Party Executive—minutes 1916–19, 89-040-2/18, ATL.
99 *Maoriland Worker*, 26 July 1916, p.7; Vowles, pp.47–9; Gustafson, *Labour's Path*, p.93.
100 Plumridge, pp.57–67.
101 *Sun*, 19 June 1917, p.2; *Maoriland Worker*, 4 July 1917, p.3, 8 Aug. 1917, p.3, 22 Aug. 1917, p.6, 5 Sept. 1917, p.2; *Auckland Star*, 22 June 1917, p.3, 26 June 1917, p.2, 29 June, p.6. The Auckland situation remains under-researched.
102 *Sun*, 18 July 1916, p.3.
103 *Sun*, 6 June 1916, p.12, commenting on Jutland; *Sun*, 24 Oct. 1916, p.3.
104 Plumridge, pp.104–9.
105 *Grey River Argus*, 24 May 1917, p.3.
106 This outline relies on Gustafson, *Labour's Path*, p.133, from which the quotation is drawn. James Thorn was treated in a similar fashion, being first imprisoned for sedition and then conscripted; Thorn went on the run.
107 Gustafson, *Labour's Path*, pp.132, 134–6.
108 *Evening Post*, 20 Dec. 1918, p.3; Gustafson, p.136.
109 The source is John A. Lee, *Rhetoric at the Red Dawn*, Collins, Auckland, 1965, p.70, so we may assume there is some embroidery.
110 Gustafson, *Labour's Path*, p.139.
111 Ibid., p.141.
112 The 1919 election results are covered in Gustafson, *Labour's Path*, ch.13, and newspapers for 18 December 1919. Mitchell had inflicted the notorious no.1 field punishment on Archibald Baxter and his three comrades in France.

Chapter 3: Building a Party, 1919–35

1 *Maoriland Worker*, 12 July 1922, p.5, 19 July 1922, p.5.
2 *NZPD*, vol.186, 1920, p.157.
3 This analysis is based on the *Maoriland Worker*, 24 Dec. 1919, p.5 and *Evening Post*, 18 Dec. 1919, p.9.
4 *Maoriland Worker*, 13 Dec. 1922, p.8; the discussion of the 1922 results is drawn from this issue of the *Worker* and the official return in *AJHR*, 1923, H–33.
5 *NZPD*, vol.186, 1920, p.155.
6 Ibid., vol.199, 1923 (William Downie Stewart), p.71.
7 Ibid., pp.3–9.

8 Michael Bassett, *Coates of Kaipara*, Auckland University Press, Auckland, 1995, p.100, emphasises the extent of business funding for Coates.
9 *Press*, 11 Mar. 1926, p.8, 15 Mar. 1926, p.7.
10 *New Zealand Herald*, 5 Nov. 1925, p.9.
11 Bassett, *Coates*, pp.105, 106.
12 *Auckland Star*, 30 Sept. 1927, p.5.
13 The Raglan by-election is briefly discussed in Bassett, *Coates*, p.125, from which this is drawn.
14 *New Zealand Herald*, 15 Nov. 28, p.11.
15 Robert Chapman, 'The sad, slow end of the twenties', in Elizabeth McLeay (ed.), *New Zealand Politics and Social Patterns: selected works by Robert Chapman*, Victoria University Press, Wellington, 1999, p.121.
16 Chapman, p.124.
17 This is implied by Holland, *NZPD*, vol.220, 1928, pp.47–9.
18 Chapman, p.124; P.J. O'Farrell, *Harry Holland: militant socialist*, Australian National University Press, Canberra, 1964, p.178.
19 Holland, *NZPD*, vol.220, 1928, pp.47–9.
20 Erik Olssen, *John A. Lee*, University of Otago Press, Dunedin, 1977, p.56.
21 1926/09/Ch, 1926/05/Ak, in ADMO W5933 21007 Box 6 21/2/33 pt 2 SIS: Communist Party of New Zealand—Policy on other political parties in New Zealand, Archives New Zealand.
22 Det. Sgt W.E. Lewis to the chief detective, Wellington, 3 Mar. 1921, in ibid.
23 As is evident from ADMO W5933 21007 Box 6 21/2/33 pt 2 SIS: Communist Party of New Zealand—Policy on other political parties in New Zealand. We thank Jared Davidson for his assistance with these files.
24 *Maoriland Worker*, 21 July 1920, p.7.
25 Ibid., 9 July 1919, p.5, 23 July 1919, p.5, 13 Aug. 1919, p.3, 24 Aug 1921, p.7.
26 Ibid., 3 Aug. 1921 p.7.
27 Colin Brown, 'Ayrton, Moses', from *The Dictionary of New Zealand Biography*, Te Ara—the Encyclopedia of New Zealand, http://www.TeAra.govt.nz/en/biographies/4a26/ayrton-moses.
28 National office report, 1923 annual conference; national executive report, 1924 conference, Labour Party archive, New Zealand Labour Party head office.
29 National executive report 1925 conference; report of the 1929 conference, Labour Party archive.
30 Minutes, 18 June 1925, New Zealand Labour Party Auckland women's branch minute book 1917–26, qMS-1486, ATL.
31 *Maoriland Worker*, 23 July 1919, p.5.
32 Ibid.; minutes, 28 Sept. 1922, Auckland women's branch minute book 1917–26.
33 Remits, 1924 conference; report of the 1927 annual conference, Labour Party archive.
34 Elizabeth R. McCombs, *Women and the Labour Movement*, Labour Book Room, Wellington, 1933.
35 Michael Bassett with Michael King, *Tomorrow Comes the Song: a life of Peter Fraser*, Penguin, Auckland, 2000, p.107.
36 Report of the 1924 conference, Labour Party archive; Claudia Orange, 'Mawhete, Rangiputangatahi', from *The Dictionary of New Zealand Biography*, Te Ara—the Encyclopedia of New Zealand, http://www.TeAra.govt.nz/en/biographies/4m48/mawhete-rangiputangatahi.
37 Letter in the 1925 conference minutes, signed by Kipa Roera, Paratene Wihonga, Pita Te

Kopu, Rota Te Rangi, Pepene Ruka, W.D. Parete, Rangi Mawhete, Toroa Ngataua, John Morgan, Wi Neepa, Mua Carr, Labour Party Archive, NZLPHO.

38 Report of the 1925 conference, Labour Party archive. The committee was McCombs, O'Brien, Armstrong, Monteith, Mawhete, Kipa Roera and John Morgan.

39 *New Zealand Worker*, 29 Apr. 1925, p.1.

40 Ralph Ngātata Love, 'Policies of Frustration: the growth of Maori politics: the Ratana/ Labour era', PhD thesis, Victoria University of Wellington, 1977.

41 North Canterbury LRC minutes, 6 Feb. 1930, 1a, MB-40, Macmillan Brown Library.

42 Report of the 1932 conference, Labour Party archive.

43 *Maoriland Worker*, 23 July 1919, p.5, 21 July 1920, p.7, 28 July 1920, p.7. A specimen is at http://www.nzmuseums.co.nz/account/4033/object/497275/New_Zealand_Labour_Party_Bond_1919.

44 Financial report, 1923 annual conference, Labour Party archive.

45 Financial report, 1924 annual conference, Labour Party archive.

46 National office report, 1926 annual conference, Labour Party archive.

47 Report of the 1929 conference, Labour Party archive.

48 National office report, 1930 annual conference, and conference minutes, Labour Party archive.

49 National executive report, 1933 conference, Labour Party archive.

50 Bassett and King, p.126, and also pp.130–1.

51 P.J. O'Farrell, *Harry Holland: militant socialist*, Australian National University Press, Canberra, 1964, pp.196–200.

52 National executive report, 1933 conference and 1934 conference; report of the 1932 conference, Labour Party archive.

53 Report of the annual conference, 1935 and 1936, Labour Party archive.

54 For examples, see Olssen, *John A. Lee*, pp.56–60.

55 See O'Farrell.

56 Keith Sinclair, *Walter Nash*, Auckland University Press, Auckland, 1976, p.112.

57 *NZPD*, vol.186, 1920, pp.99–100 (Holland).

58 *Maoriland Worker*, 10 Aug. 1921, p.7, 7 Sept. 1921, p.7.

59 Bruce Brown, *The Rise of New Zealand Labour: a history of the New Zealand Labour Party from 1916 to 1940*, Price Milburn, Wellington, 1962, pp.55–7; V.I. Lenin, *Collected Works*, vol.31, Progress Publishers, Moscow, 1977, pp.206–11.

60 Remits, 1923 annual conference, Labour Party archive.

61 Minutes and national executive report, 1924 annual conference, Labour Party archive.

62 *NZPD*, vol.186, 1920, pp.158, 192.

63 Report on defence policy, 1924 conference, Labour Party archive.

64 Annual conference 1930, 1931, 1934, Labour Party archive.

65 Nicholas Hoare, 'Harry Holland's "Samoan complex"', *Journal of Pacific History*, 49 (2), 2014, p.152. This paragraph is based on Hoare's article.

66 Ibid., p.163.

67 Ibid., p.169.

68 *NZPD*, vol.191, 1921, pp.430–1 (Munro).

69 Ibid., vol.186, 1920, pp.213–15 (Savage), pp.188–93 (Sullivan); vol.203, 1923, p.315 (Sullivan).

70 Ibid., vol.218, 1928, p.209 (McCombs).

71 Quoted by McCombs, ibid., pp.210–11. William Trufant Foster and Waddill Catchings, *Profits*, Houghton Mifflin, Boston and New York, 1925 was in the library, as McCombs confirmed: ibid., vol.227, 1931, p.166 (McCombs).

72 Ibid., vol.227, 1931, pp.166–75 (McCombs).
73 Ibid., vol.231, 1932, p.340 (McCombs).
74 Jean Garner, 'McCombs, James', from *The Dictionary of New Zealand Biography*, Te Ara—the Encyclopedia of New Zealand, http://www.TeAra.govt.nz/en/biographies/3m3/mccombs-james. See also Barry Gustafson, *Labour's Path to Political Independence*, Auckland University Press, Auckland, 1980.
75 *Auckland Star*, 7 July 1919, p.11. See also Barry Gustafson, *From the Cradle to the Grave: a biography of Michael Joseph Savage*, Reed Methuen, Auckland, 1986, p.144.
76 *Maoriland Worker*, 1 Sept. 1920, p.5.
77 Ibid., 17 Aug. 1921, p.10, 24 Aug. 1921, p.7.
78 Annual conference 1925, land policy committee report; annual conference 1926, Labour Party archive.
79 Annual conference 1927, Labour Party archive.
80 National executive report, 1929 conference, Labour Party archive.
81 *NZPD*, vol.209, 1926, pp.671–3 (Holland).
82 Ibid., vol.231, 1932, p.255 (Armstrong).
83 Holland's second major speech is in *NZPD*, vol.233, 1932, pp.59–71.
84 Ibid., vol.231, 1932, pp.167–78 (Holland).
85 Ibid., vol.224, 1930, pp.44–8 (Nash).
86 Noel Thompson, 'Hobson and the Fabians, two roads to socialism in the 1920s', *History of Political Economy*, 26 (1994), p.214. On Keynes, see Donald Moggridge, *Maynard Keynes: an economist's biography*, Routledge, London and New York, 1992, p.461.
87 Moggridge, pp.482–90; John Maynard Keynes, *The Collected Writings of John Maynard Keynes*, Cambridge University Press, London, 1972, vol.9, pp.89–116 ('Lloyd George') and 126–49 (*Nation* articles); vol.20, pp.283–309 (Macmillan Committee).
88 *NZPD*, vol.231, 1932, pp.247–50 (Nash).
89 Warren Hogan, 'Allan George Barnard Fisher', in J.E. King (ed.), *A Biographical Directory of Australian and New Zealand Economists*, Edward Elgar, Cheltenham, 2007; A.G.B. Fisher, *The Clash of Progress and Security*, London, Macmillan, 1935; see also S. Herbert Frankel's summary in *South African Journal of Economics*, 4 (3), 1936. For Lee see Olssen, *John A. Lee*, pp.48–51.
90 R. Clifton, 'Douglas Credit and the Labour Party 1930–35', MA thesis, Victoria College, 1961, p.218. This paragraph relies on Clifton's thesis.
91 The affirmations are given in *NZPD*, vol.237, 1933, pp.246–7 (Nash).
92 Olssen emphasises the differences in *John A. Lee*, p.54.
93 Sinclair, *Walter Nash*, p.116.
94 Ibid., p.110.
95 *Auckland Star*, 28 Nov. 1935, p.11.
96 Western and Southern Māori were won by Rātana candidates on minority votes, but it must be remembered that the secret ballot did not exist for Māori seats until 1938.
97 *Auckland Star*, 28 Nov. 1935; *Evening Post*, 30 Nov. 1935, p.10.
98 *Auckland Star*, 28 Nov. 1935.
99 R.H. Tawney, quoted in Lawrence Goldman, *The Life of R.H. Tawney: socialism and history*, Bloomsbury, London, 2014, p.156.
100 We draw here on Sheri Berman, *The Primacy of Politics: social democracy and the making of Europe's twentieth century*, Cambridge University Press, New York, 2006; annual conference 1930, Labour Party archive.

Chapter 4: The Welfare State: the Savage Years, 1935–40

1 *Standard*, 4 Dec. 1935.
2 J.O. Wilson, *New Zealand Parliamentary Record 1840–1984*, Government Printer, Wellington, 1985, p.82.
3 Barry Gustafson, *From the Cradle to the Grave: a biography of Michael Joseph Savage*, Reed Methuen, Auckland, 1986, pp.179–80.
4 Michael Bassett with Michael King, *Tomorrow Comes the Song: a life of Peter Fraser*, Penguin, Auckland, 2000, p.140.
5 J.B. Condliffe, *The Welfare State in New Zealand*, Allen & Unwin, London, 1959, p.62.
6 Gustafson, *From the Cradle to the Grave*, p.183.
7 *Parliamentary Labour Party Report to Twentieth Annual Conference*, Apr. 1936, MS-Papers-0270-023, ATL.
8 Jim McAloon, *Judgements of All Kinds: economic policy-making in New Zealand 1945–1984*, Victoria University Press, Wellington, 2013, p.43.
9 David Wilson, *History in the Making: a summary of the legislative and administrative actions of the first Labour government during its first year of office*, Labour Bookroom, Wellington, 1937.
10 Keith Sinclair, *Walter Nash*, Auckland University Press/Oxford University Press, Auckland and New York, 1976, p.130.
11 McAloon, *Judgements of All Kinds*, pp.44–5.
12 Bassett and King, p.143.
13 Gustafson, *From the Cradle to the Grave*, pp.193–8.
14 Adrian Rurawhe interview, 17 Sept. 2015.
15 Gustafson, *From the Cradle to the Grave*, p.189.
16 1937 budget, quoted in McAloon, *Judgements of All Kinds*, p.43.
17 Peter Franks, 'Predominance of support for moderate policy: the formation of the New Zealand Federation of Labour, 1937', in Peter Franks and Melanie Nolan (eds), *Unions in Common Cause: the New Zealand Federation of Labour 1938–88*, Steele Roberts, Wellington, 2011, pp.89–90.
18 Gustafson, *From the Cradle to the Grave*, p.186.
19 New Zealand Labour Party, *Twenty-first Annual Conference Report, held in the Town Hall, Wellington, New Zealand, March 29 to April 1 1937*, p.14, MS-Papers-0270-387, ATL.
20 *Annual Report of the National Executive to Twentieth Annual Conference*, 1936, MS-Papers-0270-023, ATL.
21 Keith Newman, *Rātana Revisited: an unfinished legacy*, Reed Publishing, Auckland, 2006.
22 Angela Ballara, 'Paikea, Paraire Karaka', from *The Dictionary of New Zealand Biography*, Te Ara—the Encyclopedia of New Zealand, http://www.TeAra.govt.nz/en/biographies/4p1/paikea-paraire-karaka.
23 *Twenty-first Annual Conference Report*, 1937, p.27.
24 Ibid., p.14.
25 *Standard*, 21 Jan. 1937.
26 Franks, 'Predominance of support for moderate policy', pp.91–8.
27 Ibid., pp.98–110.
28 Tawa Flat branch minutes, 25 May 1937, 2006-036-15/1, ATL; Karori branch minutes, 16 Nov. 1937, 89-040-3/02, ATL; Island Bay branch minutes, 10 July, 14 Aug., 11 Sept. 1939, MSX-4412, ATL; Karori branch minutes, 24 May 1938, 89-040-3/02, ATL.
29 Elizabeth McCombs Club minutes, 1939–1948, MSX-9100, ATL.
30 St Andrews branch minutes, 18 Sept. 1937, 89-040-1/05, ATL.

31 Dunedin Women's branch minutes, 3 Apr. 1935, AG-645/004, Hocken Collections; Purakanui branch minutes, 25 June 1937, 25 Apr. 1938, 89-040-2/20, ATL.
32 Ōwhango branch minutes, 23 Apr., 5 July 1938, 89-040-4/20, ATL.
33 Auckland LRC picnic committee minutes, 25 Nov., 7 Dec. 1936, MSS & Archives A-65, vol.2, UAL.
34 Auckland Labour Club (Inc.), *Annual Report and Balance Sheet for year ending June 22nd 1937*, 2007-115-7/04, ATL.
35 *Twenty-first Annual Conference Report*, p.4.
36 Sinclair, *Walter Nash*, p.132.
37 Gustafson, *From the Cradle to the Grave*, pp.219–21.
38 Sinclair, *Walter Nash*, p.166.
39 *Twenty-second Annual Conference Report*, 1938, pp.5–6, 19.
40 *Evening Post*, 21 Apr. 1938.
41 Gustafson, *From the Cradle to the Grave*, p.222.
42 National executive minutes, 29 Oct. 1938, 89-040-3/04, ATL.
43 Karori branch minutes, 4 July, 22 Aug. 1938, 89-040-3/02, ATL; Māngere branch minutes, 8 Aug. 1938, MSS & Archives A-246, UAL; Te Whetu branch minutes, 8 Feb. 1938, 89-040-3/03, ATL; St Andrews branch minutes, 24 Sept. 1938, 89-040-1/05, ATL; Oxford branch minutes, 11 Oct. 1938, 89-040-3/04, ATL; Purakanui branch minutes, 28 Sept. 1938, 89-040-2/20, ATL; Tawa Flat branch minutes, 28 Sept. 1938, 2006-036-15/1, ATL.
44 National executive report to the 1936 annual conference, MS-Papers-0270-023, ATL; *Twenty-third Annual Conference Report, minutes of meeting held in the Town Hall, Wellington, New Zealand, April 10 to 14, 1939*, p.18.
45 Franks and Nolan, p.6.
46 John Pell to John A. Lee, 23 Oct. 1938, 441/13, Auckland City Libraries.
47 Gustafson, *From the Cradle to the Grave*, p.228.
48 *The Call: the Onekaka People's Press*, 17 Oct. 1938.
49 Gustafson, *From the Cradle to the Grave*, pp.214–17.
50 McAloon, *Judgements of All Kinds*, pp.45–6.
51 Sinclair, *Walter Nash*, p.123.
52 Letter from Labour MPs to Savage, 8 Sept. 1938, 441/29, Auckland City Libraries.
53 Gustafson, *From The Cradle to The Grave*, pp.232–3; *New Zealand Herald*, 15 Dec. 1938.
54 F.P. Walsh to F.G. Young, 8 Nov. 1938, MS-Papers-2151-292, ATL.
55 Gustafson, *From the Cradle to the Grave*, pp.234-235.
56 John A. Lee, 'The conflict between caucus and cabinet', 15 Dec. 1938, 441/5, Auckland City Libraries.
57 Gustafson, *From the Cradle to the Grave*, p.236.
58 *Twenty-third Annual Conference Report,* 1939, p.39; annex to annual report of national executive, return showing affiliated membership 1938–1939, 94-106-22/02, ATL.
59 *Twenty-third Annual Conference Report*, 1939, pp.35, 8, 14–15.
60 Ibid., pp.21–2.
61 Gustafson, *From the Cradle to the Grave*, pp.239–40.
62 *Summarised Report of Proceedings, 1939 Annual Conference issued by D. Wilson, National Secretary*, MS-Papers-0270-032, ATL.
63 John A. Lee to C.G. Scrimgeour, 17 Apr. 1939, 441/29, Auckland City Libraries.
64 Henry Hayward to Lee, 14 June, 11 July 1939, 441/17, Lee to Hayward, 15 June, 23 June 1939, 441/29, Auckland City Libraries.
65 Young to Walsh, 29 May 1939, MS-Papers-2151-293, ATL.
66 C.G. Fellows, secretary, Northcote branch to Lee, 5 May 1939, H. Dunlop, secretary,

Waiuku branch to Lee, 23 May 1939, 441/11A, Auckland City Libraries; Island Bay branch minutes, 1 May 1939, MSX-4412, ATL; Greenhithe branch minutes, 15 May 1939, MSS & Archives A-37, UAL; St Andrews branch minutes, 29 May 1939, 89-040-1/05, ATL; Albany branch minutes, 28 June 1939, MSS & Archives A-36, UAL.

67 Young to Peter Fraser, 6 July 1939, MS-Papers-2151-293, ATL. An unsigned report of McMillan's comments is in Walsh's papers, MS-Papers-0274-378, ATL.

68 *Tomorrow*, 5 July 1939. Lee's handwritten manuscript is in his papers, 441/8 part 2, Auckland City Libraries.

69 Gustafson, *From the Cradle to the Grave*, pp.241, 256.

70 T. Anderson to Walsh, 8 Aug. 1939, MS-Papers-2151-135, ATL.

71 Bassett and King, pp.166–71.

72 M. Moohan, acting secretary, to all branches and LRCs, 25 Sept. 1939, 94-106-20/12, ATL.

73 R. Brooks to Walsh, 18 Sept. 1939, MS-Papers-2151-289, ATL.

74 Otago LRC minutes, 26 Oct. 1939, AG-56-1-2, Hocken Collections.

75 Gustafson, *From the Cradle to the Grave*, p.255.

76 Nominations for Lee and Mollie Lee from 56 branches, LRCs and unions are in his papers, 441/27, Auckland City Libraries.

77 Walsh to Brooks, 11 Nov. 1939, MS-Papers-2151-289, ATL.

78 Lee to C. Croall, 23 Nov. 1939, 441/11B, Auckland City Libraries.

79 *Tomorrow*, 6 Dec. 1939.

80 Anderson to Walsh, 12 Dec. 1939, MS-Papers-2151-135, ATL.

81 Gustafson, *From the Cradle to the Grave*, p.261.

82 Auckland LRC minutes, 11 Jan. 1940, vol.5, MSS & Archives A-65, UAL.

83 Gustafson, *From the Cradle to the Grave*, p.261.

84 Anderson to Walsh, 12 Jan. 1940, MS-Papers- 2151-136, ATL.

85 *24th Annual Conference Report, March 25th to March 27th 1940*, pp.10–11; Gustafson, *From the Cradle to the Grave*, p.262.

86 *24th Annual Conference Report*, 1940, p.28; affiliation fees statement, annex to annual report of national executive, 14 Apr. 1941, 94-106-20/13, ATL.

87 *24th Annual Conference Report*, 1940, pp.11, 15.

88 Gustafson, *From the Cradle to the Grave*, p.267.

89 *Standard*, 28 Mar. 1940.

90 'Delegates report', an unsigned report on the conference attributed to Norman Proctor, MSS & Archives A-121, UAL.

91 *24th Annual Conference Report*, 1940, p.23; *Standard*, 28 Mar. 1940.

92 Gustafson, *From the Cradle to the Grave*, p.268.

93 Ibid., pp.269–71.

94 Erik Olssen, 'The impact of John A. Lee's expulsion upon the New Zealand Labour Party', *New Zealand Journal of History*, 12 (1), Apr. 1978, pp.34–6.

95 Walsh to Brooks, 25 Apr. 1940, MS-Papers-2151-289, ATL.

96 John A. Lee, *Simple on a Soapbox*, Collins, London, 1964, p.208.

97 Bruce S. Taylor, 'The Expulsion of J.A. Lee and its Effects on the Development of the New Zealand Labour Party', MA thesis, University of Canterbury, 1970, p.61.

98 New Plymouth LRC minutes, 27 Apr. 1940, ARC 2007-100, Puke Ariki; North Canterbury LRC minutes, 18 Apr., 2 May, 13 June 1940, MB-40, Macmillan Brown Library.

99 Eden branch minutes, 7 May 1940, MSS & Archives A-120, UAL; Island Bay branch minutes, 8 Apr. 1940, MSX-4412, ATL; Karori branch minutes, 7 May 1940, 89-040-2/14, ATL; Tawa Flat branch minutes, 2 Apr. 1940, 2006-035-15/1, ATL. Some Canterbury branches also supported a special conference: Taylor, 'The expulsion of J.A. Lee', p.62.

100 Otago LRC minutes 24 Apr., 27 June 1940, AG-56-1-2, Hocken Collections; D.R. McDairmid to Lee, 27 June 1940, 441/30, Auckland City Libraries.
101 Olssen, 'The impact of John A. Lee's expulsion', pp.38–9; Peter Franks, *Print and Politics: a history of trade unions in the New Zealand printing industry 1865–1995,* Victoria University Press, Wellington, 2001, p.125.
102 Taylor, 'The Expulsion of J.A. Lee', pp.71–9.
103 Ibid., pp.46–7.
104 St Andrews branch minutes, 17 Apr. 1940, 89-040-1/05, ATL.
105 *Summarised Report of Proceedings of the 1940 Annual Conference issued by D. Wilson, Retiring National Secretary*, 2007-115-8/07, ATL.
106 *Standard*, 11 Apr. 1940.
107 Tawa Flat branch minutes, 24 Apr., 29 May, 28 Aug. 1940, 2006-035-15/1, ATL.
108 Island Bay branch minutes, 15 May, 30 May, 10 June 1940, MSX-4412, ATL.
109 Taylor, 'The Expulsion of J.A. Lee', pp.68–70.
110 W.J. Lyon to J.T. Head, 1 Jan. 1941, MSS & Archives A-29, UAL.

Chapter 5:
War and Recovery: the Fraser Years, 1940–49

1 Michael Bassett with Michael King, *Tomorrow Comes the Song: a life of Peter Fraser*, Penguin, Auckland, 2000, p.185.
2 Ibid., pp.189–90.
3 Ibid., p.251.
4 *Standard*, 29 Feb. 1940.
5 Nancy M. Taylor, *The Home Front*, vol.1, Historical Branch, Department of Internal Affairs, Wellington, 1986, pp.92–109.
6 Bassett and King, p.196.
7 Herbert Roth, *Trade Unions in New Zealand Past and Present*, Reed Education, Wellington, 1974, p.62.
8 New Zealand Labour Party, *Minutes of Emergency Conference held in the Town Hall, Wellington on Monday, June 3rd 1940.*
9 New Zealand Federation of Labour, *Minutes of Special Conference, Trades Hall, Wellington, 1st June 1940*, MSX-238, ATL.
10 Anderson to Walsh, 3 Jan. 1940, MS-Papers-2151-136, ATL.
11 Walsh to Anderson, 26 May 1940, ibid.
12 Nancy M. Taylor, 'Human rights in World War II in New Zealand', *New Zealand Journal of History*, 23 (2), Oct.1989.
13 J.R.S. Daniels, 'The General Election of 1943', MA thesis, Victoria College, 1951, pp.7–12; Walsh to Anderson, 26 May 1940, MS-Papers-2151-136, ATL.
14 Jim McAloon, *Judgements of All Kinds: economic policy-making in New Zealand 1945–1984*, Victoria University Press, Wellington, 2013, p.47; Bassett and King, pp.200–1.
15 New Zealand Labour Party, *Report of the 25th Annual Conference of the New Zealand Labour Party held in the Town Hall, Wellington, from April 14 to 17 1941*, pp.2, 21.
16 Ibid., p.15; J.T. Head to W.J. Lyon, 29 Apr. 1941, MSS & Archives A-29, UAL.
17 *Report of the 25th Annual Conference*, 1941, pp.23–4.
18 Head to Lyon, 29 Apr. 1941.
19 *Report of the 26th Annual Conference of the New Zealand Labour Party held in the Town Hall, Wellington from April 6 to 9, 1942*, p.19.
20 Bassett and King, pp.215–17.
21 Ibid., pp.204–5.

22 *Evening Post*, 19 May 1941.
23 Karori branch minutes, 9 June, 24 June 1941, 89-040-2/14, ATL.
24 Daniels, pp.12–15.
25 Bassett and King, p.226.
26 Taylor, *The Home Front*, vol.2, pp.663–6, 788–96.
27 Roth, *Trade Unions in New Zealand*, p.62.
28 'Memorandum of a meeting held in Parliament Buildings, Wellington, between the Federation of Labour, the executive of the Labour Party and Cabinet, on Friday and Saturday, January 9th and 10th, 1942', MS-Papers-8771, ATL.
29 Roth, *Trade Unions in New Zealand*, p.63.
30 McAloon, *Judgements of All Kinds*, p.47.
31 Ibid., p.49.
32 Bassett and King, pp.230–1.
33 Karori branch minutes, 7 July 1942, 89-040-2/14, ATL.
34 Auckland Trades Council minutes, special meeting, 21 Sept. 1942, MS-Papers-4100-19/1/2, ATL.
35 Bassett and King, p.232.
36 Ibid., pp.240–5.
37 Ibid., p.249.
38 Otago LRC minutes, 8 Apr. 1943, AG-56-1-2, Hocken Collections.
39 *Report of the 27th Annual Conference of the New Zealand Labour Party held in the Trades Hall, Wellington, April 26th to 29th, 1943*, p.22.
40 Bassett and King, p.246.
41 *Report of the 27th Annual Conference*, 1943, p.13.
42 Bassett and King, p.241.
43 Bruce S. Taylor, 'The Expulsion of J.A. Lee and its Effects on the Development of the New Zealand Labour Party', MA thesis, University of Canterbury, 1970', p.69.
44 New Zealand Labour Party, *Labour's March to Social and Economic Security, Standard Press*, 1943, 94-106-22/02, ATL.
45 Daniels, p.281.
46 Copies are in the Lee papers, 441/1, Auckland City Libraries.
47 National executive, New Zealand Labour Party, *General Election 1943, Standard Press*, Wellington, 1943, 94-106-22/02, ATL.
48 Bassett and King, p.256.
49 Daniels, pp.264–79, 306.
50 W.L. Renwick, *Scrim: the man with a mike*, Victoria University Press, Wellington, 2011, makes it plain that Scrimgeour had been hoist by his own petard. Close to Savage, he had insisted on terms of appointment that varied from the public service norm, making it effectively a political appointment.
51 *General Election 1943*; *Report of the Twenty-eighth Annual Conference in the Trades Hall, Wellington, 6th to 10th November, 1944,* p.34.
52 Glen Rockley, 'Political currents in New Zealand', *Far Eastern Survey*, 17 Nov. 1943.
53 Bassett and King, pp.257–60.
54 Ibid., pp.266–71.
55 Keith Sinclair, *Walter Nash*, Auckland University Press/Oxford University Press, Auckland and New York, 1976, pp.237–43.
56 Bassett and King, p.277.
57 *Report of the Twenty-eighth Annual Conference*, 1944, pp.23–5.
58 Sinclair, *Walter Nash*, p.244.

59 *Report of the Twenty-ninth Annual Conference in the Trades Hall, Wellington, 12th to 15th November 1945*, p.10.
60 Bassett and King, p.292.
61 Ibid., p.298.
62 J.W. Davidson, *Samoa mo Samoa: the emergence of the independent state of Western Samoa*, Oxford University Press, Melbourne, 1967, p.158.
63 Bassett and King, pp.281–3; Doug Munro, 'J.W. Davidson: the making of the participant historian', in Brij V. Lal and Peter Hempenstall (eds), *Pacific Lives, Pacific Places: bursting boundaries in Pacific history*, Journal of Pacific History, Canberra, 2001, pp.98–116; Davidson, chs 6–7; Colin Aikman, 'Powles, Guy Richardson', from *The Dictionary of New Zealand Biography*, Te Ara—the Encyclopedia of New Zealand, http://www.TeAra.govt.nz/en/biographies/5p37/powles-guy-richardson.
64 McAloon, *Judgements of All Kinds*, pp.55–6.
65 Roth, *Trade Unions in New Zealand*, p.172.
66 Roy McLennan, 'The Last Years of the First Labour Government, 1945–1949', MA thesis, University of Auckland, 1963, pp.xi-xii.
67 McAloon, *Judgements of All Kinds*, pp.56–7.
68 Bassett and King, p.276.
69 Ibid., pp.271–9.
70 Peter Franks and Melanie Nolan (eds), *Unions in Common Cause: the New Zealand Federation of Labour 1938–88*, Steele Roberts, Wellington, 2011, pp.108–9.
71 Auckland Trades Council minutes, 18 Oct. 1945, MS-Papers-4100-19/1/3, ATL; *Auckland Star*, 3 Dec. 1945.
72 *Evening Post*, 1 Dec. 1945.
73 *Report of the Thirty-first Annual Conference in the Trades Hall, Wellington, 9th to 12th June 1947*, p.5.
74 *Report of the 25th Annual Conference*, 1941, p.7.
75 *Report of the Twenty-ninth Annual Conference*, 1945, pp.25–6.
76 Circular from P. Dowse, secretary, New Zealand Labour Newspapers Ltd to all LRCs and trades councils, 18 July 1946, 2007-115-8/07, ATL.
77 Alice Clayton, 'Red ink: the Southern Cross labour newspaper within the 1940s social background', MS-Papers-11651-384, ATL.
78 *Standard*, 21 Mar. 1951.
79 McLennan, pp.6–26.
80 Bassett and King, p.305.
81 Ibid., p.301; R.M. Chapman, *The Political Scene 1919–1931*, Heinemann Educational Books, Auckland, 1969, pp.66–8.
82 McLennan, pp.136–7.
83 *Report of the Thirty-first Annual Conference*, 1947, p.9.
84 McLennan, pp.138–9.
85 *Report of the Thirty-first Annual Conference*, 1947, pp.9–12.
86 Bassett and King, 1947, pp.315–16.
87 Warren Freer, *A Lifetime in Politics: the memoirs of Warren Freer*, Victoria University Press, 2004, pp.37–40; Bassett and King, p.317.
88 *Report of the Twenty-ninth Annual Conference*, 1945, pp.34–6.
89 Claudia Orange, 'A Kind of Equality: Labour and the Maori People 1935–1949', MA thesis, University of Auckland, 1977, pp.224–5.
90 Bassett and King, pp.303–5.
91 Report of the Māori Advisory Council to the Twenty-fourth Annual Conference, annual

conference file 1940, Labour Party archive, New Zealand Labour Party head office.

92 Orange, 'A Kind of Equality', pp.215–20.
93 *Report of the Thirty-first Annual Conference*, 1947, p.30.
94 McLennan, p.152.
95 McAloon, *Judgements of All Kinds*, pp.68–71.
96 McLennan, p.167.
97 Ibid., pp.168–74.
98 Ibid., pp.180–7.
99 Roth, *Trade Unions in New Zealand*, p.172.
100 Ibid., p.67.
101 Auckland Trades Council minutes, 15 Apr. 1948, MS-Papers-4100-19/1/5, ATL
102 *Report of the Thirty-second Annual Conference held in the Concert Chamber, Town Hall, Dunedin, May 3–7, 1948*, p.20.
103 Ibid., p.5; *Report of the Thirty-third Annual Conference held in the Town Hall, Wellington, May 21 to 26, 1949*, p.7.
104 For example, Blenheim branch minutes, 19 Feb. 1947, MSX-3701, ATL; Carterton branch minutes, 14 May 1947, 2000-150-30/08, ATL; Gonville branch minutes, 15 July 1948, 89-040-1/02, ATL; Island Bay branch minutes, 13 Apr. 1948, MSX-4412, ATL; Waipukurau branch minutes, 15 Sept. 1948, 89-040-3/01, ATL.
105 Warren Freer, *A Lifetime in Politics: the memoirs of Warren Freer*, Victoria University Press, Wellington, p.25.
106 Karori women's branch minutes, 25 Oct., 22 Nov. 1947, 2003-244-02/08, ATL; Island Bay branch minutes, 10 Mar. 1947, MSX-4412, ATL; *Report of the Thirty-second Annual Conference*, 1949, p.24.
107 Roth, *Trade Unions in New Zealand*, pp.69–70.
108 Bassett and King, pp.216, 328–32.
109 McLennan, p.258.
110 *Report of the Thirty-third Annual Conference*, pp.17, 19–20.
111 Martyn Finlay to Peter Franks, 27 Jan. 1972.
112 McLennan, p.257.
113 Island Bay branch minutes, 11 July 1949, MSX-4412, ATL.
114 Freer, p.38.
115 Blenheim branch minutes, 20 July 1949, MSX-3701, ATL; Waipukurau branch minutes, 20 July 1949, 89-040-3/01, ATL.
116 Roskill branch minutes, 11 July 1949, MSS & Archives A-154, UAL; Dunedin West branch minutes, 13 July 1949, ARC-053, Hocken Collections; Otago LRC minutes, 25 Aug. 1949, AG-56-1-4, Hocken Collections.
117 Interview with Peter Franks, 16 Mar. 1972.
118 Bassett and King, p.339.
119 New Zealand Labour Party, *Election Manifesto 1949*, MS-Papers-0274-378, ATL.
120 McLennan, pp.268–74.
121 Ibid., pp.275–6.
122 *Report of the Thirty-first Annual Conference*, 1947, pp.17–19.

Chapter 6:
Terminal Affluence? Labour in Opposition, 1949–57

1 Arnold Nordmeyer to Mick Connelly, 24 Jan. 1950, MB-96 22/4, Macmillan Brown Library.
2 New Zealand Labour Party, *Report of the Forty-fifth Annual Conference held in the Town*

Hall, Wellington on May 8, 9, 10, 11, 1961, pp.3–4.
3 *Report of the Thirty-fourth Annual Conference*, 1950, p.10.
4 Ibid., pp.19–20.
5 *Standard*, 22, 29 Nov. 1950.
6 Ibid., 22 Nov. 1950.
7 Michael Bassett with Michael King, *Tomorrow Comes the Song: a life of Peter Fraser*, Penguin, Auckland, 2000, pp.350–2.
8 *Standard*, 24 Jan. 1951.
9 Bassett and King, p.351.
10 Michael Bassett, *Confrontation '51: the 1951 waterfront dispute*, A.H. & A.W. Reed, Wellington, 1972, p.190.
11 John Roberts, '1951: the storm before the calm', *New Zealand Listener*, 29 May 1976.
12 Bassett, *Confrontation '51*, pp.174–5.
13 Bruce Brown, 'The lockout and Walter Nash', in David Grant (ed.), *The Big Blue: snapshots of the 1951 waterfront lockout*, Canterbury University Press, Christchurch, 2004, p.107.
14 Herbert Roth, 'The New Zealand Trade Union Congress, 1950–51', in Eric Fry (ed.), *Common Cause: essays in Australian and New Zealand Labour History*, Allen & Unwin/Port Nicholson Press, Wellington, 1986, pp.124–38.
15 Bassett, *Confrontation '51*, pp.67–83.
16 Ibid., pp.99–103.
17 Ibid., p.114.
18 Ibid., pp.120–34.
19 Ibid., p.104.
20 K. Baxter, secretary, FOL to W. Nash, 22 Mar. 1951, MS-Papers-4100-22/01/2, ATL.
21 Bassett, *Confrontation '51*, p.145.
22 Ibid., p.178.
23 Ibid., pp.145–7.
24 Dick Scott, *151 Days: the great waterfront lockout and supporting strikes, February 15–July 15, 1951*, Reed Books, Auckland, 2001.
25 *Tribune* (Auckland LRC newspaper), 28 Apr. 1951.
26 Melanie Nolan, 'Shattering dreams about women in the lockout', in Grant (ed.), *The Big Blue*, pp.59–81.
27 Walter Nash, 'Waterfront dispute', Report to the 1951 Labour Party conference, pp.11–19, 1951 annual conference file, Labour Party archive, New Zealand Labour Party head office.
28 Bassett, *Confrontation '51*, pp.150–6.
29 Ibid., pp.160–71.
30 New Zealand Federation of Labour, *Minutes and Report, Fourteenth Annual Conference of the New Zealand Federation of Labour held in the Social Hall, Trades Hall, Wellington, April 24, 26, 27, 1951*, pp.3–15, MSX-2390, ATL; *Standard*, 2 May 1951.
31 Bassett, *Confrontation '51*, pp.171–3.
32 *Standard*, 16 May 1951.
33 Nash, 'Waterfront dispute', pp.1–2.
34 *Report of the 35th Annual Conference*, pp.22, 25–6.
35 Bassett, *Confrontation '51*, pp.180–8.
36 Ibid., pp.193–4.
37 Ibid., pp.194–7.
38 Ibid., p.197.
39 *Auckland Star*, 24 July 1951; *New Zealand Herald*, 25 July 1951.
40 *Who Squeaks in the Dark???*, box 1, MSS & Archives A-131, UAL.

41 Baxter to W.T. Quealy, 25 July 1951, MS-Papers-4100-22/01/3, ATL.
42 Auckland LRC minutes, 26 July 1951, vol.8, MSS & Archives A-65, UAL; *New Zealand Herald*, 26 July 1951; Quealy to Baxter, 25 July 1951, MS-Papers-4100-22/01/3, ATL; *Standard*, 1 Aug. 1951.
43 *Report of the 36th Annual Conference held in the Town Hall, Wellington on April 28, 29, 30, 1952*, p.5.
44 Auckland LRC minutes, 26 July 1951.
45 Minutes of meetings of LRCs in the Auckland metropolitan area, campaign committees and candidates, 29 July, 5 Aug., 12 Aug., 26 Aug. 1951, vol.8, MSS & Archives A-65, UAL.
46 *Standard*, 22 Aug., 15 Aug. 1951.
47 Bassett, *Confrontation '51*, p.198.
48 *Report of the 36th Annual Conference*, 1952, p.5.
49 Bassett, *Confrontation '51*, pp.203–8.
50 W.B. Sutch, *The Quest for Security in New Zealand*, Oxford University Press, Wellington, 1966, p.398.
51 *Standard*, 14 Nov. 1951.
52 *NZPD*, vol.296, 1951, pp.1219, 1230, 1275.
53 *Standard*, 20 June 1951.
54 Keith Sinclair, *Walter Nash*, Auckland University Press/Oxford University Press, Auckland and New York, 1976, p.286.
55 *Report of the 35th Annual Conference*, 1951, pp.7–11.
56 Ibid., p.14.
57 *Standard*, 20 June 1951.
58 *Report of the 35th Annual Conference*, 1951, p.16.
59 Louise Overacker, 'The New Zealand Labour Party', *American Political Science Review*, 49 (3), Sept. 1955, p.719.
60 *Report of the 35th Annual Conference*, 1951, pp.11, 22–3.
61 *Report of the Fortieth Annual Conference held in the Town Hall, Wellington on May 7, 8, 9, 1956*, pp.10–11.
62 *Where Labour Stands!*, Nov. 1952, 2007-115-8/07, ATL.
63 *Report of the 36th Annual Conference*, 1952, pp.11–12.
64 New Zealand Federation of Labour, *Minutes and Report of the Fifteenth Annual Conference of the New Zealand Federation of Labour, held in the Social Hall, Trades Hall, Wellington, April 21, 22, 23 and 24, 1952*, p.21, 28, MSX-2390, ATL; *Report of the 36th Annual Conference*, 1952, p.11.
65 Joint Council of Labour minutes, 21 July 1952, MS-Papers-4100-22/02/1, ATL.
66 *Report of the 36th Annual Conference*, p.4.
67 Overacker, p.714.
68 Auckland LRC minutes, 24 July 1952; Overacker, pp.724–7.
69 Overacker, pp.731–2.
70 Sinclair, *Walter Nash*, p.291.
71 Bruce Brown, 'Nordmeyer 1901–1989', in Margaret Clark (ed.), *Three Labour Leaders: Nordmeyer, Kirk, Rowling*, Dunmore Press, Palmerston North, 2001, p.33.
72 Sinclair, *Walter Nash*, pp.292–3.
73 Brown, 'Nordmeyer 1901–1989', p.33.
74 National executive minutes, 16, 17 Feb. 1954, national executive minutes, Apr. 1953–May 1957, Labour Party archive.
75 *Standard*, 24 Feb. 1954.
76 K. Baxter to trades councils and trade union committees, 17 Feb. 1954, MS-

Papers-0274-346, ATL.
77 FOL national executive minutes, 22 Feb., 22 Mar., 5 Apr., 26 Apr. 1954, MSZ-0150, ATL; Sinclair, *Walter Nash*, p.294.
78 National executive minutes, 13 Apr., 20 Apr., 9 May 1954, national executive minutes Apr. 1953–May 1957, Labour Party archive.
79 Brown, 'Nordmeyer 1901–1989', p.33.
80 *Standard*, 3 Nov. 1954.
81 New Zealand Labour Party, *1954 General Election Report*, ATL.
82 *Standard*, 17 Nov. 1954.
83 *Report of the Thirty-ninth Annual Conference*, 1955, p.4.
84 Ibid., pp.12–13.
85 Ibid., pp.27–8.
86 *Report of the 36th Annual Conference*, 1952, p.8.
87 *Report of the 37th Annual Conference*, 1953, p.12.
88 New Plymouth LRC minutes, 23 Aug. 1952, ARC 2007-100/2, Puke Ariki.
89 *Standard*, 2 May 1956.
90 *Report of the Forty-first Annual Conference held in the Town Hall, Wellington on May 6, 7, 8, 1957*, p.6.
91 For example, the Auckland women's branch, *Standard*, 13 Jan. 1954.
92 *Standard*, 25 May 1955.
93 *Report of the Forty-first Annual Conference*, 1957, pp.6, 8, 10.
94 *Report of the Thirty-ninth Annual Conference*, 1955, p.35.
95 Ibid., p.5; *Report of the Forty-first Annual Conference*, 1957, p.1.
96 *Report of the Fortieth Annual Conference*, 1956, pp.36–7; *Report of the Forty-first Annual Conference*, 1957, p.23.
97 Sinclair, *Walter Nash*, p.299.
98 Brown, 'Nordmeyer 1901–1989', pp.35–6.
99 Sinclair, *Walter Nash*, p.299.
100 Auckland LRC executive, '1957 election campaign report', vol.9, MSS & Archives A-65, UAL.
101 FOL national executive minutes, 6 November 1957, MSZ-0150, ATL.
102 Sinclair, *Walter Nash*, p.300.
103 *Report of the Forty-second Annual Conference held in the Town Hall, Wellington, on May 5, 6, 7, 8, 1958*, p.5.

Chapter 7: Faltering Certainties: Government and Opposition in a Changing World, 1958–69

1 Keith Sinclair, *Walter Nash*, Auckland University Press/Oxford University Press, Auckland and New York, 1976, p.304.
2 Ian McGibbon (ed.), *Unofficial Channels: letters between Alister McIntosh and Foss Shanahan, George Laking and Frank Corner 1946–1966*, Victoria University Press, Wellington, 1999, p.243.
3 Michael Hirschfeld, 'The New Zealand Labour Party in Office, 1957–60', MA thesis, Victoria University of Wellington, 1970, pp.31–2.
4 Sinclair, *Walter Nash*, pp.30–7.
5 Jim McAloon, *Judgements of All Kinds: economic policy-making in New Zealand 1945–1984*, Victoria University Press, Wellington, 2013, p.106.
6 Ibid., p.106.

7 Hirschfeld, pp.253–4.
8 Ibid., p.256.
9 New Zealand Federation of Labour, special national council meeting, 17 July 1958, MSZ-0150, ATL.
10 Melanie Nolan, 'The tyranny of averages and the politics of indexing: the Walsh years 1937–63', in Peter Franks and Melanie Nolan (eds), *Unions in Common Cause: the New Zealand Federation of Labour 1938–88*, Steele Roberts, Wellington, 2011, p.128.
11 FOL special national council meeting, 17 July 1958.
12 Sinclair, *Walter Nash*, p.310.
13 John Gould, *The Rake's Progress? The New Zealand economy since 1945*, Hodder and Stoughton, Auckland 1982, p.88.
14 Hirschfeld, p.1. A copy of Nash's final broadcast address is in Eph-B-NZ-LABOUR-1950s, ATL.
15 Hirschfeld, p.256.
16 New Plymouth LRC minutes, 25 June 1958, ARC 2007-100/2, Puke Ariki; Christchurch women's branch minutes, 3 July 1958, MB-40, 75810, Macmillan Brown Library.
17 'Promise and Performance—a policy summary', 2 Oct. 1958, 94-106-20/13, ATL.
18 Barry Gustafson, *Social Change and Party Organisation: the New Zealand Labour Party since 1945*, Sage Publications, London, 1976, p.21.
19 Auckland LRC special executive minutes, 20 Dec. 1958, 22 Jan. 1959, vol.9, MSS & Archives A-65, UAL.
20 Bob Tizard interview, 10 May 2014.
21 New Zealand Labour Party, *Report of the Forty-third Annual Conference*, 1959, pp.21–2.
22 Sinclair, *Walter Nash*, p.311.
23 Hirschfeld, pp.274–81.
24 McAloon, *Judgements of All Kinds*, pp.110–16.
25 Hirschfeld, pp.182–200.
26 Sinclair, *Walter Nash*, pp.343–5.
27 'Promise and Performance—a policy summary', 2 Oct. 1958, 94-106-20/13, ATL.
28 Sinclair, *Walter Nash*, p.319.
29 Hirschfeld, p.87.
30 Ibid., pp.68–80.
31 Ibid., pp.59–66, 100–2, 116.
32 *Report of the Forty-second Annual Conference held in the Town Hall, Wellington on May 5, 6, 7, 8, 1958*, p.10.
33 *Report of the Forty-third Annual Conference*, 1959, p.8.
34 Hirschfeld, p.109.
35 Ibid., pp.103–5.
36 Sinclair, *Walter Nash*, pp.334–5.
37 Ibid., pp.107–8.
38 National executive minutes, 11 Aug. 1959, national executive minutes June 1957 to May 1960, Labour Party archive.
39 Sinclair, *Walter Nash*, pp.335–6.
40 Ibid., pp.32–4.
41 Interview with Norman Kirk, 16 Mar. 1972.
42 Sinclair, *Walter Nash*, p.324.
43 Malcolm Templeton, *A Wise Adventure: New Zealand and Antarctica, 1920–1960*, Victoria University Press, Wellington, 2000.
44 National executive minutes, 11 Aug. 1959.

45 Sinclair, *Walter Nash*, p.349.
46 Hirschfeld, pp.148–9.
47 *Report of the Forty-fifth Annual Conference held in the Town Hall, Wellington on May 8, 9, 10, 11, 1961*, pp.8–9.
48 Gustafson, *Social Change and Party Organisation*, p.20.
49 *Report of the Forty-fourth Annual Conference held in the Town Hall, Wellington on June 8, 9, 10, 1960*, p.8.
50 Richard Northey, 'The Annual Conferences of the New Zealand Labour Party', MA thesis, University of Auckland, 1973, p.33.
51 Wellington City branch minutes, 2 Aug. 1960, MSS & Archives A-238, UAL.
52 Stan Rodger interview, 11 Aug. 2014.
53 Northey, p.391.
54 *Report of the Forty-fifth Annual Conference*, p.20.
55 Auckland Metropolitan Campaign Committee minutes, 5 Feb. 1961, vol.11, MSS & Archives A-65, UAL.
56 Auckland LRC minutes, 23 Feb. 1961; Auckland Metropolitan Campaign Committee minutes, 12 Mar. 1961.
57 Auckland Regional Advisory Council minutes, 15 Oct. 1961, 1/1, MSS & Archives A-161, UAL.
58 *Report of the Forty-sixth Annual Conference held in the Town Hall, Wellington on May 7, 8, 9, 10, 1962*, p.7.
59 Gustafson, *Social Change and Party Organisation*, pp.9–12.
60 Ibid., pp.15–18.
61 Ibid., p.22.
62 Ibid., pp.24–7, 43.
63 *Report of the Forty-sixth Annual* Conference, pp.18–20.
64 McGibbon, p.294.
65 Sinclair, *Walter Nash*, pp.354–8.
66 K. Baxter, Circular to FOL conference delegates, 10 May 1963, in the possession of Peter Franks.
67 *Report of the Forty-eighth Annual Conference held in the Town Hall, Wellington on May 11th, 12th, 13th and 14th 1964*, p.23.
68 *New Zealand Statesman*, Nov. 1963, p.1.
69 *Report of the Forty-eighth Annual Conference*, 1964, p.8.
70 Ibid., p.15.
71 *Report of the Forty-ninth Annual Conference held in the Town Hall, Wellington on May 17th, 18th, 19th and 20th 1965*, p.6.
72 Ibid., p.4.
73 Warren Freer, *A Lifetime in Politics: the memoirs of Warren Freer*, Victoria University Press, Wellington, 2004, pp.136–7.
74 Bruce Brown, 'Nordmeyer 1901–1989', in Margaret Clark (ed.), *Three Labour Leaders: Nordmeyer, Kirk, Rowling*, Dunmore Press, Palmerston North, 2001, p.42.
75 Michael Cullen, 'Brief thoughts on three leaders', in Margaret Clark (ed.), *Three Labour Leaders*, p.12.
76 Margaret Hayward, 'Norman Kirk's early life: defining experiences', in Margaret Clark (ed.), *Three Labour Leaders*, p.102.
77 Ian Templeton and Keith Eunson, *Election '69: an independent survey of the New Zealand political scene*, A.H. & A.W. Reed, Wellington, 1969, pp.70–1.
78 Norman Kirk, *Towards Nationhood*, New Zealand Books, Palmerston North, 1969, p.37.

79 *Report of the 50th Annual Conference held in the Town Hall, Wellington on May 9th to 13th, 1966*, p.3.
80 *New Zealand Labour Party Journal*, 2 (2), Apr. 1966.
81 Gustafson, *Social Change and Party Organisation*, p.35.
82 A.H. Nordmeyer, 'Report of the parliamentary members to the forty-ninth annual conference', 18 May 1965, 1965 annual conference file, Labour party archive.
83 *Report of the 50th Annual Conference*, 1966, pp.14–15.
84 Gustafson, 'Arnold Nordmeyer', in Margaret Clark (ed.), *Three Labour Leaders*, pp.20–1.
85 Jim Eagles and Colin James, *The Making of a New Zealand Prime Minister*, Cheshire Publishing, Wellington, 1973, p.36.
86 *Report of the Fifty-first Annual Conference held in the Town Hall, Wellington on May 8th, 9th, 10th and 11th 1967*, p.10.
87 McAloon, *Judgements of All Kinds*, pp.127–9.
88 Gould, pp.113–18.
89 *Report of the Fifty-first Annual Conference*, 1967, p.8.
90 *Report of the Fifty-second Annual Conference held in the Town Hall, Wellington on May 6th, 7th, 8th and 9th, 1968*, p.8.
91 New Zealand Labour Party, *Organising to Win: an outline of campaign organisation for general elections*, n.d., 92-127-13, Hocken Collections.
92 Roger Douglas interview, 16 Apr. 2015.
93 Auckland LRC, *President's Annual Report for the year 1965–1966*, 36/7, MSS & Archives A-65, UAL.
94 Auckland Regional Advisory Council, 'Recommendations for the constitutional conference 1967', Feb. 1967, copy in the possession of Stan Rodger.
95 Roger Douglas interview, 16 Apr. 2015.
96 'RAC secretary's Report', 3 April 1967, 1/1, MSS & Archives A-161, UAL.
97 Auckland LRC, *President's Annual Report for the year 1966–1967*, 36/7, MSS & Archives A-65, UAL.
98 Gustafson, *Social Change and Party Organisation*, p.27.
99 *Report of the Fifty-first Annual Conference*, 1967, pp.19–21.
100 Gustafson, *Social Change and Party Organisation*, p.28.
101 Ibid., pp.43–4.
102 Auckland Regional Advisory Council, *President's Annual Report*, 30 June 1968, 1/4, MSS & Archives A-161, UAL.
103 Auckland LRC, special meeting minutes, 4 Nov. 1968, box 1, MSS & Archives A-154, UAL.
104 'Labour Party organisation', Report to the Auckland LRC executive by the reorganisation subcommittee, 17 Feb. 1969, box 1, MSS & Archives A-154, UAL.
105 Auckland LRC minutes, 6 Mar. 1969, box 1, MSS & Archives A-154, UAL; Auckland Regional Advisory Council minutes, 9 Mar. 1969, 1/4, MSS & Archives A-161, UAL.
106 Gustafson, *Social Change and Party Organisation*, pp.33–4.
107 *Report of the Fifty-second Annual Conference*, 1968, pp.7, 9.
108 Ibid., pp.12–13.
109 *Report of the Fifty-third Annual Conference held in the Town Hall, Wellington on April 21st, 22nd, 23rd and 24th 1969*, pp.13, 30.
110 Ibid., pp.52–3.
111 *Opportunities for the Sixties: suggestions of the Princes Street branch, New Zealand Labour Party*, 1965; *Education in New Zealand: policy recommendations, Princes St branch, New Zealand Labour Party*, 1966.
112 *Report of the Fifty-third Annual Conference*, 1969, pp.53–4.

113 Ibid., pp.36–49.
114 *Report of the Fifty-first Annual Conference*, 1967, pp.10–12.
115 Templeton and Eunson, p.74.
116 *Report of the Fifty-second Annual Conference*, 1968, p.6.
117 *Report of the Fifty-fourth Annual Conference held in St Francis Hall, Wellington on May 4th, 5th, 6th and 7th, 1970*, p.3 (Norman Douglas's presidential address).
118 Ibid., p.11.
119 Eagles and James, p.57.

Chapter 8: Ruined Optimism: The Kirk Years, 1970–75

1 Jim McAloon, *Judgements of All Kinds: economic policy-making in New Zealand 1945–1984*, Victoria University Press, Wellington, 2013, p.126.
2 New Zealand Labour Party, *Report of the Fifty-fourth Annual Conference held in St Francis Hall, Hill Street, Wellington on May 4th, 5th, 6th and 7th, 1970*, p.16.
3 Ibid., pp.14, 53.
4 Annual conference files, 1970 and 1975, Labour Party archive, New Zealand Labour Party head office.
5 *Report of the Fifty-fourth Annual Conference*, 1970, p.36.
6 *Report of the Fifty-third Annual Conference held in the Town Hall, Wellington on April 21st, 22nd, 23rd and 24th 1969*, p.30.
7 John Henderson, 'Rowling, Wallace Edward', from *The Dictionary of New Zealand Biography*, Te Ara—the Encyclopedia of New Zealand, http://www.TeAra.govt.nz/en/biographies/6r1/rowling-wallace-edward.
8 Angela Ballara, 'Bennett, Charles Moihi Te Arawaka', from *The Dictionary of New Zealand Biography*, Te Ara—the Encyclopedia of New Zealand, http://www.TeAra.govt.nz/en/biographies/5b23/bennett-charles-moihi-te-arawaka.
9 *Report of the Fifty-fifth Annual Conference held in the Town Hall, Wellington on May 24, 25, 26 and 27, 1971*, p.4.
10 *Report of the Fifty-fourth Annual Conference*, 1970, p.53.
11 Richard Northey, 'The Annual Conferences of the New Zealand Labour Party', MA thesis, University of Auckland, 1973, p.350.
12 *Report of the Fifty-fourth Annual Conference*, 1970, pp.59–60; Northey, p.349.
13 *Report of the Fifty-sixth Annual Conference held in the Town Hall, Wellington on May 8, 9, 10 and 11, 1972*, p.44.
14 Northey, p.348.
15 *Report of the Fifty-fifth Annual Conference*, 1971, p.37.
16 *Report of the Fifth-fourth Annual Conference*, 1970, p.43.
17 Northey, p.356.
18 *Dominion*, 11 May 1972.
19 Northey, p.356.
20 Ibid., p.364.
21 Ibid., pp.357–9.
22 *What Does LPYS Mean?*, Labour Party Young Socialists, 1975, in the possession of Peter Franks.
23 *Report of the Fifty-fourth Annual Conference*, 1970, p.54.
24 *Report of the Fifty-fifth Annual Conference*, 1971, p.33.
25 For example, he wrongly believed that the Socialist Action League was working through the Victoria University Labour Club, which he wanted expelled from the party. Margaret

Hayward, *Diary of the Kirk Years*, Cape Catley and A.H. & A.W. Reed, Wellington, 1981, pp.38–9.

26 John Wybrow, general secretary to LRCs, IBCs and branches, 25 May 1972, copy in the possession of Stan Rodger.

27 Peter Wilson, president, VUW Labour Club to John Wybrow, 28 May 1972, 2004-024-2/08, ATL.

28 *Dominion*, 11 May 1972; Northey, p.361.

29 *Report of the Fifty-sixth Annual Conference*, 1972, pp.50–2.

30 Wellington Labour Representation Committee, 'People, Politics and Participation Study' conference, Sept. 1972; VUW Labour Club, 'Participation or proscription?', Sept. 1972, 2004-024-2/08, ATL.

31 Wellington Divisional Area Council minutes, 17 Aug. 1972, 2007-115-4/4, ATL.

32 *Report of the Fifty-sixth Annual Conference*, 1972, pp.41, 35–6.

33 Ibid., pp.40, 34.

34 Ibid., p.30.

35 Ibid., p.43; Northey, p.61.

36 Northey, p.322.

37 Ibid., pp.386–99, 460.

38 Ibid., p.453.

39 Ibid., p.463.

40 Ibid., p.333.

41 *Report of the Fifty-fifth Annual Conference*, 1971, p.12.

42 *New Zealand Listener*, 29 May 1972; *Report of the Fifty-sixth Annual Conference*, 1972, p.11; Northey, p.332.

43 Northey, pp.452, 475.

44 Horowhenua women's branch minutes, 3 Dec. 1968, 2 Sept. 1969 and annual report 1969, 2006-036/01/1, ATL; agenda for branch meeting, 6 Aug. 1974, 2006-036/04/04, ATL.

45 Tākaka branch minutes, 8 Nov. 1970, 11 Feb. 1973, 89-040-3/14, ATL.

46 Blenheim branch minutes, 28 Oct., 28 July 1970, 2000-150/31/3, ATL.

47 Tākaka branch minutes, 7 June 1971, 89-040-3/14, ATL.

48 Allenton branch minutes, 1 Dec. 1974, 89-040-3/13, ATL.

49 Blenheim branch minutes, 21 May 1973, 21 Apr. 1975, 2000-150-31/03, ATL.

50 *Report of the Fifty-sixth Annual Conference*, 1972, p.13.

51 *Evening Post*, 1 May 1972.

52 New Zealand Labour Party, *1972 Election Manifesto*, 2003-137-5/6, ATL.

53 Jim Eagles and Colin James, *The Making of a New Zealand Prime Minister*, Cheshire Publishing, Wellington, 1973, p.149.

54 *Report of the Fifty-sixth Annual Conference*, 1972, p.13.

55 Eagles and James, p.103.

56 Ibid., p.175; Hayward, *Diary of the Kirk Years*, pp.69–90.

57 Peter Franks, notes of Kirk's speech, 2004-024-2/05, ATL.

58 Eagles and James, pp.202–3, 212.

59 Michael Bassett, *The Third Labour Government: a personal history*, Dunmore Press, Palmerston North, 1976, pp.23–5.

60 Ibid., pp.25–8.

61 Ibid., p.29.

62 Hayward, *Diary of the Kirk Years*, pp.110–25.

63 Bob Tizard interview, 10 May 2014.

64 Hayward, *Diary of the Kirk Years*, pp.133–51.

65 McAloon, *Judgements of All Kinds*, pp.152–3.
66 Bassett, *The Third Labour Government*, pp.54–61.
67 McAloon, *Judgements of All Kinds*, pp.152–3.
68 *Report of the Fifty-seventh Annual Conference held in the Town Hall, Wellington on May 7, 8, 9 & 10, 1973*, pp.17–22; *Report of the Fifty-eighth Annual Conference held in the Town Hall, Wellington on May 13, 14, 15 & 16, 1974*, pp.12–28.
69 *Report of the Fifty-seventh Annual Conference*, 1973, pp.43–5; *Salient*, 30 May 1973.
70 1974 was the first conference for many years where union affiliates had a minority of the voting entitlement: *Report of the Fifty-eighth Annual Conference*, 1974, p.59.
71 Ibid., pp.31–44.
72 McAloon, *Judgements of All Kinds*, pp.154–5.
73 Roger Douglas interview, 16 Apr. 2015.
74 Bassett, *The Third Labour Government*, p.125.
75 Ibid., pp.146–9; Philip Goff, 'Labour and the Unions: the politics of industrial relations under the third Labour Government', MA thesis, University of Auckland, 1979, pp.274–304.
76 Hayward, *Diary of the Kirk Years*, pp.261–5.
77 Ibid., pp.282–305.
78 Don Milne interview, 13 May 2014.
79 David Grant, *The Mighty Totara: the life and times of Norman Kirk*, Random House, Auckland, 2014, pp.437–8.
80 On ohu see Lyman Tower Sargent, 'The ohu movement', *Journal of New Zealand Studies*, Nov. 1996.
81 Bassett, *The Third Labour Government*, pp.164–72.
82 Colin Moyle interview, 5 Mar. 2015.
83 Freer, *A Lifetime in Politics: the memoirs of Warren Freer*, Victoria University Press, Wellington, 2004, pp.199–200; Bob Tizard interview, 10 May 2014.
84 McAloon, *Judgements of All Kinds*, p.155.
85 Bryan Philpott, 'The economy', in Ray Goldstein with Rod Alley (eds), *Labour in Power: promise and performance: evaluations of the work of the New Zealand government from 1972 to 1975*, Price Milburn for New Zealand University Press, Wellington, 1975, p.48.
86 McAloon, *Judgements of All Kinds*, p.151.
87 *Report of the Fifty-ninth Annual Conference held in the Town Hall, Wellington, on May 12, 13, 14, 15 & 165, 1975*, pp.21–2.
88 *Report of the Fifty-ninth Annual Conference*, p.12.
89 Bassett, *The Third Labour Government*, pp.179–94, 230–5. See also Alison McCullough, *Fighting to Choose: the abortion rights struggle in New Zealand*, Victoria University Press, Wellington, 2013.
90 Sonja Davies, *Bread and Roses*, Australia and New Zealand Book Co., Auckland, 1984, p.225.
91 *Report of the Fifty-ninth Annual Conference*, 1975, pp.10–11.
92 *Femina*, 1, July 1975, 94-105-22/04 ATL.
93 Margaret Wilson interview, 24 July 2015.
94 Richard Thompson, 'Race relations' in Goldstein and Alley, p.99.
95 J.L. Hunt and the Labour Party Research Unit (eds), *Labour Leads: policies at work, December 1972–May 1975*, New Zealand Labour Party, May 1975, p.38.
96 Claudia Orange, 'A Kind of Equality: Labour and the Maori people 1935–1949', MA thesis, University of Auckland, 1977, p.223.
97 *NZPD*, vol. 395, 1974 (Matiu Rata), p.5725.

98 Koro Wetere, 'Norman Kirk and Maori', in Margaret Clark (ed.), *Three Labour Leaders: Nordmeyer, Kirk, Rowling*, Dunmore Press, Palmerston North, 2001, p.120.
99 *NZPD*, vol. 395, 1975 (Sir Roy Jack), p.5728.
100 *NZPD*, vol. 401, 1975 (Venn Young), p.4343.
101 Claudia Orange, *An Illustrated History of the Treaty of Waitangi*, Bridget Williams Books, Wellington, 2004, pp.144–9.
102 Bassett, *The Third Labour Government*, pp.259–60.
103 Ibid., pp.261–4.
104 Ibid., p.256.
105 Bob Tizard interview, 10 May 2014.
106 *Report of the Sixtieth Annual Conference held in the Town Hall, Wellington on May 10, 11, 12 & 13, 1976*, pp.9, 16.
107 Bassett, *The Third Labour Government*, p.253.
108 Ibid., pp.294–302.
109 Barry Gustafson, 'Education, health and social welfare' in Goldstein and Alley (eds), pp.67–71.
110 Ibid., pp.76-77.
111 Elizabeth Rowley, 'Housing' in Goldstein and Alley (eds), p.86.
112 Hunt and the Labour Party Research Unit (eds).
113 Bassett, *The Third Labour Government*, p.283.

Chapter 9: Recession, Crisis and Social Tension, 1975–84

1 Steve Maharey interview, 16 July 2015.
2 Phil Goff interview, 21 May 2015.
3 Interview with Mollie Clark, 12 Mar. 1994, OHLC-008773, ATL.
4 New Zealand Labour Party, *Report of the Sixtieth Annual Conference held in the Town Hall, Wellington on May 10, 11, 12 & 13, 1976*, p.3.
5 Peter Franks, *Print and Politics: a history of trade unions in the New Zealand printing industry 1865–1995*, Victoria University Press, Wellington, 2001, pp.205–6.
6 New Zealand Council minutes, 20 Feb., 16 July 1976, 95-229-55/03, ATL.
7 New Zealand Executive minutes, 23 Jan. 1976; New Zealand Council minutes, 28 May 1976, 95-229-55/03, ATL.
8 New Zealand Labour Party, 'A special report from the Labour Party Council', [1979], 94-105-22/04, ATL.
9 John Henderson, *Rowling: the man and the myth*, Australia and New Zealand Book Co. with Fraser Books, Auckland, 1981, p.152.
10 Alan Levett, Geoffrey Palmer, Whetu Rolleston and Margaret Shields, 'Planning for the Labour Party at mid-1976', paper in the possession of Stan Rodger.
11 Henderson, p.167.
12 Ibid., pp.162–5; Geoffrey Palmer, *Reform: a memoir*, Victoria University Press, Wellington, 2013, p.235.
13 Colin Moyle interview, 5 Mar. 2015.
14 Barry Gustafson, *His Way: a biography of Robert Muldoon*, Auckland University Press, Auckland, 2000, p.201.
15 Henderson, p.165.
16 Stan Rodger interview, 11 Aug. 2014.
17 Ibid.
18 *Report of the Sixty-first Annual Conference*, 1977, p.21.

19 Ibid., p.25.
20 Henderson, p.187.
21 New Zealand Labour Party, *Constitution and Rules*, revised edn, 1979, New Zealand Labour Party, Wellington, p.3.
22 *Report of the Sixty-third Annual Conference held in the Town Hall, Wellington on May 14, 15, 16 & 17 1979*, p.11.
23 *Constitution and Rules*, 2014, p.4.
24 *Report of the Sixtieth Annual Conference*, 1976, pp.32, 53–4; *Report of the Sixty-first Annual Conference*, 1977, p.27.
25 *Report of the Sixty-second Annual Conference held in the Town Hall, Wellington on May 8, 9, 10, 11 & 12 1978*, p.18.
26 Ibid., p.33.
27 Ibid., p.22.
28 Henderson, p.176.
29 Ibid., p.177.
30 Clifford Norton, *New Zealand Parliamentary Election Results 1946–1987*, occasional publication no.1, Department of Political Science, Victoria University of Wellington, 1988, p.6.
31 'Report on NZ Council seminar addressed by Professor R.M. Chapman, September 1979', 96-164-04/2, ATL.
32 *Report of the Sixty-third Annual Conference*, 1979, p.16.
33 Helen Clark interview, 11 Aug. 2015.
34 *New Nation*, Oct. 1980.
35 *Report of the Sixty-fourth Annual Conference held in the Town Hall, Wellington on May 12, 13, 14 & 15 1980*, p.10.
36 Interview with Dave Vallely, 25 Oct. 1991, OHLC-004237, ATL.
37 Pete Hodgson interview, 9 July 2015.
38 New Zealand Labour Party, 'Electorate and branch membership', Dec. 1979, 96-164-04/2, ATL.
39 *Report of the Sixty-fourth Annual Conference*, 1980, pp.18–19.
40 Hastings Women's branch minutes, 4 June 1980, 89-040-3/11, ATL.
41 Joan Caulfield interview, 25 May 2015.
42 Jon Fraenkel, 'Pacific Islands and New Zealand: immigration and aid', Te Ara—the Encyclopedia of New Zealand, www.TeAra.govt.nz/en/pacific-islands-and-new-zealand/page2.
43 *Report of the Sixty-third Annual Conference*, 1979, p.45.
44 Ibid., pp.56, 45.
45 *Report of the Sixtieth Annual Conference*, 1976, p.26; *Dominion*, 21 Jan. 1977.
46 'Joint Council of Labour—July 27, 1976, notes on issues to be discussed', MS-Papers-4100-22/02/2, ATL.
47 *Report of the Sixty-fourth Annual Conference*, 1980, pp.7, 37; *Report of the Sixty-fifth Annual Conference held in the Town Hall, Wellington on May 11, 12, 13 & 14, 1981*, p.28.
48 *Report of the Sixty-third Annual Conference*, 1979, p.18.
49 Ibid., pp.20, 42–3.
50 Jim McAloon, *Judgements of All Kinds: economic policy-making in New Zealand 1945–1984*, Victoria University Press, Wellington, 2013, pp.174–5.
51 Henderson, pp.13–14.
52 Russell Marshall, 'Rowling as prime minister and leader of the opposition 1974–83', in Margaret Clark (ed.), *Three Labour Leaders: Nordmeyer, Kirk, Rowling*, Dunmore Press,

Palmerston North, p.186.

53 *Report of the Sixty-third Annual Conference*, 1979, p.41.

54 'Interim Report for Northern Maori by-election for NZ Executive meeting, 13 June 1980', 96-164-04/2, ATL.

55 Roger Douglas and Louise Callan, *Toward Prosperity*, David Bateman, Auckland, 1987, pp.13–19.

56 Marshall, p.187.

57 Henderson, p.15.

58 Michael Bassett, *Working with David: inside the Lange cabinet*, Hodder Moa, Auckland, 2008, p.54.

59 *Evening Post*, 8 Dec. 1980.

60 Bassett, *Working with David*, pp.55–6.

61 Henderson, pp.18–20; *Evening Post*, 12 Dec. 1980.

62 Henderson, pp.24–5.

63 *Evening Post*, 12 Dec. 1980; New Zealand Council minutes, 19 Dec. 1980, 96-164-04/2, ATL.

64 *Report of the Sixty-fifth Annual Conference*, 1981, pp.7, 11.

65 Ibid., pp.15, 41, 53–4.

66 Hugh Oliver, 'The Labour caucus and economic policy formation, 1981–1984,' in Brian Easton (ed.), *The Making of Rogernomics*, Auckland University Press, Auckland, 1989, p.24.

67 Douglas and Callan, pp.25–7; David Lange, *My Life*, Viking, Auckland, 2005, pp.142–3.

68 Geoff Chapple, *1981: the tour*, A.H. & A.W. Reed, Wellington, 1984.

69 *Report of the Sixty-sixth Annual Conference held in the Town Hall, Wellington on May 10, 11, 12, & 13, 1982*, p.4.

70 Ibid., p.39.

71 Norton, p.6.

72 *Report of the Sixty-sixth Annual Conference*, 1982, pp.5, 36.

73 New Zealand Federation of Labour, *Minutes and Report of the Proceedings of the Forty-fifth Annual Conference held in the Town Hall, Wellington, on May 4, 5, 6 and 7, 1982*, p.26. He made similar comments in his speech to the party conference the following week.

74 Oliver, pp.24–9.

75 *Report of the Sixty-sixth Annual Conference*, 1982, p.2.

76 Aro Valley branch minutes, 27 May 1982, MSY-2396, ATL.

77 *Unity*, 19 May 1982.

78 Ray Markey, 'Troubled times: 1967–88', in Peter Franks and Melanie Nolan (eds), *Unions in Common Cause: the New Zealand Federation of Labour 1938–88*, Steele Roberts, Wellington, 2011, pp.145–81.

79 *Report of the Sixty-sixth Annual Conference*, 1982, pp.22–6.

80 Ibid., pp.18–26.

81 Bassett, *Working with David*, pp.76–82.

82 Marshall, pp.189–90.

83 Fraser Geary, 'Yes—I'm the great pretender: a socialist critique of David Lange', *Caucus*, Apr. 1983.

84 *Labour Network*, 1, Dec./Jan. 1982/83.

85 Draft letter to John Stewart, editor, *New Zealand Monthly Review*, folder 1, MSS & Archives 89/1, UAL.

86 Circular letter to ARC delegates from *Labour Network*, 5 Aug. 1983, folder 6, MSS & Archives 89/1, UAL.

87 'Appendix A', folder 1, MSS & Archives 89/1, UAL; Roger Douglas interview, 16 Apr. 2015.

88 *Labour Network*, Sept./Oct. 1983.
89 *Dominion*, 30 Aug. 1983.
90 *Report of the Sixty-seventh Annual Conference held at Trillos Downtown, Auckland, September 2, 3, 4, & 5, 1983*, p.20.
91 Ibid., pp.4–5.
92 Ibid., pp.29–30.
93 *Unity*, 25 May 1983.
94 *Report of the Sixty-seventh Annual Conference*, 1983, pp.23, 25.
95 Ibid., p.54.
96 McAloon, *Judgements of All Kinds*, pp.185–98.
97 Oliver, pp.11, 31–5.
98 Ibid., p.13.
99 Ibid., pp.16–21.
100 Ibid., pp.37–43.
101 Ibid., pp.43–4.
102 'The Labour Party's proposals for its economic strategy election 1984, memorandum from the Research Office to National Executive', 31 Jan. 1984, 95-050-14, ATL.
103 Ken Douglas, 'What were the real issues?', in Margaret Clark (ed.), *For the Record: Lange and the fourth Labour government*, Dunmore Publishing, Wellington, 2005, pp.80–1.
104 Ken Douglas to John Wybrow, 13 Feb. 1984, 95-050-14, ATL.
105 'Economic policy—trade union concerns', 16 Feb. 1984, 97-114-36/05, ATL; Joint Council of Labour minutes, 22 Feb. 1984, 95-050-13, ATL.
106 Oliver, p.48.
107 John Wybrow to Ken Douglas, 30 Apr. 1984; Douglas to Wybrow, 7 June 1984, 95-050-13, ATL.
108 Oliver, p.46; Joint Council of Labour minutes, 26 June 1984, 95-050-13, ATL.
109 Oliver, p.49.
110 Trade Union/Labour Party Liaison Committee, 'Report on 1984 campaign', 95-050-14, ATL; *Labour Network*, Spring 1984; *Unity*, 1 Aug. 1984.
111 Sam Jennings, general secretary, New Zealand Waterside Workers' Federation to Ken Douglas, 31 July 1984; Peter Cullen, general secretary, Wellington District Hotel, Hospital, Restaurant and Related Trades Employees' Union to Mike Smith, 7 Aug. 1984, 95-050-14, ATL.
112 *Report of the Victory Conference 1984*, held in the Michael Fowler Centre, Wellington, 8, 9 and 10 September 1984, p. 9.

Chapter 10: Labour and Neo-liberalism, 1984–93

1 This list, drawn from G.A. Wood, *Ministers and Members in the New Zealand Parliament*, University of Otago Press, Dunedin, 1996, p.66, omits some minor portfolios.
2 Colin James, *The Quiet Revolution: turbulence and transition in contemporary New Zealand*, Allen & Unwin, Wellington, 1986; Colin James, *New Territory: the transformation of New Zealand*, Bridget Williams Books, Wellington, 1992.
3 Michael Bassett and Judith Bassett, *Roderick Deane: his life and times*, Viking, Auckland, 2006, pp.110–19, quote at p.110.
4 Colin James and Nikitin Sallee, 'Lange's hands still steady two years further on', *National Business Review*, 11 July 1986, quoted James, *New Territory*, p.149. Jane Kelsey has made a similar suggestion: that 'without the exchange crisis of July 1984 … [t]he country's economic problems would have been subject to more leisurely assessment, and a more

pragmatic response would probably have been endorsed': Kelsey, *The New Zealand Experiment: a world model for structural adjustment?*, Auckland University Press/Bridget Williams Books, Auckland, 1997, pp.348–9.

5 Michael Bassett, *Working with David: inside the Lange cabinet*, Hodder Moa, Auckland, 2008, p.113 notes the initial approach.

6 Jim McAloon, *Judgements of All Kinds: economic policy-making in New Zealand 1945–1984*, Victoria University Press, Wellington, 2013, p.200.

7 Paul Dalziel, 'The 1984 economic summit conference: a search for policy objectives', *New Zealand Economic Papers*, 20, 1986, pp.45, 50. Suggestions that 'traditionalists' within the labour movement viewed Muldoon with a degree of nostalgia are unfounded. Jim Knox's speech to the summit was a scathing indictment of Muldoon, in terms with which no member of the Labour cabinet could have disagreed: Economic Summit Conference, *Proceedings and Conference Papers*, vol.1, 1984, pp.43–8.

8 Douglas's observation is quoted by Paul Dalziel, 'The economic summit: what people were thinking', in Brian Easton (ed.), *The Making of Rogernomics*, Auckland University Press, Auckland, 1989, p.53.

9 The seminars are emphasised by both Judy Keall and Margaret Austin: Margaret Hayward, 'Prime Ministerial Leadership in New Zealand During a Time of Change', PhD thesis, Victoria University of Wellington, 2004, pp.156–7.

10 Budget notes in Bassett, *Working with David*, pp.121–6.

11 Ibid., p.120

12 Ibid., pp.143–4 for Caygill's remark.

13 Brian Easton, 'From run to float: the making of the Rogernomics exchange rate policy', in Easton, *The Making of Rogernomics*.

14 John Martin, 'Remaking the state services', in Martin Holland and Jonathan Boston (eds), *The Fourth Labour Government*, second edn, Oxford University Press, Auckland, 1990, p.125.

15 Ibid., pp.125, 127, 124.

16 Ibid., p.135; Gary Hawke, 'Bliss at dawn: social policy in the first term of the Lange government', in Margaret Clark (ed.), *For the Record: Lange and the fourth Labour government*, Dunmore Publishing, Palmerston North, 2005, pp.101–2, suggests support.

17 Pat Walsh, 'A family fight? Industrial relations reform under the fourth Labour government', in Easton, *The Making of Rogernomics*, p.156; see also pp.159–60.

18 Ibid., p.160.

19 Bassett, *Working with David*, pp.130–4.

20 *AJHR*, 1988 G-39.

21 Hilary Stace, 'Labour owes us: the 1984 women's forums', in Clark (ed.), *For the Record*, pp.127, 128.

22 Alison J. Laurie, 'Introduction', in Alison J. Laurie and Linda Evans (eds), *Twenty Years On: histories of homosexual law reform in New Zealand*, Lesbian and Gay Archives of New Zealand, Wellington, 2009, pp.16–19.

23 Ibid., p.19.

24 The three were George Gair, Ian McLean and Katherine O'Regan. O'Regan would take over the human rights reform after Labour's defeat in 1990. Even the professed libertarian Ruth Richardson voted against the third reading, as did most so-called liberal National MPs, like Philip Burdon. The Labour noes were Fraser Colman, Stan Rodger, Peter Tapsell, John Terris, Whetū Tirikātene-Sullivan, Allan Wallbank, Trevor Young and Braybrooke. Some of the noes on both sides might have supported a differential age of consent, or said they would have. The final vote is in *NZPD*, vol.472, 1986, p.2580.

25 Bassett, *Working With David*, pp.135–6.
26 John Henderson, 'The warrior peacenik: setting the record straight on ANZUS and the Fiji coup', in Clark (ed.), *For the Record*, p.138.
27 Merwyn Norrish, 'The Lange government's foreign policy', in Clark (ed.), *For the Record*, p.151.
28 David Lange, *My Life*, Viking, Auckland, 2005, p.177, 189.
29 Ibid., p.193.
30 Ibid., p.204; the general account relies on Geoffrey Palmer, *Reform: a memoir*, Victoria University Press, Wellington, 2013, pp.468–73.
31 Lange, p.205.
32 Ibid., p.206.
33 Ibid., p.208. For the misgivings see, for example, Bruce Brown, 'The great debate at the Oxford Union', in Clark (ed.), *For the Record*.
34 Lange, quoted in Jon Johansson, *Two Titans: Muldoon, Lange and leadership*, Dunmore Publishing, Palmerston North, 2005, p.149.
35 Palmer, pp.474–5.
36 Tony Reid, 'Committed to change', *New Zealand Listener*, 25 Apr. 1987, pp.16–18. We are grateful to Charlotte Macdonald for this reference. See also Margaret Wilson, *Labour in Government, 1984–87*, Allen & Unwin/Port Nicholson Press, Wellington, 1989, p.84.
37 Wilson, p.84; Geoffrey Palmer interview, 12 June 2015.
38 Wilson, p.76; Bassett, *Working With David*, p.171.
39 Mark Gosche interview, 16 Apr. 2015; see also John C. Weaver, '"Deep in the heart of taxes": fourth Labour, the GST and fiscal reconstruction, 1981–1986', *New Zealand Journal of History*, 49 (2), Oct. 2015.
40 'Message from the president', 15 July 1985, 1985 conference papers, Labour Party archive, New Zealand Labour Party head office.
41 'Debate on economic policy', p.58, 1985 conference papers, Labour Party archive.
42 President's address, 1985 conference papers, Labour Party archive.
43 Simon Sheppard, *Broken Circle: the decline and fall of the fourth Labour government*, PSL Press, Wellington, 1999, pp.23–5.
44 President's address, 1985 conference papers, Labour Party archive.
45 Parliamentary Labour Party Report, 1985 conference papers, Labour Party archive.
46 Michael Bassett, 'Cabinet making: cabinet breaking', in Clark (ed.), *For the Record*, p.40 describes Wilson's idea of the party as 'quite close to Lenin's'. This is a libel on both Lenin and Wilson.
47 'Debate on economic policy', p.25.
48 Candidate biographies, 1986 conference papers, Labour Party archive. The candidate in question was Chris Trotter.
49 Manawatū/Rangitīkei regional representative, report for New Zealand Council, 15 Nov. 1985, Labour Party archive.
50 Murdo Macmillan, memo to New Zealand Council, 11 Feb. 1987, Labour Party archive; Murdo Macmillan, assistant general secretary, memo to Rob Allen: 'A paper on matters relating to the review of party structures as decided at the 1995 annual conference', n.d., 2006-253-5/09, ATL.
51 Waikato regional organiser, report for New Zealand Council, 15 Nov. 1985, Labour Party archive.
52 Auckland Regional Organiser, report for New Zealand Council, 15 Nov. 1985, Labour Party archive.
53 1986 conference papers, p.49; report for New Zealand Council, 15 Nov. 1985. See also Peter

Franks, 'Knox, Walter James', from *The Dictionary of New Zealand Biography*, Te Ara—the Encyclopedia of New Zealand, http://www.TeAra.govt.nz/en/biographies/5k13/knox-walter-james.

54 1986 conference papers, pp.24, 25, Labour Party archive.

55 Ibid., p.52.

56 Bassett, *Working with David*, p.247. Douglas on the political convenience of debt is quoted in Jane Kelsey, *The New Zealand Experiment: a world model for structural adjustment?*, Auckland University Press/Bridget Williams Books, Auckland, 1995, p.136.

57 Bassett, *Working with David*, p.247.

58 Ibid., pp.247–8.

59 Quoted in ibid., p.252.

60 Roger Douglas interview, 16 Apr. 2015.

61 Lange, p.230; Bassett, *Working with David*, pp.216–19.

62 Bassett, ibid., p.254 notes these selections in his inimitable style.

63 Ibid., pp.268–73; Lange, p.241, also pp.230, 240.

64 Chapman, 'A political culture under pressure', in Elizabeth McLeay (ed.), *New Zealand Politics and Social Patterns: selected works by Robert Chapman*, Victoria University Press, Wellington, 1999, pp.337–8.

65 Bassett, *Working with David*, 277–85.

66 Lange, p.245 on the cabinet.

67 Bassett, *Working with David*, p.308.

68 Kelsey, p.57.

69 Bassett, *Working with David*, pp.302–19.

70 Ibid., pp 328–32; Lange, p.247. Bassett perhaps fudges the status of the package, but Lange was not alone in his view. Compare Bassett, *Working with David*, pp.336 and 354. See also Malcolm McKinnon, *Treasury: the New Zealand Treasury, 1840–2000*, Auckland University Press, Auckland, 2003, p.337 and Sheppard, pp.45–8.

71 Lange, p.248.

72 Bassett, *Working with David*, pp.333–53. See also Roger Douglas interview; Lange, p.249.

73 The minister was David Caygill: Sheppard, p.61.

74 Bassett, *Working with David*, chs 12 and 13. Lange could be hypersensitive to criticism: in the 1990s he pursued the author of another piece, Joe Atkinson, with defamation proceedings. Jesson's article was 'Changing the world and losing a soul: the public tragedy of David Lange', *Metro*, Dec. 1987.

75 Budget 1988, *AJHR*, 1988, B-6, pp.13–14.

76 Caygill interview, 29 May 2015.

77 Kelsey, ch.12.

78 In 1986 Lange had referred to party traditionalists as 'economic neanderthals' with views little different from Muldoon's: see McKinnon, p.331.

79 Bassett, *Working with David*, pp.430–5, 445–55.

80 McKinnon, p.342.

81 Milton Friedman, 'The role of monetary policy', *American Economic Review*, 58 (1), Feb. 1968, pp.1–17, quote at p.13. See also John Singleton et al., *Innovation and Independence: the Reserve Bank of New Zealand 1973–2002*, Auckland University Press, Auckland, 2006.

82 See, for instance, Matthewson to Policy Council, 23 Dec. 1988; Timms to New Zealand Council, 22 Dec. 1988, in the authors' possession.

83 Wellington Amalgamated Watersiders' Union to general secretary, 11 Feb. 1988, in papers for New Zealand Council meeting, 19 Feb. 1988, Labour Party archive.

84 Joanna Tennant to general secretary, 19 Dec. 1987, in papers for New Zealand Council

meeting, 19 Feb. 1988. Tennant made it clear she would, out of loyalty, not go public.
85 South Island regional organiser for New Zealand Council, 27 May 1988, Labour Party archives.
86 IMRC Business House Canvass Report to New Zealand Council, 11 Nov. 1988, Labour Party archive.
87 Athol Lawrence, Area 5 representative, New Zealand Council, 29 July 1988, Labour Party archive.
88 Anderton and Sutherland to Timms, 18 Feb. 1988, in the authors' possession.
89 Austin to Anderton, 13 Dec. 1988; Anderton to Dyson, 13 Dec. 1988; Anderton to Lange, 15 Dec. 1988; Dyson to New Zealand Council, 24 Dec. 1988; Anderton to Dyson, 10 Jan. 1989; 'Opinion from Rt Hon Geoffrey Palmer, 15 Dec 1988', in the authors' possession.
90 Affiliates Council report to New Zealand Council, 25 May 1989, Labour Party archive.
91 Bassett is one minister who notes, in *Working with David*, p.493, that Lange had at that point just achieved the length of service necessary for maximum pension entitlement. Lange's health was also less good than it had been.
92 Helen Clark interview, 11 Aug. 2011.
93 Palmer to Henry Lang, 16 Sept. 1990, Lang papers, ATL.
94 Palmer, p.523.
95 Annual conference 1989 report, pp.25–6, Labour Party archive.
96 Palmer, pp.525–6; Raymond Richards, *Palmer: the parliamentary years*, Canterbury University Press, Christchurch, 2010, p.364.
97 Margaret Hayward, 'Prime Ministerial Leadership', pp.186–7; Palmer, p.527; Richards, pp.371–2, 380–1.
98 Palmer, quoted in Hayward, 'Prime Ministerial Leadership', p.184.
99 Discussed in Michael Bassett, *The Mother of All Departments: the history of the Department of Internal Affairs*, Auckland University Press, Auckland, 1997, ch.10.
100 *Dominion Post*, 19 Sept. 2015, p.C3.
101 As was rather unkindly pointed out by Richard Long, 'Labour conference lurches into dreamworld', *Dominion*, 12 Nov. 1990, p.2.
102 Bassett, *Working with David*, p.406.
103 Hayward, 'Prime Ministerial Leadership', p.209.
104 New Zealand Council, 8 Feb. 1991, Labour Party archive.
105 General secretary to New Zealand Council, 28 Feb. 1992, Labour Party archive.
106 General secretary to New Zealand Council, 22 June 1993, Labour Party archive.

Chapter 11: Rebuilding Social Democracy in a New Globalisation: The Clark Years, 1993–2008

1 1992 review of the party quoted in Rob Allen, 'Report on the New Zealand Labour Party position and state of play', 15 Nov. 1995, Labour Party archive, New Zealand Labour Party head office.
2 Seishi Gomibuchi, 'Followers and Leadership Durability: an analysis of leadership support in the New Zealand Labour Party', PhD thesis, University of Canterbury, 2001, pp.116–28.
3 Ibid., pp.107–9.
4 Ibid., pp.140–4; Maryan Street interview, 8 Aug. 2015.
5 Gomibuchi, pp.80–1.
6 Maryan Street to Mike Moore, 27 Nov. 1993; Moore to Street, 27 Nov. 1993, in the possession of Maryan Street.
7 Gomibuchi, pp.82–5.

8 Ibid., p.86; Moore to Street, undated fax, in the possession of Maryan Street.
9 Gomibuchi, pp.88–9.
10 Maryan Street interview.
11 Phil Goff interview, 21 May 2015.
12 Maryan Street interview.
13 Gomibuchi, pp.170–2.
14 Michael Gibbs, 'The Selwyn by-election', research paper, Victoria University of Wellington, 1994, 2003-24429, ATL.
15 New Zealand Labour Party, *A Working Future: New Zealand Labour Party 78th annual conference Report, 25–27 November 1994, Indian Cultural Centre, Kemp Street, Kilbirnie, Wellington*, p.9.
16 Ibid., p.29.
17 Gomibuchi, pp.176–82.
18 *Conference Report: New Zealand Labour Party 79th annual conference 17 to 19 November 1995, Ellerslie Convention Centre, Morrin Street, Ellerslie, Auckland*, pp.43–3.
19 *New Heart, New Hope, New Zealand: congress report, New Zealand Labour Party, 80th annual congress 24 to 26 May 1996, Quality Hotel, Willis Street, Wellington*, pp.7-8.
20 Gomibuchi, pp.187–92.
21 New Zealand Council minutes, 11 June 1995, Labour Party archive.
22 Trevor Mallard interview, 23 June, 12 Aug., 20 Oct. 2015.
23 Gomibuchi, pp.193–205.
24 Helen Clark to Wellington Central Labour Campaign Committee, 27 June 1996, Peter Franks files.
25 Helen Clark interview, 11 Aug. 2015.
26 Ruth Laugeson, 'A media perspective on the 1996 election campaign', in Jonathan Boston, Elizabeth McLeay and Nigel S. Roberts (eds), *From Campaign to Coalition: the 1996 MMP election*, Dunmore Press, Palmerston North, 1997, p.71.
27 Pete Hodgson interview, 9 July 2015.
28 Peter Aimer, 'Leaders and outcomes: the Clark factor in 1996', in Boston, McLeay and Roberts (eds), p.134.
29 Boston, McLeay and Roberts (eds), p.10.
30 Pete Hodgson interview, 9 July 2015.
31 Helen Clark interview.
32 *New Zealand Labour Party 1997 Annual Conference Report: 81st annual conference, 21 to 23 November 1997, Christchurch Convention Centre, Kilmore Street, Christchurch*, p.7.
33 Ibid., pp.5, 29, 70.
34 Ibid., pp.10–17.
35 *New Zealand Labour Party Conference Report 1998*, pp.10–12.
36 Helen Clark interview.
37 Jim Anderton interview, 28 May 2015.
38 Jonathan Boston and Stephen Church, 'Pre-election wheeling and dealing: the New Zealand experience', in Jonathan Boston, Stephen Church, Stephen Levine, Elizabeth McLeay and Nigel S. Roberts (eds), *Left Turn: the New Zealand general election of 1999*, Victoria University Press, Wellington, 2000, pp.233–5.
39 *New Zealand Labour Party Congress Report 1999*, pp.25–6.
40 'Introduction', in Boston, Church, Levine, McLeay and Roberts (eds), p.10.
41 O'Regan lost to Peters by 63 votes.
42 Jonathan Boston, 'Forming the coalition between Labour and the Alliance', in Boston, Church, Levine, McLeay and Roberts (eds), pp.239–70.

43 *Government Achievements 2000–2001*, New Zealand Government, Wellington, 2002, p.2, 7–8, 32.
44 Helen Clark, 'Speech from the throne', 21 Dec. 1999, at www.beehive.govt.nz.
45 Peter Aimer, 'Polls that count: from one election to the next', in Jack Vowles, Peter Aimer, Susan Banducci, Jeffrey Kemp and Raymond Miller (eds), *Voters' Veto: the 2002 election in New Zealand and the consolidation of minority government*, Auckland University Press, Auckland, 2004, pp.5–6.
46 Address by Helen Clark to the 2000 Labour Party conference, 18 Nov., Peter Franks files.
47 'Implementing a progressive agenda after fifteen years of neo-liberalism: the New Zealand experience', address to the London School of Economics, 21 Feb. 2002, 2006-253-8/04, ATL.
48 Helen Clark, Address to seminar on social policy, 1 July 2002, Peter Franks files.
49 Address to the 2003 Labour Party conference, 10 Nov., MS-Papers-11694-34, ATL.
50 Nanaia Mahuta interview, 24 Sept. 2015.
51 Address to the 2000 Labour Party conference, 18 Nov.
52 Address to the 2003 Labour Party conference, 10 Nov.
53 *Dominion*, 30 Nov. 2001; *New Zealand Labour Party Conference 2001 Report, held in the Bruce Mason Centre, Takapuna, Auckland on Friday 30th November and Saturday 1st and Sunday 2nd December 2001*, p.133, Labour Party archive.
54 Transcript of Radio New Zealand, 'Focus on Politics', 2001 annual conference file, Labour Party archive.
55 *New Zealand Herald*, 3 Dec. 2001.
56 Aimer, pp.9–11.
57 Jim Anderton interview.
58 *Government Achievements 2000–2001*, p.2; *Sunday Star-Times*, 21 July 2002.
59 *Government Achievements 2000–2001*, pp.18–21.
60 Ibid., pp.13–15, 23.
61 Ibid., pp.4, 10; Jim Anderton interview.
62 *Government Achievements 2000–2001*, pp.30–1.
63 Aimer, pp.13–14.
64 Jack Vowles, 'Estimating change during the campaign', in Vowles, Aimer, Banducci, Kemp and Miller (eds), p.36.
65 Mike Williams, 'Oddity or new paradigm: a Labour view of the 2002 election', in Boston, Church, Levine, McLeay and Roberts (eds), p.108.
66 Vowles, p.37.
67 Stephen Levine and Nigel S. Roberts, 'New Zealand votes: an overview', in Boston, Church, Levine, McLeay and Roberts (ed), pp.21, 26.
68 Levine and Roberts, 'Consistent patterns and clear trends: electoral behaviour in 2002', in ibid., p.329.
69 Jonathan Boston and Stephen Church, 'Government formation after the 2002 election', in ibid., p.333.
70 Address by Helen Clark to the 2003 Labour Party conference, 8 Nov., MS-Papers-11694-34, ATL.
71 Margaret Wilson interview, 24 July 2015.
72 Dennis Welch, *Helen Clark: a political life*, Penguin Books, Auckland, 2009, p.184.
73 Brett de Malmanche, '"Events, my dear boy": the political scene 2002–2005', in Stephen Levine and Nigel S. Roberts (eds), *The Baubles of Office: the New Zealand general election of 2005*, Victoria University Press, Wellington, 2007, p.565.
74 Maryan Street interview, 8 Aug. 2015; *Dominion Post*, 11 Nov. 2003.

75 New Zealand Council Report to the 2006 Labour Party conference, Labour Party archive.
76 *Dominion Post*, 29 Nov. 2003.
77 Stephen Levine and Nigel S. Roberts, 'The baubles of office: winning and losing under MMP', in Levine and Roberts (eds), *The Baubles of Office*, p.24.
78 Nanaia Mahuta interview.
79 De Malmanche, in Levine and Roberts (eds.), *The Baubles of Office*, p.554.
80 Address by Michael Cullen to the 2004 Labour Party conference, 15 Nov., MS-Papers-11694-34, ATL.
81 New Zealand Council report to the 2004 Labour Party conference, MS-Papers-11694-34, ATL.
82 Nanaia Mahuta interview.
83 *NZPD*, vol.617, 2004, p.13385.
84 *NZPD*, vol.624, 2005, p.20737.
85 *Press*, 13 Aug. 2005.
86 *New Zealand Herald*, 16 July 2005.
87 Colin James, 'A contest of values or a contest of wills? Factors and issues in the 2005 election', in Levine and Roberts (eds), *The Baubles of Office*, p.50.
88 *Dominion Post*, 19 Aug. 2005.
89 James, 'A context of values', p.52.
90 Ibid.
91 Steve Maharey, 'Labour: an historic third term', in Levine and Roberts (eds), *The Baubles of Office*, p.102.
92 Levine and Roberts, 'The Baubles of Office', p.47.
93 Jonathan Boston, 'An unusual government: coalition politics and inter-party arrangements following the 2005 election', in Levine and Roberts (eds), *The Baubles of Office*, pp.389–407.
94 James, 'A contest of values', pp.57–8.
95 David Capie, 'Gone by lunchtime: New Zealand's foreign policy consensus and the 2005 election', in Levine and Roberts (eds), *The Baubles of Office*, pp.318–26.
96 *New Zealand Herald*, 12 Oct. 2006.
97 New Zealand Council report to the 2006 Labour Party conference, Labour Party archive.
98 2006 and 2007 annual conference files, Labour Party archive; New Zealand Council report to the 2007 annual conference, MS-Papers-11694-40, ATL.
99 Colin James, '2008: the last baby-boomer election', in Stephen Levine and Nigel S. Roberts (eds), *Key to Victory: the New Zealand general election of 2008*, Victoria University Press, Wellington, 2010, p.44.
100 Ibid.
101 Claire Robinson, '2008: images of political leadership', in Levine and Roberts (eds), *Key to Victory*, p.141.
102 Prime minister's announcement of the 2008 general election, 12 Sept. 2008, Peter Franks files.
103 Address by Helen Clark to the 2007 Labour Party conference, 4 Nov. 2007, MS-Papers-11694-40, ATL.
104 James, '2008: the last baby-boomer election', p.50.
105 Stephen Levine and Nigel S. Roberts, '2008: key to victory' in Levine and Roberts (eds), *Key to Victory*, p.33.
106 Ibid., p.26.
107 Michael Cullen, Valedictory statement, 29 Apr. 2008, *NZPD*, vol.653, 2008, p.2740.
108 Inland Revenue and Ministry of Social Development, *Changing Families' Financial Support and Incentives for Working: the summary report of the evaluation of the Working for Families*

package, Centre for Social Research and Evaluation, Inland Revenue, 2010, p.viii.
109 Adrian Rurawhe interview, 17 Sept. 2015; Nanaia Mahuta interview.
110 Michael Cullen interview, 27 May 2015.
111 In 2014 Police Commissioner Mike Bush apologised to Tūhoe.
112 Michael Cullen interview.
113 New Zealand Labour Party head office.
114 New Zealand Council report to the 2009 Labour Party conference, MS-Papers-11694-40, ATL.
115 By 2014 Labour had seven affiliated unions: the Engineering, Printing and Manufacturing Union, the Service and Food Workers' Union, the Meat Workers' Union, the Rail and Maritime Transport Union, the Dairy Workers' Union, the Maritime Union and the Central Amalgamated Workers' Union.
116 Jim Anderton interview.

Chapter 12: A Painful Transition? Opposition, 2008–16

1 *New Zealand Herald*, 11 Nov. 2008.
2 *Press*, 22 Nov. 2008, p.19.
3 Colin James, 'Labour's big win: hard thinking for Kohn Key', http://www.colinjames.co.nz/2009/06/15/labours-big-win-hard-thinking-for-john-key/.
4 Jennifer Lees-Marshment, 'Political marketing and governance', in Jon Johansson and Stephen Levine (eds), *Kicking the Tyres: the New Zealand general election and electoral referendum of 2011*, Victoria University Press, 2012, p.186.
5 Phil Goff, 'Goff: Grey Power Palmerston North', speech, 29 Nov. 2009, www.scoop.co.nz; Patrick Gower, 'Goff faces grilling on seabed speech', *New Zealand Herald*, 7 Dec. 2009.
6 Brian Edwards, 'A dissenting view on Chris Carter's expulsion from the Labour Party', www.brianedwardsmedia.co.nz, 12 Dec. 2010; Vernon Small, 'Chris Carter suspended from caucus', www.stuff.co.nz, 20 Oct. 2010; Audrey Young, 'Suspended MP Chris Carter unbalanced—Mallard', *New Zealand Herald*, 30 July 2010; Chris Trotter, 'Chris Carter Q+A', www.bowalleyroad.blogspot.co.nz, 30 July 2010.
7 Grant Robertson, 'Labour', in Johansson and Levine (eds), p.131.
8 Johansson and Levine, 'Making New Zealand a better country?', in Johansson and Levine (eds), pp.57, 52.
9 Robertson, in Johansson and Levine (eds), p.130; Lees-Marshment, ibid, pp.187–8.
10 One author recalls driving his elderly mother along the Petone foreshore during that campaign: she looked at this billboard and said, 'I don't know what that means.'
11 Colin James, 'On a wing and a smile', in Johansson and Levine (eds), p.75.
12 We do not suggest that partial privatisation should have been meekly accepted.
13 Guyon Espiner, 'The courage born of desperation', *North & South*, Dec. 2011.
14 James, 'On a wing and a smile', p.74.
15 As both Steven Joyce and Grant Robertson say in their contributions to Johansson and Levine (eds), pp.124, 132; see also Lees-Marshment, p.187.
16 This paragraph draws on James, 'On a wing and a smile'.
17 Labour's Organisational Review 2012: summary of recommendations; recommendations agreed by New Zealand Council, July 2012, in papers relating to New Zealand Labour Party annual conference, MS-Papers-11694-49, ATL.
18 *Herald on Sunday*, 18 Nov. 2012.
19 Adopting the name of the party's former newspaper was unfortunate. Despite advice that the *Standard* was the Labour Party's newspaper, the founders of the website say: 'The

Standard … was founded by labour movement activists in the 1930s': the *Standard*.org.nz/About.

20 Tracy Watkins, Kate Chapman and Vernon Small, 'Labour leadership vote tomorrow', www.stuff.co.nz, 19 Nov. 2012; 'Gordon Campbell on the Labour Party ructions', www.scoop.co.nz, 19 Nov. 2012; for example, *Dominon Post*, 16 Nov. 2012, editorial.

21 *New Zealand Herald*, 16 Nov. 2012, pp.A12–13; 19 Nov. 2012, p.A9.

Anecdotally the authors are aware of several such returning members.

22 Tracy Watkins, Michael Fox and Angela Vance, 'Cunliffe wins Labour leadership', www.stuff.co.nz, 15 Sept. 2013.

23 Steve Kilgallon and Simon Day, 'Cunliffe: I work as hard as anyone', www.stuff.co.nz, 20 July 2014; Tracy Watkins, 'I'm working my butt off—Cunliffe', www.stuff.co.nz, 21 July 2014.

24 This is the personal observation of the authors.

25 Claire Trevett, 'Cuncliffe comes clean over donations', *New Zealand Herald*, 4 Mar. 2014; Stephen Levine, 'Moments of truth: the 2014 New Zealand general election', in Stephen Levine and Jon Johansson (eds), *Moments of Truth: the New Zealand general election of 2014*, Victoria University Press, Wellington, 2015, p.40.

26 Frank Macskasy, 'Dirty politics exclusive: the Donghua Liu affair: one year on', www.thedailyblog.co.nz, 10 July 2015; John Armstrong, 'Cunliffe's resignation may be in order', *New Zealand Herald*, 18 June 2014.

27 Kate McMillan, 'Glove puppets, black ops and textual relations: the media's election campaign 2014', in Levine and Johansson (eds) is generally helpful.

28 Levine, 'Moments of truth', p.32. See also Tim Barnett and David Talbot, 'The 2014 campaign: a Labour Party perspective', in Levine and Johansson (eds), p.139.

29 Sue Bradford left the Mana Party over the arrangement with Dotcom.

30 Colin James, 'Election in a bubble', in Levine and Johansson (eds), p.79.

31 This paragraph is based on Morgan Godfery, 'The search for stability', in Levine and Johansson (eds).

32 Levine, 'Moments of truth', p.58.

33 Stephen Mills, 'Survey findings and the 2014 election', in Levine and Johansson (eds), p.266.

34 James, 'Election in a bubble', p.84.

Bibliography

Newspapers

A large range of New Zealand newspapers is available through the National Library of New Zealand's Papers Past website, and this has been used extensively.

Official sources

Appendices to the Journals of the House of Representatives
New Zealand Parliamentary Debates

Archives and manuscripts

University of Auckland Libraries
Auckland Labout Representation Committee papers
New Zealand Labour Party Auckland Regional Council papers
Waitematā Labour Regional Council correspondence
Branch records: Albany, Eden, Roskill, Wellington City

Auckland City Libraries

John A. Lee papers

New Zealand Labour Party national office, Fraser House, Wellington

Reports of the annual conference
New Zealand Council minutes and reports
Executive minutes and reports

Archives New Zealand

SIS: Communist Party of New Zealand – Policy on Other Political Parties in New Zealand

Alexander Turnbull Library

New Zealand Labour Party head office records
New Zealand Labour Party branch minute books and related records
New Zealand Labour Party Auckland women's branch records
H.O. Roth papers

Margaret Wilson papers
Fintan Patrick Walsh papers
Conrad Bollinger papers
Peter Franks papers
New Zealand Shipowners' Federation records: Wellington Strike Committee minute book, 1913
New Zealand Federation of Labour records
Elizabeth McCombs Club records

Macmillan Brown Library, University of Canterbury

Michael Connelly papers
Christchurch women's branch records
North Canterbury Labour Representation Committee records

Hocken Collections Te Uare o Hākena, University of Otago

Dunedin women's branch records
Arthur McCarthy papers
Otago Labour Representation Committee records
Dunedin West branch records

Puke Ariki, New Plymouth

New Plymouth Labour Representation Committee minutes, 27 April 1940, ARC 2007-100

Interviews

Jim Anderton
Joan Caulfield
David Caygill
Helen Clark
Michael Cullen
Roger Douglas
Ruth Dyson
Phil Goff
Mark Gosche
Marian Hobbs
Pete Hodgson
Dorothy Jelicich
Annette King
Andrew Little
Steve Maharey
Nanaia Mahuta
Trevor Mallard
Don Milne
Mike Moore
Colin Moyle
J.B. Munro
Geoffrey Palmer
Grant Robertson
Anne Rodger
Stan Rodger

Adrian Rurawhe
Maryan Street
Bob Tizard
Cath Tizard
Judith Tizard
Koro Wetere
Margaret Wilson

Norman Kirk, 16 March 1972

Labour Movement Oral History Project, Alexander Turnbull Library:
Dave Vallely, 25 October 1991, OHLC-004237
Mollie Clark, 12 March 1994, OHLC-008773

Books, articles, essays and theses

Aikman, Colin, 'Powles, Guy Richardson', from *The Dictionary of New Zealand Biography*, Te Ara – the Encyclopedia of New Zealand, http://www.TeAra.govt.nz/en/biographies/5p37/powles-guy-richardson

Atkinson, Neill, *Adventures in Democracy: a history of the vote in New Zealand*, Otago University Press, 2003

Ballara, Angela, 'Bennett, Charles Moihi Te Arawaka', from *The Dictionary of New Zealand Biography*, Te Ara – the Encyclopedia of New Zealand, http://www.TeAra.govt.nz/en/biographies/5b23/bennett-charles-moihi-te-arawaka

Ballara, Angela, 'Paikea, Paraire Karaka', from *The Dictionary of New Zealand Biography*, Te Ara – the Encyclopedia of New Zealand, http://www.TeAra.govt.nz/en/biographies/4p1/paikea-paraire-karaka

Bassett, Michael, *Coates of Kaipara*, Auckland University Press, Auckland, 1995

Bassett, Michael, *Confrontation '51: the 1951 waterfront dispute*, A.H. & A.W. Reed, Wellington, 1972

Bassett, Michael, *The Mother of All Departments: the history of the Department of Internal Affairs*, Auckland University Press, Auckland, 1997

Bassett, Michael, *The Third Labour Government: a personal history*, Dunmore Press, Palmerston North, 1976

Bassett, Michael, *Working with David: inside the Lange cabinet*, Hodder Moa, Auckland, 2008

Bassett, Michael and Judith Bassett, *Roderick Deane: his life and times*, Viking, Auckland, 2006

Bassett, Michael with Michael King, *Tomorrow Comes the Song: a life of Peter Fraser*, Penguin, Auckland, 2000

Berman, Sheri, *The Primacy of Politics: social democracy and the making of Europe's twentieth century*, Cambridge University Press, New York, 2006

Bohan, Edmund, 'Andrews, Samuel Paul', from *The Dictionary of New Zealand Biography*, Te Ara – the Encyclopedia of New Zealand, http://www.TeAra.govt.nz/en/biographies/2a9/andrews-samuel-paul

Bohan, Edmund, *To Be a Hero: a biography of Sir George Grey 1812–98*, HarperCollins, Auckland, 1998

Boston, Jonathan, Elizabeth McLeay and Nigel S. Roberts (eds), *From Campaign to Coalition: the 1996 MMP election*, Dunmore Press, Palmerston North, 1997

Boston, Jonathan, Stephen Church, Stephen Levine, Elizabeth McLeay and Nigel S. Roberts (eds), *Left Turn: the New Zealand general election of 1999*, Victoria University Press,

Wellington, 2000

Bowman, Sylvia E. (ed.), *Edward Bellamy Abroad*, New York, Twayne, 1962

Brooking, Tom, *Richard Seddon: King of God's Own: the life and times of New Zealand's longest serving prime minister*, Penguin, Auckland, 2014

Brown, Bruce, 'The lockout and Walter Nash', in David Grant (ed.), *The Big Blue: snapshots of the 1951 waterfront lockout*, Canterbury University Press in association with the Trade Union History Project, Christchurch, 2004

Brown, Bruce, *The Rise of New Zealand Labour: a history of the New Zealand Labour Party from 1916 to 1940*, Price Milburn, Wellington, 1962

Brown, Colin, 'Ayrton, Moses', from *The Dictionary of New Zealand Biography*, Te Ara – the Encyclopedia of New Zealand, http://www.TeAra.govt.nz/en/biographies/4a26/ayrton-moses

Chapman, R.M., *The Political Scene 1919–1931*, Heinemann Educational Books, Auckland, 1969

Chapman, R.M. and Keith Sinclair (eds), *Studies of a Small Democracy: essays in honour of Willis Airey*, Paul's Book Arcade for the University of Auckland, Auckland, 1963

Chapple, Geoff, *1981: the tour*, A.H. & A.W. Reed, Wellington, 1984

Clark, Margaret (ed.), *For the Record: Lange and the fourth Labour government*, Dunmore Publishing, Wellington, 2005

Clark, Margaret (ed.), *Peter Fraser: master politician*, Dunmore Press, Palmerston North, 1998

Clark, Margaret (ed.), *Three Labour Leaders: Nordmeyer, Kirk, Rowling*, Dunmore Press, Palmerston North, 2001

Clifton, R., 'Douglas Credit and the Labour Party 1930–35', MA thesis, Victoria College, 1961

Condliffe, J.B., *The Welfare State in New Zealand*, Allen & Unwin, London, 1959

Crosland, C.A.R., *The Future of Socialism*, Jonathan Cape, London, 1956

Dalziel, Paul, 'The 1984 economic summit conference: a search for policy objectives', *New Zealand Economic Papers*, 20, 1986

Daniels, J.R.S., 'The General Election of 1943', MA thesis, Victoria University College, 1951

Davidson, J.W., *Samoa mo Samoa: the emergence of the independent state of Western Samoa*, Oxford University Press, Melbourne, 1967

Davies, Sonja, *Bread and Roses*, Australia and New Zealand Book Co., Auckland, 1984

Douglas, Roger and Louise Callan, *Toward Prosperity*, David Bateman, Auckland, 1987

Dunick, Mark E., 'The Clarion Settlers: a socialist migration to New Zealand', BA (Hons) dissertation, Victoria University of Wellington, 2014

Dunmore, John, *Norman Kirk: a portrait*, New Zealand Books, Palmerston North, 1972

Eagles, Jim and Colin James, *The Making of a New Zealand Prime Minister*, Cheshire Publishing, Wellington, 1973

Easton, Brian (ed.), *The Making of Rogernomics*, Auckland University Press, Auckland, 1989

Easton, Brian, *The Nationbuilders*, Auckland University Press, Auckland, 2001

Edwards, Brian, *Helen: portrait of a prime minister*, Exisle, Auckland, 2001

Eley, Geoff, *Forging Democracy: the history of the left in Europe, 1850–2000*, Oxford University Press, New York, 2002

Fill, Barbara, *Strike: trouble at t' mill*, GP Books, Wellington, 1989

Fisher, A.G.B., *The Clash of Progress and Security*, London, Macmillan, 1935

Franks, Peter, 'Knox, Walter James', from *The Dictionary of New Zealand Biography*, Te Ara – the Encyclopedia of New Zealand, http://www.TeAra.govt.nz/en/biographies/5k13/knox-walter-james

Franks, Peter, *Print and Politics: a history of trade unions in the New Zealand printing industry 1865–1995*, Victoria University Press, Wellington, 2001

Franks, Peter and Melanie Nolan (eds), *Unions in Common Cause: the New Zealand Federation of*

Labour 1938–88, Steele Roberts, Wellington, 2011

Freer, Warren, *A Lifetime in Politics: the memoirs of Warren Freer*, Victoria University Press, Wellington, 2004

Friedman, Milton, 'The role of monetary policy', *American Economic Review*, 58 (1), 1967

Garner, Jean, 'McCombs, James', from *The Dictionary of New Zealand Biography*, Te Ara – the Encyclopedia of New Zealand, http://www.TeAra.govt.nz/en/biographies/3m3/mccombs-james

Gibbs, Michael, 'The Selwyn by-election', research paper, Victoria University of Wellington, 1994

Goff, Philip, 'Labour and the Unions: the politics of industrial relations under the third Labour government', MA thesis, University of Auckland, 1979

Goldman, Lawrence, *The Life of R.H. Tawney: socialism and history*, Bloomsbury, London, 2014

Goldstein, Ray with Rod Alley (eds), *Labour in Power: promise and performance: evaluations of the work of the New Zealand government from 1972 to 1975*, Price Milburn for New Zealand University Press, Wellington, 1975

Gomibuchi, Seishi, 'Followers and Leadership Durability: an analysis of leadership support in the New Zealand Labour Party', PhD thesis, University of Canterbury, 2001

Gould, John, *The Rake's Progress? The New Zealand economy since 1945*, Hodder and Stoughton, Auckland, 1982

Gourevitch, Peter, *Politics in Hard Times: comparative responses to international economic crises*, Cornell University Press, Ithaca, 1986

Grant, David (ed.), *The Big Blue: snapshots of the 1951 waterfront lockout*, Canterbury University Press, Christchurch 2004

Grant, David, *Jagged Seas: the New Zealand Seamen's Union 1879–2003*, Canterbury University Press, Christchurch, 2012

Grant, David, *The Mighty Totara: the life and times of Norman Kirk*, Random House, Auckland, 2014

Gustafson, Barry, *The First 50 years: a history of the New Zealand National Party*, Reed Methuen, Auckland, 1986

Gustafson, Barry, *From the Cradle to the Grave: a biography of Michael Joseph Savage*, Reed Methuen, Auckland, 1986

Gustafson, Barry, *His Way: a biography of Robert Muldoon*, Auckland University Press, Auckland, 2000

Gustafson, Barry, *Labour's Path to Political Independence*, Auckland University Press, Auckland, 1980

Gustafson, Barry, 'Payne, John', from *The Dictionary of New Zealand Biography*, Te Ara – the Encyclopedia of New Zealand, http://www.TeAra.govt.nz/en/biographies/3p18/payne-john

Gustafson, Barry, *Social Change and Party Organisation: the New Zealand Labour Party since 1945*, Sage Publications, London, 1976

Hamer, David, *The New Zealand Liberals: the years of power 1891–1912*, Auckland University Press, Auckland, 1988

Hamer, David, 'The second ballot: a New Zealand electoral experiment', *New Zealand Journal of History*, 21 (1), April 1987

Hayward, Margaret, *Diary of the Kirk Years*, Cape Catley and A.H. & A.W. Reed, Wellington, 1981

Hayward, Margaret, 'Prime Ministerial Leadership in New Zealand During a Time of Change 1984 to 2000', PhD thesis, Victoria University of Wellington, 2004

Henderson, John, 'Rowling, Wallace Edward', from *The Dictionary of New Zealand Biography*, Te Ara – the Encyclopedia of New Zealand, http://www.TeAra.govt.nz/en/biographies/6r1/rowling-wallace-edward

Henderson, John, *Rowling: the man and the myth*, Australia and New Zealand Book Co. with Fraser Books, Auckland, 1981

Hickey, P.H., *Red Fed Memoirs*, Wellington Media Collective, Wellington, 1980

Hirschfeld, Michael, 'The New Zealand Labour Party in Office, 1957–60', MA thesis, Victoria University of Wellington, 1970

Hoare, Nicholas, 'Harry Holland's "Samoan complex"', *Journal of Pacific History*, 49 (2), 2014

Hogan, Warren, 'Allan George Barnard Fisher', in J.E. King (ed.), *A Biographical Directory of Australian and New Zealand Economists*, Edward Elgar, Cheltenham, 2007

Holland, H.E. et al., *The Tragic Story of the Waihi Strike*, Hocken Library, Dunedin, 1975

Holland, Martin and Jonathan Boston (eds), *The Fourth Labour Government*, second edition, Oxford University Press, Auckland, 1989

Hunt, J.L. and the Labour Party Research Unit (eds), *Labour Leads: policies at work, December 1972–May 1975*, New Zealand Labour Party, Wellington, 1975

James, Colin, *New Territory: the transformation of New Zealand*, Bridget Williams Books, Wellington, 1992

James, Colin, *The Quiet Revolution: turbulence and transition in contemporary New Zealand*, Allen & Unwin, Wellington, 1986

Jamieson, Rosemary, *In Command: Phil Connolly*, Steele Roberts, Wellington, 2009

Johansson, Jon, *Two Titans: Muldoon, Lange and leadership*, Dunmore Publishing, Palmerston North, 2005

Johansson, Jon and Stephen Levine (eds), *Kicking the Tyres: the New Zealand general election and electoral referendum of 2011*, Victoria University Press, Wellington, 2012

Kelsey, Jane, *The New Zealand Experiment: a world model for structural adjustment?*, Auckland University Press/Bridget Williams Books, Auckland, 1997

Keynes, John Maynard, *The Collected Writings of John Maynard Keynes*, Cambridge University Press, London, 1972

Kirk, Norman, *Towards Nationhood*, New Zealand Books, Palmerston North, 1969

Lange, David, *My Life*, Viking, Auckland, 2005

Laurie, Alison J. and Linda Evans (eds), *Twenty Years On: histories of homosexual law reform in New Zealand*, Lesbian and Gay Archives of New Zealand, Wellington, 2009

Lee, John A., *Political Notebooks*, Alister Taylor, Wellington, 1973

Lee, John A., *Simple on a Soapbox*, Collins, London, 1964

Lenin, V.I., *Collected Works*, vol.31, Progress Publishers, Moscow, 1977

Levine, Stephen and Jon Johansson (eds), *Moments of Truth: the New Zealand general election of 2014*, Victoria University Press, Wellington, 2015

Levine, Stephen and Nigel S. Roberts (eds), *The Baubles of Office: the New Zealand general election of 2005*, Victoria University Press, Wellington, 2007

Levine, Stephen, and Nigel S. Roberts (eds), *Key to Victory: the New Zealand general election of 2008*, Victoria University Press, Wellington, 2010

Logan, Mary, *Nordy: Arnold Nordmeyer: a political biography*, Steele Roberts, Wellington, 2008

Love, Ralph Ngātata, 'Policies of Frustration: the growth of Maori politics: the Ratana/Labour era', PhD thesis, Victoria University of Wellington, 1977

Martin, John E., *Honouring the Contract*, Victoria University Press, Wellington, 2010

Martin, John E., *The House: New Zealand's House of Representatives*, Dunmore Press, Palmerston North, 2004

McAloon, Jim, 'Cooke, Frederick Riley', from *The Dictionary of New Zealand Biography*, Te Ara – the Encyclopedia of New Zealand, http://www.TeAra.govt.nz/en/biographies/3c29/cooke-frederick-riley

McAloon, Jim, *Judgements of All Kinds: economic policy-making in New Zealand 1945–1984*,

Victoria University Press, Wellington, 2013
McAloon, Jim, 'A Political Struggle: Christchurch Labour Politics 1905-1913', New Zealand Journal of History, 28, (1), 1994
McAloon, Jim, *Nelson: a regional history*, Cape Catley, Whatamongo Bay, 1997
McAloon, Jim, 'Unsettling recolonisation: labourism, Keynesianism, and Australasia from the 1890s to the 1950s', *Thesis Eleven*, 92, 2008
McClure, Margaret, *A Civilised Community: a history of social security in New Zealand, 1898–1998*, Auckland University Press, Auckland, 1998
McCombs, Elizabeth R., *Women and the Labour Movement*, Labour Book Room, Wellington, 1933
McCullough, Alison, *Fighting to Choose: the abortion rights struggle in New Zealand*, Victoria University Press, Wellington, 2013
McGibbon, Ian (ed.), *Unofficial Channels: letters between Alister McIntosh and Foss Shanahan, George Laking and Frank Corner 1946–1966*, Victoria University Press, Wellington, 1999
McKinnon, Malcolm, *Treasury: the New Zealand Treasury, 1840–2000*, Auckland University Press, Auckland, 2003
McLean, Gavin, *The Southern Octopus: the rise of a shipping empire*, Wellington Maritime Museum/New Zealand Ship and Marine Society, Wellington, 1990
McLeay, Elizabeth (ed.), *New Zealand Politics and Social Patterns: selected works by Robert Chapman*, Victoria University Press, Wellington, 1999
McLennan, Roy, 'The Last Years of the First Labour Government, 1945–1949', MA thesis, University of Auckland, 1963
McNeill, Dougal, 'Labouring feeling: Harry Holland's political emotions', *Journal of New Zealand Studies*, 21, 2015
Moggridge, Donald, *Maynard Keynes: an economist's biography*, Routledge, London and New York, 1992
Morgan, Thomas J., 'Walter Thomas Mills: his record', *The Socialist*, 350, 2 Nov. 1907, p.3, www.marxisthistory.org
Munro, Doug, 'J.W. Davidson: the making of the participant historian', in Brij V. Lal and Peter Hempenstall (eds), *Pacific Lives, Pacific Places: bursting boundaries in Pacific history*, Journal of Pacific History, Canberra, 2001
Newman, Keith, *Rātana Revisited: an unfinished legacy*, Reed Publishing, Auckland, 2006
Nolan, Melanie, *Kin: a collective biography of a New Zealand family*, Canterbury University Press, Christchurch, 2006
Nolan, Melanie (ed.), *Revolution: the 1913 great strike in New Zealand*, Canterbury University Press, Christchurch, 2006
Nolan, Melanie (ed.), *War and Class: the diary of Jack McCullough*, Dunmore Press, Palmerston North, 2009
Northey, Richard, 'The Annual Conferences of the New Zealand Labour Party', MA thesis, University of Auckland, 1973
Norton, Clifford, *New Zealand Parliamentary Election Results 1946–1987*, occasional publication no.1, Department of Political Science, Victoria University of Wellington, 1988
O'Farrell, P.J., *Harry Holland: militant socialist*, Australian National University Press, Canberra, 1964
Olssen, Erik, 'Bennett, Henry Gilbert Scott', from *The Dictionary of New Zealand Biography*, Te Ara – the Encyclopedia of New Zealand, http://www.TeAra.govt.nz/en/biographies/3b30/bennett-henry-gilbert-scott
Olssen, Erik, *Building the New World: work, politics and society in Caversham, 1880s–1920s*, Auckland University Press, Auckland, 1995

Olssen, Erik, 'The impact of John A. Lee's expulsion upon the New Zealand Labour Party', *New Zealand Journal of History*, 12 (1), April 1978

Olssen, Erik, *John A. Lee*, University of Otago Press, Dunedin, 1977

Olssen, Erik, 'Mills, Walter Thomas', from *The Dictionary of New Zealand Biography*, Te Ara – the Encyclopedia of New Zealand, http://www.TeAra.govt.nz/en/biographies/3m54/mills-walter-thomas

Olssen, Erik, 'The origins of the New Zealand Labour Party: a reconsideration', *New Zealand Journal of History*, 21 (1), April 1987

Olssen, Erik, *The Red Feds: revolutionary industrial unionism and the New Zealand Federation of Labour, 1908–14*, Auckland University Press, Auckland, 1988

Olssen, Erik, 'W.T. Mills, E.J.B. Allen, John A. Lee and socialism in New Zealand', *New Zealand Journal of History*, 10 (2), October 1976

Olssen, Erik and Len Richardson, 'The New Zealand labour movement 1880–1920', in Eric Fry (ed.), *Common Cause: essays in Australian and New Zealand Labour History*, Allen & Unwin/Port Nicholson Press, Wellington, 1986

Orange, Claudia, *An Illustrated History of the Treaty of Waitangi*, Bridget Williams Books, Wellington, 2004

Orange, Claudia, 'A Kind of Equality: labour and the Maori people 1935–1949', MA thesis, University of Auckland, 1977

Orange, Claudia, 'Mawhete, Rangiputangatahi', from *The Dictionary of New Zealand Biography*, Te Ara – the Encyclopedia of New Zealand, http://www.TeAra.govt.nz/en/biographies/4m48/mawhete-rangiputangatahi

Overacker, Louise, 'The New Zealand Labour Party', *American Political Science Review*, 49 (3), September 1955

Palmer, Geoffrey, *Reform: a memoir*, Victoria University Press, Wellington, 2013

Patai, Daphne (ed.), *Looking Backward, 1988–1888: essays on Edward Bellamy*, University of Massachusetts Press, Amherst, 1998

Plumridge, E.W., 'Labour in Christchurch', MA thesis, University of Canterbury, 1979

Rennie, Hugh, 'Gillies, Thomas Bannatyne', from *The Dictionary of New Zealand Biography*, Te Ara – the Encyclopedia of New Zealand, http://www.teara.govt.nz/en/biographies/1g9/gillies-thomas-bannatyne

Renwick, W.L., *Scrim: the man with a mike*, Victoria University Press, Wellington, 2011

Richards, Raymond, *Palmer: the parliamentary years*, Canterbury University Press, Christchurch, 2010

Richardson, Len, *Coal, Class and Community: the United Mineworkers of New Zealand, 1880–1960*, Auckland University Press, Auckland, 1995

Roberts, John, '1951: the storm before the calm', *New Zealand Listener*, 29 May 1976

Roche, Stanley, *The Red and the Gold: an informal account of the Waihi strike, 1912*, Oxford University Press, Auckland, 1984

Rockley, Glen, 'Political currents in New Zealand', *Far Eastern Survey*, 17 Nov. 1943

Roth, Herbert, 'Bellamy societies abroad', in Sylvia E. Bowman (ed.), *Edward Bellamy Abroad*, Twayne, New York, 1962

Roth, Herbert, 'Buying a Labour Party: Fowlds, Mills, and the ULP', *Political Science*, 20 (1), September 1968

Roth, Herbert, 'Marx and New Zealand', *New Zealand Monthly Review*, July 1983

Roth, Herbert, 'The New Zealand Socialist Party', *Political Science*, 9 (1), March 1957

Roth, Herbert, 'The New Zealand Trade Union Congress, 1950–51', in Eric Fry (ed.), *Common Cause: essays in Australian and New Zealand Labour History*, Allen & Unwin/Port Nicholson Press, Wellington, 1986

Roth, Herbert, 'Parnell, Samuel Duncan', from *The Dictionary of New Zealand Biography*, Te Ara – the Encyclopedia of New Zealand, http://www.TeAra.govt.nz/en/biographies/1p7/parnell-samuel-duncan

Roth, Herbert, *Trade Unions in New Zealand Past and Present*, Reed Education, Wellington, 1974

Salmond, J.D., *New Zealand Labour's Pioneering Days: the history of the labour movement in N.Z. from 1840 to 1894*, ed. D.W. Crowley, Forward Press, Auckland, 1950

Sargent, Lyman Tower, 'The ohu movement', *Journal of New Zealand Studies*, November 1996

Sassoon, Donald, *One Hundred Years of Socialism: the west European left in the twentieth century*, Fontana, London, 1997

Scott, Dick, *151 Days: the great waterfront lockout and supporting strikes, February 15–July 15, 1951*, Reed Books, Auckland, 2001

Sheppard, Simon, *Broken Circle: the decline and fall of the fourth Labour government*, PSL Press, Wellington, 1999

Sinclair, F.R.J., 'Fish, Henry Smith', from *The Dictionary of New Zealand Biography*, Te Ara – the Encyclopedia of New Zealand, http://www.TeAra.govt.nz/en/biographies/2f8/fish-henry-smith

Sinclair, Keith, 'The Lee–Sutch syndrome: New Zealand Labour Party policies and politics, 1930–1940', *New Zealand Journal of History*, 8 (2), October 1974

Sinclair, Keith, *Walter Nash*, Auckland University Press/Oxford University Press, Auckland and New York, 1976

Singleton, John et al., *Innovation and Independence: the Reserve Bank of New Zealand 1973–2002*, Auckland University Press, Auckland, 2006

Stevens, Norman D., 'Labour candidates for the New Zealand House of Representatives 1890–1916, part 1: 1890–1896', *Political Science*, 7 (1), March 1955

Sutch, W.B., *The Quest for Security in New Zealand*, Oxford University Press, Wellington, 1966

Taylor, Bruce S., 'The Expulsion of J.A. Lee and its Effects on the Development of the New Zealand Labour Party', MA thesis, University of Canterbury, 1970

Taylor, James, '"To me, Socialism is not a set of dogmas but a living principle": Harry Atkinson and the Christchurch Socialist Church, 1890–1905', MA thesis, Victoria University of Wellington, 2010

Taylor, Kerry, 'The ambiguous legacy of Samuel Duncan Parnell: the eight hour day in New Zealand', in Julie Kimber and Peter Love (eds), *The Time of Their Lives: the eight hour day and working life*, Australian Society for the Study of Labour History, Melbourne, 2007

Taylor, Kerry, 'Hindmarsh, Alfred Humphrey', from *The Dictionary of New Zealand Biography*, Te Ara – the Encyclopedia of New Zealand, http://www.TeAra.govt.nz/en/biographies/3h28/hindmarsh-alfred-humphrey

Taylor, Nancy M., *The Home Front*, Historical Branch, Department of Internal Affairs, Wellington, 1986

Taylor, Nancy M., 'Human rights in World War II in New Zealand', *New Zealand Journal of History*, 23 (2), October 1989

Templeton, Ian and Keith Eunson, *Election '69: an independent survey of the New Zealand political scene*, A.H. & A.W. Reed, Wellington, 1969

Templeton, Malcolm, *Standing Upright Here: New Zealand in the nuclear age 1945–1990*, Victoria University Press, Wellington, 2006

Templeton, Malcolm, *A Wise Adventure: New Zealand and Antarctica, 1920–1960*, Victoria University Press, Wellington, 2000

Thompson, E.P., *The Making of the English Working Class*, Gollancz, London, 1963

Thompson, Noel, 'Hobson and the Fabians: two roads to socialism in the 1920s', *History of Political Economy*, 26 (1994)

Tilton, Timothy A., 'A Swedish road to socialism: Ernst Wigforss and the ideological foundations of Swedish social democracy', *American Political Science Review*, 73 (2), June 1979

Tomlinson, Jim, *Democratic Socialism and Economic Policy: the Attlee years, 1945–51*, Cambridge University Press, Cambridge, 1997

Vowles, Jack, 'Ideology and the formation of the New Zealand Labour Party: some new evidence', *New Zealand Journal of History*, 16 (1), April 1982

Vowles, Jack, Peter Aimer, Susan Banducci, Jeffrey Kemp and Raymond Miller (eds), *Voters Veto: the 2002 election in New Zealand and the consolidation of minority government*, Auckland University Press, Auckland, 2004

Weaver, John C., '"Deep in the heart of taxes": fourth Labour, the GST and fiscal reconstruction, 1981–1986', *New Zealand Journal of History*, 49 (2), October 2015

Weir, Robert, *Knights Down Under: the Knights of Labour in New Zealand*, Cambridge Scholars Publishing, Newcastle upon Tyne, 2009

Welch, Dennis, *Helen Clark: a political life*, Penguin Books, Auckland, 2009

Wilson, David, *History in the Making: a summary of the legislative and administrative actions of the first Labour government during its first year of office*, Labour Bookroom, Wellington, 1937

Wilson, J.O., *New Zealand Parliamentary Record 1840–1984*, Government Printer, Wellington, 1985

Wilson, Margaret, *Labour in Government, 1984–87*, Allen & Unwin/Port Nicholson Press, Wellington, 1989

Wood, G.A., *Ministers and Members in the New Zealand Parliament*, University of Otago Press, Dunedin, 1996

Wright, Vernon, *David Lange, Prime Minister: a profile*, Unwin Paperbacks, Port Nicholson Press, Wellington, 1984

Acknowledgements

In 2012 the New Zealand Council of the Labour Party accepted our proposal to write a centennial history of the party. It was agreed that, as established and reputable historians, we would be independent in our writing and that the book would not be an official history.

The party has given a great deal of support to this project over the past four years. We particularly thank Tim Barnett, Chris Flatt, Nigel Haworth and Paul Tolich for their assistance. At the party's head office, Dianna Lacy was always willing to share her encyclopaedic knowledge and to provide access to party records. Stan Rodger, Helen Clark and Judith Tizard were also generous in sharing their knowledge with us in the early stages of our work. We thank Andrew Little and Nigel Haworth for writing prefaces to the book.

The following people were interviewed and/or provided information: Jim Anderton, David Butcher, Joan Caulfield, David Caygill, Helen Clark, Michael Cullen, Roger Douglas, Ruth Dyson, Phil Goff, Mark Gosche, Peter Harris, Marian Hobbs, Pete Hodgson, Dorothy Jelicich, Annette King, Andrew Little, Steve Maharey, Nanaia Mahuta, Trevor Mallard, Don Milne, Mike Moore, Colin Moyle, J.B. Munro, Geoffrey Palmer, Grant Robertson, Anne Rodger, Stan Rodger, Adrian Rurawhe, Maryan Street, Bob Tizard, Cath Tizard, Judith Tizard, Koro Wetere and Margaret Wilson.

Most of the interviews were done by Peter Franks and Rob Carr. Thanks to Rob, who put hours of his own time into this work, we were able to interview a larger group of people than we initially envisaged. We thank Nanaia Mahuta for interviewing Koro Wētere and Freya Dean for helping to research interviews in the Alexander Turnbull Library.

In 2014 the New Zealand History Research Trust gave Peter Franks an award in history which enabled him to take time off work and to travel to do research and interviews. We thank Bernadette Murphy, Jim Marsh, John Hudson and Marian Hobbs for giving him a bed during his travels.

There are voluminous collections of Labour Party records, publications and images in libraries. We thank the librarians and archivists at the Alexander Turnbull Library, National Library of New Zealand; Victoria University library; Special Collections at the University of Auckland library; Puke Ariki in New Plymouth; the Macmillan Brown library at the University of Canterbury; and the Hocken library at Otago University for their assistance. We particularly acknowledge the help we received from Jocelyn Chambers, Paul Diamond, Gillian Headifen, Katherine Pawley, Erin Kimber and David Murray. We thank Peter Davis, Joe Fleetwood and Joyce Paton for giving us permission to access restricted collections of records and oral histories.

At Victoria University Press, Fergus Barrowman and Holly Hunter have been enthusiastic and supportive. We thank Rachel Barrowman for editing the manuscript, Todd Atticus for designing the cover, Timothy Vaughan-Sanders for indexing the book and Patricia Norton for proofreading.

Colin James and Melanie Nolan read and commented on the manuscript. We are indebted to them for their helpful comments and criticisms which have made this a better book. Jim McAloon is particularly grateful to Victoria University colleagues for their interest and support, and we would both like to acknowledge other New Zealand labour historians who have taught and encouraged us in various ways over many years. Here we particularly acknowledge Len Richardson, Erik Olssen, Jock Phillips and Pat Walsh and our friends and colleagues in the Labour History Project.

Our partners, Sue Piper and Jenny Dawson, have lived with this book as long as we have. We thank them for their encouragement, love and support.

Peter Franks and Jim McAloon
April 2016

Index

I1 denotes photographs in the first insert after page 80
I2 denotes photographs in the second insert after page 128
I3 denotes photographs in the second insert after page 176
I4 denotes photographs in the second insert after page 224

A

B

C

I

J

K

L

M

N

R

S

Y